Lab Manual for
CompTIA A+ Guide to
IT Technical Support
TENTH EDITION

Jean Andrews, Ph.D.

Joy Dark

Jill West

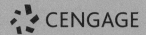
CENGAGE

Australia • Brazil • Mexico • Singapore • United Kingdom • United States

Lab Manual for CompTIA A+ Guide to IT Technical Support, Tenth Edition
Jean Andrews, Joy Dark, Jill West

SVP, Higher Education Product Management: Erin Joyner

VP, Product Management: Mike Schenk

Product Director: Lauren Murphy

Product Manager: Amy Savino

Product Assistant: Thomas Benedetto

Director, Learning Design: Rebecca von Gillern

Senior Manager, Learning Design: Leigh Hefferon

Learning Designer: Natalie Onderdonk

Vice President, Marketing – Science, Technology, & Math: Jason Sakos

Senior Marketing Director: Michele McTighe

Marketing Manager: Cassie Cloutier

Product Specialist: Mackenzie Paine

Director, Content Creation: Juliet Steiner

Senior Manager, Content Creation: Patty Stephan

Senior Content Manager: Brooke Greenhouse

Director, Digital Production Services: Krista Kellman

Digital Delivery Lead: Jim Vaughey

Developmental Editor: Dan Seiter

Art Director: Erin Griffin

Cover Designer: Joseph Villanova

Cover image: iStockPhoto.com/Tailex

Production Service/Composition: SPi Global

For product information and technology assistance, contact us at
Cengage Customer & Sales Support, 1-800-354-9706 or
support.cengage.com.

For permission to use material from this text or product,
submit all requests online at **www.cengage.com/permissions.**

Library of Congress Control Number: 2019913065
ISBN: 978-0-357-44078-0

Cengage
200 Pier 4 Boulevard
Boston, MA 02210
USA

Cengage is a leading provider of customized learning solutions with employees residing in nearly 40 different countries and sales in more than 125 countries around the world. Find your local representative at **www.cengage.com.**

Cengage products are represented in Canada by Nelson Education, Ltd.

To learn more about Cengage platforms and services, register or access your online learning solution, or purchase materials for your course, visit **www.cengage.com.**

Printed in the United States of America
Print Number: 01   Print Year: 2019

Table of Contents

CHAPTER 7

Setting Up a Local Network 195

CHAPTER 8

Network Infrastructure and Troubleshooting. 233

CHAPTER 9

Supporting Mobile Devices 263

CHAPTER 10

Virtualization, Cloud Computing, and Printers 287

CHAPTER 11

Windows Versions and Customer Service 321

CHAPTER 12

Installing Windows 351

CHAPTER 13

Maintaining Windows. 377

CHAPTER 14

Troubleshooting Windows After Startup. 405

CHAPTER 15

Troubleshooting Windows Startup . . . 441

CHAPTER 16

Securing and Sharing Windows Resources 473

CHAPTER 17

Security Strategies. 501

CHAPTER 18

macOS, Linux, and Scripting. 533

Preface

This lab manual is designed to be the best tool on the market to help you get hands-on practical experience troubleshooting and repairing personal computers, mobile and IoT devices, operating systems, and networks. The manual contains more than 120 labs, each of which targets a practical problem you're likely to face when troubleshooting systems in the real world. Every attempt has been made to write labs that allow you to use generic hardware devices. A specific hardware configuration isn't necessary to complete the labs. In learning to install, support, and troubleshoot hardware devices, operating systems, and networks, the focus is on Windows 10 and Windows 8, with minor coverage of Windows 7. Each chapter contains labs designed to provide the structure novices need, as well as labs that challenge experienced and inquisitive students.

This book helps prepare you for the new CompTIA A+ 1000 series Certification exams offered through the Computer Technology Industry Association (CompTIA): A+ 220-1001 and A+ 220-1002. The A+ 220-1001 Core 1 exam includes selecting, installing, maintaining, and troubleshooting the hardware components of computers, networks, printers, and mobile devices, along with virtualization and cloud computing. The A+ 220-1002 Core 2 exam focuses on operating systems, security, troubleshooting software, and operational procedures.

Because this certification credential is quickly growing in popularity among employers, becoming certified increases your ability to gain employment, improve your salary, and enhance your career. To find more information about A+ Certification and its sponsoring organization, CompTIA, go to the CompTIA website at *comptia.org*.

Whether your goal is to become an A+ certified technician or an IT support technician, the *Lab Manual for CompTIA A+ Guide to IT Technical Support*, Tenth Edition, along with Jean Andrews's textbooks and digital content, will take you there!

FEATURES

To ensure a successful experience for both instructors and students, this book includes the following pedagogical features:

- ◢ *Objectives*. Every lab opens with learning objectives that set the stage for students to absorb the lab's lessons.
- ◢ *Materials Required*. This feature outlines all the materials students need to successfully complete the lab.
- ◢ *Lab Preparation*. This feature alerts instructors and lab assistants to items they need to check or set up before the lab begins.
- ◢ *Activity Background*. A brief discussion at the beginning of each lab provides important background information.
- ◢ *Estimated Completion Time*. To help students plan their work, each lab includes an estimate of the total amount of time required to complete it.
- ◢ *Activity*. Detailed, numbered steps walk students through the lab. These steps are divided into manageable sections, with explanatory material between each section. Questions within each activity help students think through exactly what they are doing and why they are doing it as they follow the steps.
- ◢ *Figures*. Where appropriate, photographs of hardware or screenshots of software are provided to increase student mastery of the lab topic.
- ◢ *Review Questions*. Questions at the end of each lab help students test their understanding of the lab material.
- ◢ *Website*. For updates to this book and information about other A+ and IT products, go to *login.cengage.com*.

WHAT'S NEW IN THE TENTH EDITION

▲ Steps are updated to focus on Microsoft Windows 10 and Windows 8 and the latest versions of macOS, Ubuntu Linux, Android, and iOS.

▲ New projects are added to cover new technology and higher-level thinking skills, which reflect updates to CompTIA's A+ 220-1001 Core 1 and 220-1002 Core 2 exams.

▲ Enhanced and additional coverage on supporting cloud computing, virtualization, IoT devices, networking, and Active Directory is now included.

ACKNOWLEDGMENTS

The authors would first like to thank Dan Seiter, the developmental editor, for keeping us on track and providing a calm demeanor with the occasional comic relief. Dan, your meticulous work and encouraging attitude made the process more fun and made a significantly positive impact on the quality of the final product. Thank you to Brooke Greenhouse, Danielle Shaw, Amy Savino, Kristin McNary, and all the Cengage staff for their instrumental roles in developing this lab manual. Brooke, Danielle, Amy, and Kristin, we so appreciate all your hard work and impressive dedication to excellence. Many thanks to all the instructors who offered great suggestions for new labs and encouraged us to make other changes to the previous editions. Keep those suggestions coming!

CLASSROOM SETUP

Lab activities have been designed to explore many different Windows and hardware setups and troubleshooting problems while attempting to keep the requirements for specific hardware to a minimum. Most labs can be done alone, although a few ask you to work with a partner. If you prefer to work alone, simply do all the steps yourself. Lab activities that use a Windows desktop operating system have been designed to work in Windows 10 or Windows 8, although you can use Windows 7 for some labs. In some cases, Windows 10/8 Professional will be required.

Typical labs take 30 to 45 minutes; a few might take a little longer. For several of the labs, your classroom should be networked and provide access to the Internet. When access to Windows setup files is required, these files can be provided on a network drive made available to the computer, on the Windows installation DVD or a flash drive, or on some other type of removable storage media.

These are the minimum hardware requirements for Windows 10/8/7:

▲ 1 GHz or better Pentium-compatible computer
▲ 1 GB of RAM for 32-bit Windows or 2 GB of RAM for 64-bit Windows
▲ 16 GB of free hard drive space for 32-bit Windows or 20 GB for 64-bit Windows
▲ DirectX 9 or higher video device
▲ A user account with administrator privileges

Several labs use virtual machines installed in a hypervisor, such as Client Hyper-V in Windows 10 Professional. For these labs, extra RAM is needed. A few labs focus on special hardware. One lab requires a wireless card and router. Another lab requires the use of a multimeter, and some labs require software that can be freely downloaded from the Internet. Labs in Chapter 10 require a local or network printer.

LAB SETUP INSTRUCTIONS

CONFIGURATION TYPE AND OPERATING SYSTEMS

Each lab begins with a list of required materials. Before beginning a lab activity, each student workgroup or individual should verify access to these materials. Then, students should ensure that the correct operating system is installed and in good health. Note that in some cases, installing an operating system isn't necessary. In some labs, device drivers are needed. Students can work more efficiently if these drivers are available before beginning the lab.

PROTECTING DATA

In several labs, data on the hard drive might get lost or corrupted. For this reason, it's important that valuable data stored on the hard drive is backed up to another medium.

ACCESS TO THE INTERNET

Several labs require access to the Internet. If necessary, students can use one computer to search the Internet and download software or documentation and another computer to perform the lab procedures. If the lab doesn't have Internet access, students can download the required software or documentation before the lab and bring the files to the lab on some sort of storage medium or network share.

UTILITIES TO DOWNLOAD FROM THE WEB

The following table includes a list of software that can be downloaded free from the web. As new releases of software appear, the steps in the lab that use the software might need adjusting. It is suggested that instructors test each of these labs to make sure the software still works before students do the lab.

Lab	Software and URL
Lab 1.2: Gather and Record System Information	Belarc Advisor at *belarc.com/free_download.html*
Lab 2.1: Use the HWiNFO Hardware Information Utility	HWiNFO at *hwinfo.com*
Lab 2.4: Remove and Replace a Motherboard	CPU-Z at *cpuid.com*
Lab 2.5: Examine BIOS/UEFI Settings and Research BIOS/UEFI Updates	BIOSAgentPlus at *biosagentplus.com*
Lab 3.2: Run a Burn-In Test and Benchmark a CPU	BurnInTest at *passmark.com/download/bit_download.htm*
Lab 3.4: Benchmark RAM and Plan an Upgrade	Novabench at *novabench.com*
Lab 3.6: Troubleshoot Memory Problems	MemTest86 at *memtest86.com*
Lab 4.5: Measure Temperature and Adjust Fan Speed	SpeedFan at *filehippo.com/download_speedfan*

(Continues)

Lab 5.1: Test Hard Drive Performance Using HD Tune	HD Tune at *hdtune.com*
Lab 5.2: Examine Your Hard Drive Using Four Methods	Speccy at *ccleaner.com/speccy*
Lab 5.4: Use Hard Drive Utilities	SeaTools for Windows at *seagate.com/support/downloads/seatools*; Data Lifeguard Diagnostic for Windows at *support.wdc.com*
Lab 6.4: Use Diagnostics Software to Test I/O Devices	MonitorTest at *passmark.com/products/monitortest.htm*; KeyboardTest at *passmark.com/products/keytest.htm*
Lab 7.6: Set Up a VPN	Opera at *opera.com*
Lab 7.7: Create a Network in Packet Tracer	Packet Tracer at *netacad.com/courses/packet-tracer*
Lab 8.5: Set Up Advanced IP Scanner and Wake-on-LAN	Advanced IP Scanner at *advanced-ip-scanner.com*
Lab 9.2: Research Android Apps and Use Dropbox	Dropbox at *dropbox.com*
Lab 9.3: Explore How Android Apps Are Developed and Tested	Android Studio for Windows at *developer.android.com/studio*
Lab 9.4: Configure Email and Dropbox on Mobile Devices	Dropbox at *dropbox.com*
Lab 10.1: Create a VM in Oracle VirtualBox	Oracle VirtualBox at *virtualbox.org/wiki/Downloads*
Lab 12.1: Create a Bootable Windows 10 Setup DVD	Media Creation Tool at *microsoft.com/en-us/software-download/windows10*
Lab 12.4: Perform a Clean Installation of Windows 8.1	Windows 8.1 installation ISO file at *microsoft.com/en-us/software-download/windows8ISO*
Lab 14.6: Apply a Restore Point	CPU-Z at *cpuid.com*
Lab 14.8: Use Windows Utilities to Speed Up a System	Autoruns at *docs.microsoft.com/en-us/sysinternals/downloads/autoruns*
Lab 14.9: Research Data Recovery Software	Recuva at *ccleaner.com/recuva/download*
Lab 15.2: Create and Use a Custom Refresh Image in Windows 8	Chrome at *google.com/chrome*; Firefox at *mozilla.org/firefox*
Lab 17.7: Download and Use Microsoft Security Essentials in Windows 7	Microsoft Security Essentials at *microsoft.com/en-us/download/windows.aspx*
Lab 18.2: Investigate Linux and Create a Bootable Ubuntu Flash Drive	Ubuntu at *ubuntu.com*; LinuxLive USB Creator at *linuxliveusb.com/en/home*
Lab 18.3: Use TeamViewer to Remotely Access Another Computer	TeamViewer at *teamviewer.com*
Lab 18.6: Use Wireshark to Compare Security in Telnet and SSH	Ubuntu at *ubuntu.com*; PuTTY at *putty.org*

ONLINE RESOURCES AND STUDY TOOLS

A few labs require students to download documents and optional content to use during the lab. For example, several labs use the Computer Inventory and Maintenance form made available online. To access the form, please go to *login.cengage.com*. After signing in or creating a new account, locate the ISBN of the title on the back cover of the main textbook, and then search on the ISBN using the search box at the top of the webpage. When you get to the product page, you can locate and download the free resources you need.

THE TECHNICIAN'S WORK AREA

When opening a computer case, it's important to have the right tools and to be properly grounded to ensure that you don't cause more damage than you repair. Take a look at the items that should be part of any technician's work area:

- ◢ Grounding mat or bench (with grounding wire properly grounded)
- ◢ Grounding wrist strap, also known as an ESD (electrostatic discharge) strap, attached to the grounding mat
- ◢ Noncarpet flooring
- ◢ A clean work area (no clutter)
- ◢ A set of screwdrivers
- ◢ 1/4-inch Torx bit screwdriver
- ◢ 1/8-inch Torx bit screwdriver
- ◢ Needle-nose pliers
- ◢ Pen light (flashlight)
- ◢ Several new antistatic bags (for transporting and storing hardware)

At minimum, you must have at least two key items. The first is an ESD strap. If a grounding mat isn't available, you can attach the ESD strap to the computer's chassis and, in most cases, provide sufficient grounding for handling hardware components inside the computer case. The second key item is, of course, a screwdriver. You won't be able to open most cases without some type of screwdriver.

PROTECTING YOURSELF, YOUR HARDWARE, AND YOUR SOFTWARE

When you work on a computer, harming both the computer and yourself is possible. The most common accident when attempting to fix a computer problem is erasing software or data. Experimenting without knowing what you're doing can cause damage. To prevent these sorts of accidents as well as physically dangerous ones, take a few safety precautions. The following sections describe potential sources of damage to computers and explain how to protect against them.

POWER TO THE COMPUTER

To protect yourself and the equipment when working inside a computer, turn off the power, unplug the computer, press the power button to drain power, and always use an ESD strap. Consider the monitor and the power supply to be "black boxes." Never remove the cover or put your hands inside this equipment unless you know the hazards of charged capacitors. Both the power supply and the monitor can hold a dangerous level of electricity even after they're turned off and disconnected from a power source.

STATIC ELECTRICITY OR ESD

Electrostatic discharge (ESD), commonly known as static electricity, is an electrical charge at rest. A static charge can build up on the surface of a nongrounded conductor and on nonconductive surfaces, such as clothing or plastic. When two objects with dissimilar electrical charges touch, static electricity passes between them until the dissimilar charges are made equal. To see how this works, turn off the lights in a room, scuff your feet on the carpet, and touch another person. Occasionally, you see and feel the charge in your fingers. If you can feel the charge, you discharged at least 3000 volts of static electricity. If you hear the discharge, you released at least 6000 volts. If you see the discharge, you released at least 8000 volts of ESD. A charge of less than 3000 volts can damage most electronic components. That means you can touch a chip on an expansion card or system board and damage the chip with ESD without ever feeling, hearing, or seeing the discharge.

ESD can cause two types of damage in an electronic component: catastrophic failures and upset failures. A catastrophic failure destroys the component beyond use. An upset failure damages the component so that it doesn't perform well, even though it might still function to some degree. Upset failures are the most difficult to detect because they aren't easily observed.

PROTECTING AGAINST ESD

To protect the computer against ESD, always ground yourself before touching electronic components, including the hard drive, system board, expansion cards, processors, and memory modules, by using one or more of the following static control devices or methods:

▲ *ESD strap*. An ESD strap is a bracelet you wear around your wrist. The other end is attached to a grounded conductor, such as the computer case or a ground mat, or it can be plugged into a wall outlet. (Only the ground prong makes a connection!)

▲ *Grounding mats*. Grounding mats can come equipped with a cord to plug into a wall outlet to provide a grounded surface on which to work. Remember, if you lift the component off the mat, it's no longer grounded and is susceptible to ESD.

▲ *Static shielding bags*. New components come shipped in static shielding bags. Save the bags to store other devices that aren't currently installed in a PC.

The best way to protect against ESD is to use an ESD strap with a grounding mat. You should consider an ESD strap essential equipment when working on a computer. However, if you're in a situation where you must work without one, touch the computer case before you touch a component. When passing a component to another person, ground yourself. Leave components inside their protective bags until you're ready to use them. Work on hard floors, not carpet, or use antistatic spray on carpets.

There's an exception to the ground-yourself rule. Inside a monitor case, the electricity stored in capacitors poses a substantial danger. When working inside a monitor, you don't want to be grounded because you would provide a conduit for the voltage to discharge through your body. In this situation, be careful not to ground yourself.

When handling system boards and expansion cards, don't touch the chips on the boards. Don't stack boards on top of each other; doing so could accidentally dislodge a chip. Hold cards by the edges, but don't touch the edge connections on the card.

After you unpack a new device or software that has been wrapped in cellophane, remove the cellophane from the work area quickly. Don't allow anyone who's not properly grounded to touch components.

Hold an expansion card by the edges. Don't touch any of the soldered components on a card. If you need to put an electronic device down, place it on a grounding mat or a static shielding bag. Keep components away from your hair and clothing.

PROTECTING HARD DRIVES AND DISKS

Always turn off a computer before moving it. Doing so protects the hard drive, which might be spinning when the computer is turned on. Never jar a computer while the hard disk is running. Avoid placing a computer on the floor, where users could accidentally kick it.

Follow the usual precautions to protect CDs and DVDs. Protect the bottom of optical discs from scratches and keep them away from heat and direct sunlight. Treat discs with care, and they'll usually last for years.

Taking a Computer Apart and Putting It Back Together

Labs included in this chapter:

- **Lab 1.1:** Record Your Work and Make Deliverables
- **Lab 1.2:** Gather and Record System Information
- **Lab 1.3:** Identify Computer Parts
- **Lab 1.4:** Identify Form Factors
- **Lab 1.5:** Take a Computer Apart and Put It Back Together
- **Lab 1.6:** Investigate Computer Teardown Procedures
- **Lab 1.7:** Compare Laptops and Desktops

LAB 1.1 RECORD YOUR WORK AND MAKE DELIVERABLES

OBJECTIVES

The goal of this lab is to use different methods to create a submission file for your instructor and to familiarize yourself with your version of the operating system. After completing this lab, you will be able to:

▲ Determine what type and version of operating system your computer is running

▲ Use the Snipping Tool to take a snapshot of your screen

▲ Create a submission file for your instructor in one of four formats

MATERIALS REQUIRED

This lab requires the following:

▲ Windows 10, Windows 8, or Windows 7 operating system

LAB PREPARATION

Before the lab begins, the instructor or lab assistant needs to do the following:

▲ Verify that Windows starts with no errors

ACTIVITY BACKGROUND

The pages of this lab manual are perforated to allow students to tear off the pages and submit them to instructors for grading. However, your instructor might prefer that you submit your work using email or an online interface such as Moodle, Blackboard, or WebCT. This lab prepares you to submit your work using an electronic method.

ESTIMATED COMPLETION TIME: 20 MINUTES

 Activity

The Windows Snipping Tool lets you take screenshots or snips of the entire Windows desktop, a window, or any region of the desktop. Follow these steps to explore the Control Panel and System windows and take snips of your work on the desktop:

1. To open Control Panel, enter **Control Panel** in the Windows 10 search box on the taskbar. In Windows 8, right-click **Start** and click **Control Panel**. In Windows 7, click **Start** and click **Control Panel**.

   Notes The instructions in these labs assume that you are a knowledgeable user of computers and Windows. For example, it's assumed that you know to press Enter after typing in the Windows 10 search box and that you click an item in the search results to select it.

2. Drill down into the links, icons, and options in the Control Panel window and familiarize yourself with all the icons and options in both Icons view (also called Classic view on the A+ exam) and Category view. Figure 1-1 shows Control Panel in Small icons view in Windows 10. Explain in your own words the difference between Classic view and Category view:

_____

_____

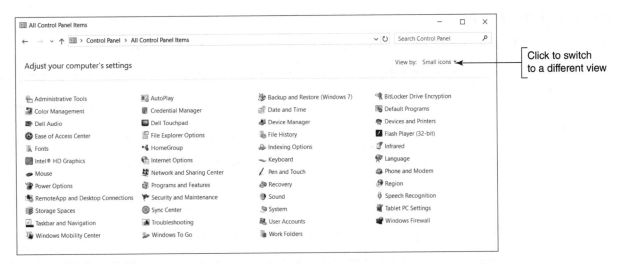

Figure 1-1 Many technicians prefer to use Control Panel in Classic view to more easily access utilities

3. In Large or Small icons view, click the **System** icon.

4. Examine the System window. What is the operating system and system type running on your computer? What processor is installed, and how much installed memory (RAM) do you have on your computer?

_____

_____

5. Leave the System window open as your active window. In Windows 10, press **Win+S** and enter **Snipping Tool** in the search box. In Windows 8, enter **Snipping Tool** in the search box. In Windows 7, click **Start,** and in the Search programs and files box, enter **Snipping Tool.** The Snipping Tool dialog box opens.

6. In the Snipping Tool dialog box, click the **Mode** drop-down arrow. (In Windows 8/7, click the **New** drop-down arrow.) What are the four types of snips you can take using the Snipping Tool?

_____

_____

_____

7. Select **Free-form Snip** from the drop-down list. Click and hold the mouse button, drag your cursor around the edges of the System window, and then release the mouse button. The Snipping Tool window opens, showing your snip.

8. On the menu bar, click **File,** and then click **Save As.**

9. Save the file on your desktop using naming and file compression standards (usually in .jpg or .png format) as directed by your instructor.

10. Email the file to your instructor, or upload it to your online interface.

11. Close all windows.

REVIEW QUESTIONS

1. What are the eight categories in the Category view in Control Panel?

   _____

   _____

   _____

2. What are the four file types that can be used to save a snip using the Windows Snipping Tool?

   _____

3. What is the purpose of the Win+S keystroke shortcut in Windows 10?

   _____

4. Search the web for information about the price of Windows 10. How much would it cost to buy your current edition (such as Home, Professional, etc.) of the Windows 10 operating system as an upgrade from Windows 8?

   _____

LAB 1.2 GATHER AND RECORD SYSTEM INFORMATION

OBJECTIVES

The goal of this lab is to document a system configuration. In this lab, you use a system's physical characteristics and operating system to determine how the system is configured. After completing this lab, you will be able to:

▲ Gather system information by observing a system

▲ Use available Windows tools to access specific system information

MATERIALS REQUIRED

This lab requires the following:

▲ Windows 10/8/7 operating system with administrator access

▲ A copy of the Computer Inventory and Maintenance form, either provided by your instructor or downloaded from *cengage.com*; for more information, see the Preface

LAB PREPARATION

Before the lab begins, the instructor or lab assistant needs to do the following:

▲ Verify that Windows starts with no errors

▲ Either verify that Internet access is available so students can download the Computer Inventory and Maintenance form or provide the form in print or digitally

 Notes The Computer Inventory and Maintenance form is used in several labs in this lab manual.

ACTIVITY BACKGROUND

When you first become responsible for a computer, you need to document its current configuration. Put this documentation in a notebook or other secure location and then use it whenever you do maintenance, upgrades, or repairs on the system. When you are responsible for several computers, it is difficult to remember the administrative passwords to each computer. In this lab, you collect system password information in your documentation. Therefore, the documentation needs to be kept confidential and secured.

In the five parts of this lab, you identify installed components and the Windows configuration by observing the system and by using Windows tools. In Part 1, you explore the physical system and Windows settings. In Part 2, you explore the network settings. In Part 3, you gather information about applications installed. In Part 4, you gather information about hardware installed. In Part 5, you examine BIOS/UEFI settings.

Save a copy of the Computer Inventory and Maintenance form because you will need it for labs in later chapters.

ESTIMATED COMPLETION TIME: 45 MINUTES

 Activity

PART 1: EXPLORE THE PHYSICAL SYSTEM AND WINDOWS SETTINGS

Observe the physical characteristics of your system, and answer the following questions:

1. Does the outside of the case have any identification indicating manufacturer, model, or component information? If so, list this information here:

_____

_____

2. How many optical drives does your system have?

_____

3. Describe the shape or type of the connection your mouse uses:

_____

4. How many USB ports are in the back of your system? How many are in the front?

_____

Most versions of Windows allow users to customize the display of information to suit their tastes. Complete the following steps to restore Windows defaults to your system:

1. Boot your system and sign in, if necessary. In Windows 10, enter **Control Panel** in the search box. In Windows 8, right-click **Start,** and then click **Control Panel.** In Windows 7, click **Start,** and then click **Control Panel.**

2. If Large icons or Small icons view has been enabled, click the **View by** drop-down menu and select **Category.** Figure 1-2 shows Control Panel in Category view for Windows 10.

Figure 1-2   Windows 10 Control Panel in Category view

3. With Category view enabled, click the **Appearance and Personalization** category. The Appearance and Personalization window opens.

4. In the Appearance and Personalization window, click **File Explorer Options** (called **Folder Options** in Windows 8/7) to open the File Explorer Options dialog box.

5. On the General tab of the File Explorer Options dialog box, click the **Restore Defaults** button (see Figure 1-3), and then click **Apply**.

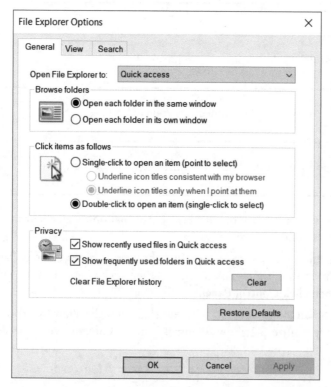

Figure 1-3   Use the File Explorer Options dialog box to restore Windows defaults to all folders

6. Click the **View** tab in the File Explorer Options dialog box. Click the **Restore Defaults** button, and then click **OK** to apply the settings and close the dialog box.

7. In the Appearance and Personalization window, click the **Taskbar and Navigation** icon (called **Taskbar and Start Menu** in Windows 7). The Taskbar and Navigation properties dialog box opens.

8. On the Taskbar tab, verify that **Lock the taskbar** is on or selected. For Windows 10, verify that **Automatically hide the taskbar in desktop mode** is off. (For Windows 8/7, verify that **Auto-hide the taskbar** is not checked.) Also verify that **Use small taskbar buttons** is off or not selected. Click **Apply** if any changes were made. Click **OK** to close the Taskbar and Navigation dialog box. Close the Control Panel window.

9. To manage Start menu settings, do one of the following:

   ◢ In Windows 10, press **Win+I** to open the **Settings** window. Click **Personalization** and then **Start**. Verify that the **Show most used apps**, **Show recently added apps**, and **Show recently opened items in Jump Lists on Start or the taskbar** options are turned **On**. Close the Settings dialog box.

   ◢ In Windows 8, open **Control Panel**, open the **Appearance and Personalization** window, and then open the **Taskbar and Navigation** dialog box. Click the **Jump Lists** tab. Verify that both check boxes under Privacy are selected. Click **OK** to apply the settings. Close all open windows.

   ◢ In Windows 7, open the **Appearance and Personalization** window and then open the **Taskbar and Start Menu Properties** dialog box. Click the **Start Menu** tab in the dialog box. Verify that both check boxes under Privacy are selected. Click **OK** to apply the settings. Close all open windows.

When you are responsible for several computers—or when several people share that responsibility— a base inventory and running record of each system's characteristics and maintenance are fundamental for quick reference. Do the following to document your system's configuration:

1. If your instructor hasn't already provided the Computer Inventory and Maintenance form, download and print it from *cengage.com*. For detailed instructions on how to use the website, see the Preface.

2. *Computer identification:* Fill in the first page of the Inventory form with information about your computer. Also fill in the administrator account name and password under the Windows and Windows Settings heading. (Because this information is confidential, you must be careful to protect this form from unauthorized viewing.)

3. *System:* Open **Control Panel** in Classic view and open the **System** window. Using the information shown in Figure 1-4 for Windows 10, fill in the System subsection under the Windows and Windows Settings heading of your Inventory form. Note that in Windows 7, this window also links to the Windows Experience Index, which rates your system's performance on a scale from 1.0 to 7.9. Close the Control Panel window.

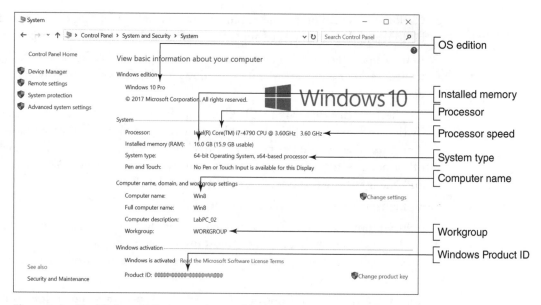

Figure 1-4 The Windows 10 System applet provides basic system information

4. *Windows Update:* To find update settings, do one of the following:

   ◢ In Windows 10, press **Win+I** to open the Settings window. Click **Update & Security**, **Windows Update**, and **Advanced options**. Record how updates are installed on your Inventory form. Close the Settings window.

   ◢ In Windows 8/7, open the **System** window and click **Windows Update**. In the Windows Update window, click **Change settings** in the left pane. The Change settings window shows the schedule for updates to Windows. Record this information in your Inventory form. Close all windows.

5. *File History or Backup and Restore:* To find backup settings, open Control Panel in Classic view. In Windows 10, click **Backup and Restore (Windows 7)**. In Windows 8, click **File History**. In Windows 7, click **Backup and Restore**. If your computer is set to back up automatically, record the information requested in your Inventory form in the File History/Backup and Restore subsection.

6. Notice at the top of the Control Panel window that you'll always see a path in the address bar for whatever window is active. You can click on various parts of this path to go to those levels of Control Panel. The Inventory form lists the corresponding path for each section's information. To return to the main Control Panel window, click **Control Panel** at the beginning of the path.

7. *User accounts:* To complete the Windows and Windows Settings section of the Inventory form, click **User Accounts**, and then click **Manage another account**. (For Windows 7, click **User Accounts and Family Safety**, and then click **Add or remove user accounts**). The Manage Accounts window shows all local user accounts in the system. Record this information on your Inventory form.

PART 2: EXPLORE NETWORK SETTINGS

Follow these steps to gather information about network settings:

1. To access the network settings on your computer, return to **Control Panel** in Classic view and click **Network and Sharing Center**.

> **Notes** If you are using the address bar to navigate options in Control Panel and you can't see the beginning of the path in the address bar, click the double left arrows on the left of the address bar to display the entire path in a drop-down list.

2. In the Network and Sharing Center window, click **Change adapter settings** in the left pane to access the Network Connections window.

3. *Network TCP/IP settings:* Right-click the active network connection, whether it's an Ethernet connection or a Wi-Fi connection, and then click **Properties** from the shortcut menu to open the connection's Properties dialog box. Select **Internet Protocol Version 4 (TCP/IPv4)**, and then click the **Properties** button to view the Internet Protocol Version 4 (TCP/IPv4) Properties dialog box, shown in Figure 1-5. If the radio button for *Obtain an IP address automatically* is selected, then the connection has a dynamic configuration, meaning Windows will request an IP address from a server each time it connects to the network. If the radio button for *Use the following IP address* is selected, an administrator has assigned a static IP address that the computer will always use when connecting to this network. Add the appropriate information in this subsection of your Inventory form, and then click **Cancel** twice to return to the Network Connections window. Repeat this step for any other available network connection.

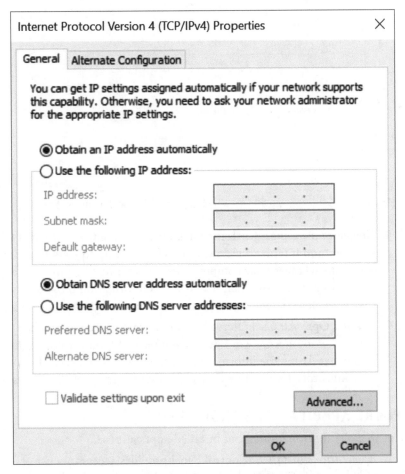

Figure 1-5 TCP/IP is a group of protocols that controls various aspects of communication between two devices on a network

4. *Wireless security settings:* Complete the following if your computer is currently connected to a wireless network; if not, skip to Step 5. To return to the Network and Sharing Center, click **Network and Internet** in the address bar path, and then click the **Network and Sharing Center** category. Under View your active networks, click the wireless connection and then click **Wireless Properties**.

> 📄 **Notes** If the connection is not secured, the Wireless Properties button will not be available.

Click the **Security** tab to find the security information for this network to fill in the Wireless Network Connection subsection of your Inventory form. You can select the **Show characters** check box, as shown in Figure 1-6, to see the Network security key. Click **Cancel** and then click **Close** to return to the Network and Sharing Center.

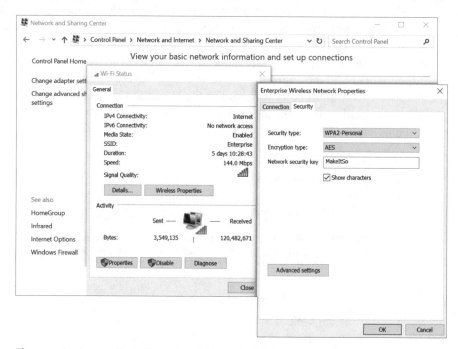

Figure 1-6 Secure all wireless networks to protect data and equipment

5. *Homegroup settings:* Click the **Back** button in the Control Panel window to return to the Network and Internet window. Click **HomeGroup** to view the HomeGroup window and determine whether your computer belongs to a homegroup. If it does, click **View or print the homegroup password** and record this information on your Inventory form. Click **Cancel** to close the View and print your homegroup password window.

6. *Internet Options:* Click **Network and Internet** in the address bar to return to the Network and Internet window. Click **Internet Options** to open the Internet Properties dialog box. Using the information on the General tab, record the home page or pages on your Inventory form. Click **Cancel** to close the Internet Properties dialog box.

PART 3: EXPLORE APPLICATIONS INSTALLED

Follow these steps to gather information about installed applications:

1. *Applications installed:* Control Panel provides access to a list of all programs installed on the system. Open **Control Panel** in Classic view and click **Programs and Features**. Scroll down to find the version of Microsoft Office installed on your computer, and enter

this information on your Inventory form. Search the list for anti-malware software, such as McAfee, Norton, or Microsoft Security Essentials for Windows 7. (Note that Windows Defender is embedded in Windows 10/8 and will not appear in the list of installed applications.) Also look for web browsers, such as Mozilla Firefox and Google Chrome. Then list any other productivity applications (like Dropbox or a graphic design program) installed on the computer, along with their publishers. When you are finished, close the Programs and Features window.

> **Notes** Your inventory of installed applications should include any productivity software or anti-malware software installed. However, it is not necessary to record every item listed in the Programs and Features window.

2. *Anti-malware software:* If applicable, open an anti-malware program you found on the list of programs and determine whether the program updates automatically and, if so, when scans are scheduled to occur. Often, this information will be on the program's home page or in the Settings menu. Record this information on your Inventory form. Close the program when you are finished.

PART 4: EXPLORE HARDWARE INSTALLED

The System Information Utility provides additional information about hardware components and configuration of your system. Do the following to gather this information:

1. *System manufacturer and model:* To open the System Information Utility, enter **msinfo32.exe** in the Windows 10/7 search box or the Windows 8 Run box. (To open the Run box in Windows 8, right-click **Start** and click **Run**.) The System Information window opens. On the System Summary page, find your system's manufacturer and model number, and record this information on your Inventory form.

2. *Drives:* Click the **+** sign next to the Components node on the navigation tree in the left pane. Click the **+** sign next to the Storage node, and then click **Drives**, as shown in Figure 1-7. Add the information requested on your Inventory form for this subsection.

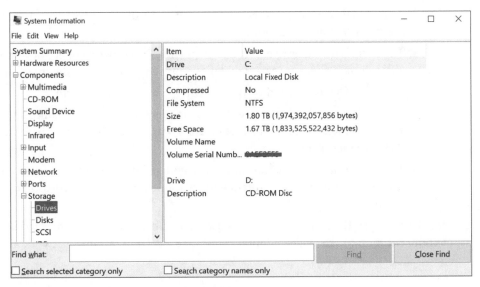

Figure 1-7 A computer may have several drives

3. *Disks:* Click **Disks** in the navigation tree and add the remaining information requested for the System Information Utility section. Close the System Information window.

Use Device Manager to complete the next portion of Part 4.

    1. To open Device Manager, right-click **Start** and click **Device Manager**. The Device Manager console opens, as shown in Figure 1-8.

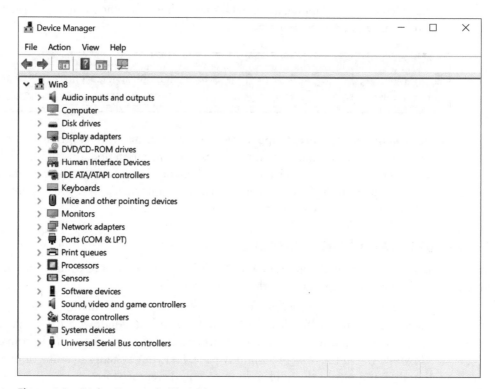

Figure 1-8   Device Manager in Windows

    2. Expand **Display adapters,** and record the name of the adapter(s) on the Computer Inventory and Maintenance form.

    3. Right-click the adapter name, and then click **Properties** to open the adapter's Properties dialog box. (If you have more than one display adapter, use the first adapter listed.)

    4. Click the **Driver** tab, and record the driver version on the form.

    5. On the Driver tab, click **Driver Details** to view the driver file names and the paths to those files. Record that information for up to three files on the Computer Inventory and Maintenance form.

    6. Repeat the same procedure to collect similar information on your computer's wired and wireless network adapters and its sound controller. Record that information on the form.

To complete Part 4, open the computer case and use visual observations of connected hardware to record information about the monitor, the video adapter if installed, and any installed network adapters.

PART 5: EXPLORE BIOS/UEFI SETTINGS

BIOS/UEFI is firmware on the motherboard that manages basic hardware components and the boot process before Windows is launched. Complete the following steps to access BIOS/UEFI settings:

1. To enter the UEFI setup utility from Windows 10, do the following:

   a. Open the **Settings** app and click **Update & Security**. In the left pane, click **Recovery**. Under Advanced startup, click **Restart now**. The computer restarts into the Windows Recovery Environment.

   b. In Windows RE, click **Troubleshoot**, and then click **Advanced options**. On the Advanced options screen, click **UEFI Firmware Settings**, and then click **Restart**. The computer reboots into UEFI setup. When you attempt to access UEFI setup and password protection has been enabled, you must enter a valid password to continue.

2. For Windows 10/8/7, follow these steps to access BIOS/UEFI setup:

   a. Shut down Windows.

   b. Turn on the computer and press the key(s) that launches the BIOS/UEFI setup utility. The key(s) to press usually appears on the screen early in the boot process—for example, "Press Del or F2 to enter setup."

3. Browse through the BIOS/UEFI screens and fill in all the information required in the BIOS/UEFI Settings and Data section of the Computer Inventory and Maintenance form.

4. Exit BIOS/UEFI setup without saving any changes to prevent saving any accidental changes made while you were exploring the BIOS/UEFI setup utility.

Record today's date and your name in the Routine Maintenance section of the Computer Inventory and Maintenance form beginning on page 5, next to Initial Inventory taken. Make a habit of documenting all maintenance and troubleshooting activities for any computer you work on.

ESTIMATED COMPLETION TIME: 15 MINUTES

CHALLENGE ACTIVITY

Programs are available to collect most, if not all, of the configuration information about a computer for you. One of the more popular programs is Belarc Advisor, which compiles information on system components, including manufacturer names, license numbers, and product keys. The program also analyzes your system for weaknesses and may suggest improvements or maintenance. To download and use Belarc Advisor, do the following:

1. Go to **www.belarc.com/free_download.html** and click the free download icon.

2. When the file has completed downloading, use File Explorer (Windows Explorer in Windows 7) to find the .exe file that you just downloaded. At the time of this writing, the file name was **advisorinstaller.exe**. What is the exact path and name of the downloaded file?

   _____

3. Double-click the file to install the program. If a UAC box appears, click **Yes**.

4. When the License Agreement window appears, click **I Agree**. Click **Install**.

5. If the program asks to check for new definitions, click **Yes**. When it reports that it is up to date, click **OK**.

6. The program creates a profile for your system and proceeds with the analysis. The process might take a few minutes. Once the analysis is presented in your browser, print your analysis and file it with your other documentation for this computer. See Figure 1-9 for a sample report.

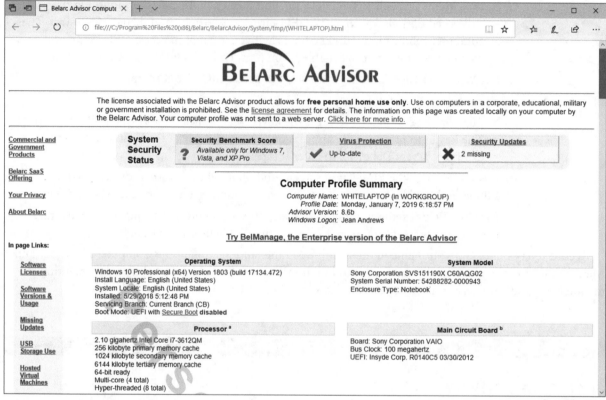

Figure 1-9   Belarc Advisor is free for personal use only

> **Notes**   When using Belarc Advisor, your information remains on your local computer and is not transmitted over the Internet. The program simply uses your computer's browser to display the data.

REVIEW QUESTIONS

1. List two categories available in Control Panel that were not mentioned in the lab:

_____

_____

2. (Windows 7 only) Based on the Windows Experience Index, what component of your computer would you upgrade first? Why?

_____

_____

3. Based on what you found while taking inventory of your computer's system, what maintenance does this computer currently need?

_____

_____

4. Besides the Computer Inventory and Maintenance form, what other documentation should you keep on each computer? How might you store that information?

_____

_____

_____

5. What differences, if any, are there between a list of components derived from a physical inspection and a list of components derived from Control Panel and System Properties?

_____

_____

6. Why is it important for IT technicians to keep documentation on computers for which they are responsible?

_____

_____

_____

_____

LAB 1.3 IDENTIFY COMPUTER PARTS

OBJECTIVES

The goal of this lab is to examine your computer to identify the parts inside and outside the case. After completing this lab, you will be able to:

▲ Identify computer components outside the case

▲ Identify computer components inside the case

MATERIALS REQUIRED

This lab requires the following:

▲ A computer that can be disassembled

▲ A Phillips-head screwdriver

▲ An ESD strap

▲ Measuring tape or ruler

▲ A workgroup of two to four students

◢ A display of six or more computer parts to be identified by students

◢ Internet access on a separate computer (if needed to look up more information)

LAB PREPARATION

Before the lab begins, the instructor or lab assistant needs to do the following for each workgroup:

◢ Gather six or more computer parts for display on a table in the lab area

◢ Put a number on each computer part, from one to six or more

◢ Provide a computer that can have the cover removed

◢ Verify that Internet access is available

ACTIVITY BACKGROUND

When working with a computer system, you must be able to identify the hardware components, both inside and outside the case. Components are not always labeled adequately, especially those inside the case. This lab helps you learn to recognize these components.

ESTIMATED COMPLETION TIME: 30 MINUTES

 Activity

Using the assorted computer parts your instructor has prepared and displayed, fill in the following chart:

Identify the Part	Describe the Computer Component and Its Use
1.	
2.	
3.	
4.	
5.	
6.	

Next, observe the external physical characteristics of your computer system and answer the following questions:

1. What is the size of your monitor? Use your measuring tape or ruler to measure from the upper-left corner to the lower-right corner (the diagonal) on the monitor screen. Is the measurement what you expected based on the size of the monitor?

_____

2. What other external components does your computer have (speakers, printer, and so forth)? Describe each component with as much detail as you can.

_____

_____

3. Look at the back of your computer, and locate all the cables and cords connected to ports and other connections. Fill in the following chart:

Describe the Port or Connector to Which the Cable or Cord Is Connected	Purpose of the Cable or Cord
1.	
2.	
3.	
4.	
5.	
6.	

4. What other ports on the computer are not being used? List them:

_____

_____

Next, you'll open the computer case and examine the components inside. As you work, make sure you do not touch anything inside the case unless you're wearing an ESD strap that's clipped to the case, so that any electrical difference between you and the case is dissipated.

To remove the computer cover when it's attached with screws, follow these steps:

1. Power down the computer and unplug it. Next, unplug the monitor, the printer, and any other device that has its own external power supply. After all power sources are unplugged, press the power button on the computer for three seconds to drain any remaining power.

2. The method required to open a computer case varies depending on the manufacturer. Many cases require that you remove the faceplate on the front of the case first. Other cases require removing a side panel first, and very old cases require removing the sides and top as a single unit first. Study your case for the correct approach.

> **Notes** In the steps that follow, you will find general guidelines for disassembling a computer. If any of these steps do not seem to apply to your system, you'll need to consult the user manual or download a PDF of the manual from the manufacturer's website for more detailed instructions.

3. For a desktop or tower case, locate and remove the screws on the back of the case on the opposite side from the ports. Be careful not to unscrew any screws besides the ones attaching the cover. The other screws are probably holding the power supply in place.

4. After you remove the cover screws, slide the side panel back to remove it from the case, as shown in Figure 1-10.

Figure 1-10   Slide a side panel to the rear and then lift it off the case

To remove the cover from a tower computer that has no visible case screws, follow these steps:

1. Power down the computer and unplug it from its power outlet. Next, unplug the monitor and any other device with an external power source from the power outlet. After all power sources are unplugged, press the power button on the computer for three seconds to drain any remaining power.

2. On some cases, you must pop the front panel off the case before removing the side panels. Look for a lever on the bottom of the panel and hinges at the top. Squeeze the lever to release the front panel and lift it off the case (see Figure 1-11). Then remove any screws holding the side panel in place, as shown in Figure 1-12, and slide the side panel to the front and then off the case.

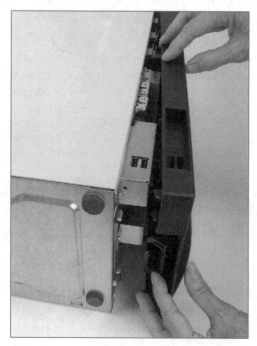

Figure 1-11   Some cases require removing the front panel before removing the side panels of a computer case

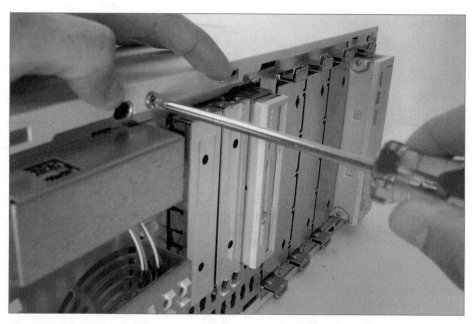

Figure 1-12 Screws hold the side panel in place

> **Notes** Some case panels don't use screws at all; these side panels usually have buttons or tabs to release the cover.

With the cover removed, you're ready to look for some components. As you complete the following, you might want to refer to drawings and photos on the Internet for additional information on the specific components in your system:

1. Put on your ESD strap and connect the clip to the side of the computer case.

2. Identify and describe the following major components. List any other components you find inside the case. Fill in the following chart. For any drives you find installed, describe the type of interface used (for example, SATA or IDE):

Component	Description—Include the Manufacturer and Model Name (if Listed) as Well as Its Distinguishing Characteristics
Power supply	
Motherboard	
Hard drive(s)	
CD/DVD drive(s)	
RAM	
System fan (not inside the power supply)	
Video card (if not integrated)	
Network card (if not integrated)	
Sound card (if not integrated)	

REVIEW QUESTIONS

1. How did you decide which expansion card was the video card?

2. How did you identify the type of CPU you have?

3. Does your system have much room for adding new components? What types of expansion slots are available for adding new cards?

4. Is there space for upgrading the RAM? If there isn't, what could you do instead to upgrade?

5. Where (specifically) would you go on the Internet to download a PDF of the motherboard manual or system manual? What information would you need to identify which manual to download?

LAB 1.4 IDENTIFY FORM FACTORS

OBJECTIVES

The goal of this lab is for you to gain experience in identifying form factors. After completing this lab, you will be able to:

- Identify the form factor of the case, motherboard, and power supply
- Select appropriate components to match an existing form factor

MATERIALS REQUIRED

This lab requires the following:

- A computer designated for this lab
- A computer toolkit with ESD strap
- Internet access

LAB PREPARATION

Before the lab begins, the instructor or lab assistant needs to do the following:

- Verify that Windows starts with no errors
- Verify that Internet access is available

ACTIVITY BACKGROUND

A form factor is a set of specifications for the size, shape, and configuration of the components that make up a computer system. Sharing a common standard allows components such as the case, motherboard, and power supply to fit together and function properly. Some common form factors are ATX, microATX, and Mini-ITX. Each comes in several variations that determine characteristics such as size and shape. In this lab, you identify your system's form factor and research some identifying characteristics of common form factors.

ESTIMATED COMPLETION TIME: 30 MINUTES

 Activity

1. Open your browser and go to your favorite search engine, such as *google.com*.

2. Use the Internet to research the main differences between ATX and microATX, and list them here:

   _____

   _____

   _____

3. Now explain the main differences between ATX and Mini-ITX (also known as ITX):

   _____

   _____

   _____

4. Each form factor comes in several sizes. How could you tell whether a system was regular ATX, microATX, or Mini-ITX?

   _____

   _____

   _____

5. Form factors are also available in various shapes. What slimline form factor is similar to but not compatible with ATX?

   _____

6. Now turn the computer off and unplug the power cord.

7. Disconnect all peripherals and remove the case cover.

8. Examine the case, motherboard, and power supply.

9. What is the form factor of this system?

   _____

10. Close the case, reattach the peripherals, and test the system to make sure it boots without errors.

REVIEW QUESTIONS

1. Why is it important that your case and motherboard share a compatible form factor?

   _____

2. When might you want to use a slimline form factor?

   _____

3. What advantages does ATX have over microATX?

   _____

4. What are two operating systems that can be installed in systems using a Mini-ITX motherboard?

   _____

5. Is it possible to determine the form factor without opening the case?

   _____

LAB 1.5 TAKE A COMPUTER APART AND PUT IT BACK TOGETHER

OBJECTIVES

The goal of this lab is to make you comfortable working inside a computer case. After completing this lab, you will be able to:

◢ Take a computer apart
◢ Recognize components
◢ Reassemble the computer

MATERIALS REQUIRED

This lab requires the following:

◢ A computer designated for disassembly
◢ A computer toolkit with an ESD strap and mat
◢ A marker and masking tape
◢ Small containers, such as paper cups, to hold screws as you work
◢ A workgroup of two to four students; an individual student can work this lab as well

LAB PREPARATION

Before the lab begins, the instructor or lab assistant needs to do the following:

◢ Verify that a computer designated for disassembly is available to each student or workgroup

ACTIVITY BACKGROUND

If you follow directions and take your time, there's no reason to be intimidated by working inside a computer case. This lab takes you step by step through the process of disassembling and reassembling a computer. Follow your computer lab's posted safety procedures when disassembling and reassembling a computer, and remember to always wear your ESD strap. Also, never force a component to fit into its slot. Doing so might damage the card or the motherboard.

You begin this lab by removing the cover of your computer and then removing the components inside. Next, you reassemble the components and replace the cover. This lab includes steps for working with a desktop computer and a tower computer. Follow the steps that apply to your computer.

In this lab, you're instructed to disassemble your computer in this order: case cover, interior cables and cords, expansion cards, motherboard, drives, power supply, and case fans. Because some systems require a different disassembly order, your instructor might change the order. For example, you might not be able to get to the power supply to remove it until drives or the motherboard are out of the way. Be sure to follow any specific directions from your instructor.

> **Notes** In a lab environment, the instructor might consider giving a demonstration of tearing down a computer and putting it back together before students begin this lab.

When you remove a screw in the following activity, place it in a paper cup or on a piece of paper so that you can keep different-sized screws separated. Later, when you reassemble your computer, having the screws organized in this way makes it easier to match the right screw to the hole.

ESTIMATED COMPLETION TIME: 60 MINUTES

 Activity

Follow the procedure outlined in the following steps to remove the case cover and expansion cards. (If you're working with a tower case, lay it on its side so that the motherboard is on the bottom.)

1. Remove the cover from your computer and attach your ESD strap to the side of the case.

2. To make reassembly easier, take notes or make a sketch (or take a picture) of the current placement of boards and cables, and identify each board and cable. You can use a marker to indicate the location of a cable on an expansion card or the motherboard. Note the orientation of the cable. Each cable for an IDE hard drive or optical drive has a colored marking on one side of the cable called the "edge color." This color marks pin 1 of the cable. On the board, pin 1 is marked with the number 1 or 2 beside the pin or with a square soldering pad on the back side of the board, as shown in Figure 1-13. You might not be able to see this soldering pad now.

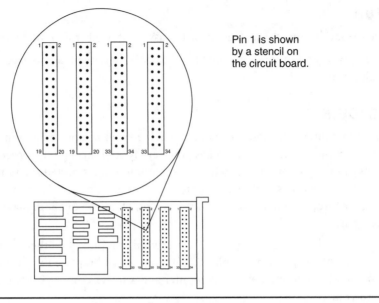

Pin 1 is shown
by a stencil on
the circuit board.

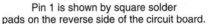

Pin 1 is shown by square solder
pads on the reverse side of the circuit board.

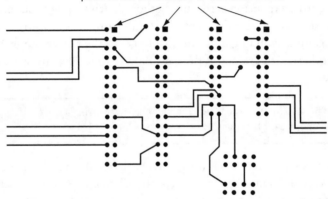

Figure 1-13   How to find pin 1 on an expansion card

> **📝 Notes** Unless your system is really old, it most likely does not have IDE drives. Most modern computers have SATA drives.

3. Remove any cables from the expansion cards. There's no need to remove the other end of the cable from its component (hard drive or optical drive). Lay the cable over the top of the component or case.

4. Remove the screw holding the first expansion card to the back of the case.

5. Grasp the card with both hands, and remove it by lifting straight up and rocking the card from end to end (not side to side). Rocking the card from side to side might spread the slot opening and weaken the connection. When you remove the card, be sure you don't touch the edge connectors on the card. (Oil from fingers can tarnish or corrode these connectors.)

6. If the card had a cable attached, examine the card connector for the cable. Can you identify pin 1? Lay the card aside on a flat surface. Don't stack cards.

7. Remove any other expansion cards the same way.

8. In some proprietary systems, a riser card assembly attaches to the motherboard, with each card attached to the assembly. If your system has this arrangement, remove it now. It's probably held in place by screws or clips and may or may not have a rail guide you can use to locate the assembly in the case.

9. Unplug any case fans.

In some systems, it's easier to remove the drives first and then the motherboard. In other systems, it's easier to remove the motherboard first. In these instructions, to make sure you don't risk dropping a drive on the motherboard when removing the drive, you're directed to remove the motherboard first and then the drives. Your instructor, however, might prefer that you remove the drives first and then the motherboard.

1. Begin removing the motherboard by removing any remaining wires or cables such as power cables, audio wires, or wires from the front of the case. Be sure to make notes or label the cables so that you can reinstall them correctly.

2. Finish removing the motherboard by removing the screws holding the board to the spacers or standoffs. Usually six to nine screws attach the motherboard to the case. Be careful not to gouge the board or damage components with the screwdriver. Because the screws on the motherboard are often located between components, they can be hard to reach. Be very careful not to damage the motherboard. See Figure 1-14.

Figure 1-14 Remove the screws that hold the motherboard to the case

> **Notes** Before you remove the motherboard, it is not necessary to remove the RAM or processor from it, or to remove the cooler on top of the processor. However, if the cooler has a large fan and is very heavy, you might need to remove it before you remove the motherboard. Follow your instructor's directions about removing the cooler.

3. The motherboard should now be free, and you can carefully remove it from the case. See Figure 1-15.

Figure 1-15 Carefully remove the motherboard from the case

4. To remove drives, remove the data cable if it's still attached. Many cases have a removable drive bay. The drives are attached to this bay, and the bay can be removed with all the drives attached. This arrangement makes it easy to get to the drive-mounting screws that hold the drives in place. If your case has a removable drive bay, this removal method is preferred. Otherwise, remove each drive separately. Be careful not to jar the drive as you remove it from the case.

5. Remove any CD, DVD, or Blu-ray drives from the case. These drives are usually in the 5-inch drive bays and are normally held in place by two or four screws. After the screws are removed, the drive slides out the front of the case.

6. Support the power supply with one hand, and remove the screws attaching it to the case. You can then remove the power supply from the case.

7. Remove any other components, such as a case fan.

Now that you have removed all the components, you're ready to reassemble the computer. Replace each component carefully. Take care to install each component firmly without overtightening the screws. Don't force components to fit. If a component won't fit easily the way it should, look for some obstruction preventing it from falling into place. Look carefully for the reason the component won't fit correctly and make any small adjustments as necessary. The following steps outline the assembly procedure, which is essentially the reverse of the disassembly procedure:

1. Install the case fan.

2. Install the power supply, and replace the screws holding it in position.

3. Install the drives in their bays and then install the motherboard, unless your instructor prefers that you install the motherboard first.

4. Connect wires from the front of the case to the front panel header on the motherboard.

5. Connect the power cables from the power supply to the drives and the motherboard. Double-check to make sure all the power supply connectors to the motherboard are connected correctly.

6. Place each card in its slot (it doesn't have to be the same slot, just the same type of slot), and replace the screw. If possible, don't place a video card near the power supply; otherwise, electromagnetic interference (EMI) from the power supply might affect the video picture. Also, because video cards produce so much heat, don't place another card adjacent to it; leave room for airflow.

7. Replace any cables to expansion cards, being sure to align the colored edge with pin 1. (In some cases, it might work better to connect the cable to the card before you put the card in the expansion slot.)

8. Check to make sure no cables are interfering with any fan's ability to turn. A common cause of an overheated system is a fan that can't move air because a cable is preventing it from spinning.

9. When all components are installed, you should have refitted all the screws you removed earlier. If some screws are missing, it's important to turn the case upside down and gently shake it to dislodge any wayward screws. Any screw left lying on a board has the potential to short out that board when power is applied. Don't use a magnet to try to find missing screws in the case because you might damage data on hard drives.

10. Plug in the keyboard, monitor, and mouse.

11. In a classroom environment, have the instructor check your work before you power up.

12. Plug in the power cord to the computer and to the power outlet or surge protector. Verify that any voltage selector switch on the rear of the case is set to 115 V, and turn on the power switch.

13. Using the power button on the front of the case, turn on the power and check that the computer is working properly before you replace the cover. Don't touch the inside of the case while the power is on.

14. If all is well, turn off the computer and replace the cover and its screws. If the computer doesn't work, don't panic. Turn off the power, and then go back and check each cable connection and each expansion card. You probably haven't seated a card solidly in the slot. After you have double-checked everything, try again.

REVIEW QUESTIONS

1. When removing the cover, why should you take care to remove only the screws that hold the cover on?

_____

_____

2. How should you rock a card to remove it from its slot? Why is it important to know how to remove a card correctly?

_____

_____

3. What should you do to help you remember which components connect to which cables?

_____

4. What marking on a ribbon cable identifies pin 1?

_____

5. What component(s) defines the system's form factor?

_____

_____

6. What form factor does your computer use?

_____

7. Why would an IT technician ever have to change out a computer's motherboard?

_____

_____

_____

LAB 1.6 INVESTIGATE COMPUTER TEARDOWN PROCEDURES

OBJECTIVES

The goal of this lab is to increase your familiarity with the process of taking apart a computer and reassembling it. After completing this lab, you will be able to:

▲ Identify multiple factors that affect the teardown process

▲ Distinguish between best practices and potentially problematic shortcuts

▲ Anticipate additional considerations for disassembling a laptop as compared to a desktop computer

MATERIALS REQUIRED

This lab requires the following:

▲ Internet access

LAB PREPARATION

Before the lab begins, the instructor or lab assistant needs to do the following:

▲ Verify that Internet access is available

ACTIVITY BACKGROUND

With such a variety of computer cases and parts options available, it helps to become familiar with as many different systems as possible before working in the field. Familiarity, however, can breed its own challenges. Some technicians, as they become more comfortable working inside a computer case, start to take shortcuts that can damage equipment or cause injury.

In this lab, you find and review an online video showing the teardown of a desktop or tower computer and then evaluate the technician's teardown process. Watch for errors the technician makes, such as not using an ESD strap or having screws left over after reassembly. Refer to the text as needed to help you remember the various guidelines and safety precautions.

Finally, you select an online video of a laptop teardown, and identify significant differences in the process compared to taking apart a desktop computer.

> **Notes** This lab should be completed after you've completed Lab 1.5 so that you can identify what is different about the system in your selected video compared to the system you worked on.

ESTIMATED COMPLETION TIME: 30 MINUTES

 Activity

Complete the following steps to investigate different procedures for taking apart a computer and putting it back together:

1. Review the portions of the chapter that discuss the proper procedures for taking apart and reassembling a computer. Pay particular attention to the safety precautions, and take notes as needed.

2. Search the web to find a video that shows the entire process of taking apart a desktop or tower computer and putting it back together. Some videos can be found on *youtube.com*. Try to find a video that is done well, with good camera angles and useful discussion about the parts shown in the video. What is the URL for the video you selected?

   _____

3. Describe at least four mistakes made by the technician in the teardown or reassembly process. Sometimes the technician will notice a mistake himself, such as missing screws that should have been loosened before attempting to remove the motherboard. Sometimes the technician doesn't seem to be aware—or chooses to ignore—that he is risking damage to expensive parts or taking unnecessary safety risks.

   _____

   _____

   _____

   _____

4. Identify the possible consequences of each mistake along with ways to prevent those mistakes in the future:

   _____

   _____

   _____

   _____

   _____

   _____

   _____

5. Identify at least two significant differences between the system you worked on for Lab 1.5 and the system shown in the video. Are there different drives in the case, such as multiple hard disk drives or optical drives? Was there a graphics card or a riser card? Was a different order of steps needed because of component placement inside the case?

_____

_____

_____

6. Select a video showing the disassembly and reassembly of a laptop computer. What is the URL for the video you selected?

_____

_____

_____

7. What are three significant differences you notice about the parts or their arrangement inside a laptop compared to the desktop computer you worked with in Lab 1.5? What is one significant difference about the process of taking apart a laptop compared to taking apart a desktop?

_____

_____

_____

_____

REVIEW QUESTIONS

1. What are three notable characteristics of the system shown in the first video you selected? For example, was this an older or newer system? How can you tell? Who is the manufacturer of the system, the case, and/or the components? What drives or other optional components were included in the system?

_____

_____

_____

_____

2. What tools did the technician use in each video? What additional tools would you recommend having on hand to take apart and reassemble a computer?

_____

_____

_____

3. Which two components of a computer should be treated as "black boxes" and not opened without specialized training?

_____

_____

4. What are two methods for keeping track of screws during disassembly so that reassembly goes more smoothly?

_____

_____

LAB 1.7 COMPARE LAPTOPS AND DESKTOPS

OBJECTIVES

The goal of this lab is to compare the specifications and costs for laptop and desktop computers. After completing this lab, you will be able to:

▲ Compile a list of specifications for a computer according to its purpose

▲ Locate a desktop computer and a laptop computer with similar specifications

▲ Compare the price of a desktop computer to that of a similar laptop computer and decide which you would purchase

MATERIALS REQUIRED

This lab requires the following:

▲ Internet access

▲ Access to a printer (optional)

LAB PREPARATION

Before the lab begins, the instructor or lab assistant needs to do the following:

▲ Verify that Internet access is available

ACTIVITY BACKGROUND

When you shop for a computer, your purchasing decisions are generally driven by questions such as the following: For what purposes will the computer be used? What features are required to accomplish your goals? What features would be nice to have but aren't essential? On what features are you willing to compromise to gain others? What future needs do you anticipate? If you understand your needs before you start shopping, you're less likely to regret your purchase.

One of the most basic decisions is whether to choose a laptop computer or a desktop computer. Unlike desktops, laptops are portable; however, to make laptops portable, manufacturers often sacrifice performance, storage space, or other features. In addition, you usually pay more for a laptop than for a desktop computer with comparable features. In this lab, you compile a list of requirements for a computer, locate a laptop computer and a desktop computer with those features, and compare the two systems.

Activity

Pretend you are about to buy a computer. The two most important criteria to determine which computer to buy are usually how it will be used and the price. Do the following to determine your requirements for your new computer:

1. You first need to decide how the computer will be used. Answer the following questions:

   ◢ For what purposes will the computer be used? (Possible uses include office applications, video playback, high-end gaming, and software development.)

   _____

   _____

   _____

   ◢ What features are required to make the computer usable for its intended purpose? Include in your list the amount of memory and hard drive space you want. (Some features you might consider include wireless [Wi-Fi, Bluetooth, or cellular] support, the display or screen type, software packages supported, and I/O ports.)

   _____

   _____

   _____

   _____

   ◢ List any additional features you would like to have but don't require:

   _____

   _____

   _____

   ◢ Which operating system do you want to use with your computer?

   _____

2. Use computer manufacturers' websites or comparison websites (such as *cnet.com* or *pricewatch.com*) to find one laptop and one desktop computer that fulfill as many of your requirements as possible and are as similar to each other as possible. Summarize your findings in Table 1-1. Save or print the webpages that support your gathered information.

Features	Desktop Computer	Laptop Computer
Manufacturer and model		
Processor type and frequency		
Memory installed		
Hard drive space		
Operating system		
Video card		
Optical drive		
Display size		
External ports		
Preinstalled applications		
Price		

Table 1-1 Desktop and laptop computer specifications

3. Online reviews of a computer can help you find out what others think of the computer, how it performs, and what problems to expect. Find two or three reviews for each of the two computers you researched in Step 2, and summarize the best review you found for each computer:

   ◢ For the desktop computer, what is the URL of the review?

   _____

   ◢ List the major points in the review about the desktop computer:

   _____

   _____

   _____

   ◢ How does this review affect your opinion of this desktop computer, its warranty, online support of the desktop, or the computer's manufacturer?

   _____

   _____

   ◢ For the laptop computer, what is the URL of the review?

   _____

◢ List the major points in the review about the laptop:

_____

_____

_____

◢ How does this review affect your opinion of this laptop, its warranty, online support of the laptop, or the computer's manufacturer?

_____

_____

4. If the desktop computer package does not include the monitor, keyboard, and mouse, you need to include the price of these peripherals so that you can make a fair comparison between the cost of a desktop and the cost of a laptop. Answer the following:

◢ Are the monitor, keyboard, and mouse included in the desktop computer package?

_____

◢ If not, what is the total price of these three peripherals? Provide webpages to support your answer.

_____

5. Based on your requirements and the research you recorded in Table 1-1, would you buy the desktop computer or the laptop? Explain your answer.

_____

_____

_____

6. How did the reviews of the desktop and laptop affect your decision? Explain your answer.

_____

_____

_____

7. For an operating system, you might want to consider using Windows by Microsoft or macOS by Apple. Compare two laptop computers that are similar in features except that one uses Windows and the other uses macOS. Fill in Table 1-2 with the results of your research. You may use the laptop from Table 1-1.

Installed Features	Windows	macOS
Website (URL)		
Brand and model		
Operating system		
Processor type		
Processor speed		
RAM		
Hard drive type/speed		
Optical drive type		
Networking		
I/O ports		
Warranty		
Other features		
Installed software		
Price		

Table 1-2 Windows and macOS laptop computer comparison

8. Based on the research you recorded in Table 1-2, which is the better buy, a Windows laptop or a macOS laptop? Explain your answer.

_____

_____

_____

REVIEW QUESTIONS

1. What are the two most important criteria when deciding which computer to buy?

_____

_____

2. Why do laptop computers cost more than desktop computers?

_____

_____

3. List three reasons why it is easier to upgrade a desktop computer than a laptop computer.

   _____

   _____

4. Other than price, what factors might someone consider when deciding whether to buy a Windows laptop or a macOS laptop?

   _____

   _____

   _____

5. In this lab, was it easier comparing a desktop computer to a laptop, or comparing a Windows laptop to a macOS laptop? Explain your answer.

   _____

   _____

   _____

CHAPTER 2

All About Motherboards

Labs included in this chapter:

- **Lab 2.1:** Use the HWiNFO Hardware Information Utility

- **Lab 2.2:** Identify Motherboard Components

- **Lab 2.3:** Identify a Motherboard and Find
  Documentation and Drivers on the Web

- **Lab 2.4:** Remove and Replace a Motherboard

- **Lab 2.5:** Examine BIOS/UEFI Settings and Research
  BIOS/UEFI Updates

- **Lab 2.6:** Flash BIOS/UEFI

LAB 2.1 USE THE HWiNFO HARDWARE INFORMATION UTILITY

OBJECTIVES

The goal of this lab is to use a hardware information utility to examine a system. After completing this lab, you will be able to:

▲ Download and install the HWiNFO utility

▲ Use the HWiNFO utility to examine your system

MATERIALS REQUIRED

This lab requires the following:

▲ A computer designated for this lab

▲ Windows 10/8/7 operating system

▲ Internet access for file downloading only

LAB PREPARATION

Before the lab begins, the instructor or lab assistant needs to do the following:

▲ Verify that Windows starts with no errors

▲ Verify that Internet access is available

▲ For labs that don't have Internet access, download the latest version of HWiNFO from *hwinfo.com* to a file server or other storage media available to students in the lab.

ACTIVITY BACKGROUND

A hardware information utility can be useful when you want to identify a hardware component in a system without having to open the computer case. Also, a hardware information utility can help you identify features of a motherboard, video card, or processor installed in a system and establish benchmarks for these components. In this lab, you learn to use HWiNFO, which was written by Martin Malík from the Slovak Republic. The utility comes in a Windows version and a DOS version. You can use the Windows version on Windows 10/8/7 computers, and you can install the portable version on a USB flash drive or CD so that the utility is available on any computer you're troubleshooting.

In this lab, you download a shareware Windows version of HWiNFO from the web and then learn how to use it. Websites sometimes change, so as you follow the instructions in this lab, you might have to adjust for changes to the *hwinfo.com* site. If your lab doesn't have Internet access, ask your instructor for the location of the file downloaded previously for your use. Write the path to that file here:

ESTIMATED COMPLETION TIME: 30 MINUTES

 Activity

Follow these steps to download and run the Windows HWiNFO utility:

1. Go to the HWiNFO website at *hwinfo.com*. Be careful not to click links to ads or to other downloads. Read more about HWiNFO. Click **Download for FREE**.

2. In the Installer column, highlight **Download for Free** and click **Local (U.S.)**. The executable file downloads to your Downloads folder. Open the folder and double-click the downloaded file to start the installation.

> **Notes** At the time of publication, the latest version of HWiNFO was 6.02, and the name of the downloaded file was hwi_602.exe. However, your downloaded file might have a different name.

3. If the UAC dialog box opens, click **Run** or **Yes** to start setup. Follow the directions on the screen to install the software. Retain all the default settings. The utility launches a Welcome dialog box after the installation completes.

4. To view and change HWiNFO settings, click **Settings**. Notice that the utility is set to display system summary information when it first launches. Click **OK** to close the Settings box.

5. To run HWiNFO, click **Run** in the Welcome dialog box. When the utility runs, it examines your system, and then the HWiNFO boxes shown in Figure 2-1 open.

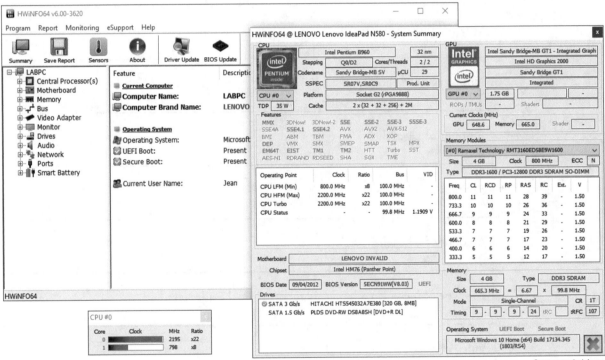

Figure 2-1 HWiNFO for Windows hardware information's initial display

Often, you are not given step-by-step directions when using utility software but must learn how to use it by exploring menus and using the software's help functions. The following steps give you practice in doing that.

1. Use the HWiNFO utility to find the following information about your system:

◢ Motherboard or laptop model and manufacturer:

_____

◢ Motherboard chipset:

_____

◢ Motherboard slots (desktop system):

_____

◢ BIOS/UEFI manufacturer:

_____

◢ BIOS/UEFI version:

_____

◢ BIOS/UEFI release date:

_____

◢ CPU brand name:

_____

◢ Processor socket (platform):

_____

◢ Original processor frequency:

_____

◢ Number of CPU cores:

_____

◢ Amount of L1 cache:

_____

◢ Amount of L2 cache:

_____

◢ Amount of L3 cache:

_____

◢ Bus type of the video adapter, as reported by the adapter:

_____

◢ Video chipset:

_____

◢ Amount of video memory (RAM):

_____

2. If you have a desktop system, identify your motherboard's serial number. Expand **Motherboard, SMBIOS DMI,** and then click **Mainboard.** What is your motherboard's serial number?

_____

3. Exit the utility.

REVIEW QUESTIONS

1. List three reasons you might use HWiNFO when troubleshooting or upgrading a computer:

   _____

   _____

   _____

2. You are considering upgrading memory on a laptop. What are three attributes of currently installed memory that HWiNFO can give to help you with this decision?

   _____

3. You suspect a hard drive in a system might be failing. What type of data about the hard drive can HWiNFO give you to help you diagnose the problem? Which button on the main menu do you select to get this data?

   _____

   _____

   _____

4. List two precautions you should take when using free utility software available on the web.

   _____

   _____

LAB 2.2 IDENTIFY MOTHERBOARD COMPONENTS

OBJECTIVES

The goal of this lab is to practice identifying motherboard form factors and components. After completing this lab, you will be able to:

◢ Identify a motherboard's CPU type

◢ Identify connectors

◢ Identify the form factor based on component type and placement

MATERIALS REQUIRED

Instructors are encouraged to supply a variety of motherboards, some common and others not as common. At the very least, this lab requires the following:

◢ Three different motherboards

> **Notes** If three motherboards aren't available, refer to the websites of three motherboard manufacturers.

LAB PREPARATION

Before the lab begins, the instructor or lab assistant needs to do the following:

◢ Gather an assortment of motherboards, with as many form factors as possible, and label the motherboards as Motherboard 1, Motherboard 2, and Motherboard 3

ACTIVITY BACKGROUND

As an IT technician, you should be able to look at a motherboard and determine what type of CPU, RAM, and form factor you're working with. You should also be able to recognize any unusual components the board might have. In this lab, you examine different motherboards and note some important information about them.

ESTIMATED COMPLETION TIME: 30 MINUTES

 Activity

Fill in the following chart for your assigned motherboards. If you have more than three motherboards, use additional paper. When the entry in the Item column is a question (such as "Parallel ATA (IDE) connector?"), write a number or a Yes or No answer.

Item	Motherboard 1	Motherboard 2	Motherboard 3
Manufacturer/model			
BIOS/UEFI manufacturer			
CPU socket			
Chipset			
RAM slot type			
How many RAM slots?			
How many RAM channels?			
How many PCI slots?			
How many PCIe ×1 slots?			
How many PCIe ×16 slots?			
How many M.2 slots?			
Parallel ATA (IDE) connector?			
How many SATA connectors?			
How many SATA Express connectors?			
Embedded video? How many video ports?			
Embedded audio? How many audio ports?			
Form factor			
Describe any unusual components			

REVIEW QUESTIONS

1. What are the two main differences between an ATX and microATX board?

   _____

   _____

2. How can you determine the chipset if it's not written on the board?

   _____

   _____

3. Of the motherboards you examined, which do you think is the oldest? Why?

   _____

   _____

   _____

4. Which motherboard best supports old and new technology? Why?

   _____

   _____

   _____

5. Which motherboard seems to provide the best possibility for expansion? Why?

   _____

   _____

   _____

6. Which motherboard is most likely the easiest to configure? Why?

   _____

7. Which motherboard do you think is the most expensive? Why?

   _____

8. What are some considerations a motherboard manufacturer has to contend with when designing a motherboard? (For example, consider room for large CPUs and cooling fans, where the power supply is located in relationship to the power connector, new technologies, and so forth.)

   _____

   _____

LAB 2.3 IDENTIFY A MOTHERBOARD AND FIND DOCUMENTATION AND DRIVERS ON THE WEB

OBJECTIVES

The goal of this lab is to explain how to identify a motherboard and find online documentation for it. After completing this lab, you will be able to:

▲ Identify a motherboard by examining it physically

▲ Determine a motherboard's manufacturer and model

▲ Search the web for motherboard documentation

MATERIALS REQUIRED

This lab requires the following:

▲ A computer designated for disassembly

▲ Internet access

▲ Adobe Acrobat Reader

▲ A computer toolkit with ESD strap

▲ Ability to print (optional)

LAB PREPARATION

Before the lab begins, the instructor or lab assistant needs to do the following:

▲ Verify that Windows starts with no errors

▲ Verify that Internet access is available

▲ Verify that Adobe Acrobat Reader is installed

ACTIVITY BACKGROUND

Often, an IT technician is asked to repair a computer for which the documentation is lost or not available. Fortunately, you can usually find documentation for a device online, as long as you have the device's manufacturer name and model number. In this lab, you learn how to find the manufacturer's name and model number on a motherboard, and then locate documentation for that device on the Internet.

ESTIMATED COMPLETION TIME: 30 MINUTES

 Activity

Follow these steps to gather information about your motherboard and processor:

1. Windows can identify a system's installed processor and might be able to identify the motherboard installed. Boot your computer to the Windows desktop. In the Windows 10/8 Run box or the Windows 7 search box, enter **msinfo32.exe**. The System Information window opens. Write down the following information:

   ▲ Processor installed:

◢ System manufacturer (likely to be the motherboard manufacturer):

_____

◢ System model (likely to be the motherboard model):

_____

◢ BIOS/UEFI version/date (might help identify the motherboard):

_____

2. Shut down the system, unplug the power cord, and then press the power button for three seconds to drain residual power.

3. Following safety precautions, including using an ESD strap, remove the computer's case cover, and then remove any components obscuring your view of the motherboard. In some cases, you might have to remove the motherboard itself, but this step usually isn't necessary. If you think it is necessary to remove the motherboard, ask your instructor for guidance.

4. Look for a stenciled or silk-screened label printed on the circuit board that indicates the manufacturer and model. Note that other components sometimes have labels printed on an affixed sticker. On a motherboard, the label is usually printed directly on the circuit board. Common motherboard manufacturers include ASUS, Intel, and ASRock.

> **Notes** Note that the manufacturer name is usually printed in much larger type than the model number. Model numbers often include both letters and numbers, and many indicate a version number as well. Figure 2-2 shows an example of a motherboard label.

Source: newegg.com

Figure 2-2 A label printed directly on a motherboard

5. Record the information on the motherboard label:

_____

6. Take your information to a computer with Internet access and open a web browser.

7. If you know the manufacturer's URL, go directly to the manufacturer's website. (Table 2-1 lists the URLs for some motherboard manufacturers.) If you don't know the manufacturer's URL, search using the manufacturer or model, as shown in Figure 2-3. In the search results, click a link associated with the manufacturer. If this link doesn't take you directly to the documentation, it usually gets you within two or three links. Continue until you find the manufacturer's website.

Manufacturer	Web Address
ASRock	*asrock.com*
ASUS	*asus.com*
BIOSTAR	*biostar-usa.com*
EVGA	*evga.com*
Gigabyte Technology Co., Ltd.	*gigabyte.com*
Intel Corporation	*intel.com*
Micro-Star International (MSI)	*us.msi.com*

Table 2-1   URLs for major motherboard manufacturers

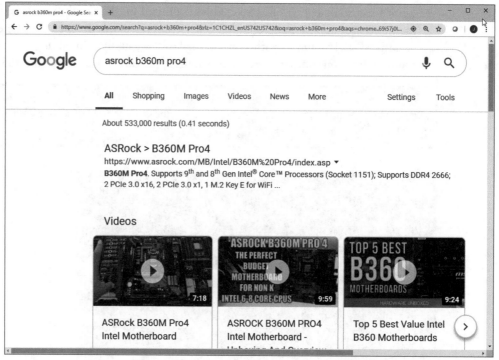

Source: google.com

Figure 2-3   Search results using the manufacturer name and model number

8. When you have found the site of your motherboard's manufacturer, look for a link for service or support. Click this link, and, if necessary, select a product category and model number. Sometimes, knowing the type of processor the board supports can be useful in finding the right motherboard.

9. Continue working your way through the site until you find the motherboard documentation. The documentation might include a variety of documents covering technical specifications and installation instructions. Often the documentation includes a basic manual, which is usually a combination of technical and installation specifications.

10. When you find the documentation, you might also find a link to updated drivers. If you see this link, click it and note the release date of the drivers. If they are newer than your system's current drivers, it's often advisable to update the drivers as well. If available, record the release dates for updated drivers:

_____

11. Return to the main documentation page and select the manual if it's available. If it isn't, select the installation instructions.

12. The manual is probably in PDF format, so you may need to have Adobe Acrobat Reader installed. If you have the Adobe browser plug-in, you can open the document from the source location; if not, you can download the manual to your computer and then open it. Using your preferred method, open the document. Either save or print the document because you will need it in Lab 2.4.

REVIEW QUESTIONS

1. How is the label usually applied to or written on a motherboard? How is it most often applied to other components?

_____

2. What type of link on a manufacturer's website usually leads you to manuals and other documentation?

_____

3. What other downloads about your motherboard might you want to find on the manufacturer's website?

_____

4. In what format is documentation most often available for download?

_____

5. When supporting motherboards, what helpful information besides downloads can be found on the manufacturer's website?

_____

LAB 2.4 REMOVE AND REPLACE A MOTHERBOARD

OBJECTIVES

The goal of this lab is to familiarize yourself with the process of replacing an old or faulty motherboard. After completing this lab, you will be able to:

◢ Use CPU-Z to identify the motherboard

◢ Find the motherboard manual on the web

◢ Remove a motherboard

▲ Install a replacement motherboard

▲ Configure a new motherboard according to its documentation

MATERIALS REQUIRED

This lab requires the following:

▲ A computer designated for this lab

▲ Motherboard manual (see manufacturer's website or use documentation from Lab 2.3)

▲ Two workgroups of two students each

▲ A computer toolkit with ESD strap

▲ Internet access to download CPU-Z

LAB PREPARATION

Before the lab begins, the instructor or lab assistant needs to do the following:

▲ Verify that Windows starts with no errors

▲ Verify that Internet access is available or provide the downloaded CPU-Z installation file from *cpuid.com*

ACTIVITY BACKGROUND

In this lab, you exchange a motherboard with another workgroup to simulate the process of replacing a faulty motherboard. After you install the new motherboard, you must configure it for your system by adjusting BIOS/UEFI settings as needed.

ESTIMATED COMPLETION TIME: 60 MINUTES

 Activity

In this lab, you download and install CPU-Z, locate the motherboard manual, remove the motherboard, and install and configure a replacement motherboard. While removing the motherboard, follow the safety precautions discussed in Chapter 1 as well as those outlined in the motherboard's documentation. Be sure to use an ESD strap to protect the motherboard, as well as other devices, from ESD. Follow these steps to gather information about your motherboard:

1. Go to **cpuid.com**.

2. Be careful not to click an advertisement that has a download link. Under CPU-Z, click **for WINDOWS**. Locate the download section on the CPU-Z page and click the **SETUP * ENGLISH** link to start the download. At the time of this revision, the latest version was 1.87 and the file name was cpu-z_1.87-en.exe. This file contains both the 32-bit and 64-bit versions. Execute the file to install CPU-Z, following directions on the screen. Accept all default settings.

3. Run the CPU-Z program. CPU-Z results display, as shown in Figure 2-4.

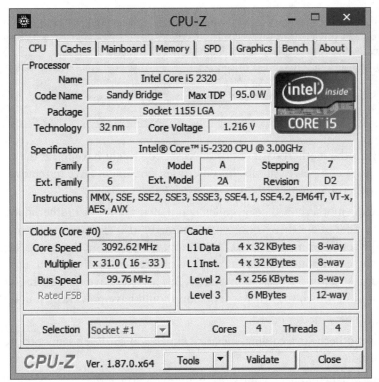

Source: CPU-Z by CPUID

Figure 2-4 CPU-Z initially displays CPU information

4. Click the **Mainboard** tab in CPU-Z, and record information about the motherboard:

   ◢ Manufacturer: _____

   ◢ Model: _____

5. If this is a different motherboard than the one you used in Lab 2.3, use the motherboard information to search for the documentation on the manufacturer's website. Save or print the documentation; you will give it to the other workgroup after you remove the motherboard from your system.

Follow these steps to remove your motherboard from your computer:

1. Power down the system, unplug all cords and cables connected to the computer, press the power button for three seconds to drain any remaining power, and remove the case cover. Take all necessary precautions (including using an ESD strap) and make a sketch of cabling and component placement. Then remove the cabling and expansion cards from the motherboard. If the cooler is not too heavy and bulky, leave it installed on the motherboard. You can also leave the CPU and memory installed. Follow your instructor's directions as to what to remove from the motherboard.

2. Six to nine screws usually attach the motherboard to the case via spacers or standoffs. The spacers prevent the printed circuitry from shorting out on the metal case and provide space for air circulation. Also, it's important that the motherboard be securely attached to the case with enough spacers and screws so that the motherboard won't crack when expansion cards are being inserted. Remove the screws that connect the motherboard to the case, and set them aside in a cup, bag, or bowl so that you don't lose any of them.

> **Notes** In this lab, it's not necessary to remove the spacers from the holes in the computer case. However, sometimes you might have to move a spacer from one hole to another, such as when you're replacing a motherboard and the new board lines up over different holes in the computer case. To remove a plastic spacer held in place with barbs, use needle-nose pliers to pinch the spacer and slide it out of the hole. To install it in a new hole, push the spacer into the hole until it pops into place. For metal spacers, carefully squeeze each spacer with pliers and remove it from the bracket holding it to the computer case.

3. Carefully lift the motherboard out of the case. You might have to tilt the board to clear the drive bays and power supply. In some cases, you might have to remove the drives to get the motherboard out.

4. Exchange the motherboard, its installed components, and the motherboard documentation with that of another workgroup. You might also exchange the components, such as the cooler or memory, that you removed from the motherboard, depending on whether these components are compatible with the new motherboard. Follow directions from your instructor on what to exchange. Be sure you have the new motherboard's documentation, which the other workgroup should have previously found on the web.

Follow these steps to install the new motherboard:

1. Install the motherboard, cabling, memory, expansion cards, and any other components you removed.

2. Have your instructor check your work before you attach the case cover and turn on the power.

3. Boot the system and enter the BIOS/UEFI setup utility. Make any adjustments in BIOS/UEFI needed for your system.

4. Save your settings and exit BIOS/UEFI setup.

5. Reboot the system and verify that the system is functioning correctly. Describe any error messages:

_____

_____

6. If an error appears, what steps do you plan to take to troubleshoot this error?

_____

_____

_____

After you have the system working, follow these steps to update the motherboard drivers:

1. Go to the website of the motherboard manufacturer and search for the drivers for the board.

2. Download and run the installation program(s) to update the motherboard drivers. Which drivers did you update?

_____

_____

_____

REVIEW QUESTIONS

1. How many screws usually attach the motherboard to the computer case?

   _____

2. What is the purpose of spacers?

   _____

3. When replacing a motherboard in the field, why would you want the replacement board to use the same processor that the older board used?

   _____

4. List three tools or methods you can use to identify a motherboard so that you can find its documentation on the web.

   _____

   _____

   _____

5. A motherboard has an onboard DVI port that is currently used for a single monitor. Sometimes the video does not come on after a Windows restart. To solve the problem, which of the following should you try first?

   a. Flash BIOS/UEFI.

   b. Update the motherboard drivers.

   c. Reinstall Windows.

   d. Replace the motherboard.

LAB 2.5 EXAMINE BIOS/UEFI SETTINGS AND RESEARCH BIOS/UEFI UPDATES

OBJECTIVES

The goal of this lab is to explore and modify BIOS/UEFI settings. After completing this lab, you will be able to:

▲ Enter the BIOS/UEFI setup utility

▲ Navigate the BIOS/UEFI setup utility

▲ Examine some setup options

▲ Research BIOS/UEFI update information

MATERIALS REQUIRED

This lab requires the following:

▲ A Windows 10/8/7 computer designated for this lab

▲ Any necessary BIOS/UEFI passwords (may need to be obtained from your instructor)

▲ A copy of the Computer Inventory and Maintenance form used in Lab 1.2

▲ Motherboard documentation

▲ Internet access

▲ A computer toolkit with ESD strap (optional)

LAB PREPARATION

Before the lab begins, the instructor or lab assistant needs to do the following:

▲ Verify that Windows starts with no errors

▲ Verify that Internet access is available

▲ Provide the Computer Inventory and Maintenance form in print or digital format, or verify that students can download the form online

ACTIVITY BACKGROUND

BIOS/UEFI firmware is UEFI firmware that is backward compatible with older BIOS firmware used on older computers. The UEFI setup utility interface can be accessed through Windows 10/8 after the computer has booted. While you can still use the traditional function keys during the boot process to access BIOS/UEFI setup, entering BIOS/UEFI setup through Windows 10/8 can sometimes save you time.

Some BIOS/UEFI utilities are protected with a supervisor password and a user password (also called a power-on password). A supervisor password allows full access to BIOS/UEFI setup, whereas a user password only allows you to view BIOS/UEFI setup screens. In most cases, you can't change any settings with a user password, although in some instances you are allowed to change certain settings. (In addition, if the user password is also set to be a power-on password and you don't know this password, you won't be able to boot the system.) When you attempt to access BIOS/UEFI setup and password protection has been enabled, you must enter a valid password to continue.

> **Notes** BIOS/UEFI setup supervisor, user, and power-on passwords are different from the Windows password required to sign in to Windows. Also, if you're responsible for a computer and have forgotten the supervisor password, you can move a jumper on the motherboard to return all BIOS/UEFI settings to their default values, which erases any BIOS/UEFI passwords.
> Another way to cause BIOS/UEFI setup to return to default settings and erase passwords is to remove the CMOS battery, which powers the memory in the firmware when electrical power is disconnected.

In this lab, you learn to use two methods to access BIOS/UEFI setup, examine BIOS/UEFI settings, research updates to the BIOS/UEFI firmware and drivers, and learn how to troubleshoot a problem with BIOS/UEFI settings.

ESTIMATED COMPLETION TIME: 30 MINUTES

 Activity

PART 1: ACCESS BIOS/UEFI SETUP

One way to enter BIOS/UEFI setup is to press a key or key combination after you start the computer with a cold start and before Windows is launched. Follow these steps:

1. Power down your computer. Press the power button to turn it on, and watch for a message on your screen, such as "Press F2 to access setup" or "Press Del to change BIOS settings." When you press this key or key combination, the BIOS/UEFI setup main screen appears.

2. If you don't see the key name(s) displayed on the screen, you can find the key or key combination documented in your motherboard manual. If you cannot find this information, Table 2-2 can help.

BIOS/UEFI Brand	Method for Entering BIOS/UEFI Setup
Intel BIOS	Boot the computer, and then press the F2 key.
AMI BIOS	Boot the computer, and then press the Delete key.
Award BIOS	Boot the computer, and then press the Delete key.
Phoenix BIOS	Boot the computer, and then press the F2 or F1 key.

Table 2-2   Methods for entering BIOS/UEFI setup

3. While you are in the BIOS/UEFI setup utility and you have not made any changes you want to keep, you can safely turn off your computer using the power switch on the back of a desktop or the power button on a laptop. Power down your computer now.

If you are using a Windows 10/8 computer and the motherboard firmware supports the feature, you can access BIOS/UEFI setup from Windows. Follow these steps:

1. Start your computer normally and sign in to Windows 10/8. Do one of the following:

   ◢ For Windows 10, open the **Settings** window, click **Update & Security**, and click **Recovery**. On the Recovery page, click **Restart now** under Advanced startup.

   ◢ For Windows 8, click **Settings** on the charms bar. Click **Change PC settings**. In the left pane, click **Update and recovery**, and then click **Recovery**. Under Advanced start-up, click **Restart now**.

2. When the system restarts, click **Troubleshoot**. On the Troubleshoot page, click **Advanced options**. On the Advanced options page, examine the various options available. Click **UEFI Firmware Settings**, and then click **Restart** on the UEFI Firmware Settings page. The system will restart again and boot to the BIOS/UEFI user interface.

PART 2: EXAMINE BIOS/UEFI SETTINGS

After you have entered BIOS/UEFI setup, follow these steps to explore the BIOS/UEFI menus and screens:

1. Examine the information and options available on the first screen. Each manufacturer's BIOS/UEFI interface has its own variations, but much of the elemental information is common to all utilities. Some manufacturers, such as ASRock, include a tutorial within the BIOS/UEFI itself. If your version provides this feature, explore it now and take notes of significant options and menus.

2. Look for some or all of the following information. Be aware that some BIOS/UEFI utilities offer an advanced mode that provides additional information. However, some BIOS/UEFI interfaces provide only limited information.

   ◢ Date: _____

   ◢ Time: _____

   ◢ BIOS/UEFI brand: _____

   ◢ BIOS/UEFI version: _____

   ◢ Revision date: _____

   ◢ CPU temperature: _____

▲ CPU voltage: _____

▲ Motherboard temperature: _____

▲ Memory summary: _____

_____

▲ Does the BIOS/UEFI support RAID configurations? If so, which type of RAID is supported (RAID 0, RAID 1, RAID 5, RAID 10)?

_____

▲ For each installed SATA drive, record the drive size and SATA port:

_____

_____

▲ Virtualization support:

_____

▲ Boot sequence (drives or network that BIOS/UEFI searches for an OS):

_____

▲ Fast boot setting: _____

▲ CSM setting: _____

▲ Secure boot setting: _____

▲ Temperature and fan speed (for all fans listed): _____

▲ System performance settings (energy saving, performance, etc.): _____

_____

▲ What password options are available? _____

_____

3. Fill in all the information required in the "BIOS/UEFI Settings and Data" section of the Computer Inventory and Maintenance form that you used in Lab 1.2.

4. Exit BIOS/UEFI setup without saving any changes to prevent saving accidental changes made while you were exploring the setup utility.

PART 3: EXPLORE A BIOS/UEFI UPDATE

BIOSAgentPlus is a free tool that scans a computer to determine if BIOS/UEFI or driver updates are available for that system. To determine whether an update is available for your computer, complete the following steps:

1. Go to the website at **biosagentplus.com**, and download the free BIOSAgentPlus program.

2. Locate the executable file on your computer and install the application. At the time of this writing, the file name was biosagentplus.exe. The scan will run automatically, and results will be presented in your browser. Is a BIOS/UEFI update available for your system?

▲ What is the make and model of your computer?

_____

▲ What is the chipset?

_____

◢ How does this information compare to information you have already gathered about your system (for example, the information given by HWiNFO in Lab 2.1)?

_____

3. The BIOS/UEFI update files available at the manufacturer's website are most likely to be free of adware, which makes them safer than using links from other websites or scanning tools. Explore the manufacturer's website for your desktop motherboard or laptop brand and model and attempt to locate the update files. If a readme.txt file is available or if other update instructions are available, read through these instructions. It is not necessary to download the update files for this lab. Answer the following questions:

◢ If you were to proceed with the download, what is the name of the file(s) you would need to download in order to install the update?

_____

◢ Where would you store the BIOS/UEFI update file(s)? For example, sometimes the file must be installed on the hard drive and sometimes on a USB drive before you start the update.

_____

◢ How do you start the update? (Most updates are started from BIOS/UEFI setup.)

_____

_____

◢ Is it possible to make a backup of the current BIOS/UEFI version in case you need to undo the update (called a flashback)? Where is the backup stored?

_____

_____

PART 4: TROUBLESHOOT BIOS/UEFI SETTINGS

Form workgroups of two to four people and do the following to practice troubleshooting problems with BIOS/UEFI:

1. Propose a change you could make to BIOS/UEFI setup that would prevent a computer from booting successfully. What change did you propose?

_____

2. Have your instructor approve the change because some changes might cause information written to the hard drive to be lost, making it difficult to recover from the problem without reloading the hard drive. Did your instructor approve the change?

_____

3. Now go to another team's computer and make the change to BIOS/UEFI setup while the other team makes a change to your system.

4. Return to your computer and troubleshoot the problem. Describe the problem as a user would:

_____

_____

5. What steps did you go through to discover the source of the problem and fix it?

_____

_____

6. If you were to encounter this same problem in the future, what might you do differently to troubleshoot it?

_____

_____

ESTIMATED COMPLETION TIME: 30 MINUTES

CHALLENGE ACTIVITY

A technician is often called on to recover from a forgotten power-on password. Do the following to practice this skill:

1. Ask your instructor to configure a power-on password on your computer.
2. Without knowing the password, boot the computer.
3. List the steps required to boot the computer without the power-on password:

_____

_____

_____

_____

REVIEW QUESTIONS

1. Why does a computer need BIOS/UEFI?

_____

_____

2. When troubleshooting a computer, why might you have to enter BIOS/UEFI setup? List at least three reasons:

_____

_____

_____

3. What happens automatically after you exit BIOS/UEFI setup?

_____

4. You plan to use Microsoft Hyper-V Manager to install a virtual machine on your laptop. Which settings should you verify or change in BIOS/UEFI before you launch Hyper-V Manager?

_____

_____

_____

5. Bluetooth on a laptop computer refuses to work. Which should you do first, update the Bluetooth drivers or update BIOS/UEFI? Why?

_____

_____

6. Where should you go online to get BIOS/UEFI update files?

_____

7. List at least two precautions you should take before or during the update process to help reduce the chance of problems occurring during the update.

_____

_____

8. Older motherboards used many jumpers to configure the board, but today's motherboards are likely to have only a single jumper group. What is the purpose of this group of jumpers?

_____

LAB 2.6 FLASH BIOS/UEFI

OBJECTIVES

The goal of this lab is to examine the process of flashing BIOS/UEFI. After completing this lab, you will be able to:

▲ Gather motherboard information

▲ Gather BIOS/UEFI string information

▲ Research correct BIOS/UEFI update information

▲ Record current BIOS/UEFI settings

▲ Flash your BIOS/UEFI, if permitted by your instructor

MATERIALS REQUIRED

This lab requires the following:

▲ Windows 10/8/7 operating system

▲ Motherboard documentation or Speccy by CCleaner

◢ A copy of the Computer Inventory and Maintenance form used in Lab 1.2 in Chapter 1

◢ Internet access

◢ Some BIOS/UEFI updates may require a bootable USB or CD drive

◢ Printer access (optional)

LAB PREPARATION

Before the lab begins, the instructor or lab assistant needs to do the following:

◢ Verify that Windows starts with no errors

◢ Verify that Internet access is available

◢ Determine if the flash program will require any external media

ACTIVITY BACKGROUND

The BIOS/UEFI on a motherboard controls many of the system's basic input/output (I/O) functions. You can update the BIOS/UEFI programming by downloading the latest update from the BIOS/UEFI, motherboard, or laptop manufacturer's website and then following specific procedures to update (or "flash") the BIOS/UEFI. Flashing a computer's BIOS/UEFI is necessary when troubleshooting an unstable motherboard. You might also need to flash a computer's BIOS/UEFI to provide support for new hardware (such as a processor, hard drive, or optical drive) or an operating system you're about to install. For example, before upgrading the processor, you might need to flash BIOS/UEFI so that the motherboard can support the new processor. Because flashing BIOS/UEFI sometimes causes problems of its own, don't flash the BIOS/UEFI unless you have a good reason to do so. Do not update BIOS/UEFI on computers that do not need it.

In this lab, you gather information about your system, including what BIOS/UEFI your computer is using and how to flash it. If your instructor permits, you also flash your BIOS/UEFI.

ESTIMATED COMPLETION TIME: 30 MINUTES

 Activity

Before making hardware, software, or BIOS/UEFI changes to a system, it's important to know your starting point so that if problems occur, you know if the problems already existed or if you created them by making changes to the system. Complete the following steps to verify that your computer is functioning:

1. Verify that your computer can boot successfully to a Windows desktop with no errors.

2. How long does it take your computer to boot?

When flashing BIOS/UEFI, using the correct BIOS/UEFI update is critical. Using the wrong update can render your system inoperable. Follow these steps to gather information on the motherboard chipset and BIOS/UEFI:

1. Use motherboard documentation or information you gathered in earlier labs to find and record the following:

◢ Motherboard manufacturer:

◢ Motherboard model number and version/revision:

_____

◢ Chipset manufacturer:

_____

◢ Chipset model number and version/revision:

_____

> **📝 Notes** If you can't find the BIOS/UEFI and motherboard information you need, you should download, install, and use a system analyzer such as Speccy (*ccleaner.com/speccy*) to obtain information on your computer. In Speccy, you'll find Manufacturer, BIOS/UEFI, and Revision data under the Motherboard section.

Next, you need to record the BIOS/UEFI manufacturer and version as BIOS/UEFI reports it. Follow these steps:

1. Reboot the system and enter BIOS/UEFI setup.
2. Look on the main screen of BIOS/UEFI setup. What is the BIOS/UEFI identifying information?

_____

◢ BIOS manufacturer and version:

_____

◢ BIOS release date:

_____

◢ Motherboard identification string:

_____

Using the information you gathered, you can search the web to determine what files you need to update your BIOS:

1. The motherboard manual gives detailed directions for how to flash BIOS/UEFI. If you have the manual saved from earlier labs, use it to answer the following questions.

   If you don't have the manual or the manual does not give the information you need, search the Support sections of the motherboard manufacturer's website and then the BIOS/UEFI manufacturer's website for information on updating your BIOS/UEFI. Alternatively, search by motherboard model number or BIOS/UEFI version number. Answer the following questions:

   ◢ Which manufacturer provides BIOS/UEFI for this system: the BIOS/UEFI manufacturer or the motherboard manufacturer?

   _____

   ◢ What is the latest BIOS/UEFI version released? What is the release date of the latest version?

   _____

◢ Is the latest BIOS/UEFI version a later version than the one you have installed?

_____

◢ Do you think your system would benefit from flashing BIOS/UEFI? Explain your answer.

_____

_____

2. Download the files to update your BIOS/UEFI or, if your computer is running the latest BIOS/UEFI version, download the files to refresh your existing BIOS/UEFI.

◢ Were the files you downloaded to update or refresh your BIOS/UEFI? What is the path and name of the files you downloaded?

_____

3. Search the motherboard manual or the manufacturer's website for the steps to flash your BIOS/UEFI. Print this procedure so that you can use it during the upgrade. Download any additional BIOS/UEFI utility or flash utility the procedure requires, as documented in the manual or on the website.

4. If you are having problems finding the directions to flash your BIOS/UEFI, research flash utilities on _wimsbios.com_. Wim's BIOS is an excellent website for researching BIOS information in general. List the names and descriptions of three BIOS utilities available on this site:

_____

_____

_____

5. The next step is to record any changes you have made previously to BIOS/UEFI settings. Generally, when BIOS/UEFI is updated, settings are returned to their default state, so you probably will need to return the settings to their present state after you have flashed BIOS/UEFI. Use the "BIOS/UEFI Settings and Data" section of the Computer Inventory and Maintenance form from Lab 1.2 to record any settings you know you changed, any hard drive settings that might have to be reconfigured after you update BIOS/UEFI, and any additional settings specified by your instructor. For example, after you update BIOS/ UEFI on a system that supports motherboard RAID, you will need to turn RAID back on after the update.

Record the following information:

◢ Hard drive information:

_____

◢ Settings you have changed:

_____

_____

◢ Settings specified by your instructor:

_____

_____

6. At this point, if your update procedure requires using an external medium, verify that the boot order allows you to boot from it before the local hard drive.

7. Sometimes you need to recover from a failed BIOS/UEFI update, which can be tricky. What directions, if any, does the documentation give about recovering from a failed BIOS/UEFI update?

_____

_____

8. Before you flash BIOS/UEFI, find out if the manufacturer offers a way to save the current BIOS/UEFI code. If so, list these steps to save BIOS/UEFI before you flash it:

_____

_____

_____

◢ On what storage media does the manufacturer recommend you save the BIOS/UEFI code?

_____

9. Why would you want to save the current BIOS/UEFI before you update it?

_____

10. Prepare to update your BIOS/UEFI. Uncompress any files, double-check the necessary procedures, read any readme.txt files included in the upgrade files (which often contain last-minute adjustments to the procedure), and create the upgrade boot disk, if necessary.

11. If your instructor permits, follow the BIOS/UEFI update procedure to flash your BIOS/UEFI. During the procedure, if you're given the opportunity to save your old BIOS/UEFI, do so. This information makes it possible to return to the previous BIOS/UEFI version if you encounter problems with the new BIOS/UEFI.

12. Reboot, verify BIOS/UEFI settings, make any changes, and verify that the computer boots to a Windows desktop successfully.

REVIEW QUESTIONS

1. At what point in the boot process is BIOS/UEFI information displayed?

_____

2. Why is it so important to record BIOS/UEFI and motherboard information correctly?

_____

3. What file might contain last-minute adjustments to the upgrade procedures?

_____

4. In what state are BIOS/UEFI settings usually placed after an update?

_____

5. Why should you not update BIOS/UEFI unless a computer needs it?

_____

6. When flashing BIOS/UEFI, why is it always important to save the old version of the BIOS/UEFI code?

_____

Supporting Processors and Upgrading Memory

Labs included in this chapter:

LAB 3.1 REMOVE AND REPLACE A CPU

OBJECTIVES

The goal of this lab is to practice the correct procedure for removing and reinstalling a CPU. After completing this lab, you will be able to:

▲ Remove the CPU from your system

▲ Install a CPU into your system

MATERIALS REQUIRED

This lab requires the following:

▲ A computer designated for disassembly in this lab

▲ Flathead screwdriver

▲ ESD strap

▲ Masking tape and marker, or another method of labeling parts

▲ Another computer, which has Internet access

▲ Alcohol wipe to remove thermal compound from the CPU

▲ Additional thermal compound (if necessary)

LAB PREPARATION

Before the lab begins, the instructor or lab assistant needs to do the following:

▲ Verify that Windows starts with no errors

▲ Verify that Internet access is available

ACTIVITY BACKGROUND

Removing and installing a CPU isn't difficult after you have done it a time or two. In today's systems, it's fairly rare for the CPU to malfunction and need to be replaced. Instead, a CPU is usually replaced as an upgrade to increase the system's operating speed. In this lab, you remove the CPU and cooling unit (heat sink and fan, or HSF), and then replace both. When you're considering upgrading the CPU in a system, be aware that an upgrade alone might not unleash the new processor's full potential if other components remain outdated. Also, be aware you might need to first flash BIOS/UEFI so that the motherboard can support the new CPU.

Often, when disassembling or assembling parts in a system, you won't have step-by-step directions for completing a particular task. Removing the heat sink and fan for the CPU is one of these tasks. Because of the overwhelming number of models on the market, you might need to refer to the manufacturer's documentation for exact details on how to remove the cooling unit.

> ⚡ **Caution** **An important note on electrostatic discharge (ESD):** The CPU is an intricate and complicated array of wires and transistors. When you feel a static shock, you're feeling somewhere in the neighborhood of 3000 volts or more. The CPU can be damaged by a shock of 10 to 1000 volts, which is a discharge you would never feel. It's important to wear your ESD strap while handling the CPU and memory. Without it, you could easily damage components by ESD and never know that you have done so. The damaged CPU might still work but not be reliable.

ESTIMATED COMPLETION TIME: 45 MINUTES

 Activity

Because the CPU is a delicate component and is easily damaged, watch your instructor demonstrate how to remove and replace one before you attempt to do so.

> **Notes** Alternately, your instructor might suggest you watch a video on *youtube.com* showing a CPU replacement rather than viewing a demonstration in the lab.

Answer the following questions about the demonstration:

1. What CPU did the instructor remove and replace?

   _____

2. What type of heat sink or cooler was attached to the CPU?

   _____

3. How was the heat sink or cooler attached to the motherboard?

   _____

4. What precautions did the instructor take to protect the CPU against ESD?

   _____

   _____

5. How did the instructor protect the CPU while it was out of its socket?

   _____

   _____

Do the following to remove the CPU from your system:

1. Power down the computer.

2. Unplug any cords or cables connected to it.

3. Press the power button for three seconds to drain any remaining power.

4. Remove the case cover.

5. Examine the inside of the case and decide what you need to remove so that you have easy access to the CPU. Next, remove and carefully label any wires or other parts that need to be removed to expose the CPU. Later, these labels can help you remember how to reconnect or reinstall any wires or parts you remove. With some system cases, the power supply needs to be removed before you can proceed. (Removing a power supply is covered in Chapter 1.)

6. Disconnect the power cord from the cooler to the motherboard.

7. The steps required to remove and install a cooler vary by CPU. Some units can be removed simply by opening the levers that attach them to the socket. Other units require you to use the eraser end of a pencil to carefully dislodge the unit from the retaining mechanism hooks. Typically, the cooler is latched on two sides or uses pins on all four corners. Those with latches on two sides unlatch easily after the pressure is removed from the main latch. Rather than use a screwdriver or other metal object to unlatch a stubborn latch, the preferred method is to use the eraser end of a pencil. Be careful because if you

slip while releasing the latch mechanism, the motherboard might be damaged beyond repair. Also, some heat sinks are permanently glued to the processor and aren't intended to be removed. In this case, leave the heat sink attached. Decide how to proceed, and, if appropriate, carefully remove the heat sink and fan unit.

8. After you have removed the cooler, you can proceed to removing the CPU. Handling the CPU requires your full attention. Some CPUs have tiny pins on the bottom of the chip that can be bent easily and need to be handled with care. Typically, CPUs and motherboards are shipped with antistatic foam, which is an ideal surface to set CPU pins into for protection. If you don't have this shipping container, plan to remove the CPU by laying it bottom-side up so that the pins aren't sitting on your work surface. Before removing the CPU, find the CPU shipping container or plan for another way to store the CPU safely.

9. You'll see a metal bar right next to the socket of the base of the CPU. This metal bar is the lever for the zero insertion force (ZIF) socket. Push the lever down and then out slightly to release it from its latch. Then pull the lever up 90° to release the CPU in the socket. (Figure 3-1 shows the lever being pushed down in an empty LGA1151 socket.)

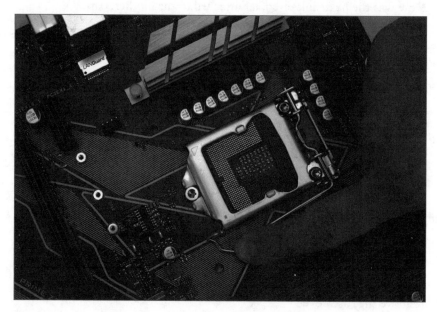

Figure 3-1   Push down and out on the socket lever to release and open it

10. Carefully grasp the sides of the CPU and gently pull straight up to remove it from the socket.

11. Using an alcohol wipe, carefully remove any thermal compound (also called thermal grease) that's smeared on the top of the CPU. Wipe in a direction from the outside toward the center so thermal compound doesn't accidentally spread over the edge. You can now safely store the CPU.

12. In the same way, carefully remove any thermal compound that is smeared on the bottom of the cooler.

Now you're ready to install the new CPU or, for this lab, to replace the CPU. If you're actually upgrading to a new CPU, you need to make certain that the CPU you are installing is approved by the manufacturer for this model of motherboard.

In this lab, you're replacing the existing CPU; however, as a technician, you need to be able to determine that a motherboard supports a CPU you are installing. Go through the following steps to practice as though you were installing a new, upgraded CPU:

1. Remember that the CPU is a delicate piece of equipment. If there are pins on the processor, they can be bent easily, and if the cooler isn't connected properly, you run the risk of the CPU overheating. Inspect the new CPU to verify that it has no bent pins. (Some CPUs will have landing pads instead, in which case you will need to check the pins on the socket for signs of damage.) If you suspect the CPU has been damaged, or if the pins are bent, you might need to replace the CPU.

2. Visually inspect the socket on the motherboard to determine what type it is. Usually, the socket type is clearly marked. Double-check that the new CPU was manufactured for the type of socket on the motherboard. What CPU socket is this motherboard using?

   _____

3. Examine the top of the CPU for the brand and model and then search the website of the CPU manufacturer. Your CPU is most likely manufactured by Intel (*ark.intel.com*) or AMD (*amd.com*). Write down the following information:

   ◢ What is the brand and model of the CPU you are installing?

   _____

   ◢ Processor base frequency:

   _____

   ◢ Number of cores:

   _____

4. To verify that the CPU is supported by the motherboard, search the motherboard manufacturer's website for the model of motherboard you are using. Look for the list of CPUs supported by the motherboard. What information in the motherboard documentation lets you know the CPU you are installing is supported by the motherboard? For example, the documentation might say the board supports all Intel 4th generation Core i5 processors.

   _____

5. Sometimes the motherboard documentation informs you that BIOS/UEFI must be updated before a particular processor can be installed. Is a BIOS/UEFI update required for this CPU? If so, what is the version of the BIOS/UEFI update? In this lab, you can assume the update has already been applied.

   _____

You're now ready to install the CPU. Follow these steps:

1. Before you install the CPU in the socket, practice raising and lowering the socket lever so that you can feel how much force is necessary to close the lever.

2. Verify that the power cable has been removed from the machine. Unlatch the ZIF lever and bring it to the open position. For AMD processors, a small, gold triangle on one corner lines up with a triangle on one corner of the socket. For Intel CPUs, the CPU and motherboard usually have notches to clearly align the CPU to the socket. Align the CPU with the socket (see Figure 3-2), and allow it to fall gently into place.

— Right notch

— Right post

Figure 3-2 Align the CPU over the socket

3. Carefully replace the socket lever so that force is applied to the top of the CPU and the CPU is installed securely in the socket. You need to place a little more pressure on the lever than you did when no CPU was present, but don't force it! If you have to force it, the CPU is probably not oriented in the socket correctly.

4. Now you're ready to install the cooler. First, examine the underside of the cooler for any foreign matter. New coolers often come with a thermal pad that's covered by a protective film of plastic. Always remember to remove this protective film, because if it isn't removed, you run the risk of damaging your CPU. If there's no thermal pad, gently apply a small amount of thermal compound—about the size of a grain of rice or small pea—to the center of the CPU. It is not necessary to spread the compound, and it's important not to use too much. Be careful that you don't apply so much that the thermal compound later squeezes out the sides and comes in contact with the edges of the processor or the socket. You don't want grease to get down into the CPU socket. Figure 3-3 shows just about the right amount of thermal grease applied.

Notes It's important that no thermal compound gets down into the socket or on the bottom of the CPU. If this happens, let the paste dry for a few days and then blow it out with compressed air.

Four holes in motherboard to attach cooler assembly

Thermal compound applied

Figure 3-3 If the cooler does not have preapplied thermal compound, apply it on top of the processor

5. Carefully align the bottom of the cooler with the socket and attach the cooler. Plug the cooler fan's power cord into the motherboard.

6. Have your instructor inspect your work to make sure the cooler is attached correctly. Booting up a system with an incorrectly attached cooler can cause damage to the processor because it will overheat.

7. It's always a good idea to test the CPU operating temperature after replacing the cooler. Most BIOS/UEFI programs display the current temperature of the CPU. Boot your machine to the BIOS/UEFI setup screen and make sure the CPU is not overheating. The CPU temperature should not exceed 43°C or 110°F.

REVIEW QUESTIONS

1. Why shouldn't you use a screwdriver to remove a heat sink?

2. What is the minimum voltage of an electrostatic discharge (ESD) that you can feel?

3. What is the voltage range in which ESD can affect electronic components?

4. What was the operating temperature of the CPU?

5. Why is it important to double-check the bottom of the heat sink before attaching it to the CPU socket?

LAB 3.2 RUN A BURN-IN TEST AND BENCHMARK A CPU

OBJECTIVES

The goal of this lab is for you to make sure the CPU is stable, learn how to compare your CPU's performance in relation to other processors, and ensure that the heat sink and fan are working correctly. After completing this lab, you will be able to:

▲ Run a burn-in test on a CPU

▲ Benchmark a CPU

MATERIALS REQUIRED

This lab requires the following:

▲ A computer running Windows 10/8/7

▲ Internet access

LAB PREPARATION

Before the lab begins, the instructor or lab assistant needs to do the following:

▲ Verify that Windows starts with no errors

▲ Verify that Internet access is available

ACTIVITY BACKGROUND

Although today's CPUs are very reliable, you should test the CPU for stability after completing a system build or installing a new CPU, and before sending it out to the end user. This testing is known as burn-in testing or stress testing.

An unstable system might boot without any errors; however, it might show problems when a load is placed on the system. Before running a burn-in test, you should back up any important data on the computer in case it has irrecoverable problems during the test. Older systems required that you carefully monitor the temperature during a stress test so you didn't damage the CPU if a problem caused the processor to overheat. Newer computers automatically shut down when the CPU overheats.

ESTIMATED COMPLETION TIME: 45 MINUTES

 Activity

For this lab, you download a trial version of BurnInTest Professional edition and run a burn-in test. After the burn-in is complete, you compare the performance of your CPU with that of similar CPUs. This process is called benchmarking the CPU. Follow these steps:

1. Go to **passmark.com/download/bit_download.htm**.

2. In the BurnInTest Software Download section, click **Download BurnInTest Professional edition**. At the time this lab was written, the file name was bitpro.exe, and the version was version 9. A newer version might be available.

3. Download the file to your computer, launch it, and follow the on-screen instructions to install and launch the software. Close the Readme file that appears.

4. When BurnInTest launches, you will be using the trial version, which is valid for 30 days. Click **Continue**.

5. The BurnInTest Evaluation window shows six tests are selected (CPU, 2D Graphics, Disk, Sound, Memory, and Network 1). A burn-in test allows you to simultaneously stress-test all major subsystems of a computer for endurance, reliability, and stability. To run all the tests, click **Go**. The tests take about 15 minutes to complete. Test results for one system are shown in Figure 3-4.

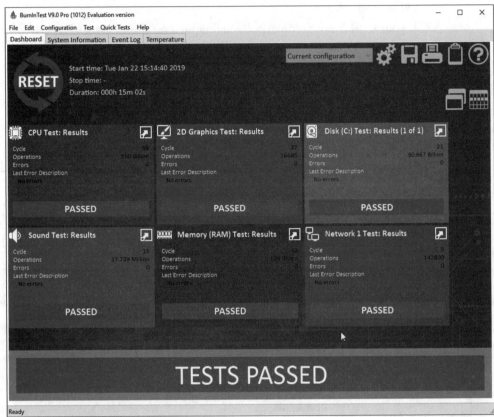

Source: PassMark Software

Figure 3-4   BurnInTest results

6. After your test has completed, answer the following questions using the results from your test:

   ◢ Did your system pass or fail the burn-in test? If your system failed, use the report to outline the reasons why:

   _____

   _____

   _____

   ◢ Using the Temperature tab, record the average temperatures during the burn-in test:

   ◢ Minimum: _____

   ◢ Current: _____

   ◢ Maximum: _____

Benchmarking a CPU is the process of assessing and comparing its performance characteristics with that of other CPUs. To benchmark your CPU using BurnInTest Pro, follow these steps:

1. Using the System Information tab, record the CPU type:

   _____

2. Beside the name of the CPU manufacturer, click **Online CPU comparison** to open *cpubenchmark.net*.

3. If your CPU is not automatically highlighted on the *cpubenchmark.net* website, click the **Select A Page** list arrow in the upper-right corner of the page, and choose **Searchable CPU List**.

4. Enter your CPU type in the search box and click **Find CPU**. Click on your CPU name once, and then once again to display CPU benchmark information, as shown in Figure 3-5. Using this information, answer the following questions:

   ◢ What is the overall rank of your CPU?

   _____

   ◢ What is the estimated value of your CPU?

   _____

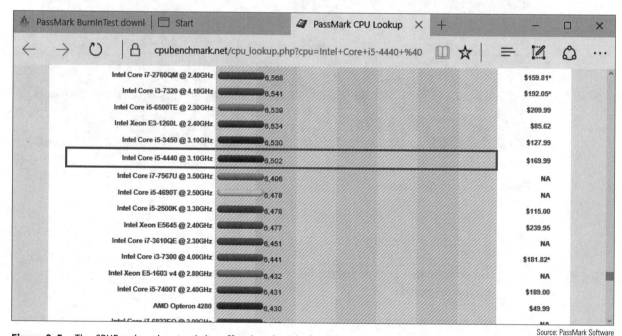

Figure 3-5 The *CPUBenchmark.net* website offers benchmarks for CPUs

Source: PassMark Software

REVIEW QUESTIONS

1. Why do you place a system under a load when you are testing for errors?

   _____

   _____

2. Why shouldn't a technician simply put the least expensive CPU into a machine to save costs?

_____

_____

3. What is the purpose of benchmarking a CPU?

_____

_____

4. It seems that for the best performance, you could simply choose the fastest model in each category. Why isn't this method a good way to choose a CPU?

_____

_____

5. What will likely happen if the CPU overheats during a stress test?

_____

6. Why is it important to back up data on a computer before you run a burn-in test on the CPU?

_____

_____

LAB 3.3 RESEARCH A RAM UPGRADE ON THE WEB

OBJECTIVES

The goal of this lab is to practice finding important information about RAM that you need when upgrading memory. After completing this lab, you will be able to:

◢ Find documentation on your system's motherboard

◢ Read documentation for your system's RAM specifications

◢ Search the web for RAM prices and availability

MATERIALS REQUIRED

This lab requires the following:

◢ A computer running Windows 10/8/7, with CPU-Z installed (CPU-Z was installed in Lab 2.4 in Chapter 2)

◢ Internet access

LAB PREPARATION

Before the lab begins, the instructor or lab assistant needs to do the following:

◢ Verify that Windows starts with no errors

◢ Verify that CPU-Z is installed

◢ Verify that Internet access is available

ACTIVITY BACKGROUND

As an IT technician, you will find that a computer's performance can often be improved by installing more RAM. Upgrading the system RAM is probably one of the easiest and most cost-effective upgrades that you can perform on a workstation. To install RAM, you need to know not only the maximum amount of memory you can install, but also which memory technology will match the motherboard. Ignoring the demands of the motherboard or compatibility with existing memory modules may jeopardize the goal of increased performance. In this lab, you determine the characteristics of the memory that is currently installed and the maximum memory the motherboard can support. Then you research the web to find the memory you need for the upgrade and the price of the upgrade.

ESTIMATED COMPLETION TIME: 30 MINUTES

 Activity

Follow these steps to find information about the installed RAM and motherboard in your system:

1. Open the CPU-Z software on your computer to determine the attributes of the RAM currently installed. Using information on the Memory tab, record the following attributes of RAM here:

   ▲ RAM type: _____

   ▲ RAM size: _____

   ▲ RAM channel #: _____

   ▲ DRAM frequency: _____

   ▲ CAS# latency (CL) rating: _____

   ▲ RAS# to CAS# delay rating: _____

2. Open the SPD tab, and complete Table 3-1 for each memory slot. If a slot is empty, write "empty" across that row in the table.

Slot #	Memory Type	Module Size	Max Bandwidth	Speed	Manufacturer
1					
2					
3					
4					

Table 3-1 Attributes of installed memory

Notes CPU-Z clocks the detected speed of each module and reports that information in the same cell as the Max bandwidth. The actual speed of a DDR, DDR2, DDR3, or DDR4 module, however, will be twice the number reported by the software because these modules transfer data on both the upside and the downside of the clock signal.

3. Using skills you learned in previous lab activities, determine your motherboard's manufacturer and model number, and record that information here. (If you don't have the motherboard documentation available, search for it on the web.)

   ▲ Manufacturer: _____

   ▲ Model #: _____

Use the documentation for your motherboard or research your motherboard on the web to answer these questions:

1. Does your motherboard support dual, triple, or quad channels? Explain how this affects the memory modules you need to install:

   _____

   _____

2. What type (or types) of memory does your motherboard support? Be sure to include details such as physical type (for example, DDR3 or DDR4), speed, ECC or non-ECC, unbuffered, or registered:

   _____

   _____

   _____

   _____

   _____

3. What is the maximum amount of memory your motherboard supports?

   _____

4. To install the maximum amount of memory the board supports, it might be necessary to replace a smaller-capacity module with a larger-capacity module. Can you use the existing memory modules to upgrade to the maximum amount of supported memory? Explain your answer:

   _____

   _____

5. What size and how many memory modules would be needed to upgrade your system to the maximum amount of supported memory and make use of the dual, triple, or quad channels that the board might support?

   _____

Now that you have the necessary information about your system's memory, go to *pricewatch.com*, *newegg.com*, or a similar website, and answer the following questions:

1. Suppose you need to replace all the modules on the board. What size and how many modules should you purchase? What is the total price of the upgrade? Be sure to take advantage of dual, triple, or quad channels the board might support.

   _____

2. Suppose you want to install the maximum amount of memory the board supports and, if possible, use the old modules already installed. What size and how many modules should you purchase? What is the total price of the upgrade?

   _____

3. If there are empty memory slots on your motherboard, you might want to buy additional memory to fill these empty slots. Search for matching modules of the same

manufacturer, style, speed, and latency ratings that are currently installed in your system. List the details and price of one memory module that matches a module already installed in your system:

_____

Explore other types of memory on *pricewatch.com*, *newegg.com*, *crucial.com*, or another similar website, and answer the following questions:

1. On average, what is the least expensive type of memory per MB you can find? What is its price?

_____

2. On average, what is the most expensive type of memory per MB you can find? What is its price?

_____

3. Pick one of the DIMMs that you selected for purchase in this lab. Search for a SO-DIMM for a laptop computer that is of the same size (in MB or GB), speed, and type (DDR2, DDR3, or DDR4) as the DIMM. Do you find that SO-DIMM for a laptop is more or less expensive than an equivalent DIMM for a desktop computer? List the DIMM and SO-DIMM you are comparing, and give their prices:

_____

_____

REVIEW QUESTIONS

1. Why might you want to upgrade RAM on a system?

_____

_____

2. Why is it important to match the latencies of the older modules to the newer modules?

_____

_____

3. What must be true before a motherboard can take advantage of the triple memory channels on the board?

_____

4. Explain the following description of a memory module: DDR3 PC10600 1333MHz.

_____

_____

5. Explain the differences between ECC memory and non-ECC memory.

_____

_____

LAB 3.4 BENCHMARK RAM AND PLAN AN UPGRADE

OBJECTIVES

The goal of this lab is to show the effects of a memory upgrade (or downgrade) on the speed of your system, and to plan and price a memory upgrade. After completing this lab, you will be able to:

▲ Install and remove RAM modules and record the effects

▲ Determine how much and what kind of memory is needed for an upgrade

MATERIALS REQUIRED

This lab requires the following:

▲ Windows 10/8/7 operating system

▲ An account with administrator privileges

▲ Internet access

▲ A computer designated for disassembly

▲ A computer toolkit and ESD strap

▲ A clock with a second hand or a smartphone stopwatch app to be used to measure the computer boot time

▲ One of the following:

    ▲ An additional memory module compatible with your system

    ▲ A system with two memory modules already installed

    ▲ A partner's system that has a memory module compatible with yours

LAB PREPARATION

Before the lab begins, the instructor or lab assistant needs to do the following:

▲ Verify that a computer designated for disassembly is available

▲ Verify that each student has access to a user account with administrator privileges

▲ Verify that the student has access to two compatible memory modules. This can be done in one of three ways:

    ▲ The instructor provides an additional compatible memory module for each student

    ▲ The student system already has two or more memory modules installed

    ▲ The student works with a partner who has a system with a compatible memory module

▲ Verify that each student has a clock or watch with a second hand or a smartphone stopwatch app to measure the system boot time

▲ Verify that Internet access is available

ACTIVITY BACKGROUND

In Part 1 of this lab, you time how long it takes your system to boot up. Then you download, install, and run Novabench to benchmark the speed of your system. In Part 2, you add or remove RAM from your system. In Part 3, you restart the system, time how long it takes your system to boot after the memory change, run Novabench again, and compare the results. In Part 4, you research the documentation for your system to gather information on its memory subsystem and determine the maximum amount of RAM it will accept. Finally, you shop online to determine the cost of the upgrade.

ESTIMATED COMPLETION TIME: 45 MINUTES

 Activity

PART 1: USE NOVABENCH TO BENCHMARK THE SYSTEM

In this part of the lab, you time how long it takes your system to boot up:

1. Power off your computer if it is not already powered off.

2. Prepare your stopwatch so that you will be ready to start timing as soon as you press the power button on your computer.

3. Start your computer, and immediately start your stopwatch. Time how long it takes for the Windows sign-in screen to appear (or the desktop, if set to automatic logon), and record the time:

Follow these steps to download, install, and run Novabench on your computer:

1. Sign in to your computer with a user account that has administrator privileges.

2. Use your web browser to go to **novabench.com**.

3. Click **Download for Free** and select the **Personal Use Free** download. Then click **Download for Windows**. The program downloads to your Downloads folder. What is the name of the file?

---

4. To install the application, double-click the application file for Novabench in the Downloads folder. Follow the on-screen directions to install the software, accepting all default settings. Novabench automatically launches.

5. In the Novabench window, take a minute to explore the various testing options under the Tests menu. What four tests are available under Individual Tests?

Now you are ready to begin the testing. Follow these steps to run the Novabench tests and record the results:

1. In the Novabench window, click **Start Tests**.

2. Novabench checks to see if you have any programs running that could interfere with the testing and prompts you to close them, if necessary. After closing any recommended programs, click **Proceed** to continue. You will see progress bars appear as Novabench tests various components of your system.

3. When complete, the Novabench Score results screen will appear (see Figure 3-6). Using this data, record the following information:

   ◢ List the four main categories that were tested, and record their scores:

◢ Record the RAM speed in MB/s:

◢ Record the drive write speed in MB/s:

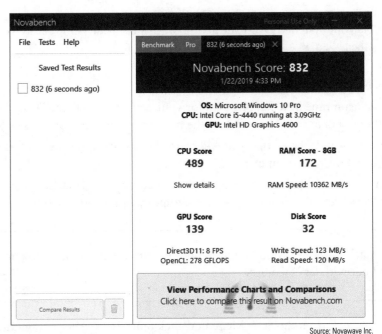

Source: Novawave Inc.

Figure 3-6   Novabench displays scores of four components of your system and an overall score of your system

PART 2: ADD OR REMOVE RAM FROM YOUR COMPUTER

If your computer started with two or more RAM modules, you now remove the extra module(s), leaving one in your system. If your computer started with one RAM module, you now install a second module. You upgrade (or downgrade) the memory by following these steps:

1. Shut down your system and remove all exterior cabling. Press and hold the power button for three seconds to drain any remaining power.

2. Be sure you're wearing your ESD strap. Open the system case and locate the slots for memory modules.

3. Remove any data cabling and other devices preventing you from accessing the slots. Answer the following questions:

   ◢ How many modules are currently installed?

   ◢ Are there any empty slots to install an additional module?

4. Most memory slots have a retaining mechanism at each end to secure each module in the slot. Typically, these mechanisms are plastic levers that you spread outward to unseat and remove the module. Modules are inserted and removed straight up and down. Spread the plastic levers apart before inserting or removing the memory modules.

5. Examine an empty slot and note the raised ridges that line up with notches on the memory module's pin edge. Because modules are designed to be inserted in only one orientation, these ridges prevent them from being inserted incorrectly.

6. If you are inserting a module, verify that the module is oriented correctly to the slot. Insert the module, and gently but firmly push it in. You can feel the module snap into position. If you are removing a module, carefully spread the levers apart, and then remove it.

7. Reassemble your system. Have your instructor inspect your work before you put the case back together.

PART 3: COMPARE BENCHMARK RESULTS

In this part of the lab, you again time how long it takes for your computer to boot. Then, you run Novabench, and compare the results to those from before the memory change. Follow these steps:

1. Prepare your stopwatch so that you will be ready to start timing as soon as you press the power button on your computer.

2. Start your computer and immediately start your stopwatch. Time how long it takes for the Windows sign-in screen (or desktop) to appear, and record the time here:

_____

▲ How much faster did your computer boot with more memory, or how much slower did it boot with less memory?

_____

3. Start Novabench from the Start Menu and click **Start Tests**. After closing the recommended programs (if any), click **Proceed** to continue.

4. When complete, the Novabench Score results screen will appear. Using this data, record the following information:

▲ Record the score for each of the four categories and the difference from the first set of information:

_____

_____

_____

_____

▲ Record the RAM speed in MB/s and the difference from the first test:

_____

▲ Record the drive write speed in MB/s and the difference from the first test:

_____

5. Repeat Part 2 to restore your computer to its original condition when you started this lab.

PART 4: PLAN AND PRICE A MAXIMUM MEMORY UPGRADE

In this part of the lab, you use your web browser to research the documentation for your system, gather information on its memory subsystem, and determine the maximum amount of RAM it will accept.

The best way to do this is to go to the manufacturer's website and look for the support page. In most cases, it is best to search using the serial number or service tag number of your system, and then to look for any links referring to upgrades or system configuration. After you have found the information on upgrading your memory, answer the following questions:

1. What is the type and maximum speed of RAM your hardware supports—for example, DDR3 1600 (PC3 12800)?

_____

2. How many total memory slots are on your motherboard?

_____

3. What is the maximum amount of RAM (GB) each slot supports?

_____

4. What is the maximum amount of RAM (GB) your system supports?

_____

5. Will you need to remove any existing RAM to upgrade to the system maximum?

_____

6. What is the maximum amount of RAM your OS supports?

_____

7. Taking into account the preceding information, what type of memory modules and how many of each will you need to buy to upgrade your system to maximum RAM at maximum speed?

_____

You are now ready to shop online for the best price for your RAM upgrade. Using high-quality, name-brand RAM for your upgrade will help avoid potential problems. Record the total price of the RAM upgrade if you were to purchase it from the following vendors:

◢ Your system manufacturer's website: _____

◢ *kingston.com*: _____

◢ *memory4less.com*: _____

REVIEW QUESTIONS

1. What feature is used on memory slots and modules to prevent modules from being inserted incorrectly?

_____

_____

2. Why was the drive write speed affected by the RAM?

_____

_____

_____

3. Why does the amount of RAM installed affect boot time?

_____

_____

4. Which website gave you the best buy for the memory upgrade? Which website would you use to make the purchase? Why?

_____

_____

LAB 3.5 EXAMINE LAPTOP DOCUMENTATION

OBJECTIVES

The goal of this lab is to find documentation for a laptop on a manufacturer's website and become familiar with it. After completing this lab, you will be able to:

- Locate documentation for two specific laptop computer models running Windows
- Download the documentation
- Use the documentation to find critical information
- Compare supporting a Windows laptop with one running Apple's macOS

MATERIALS REQUIRED

This lab requires the following:

- Internet access

LAB PREPARATION

Before the lab begins, the instructor or lab assistant needs to do the following:

- Verify that Internet access is available

ACTIVITY BACKGROUND

Laptops are designed for portability, compactness, and energy conservation, and their designs are often highly proprietary. Therefore, establishing general procedures for supporting laptops is more difficult than for desktop computers. Often, consulting the documentation for a particular model is necessary to get information on technical specifications and support procedures. In this lab, you locate and download documentation for two different Windows laptop computers, and then use that documentation to answer questions about each model. You also compare documentation for supporting a Windows laptop with that of an Apple laptop using macOS.

ESTIMATED COMPLETION TIME: 30 MINUTES

 Activity

Some major manufacturers of laptop computers are listed in Table 3-2. Of these, Lenovo, Dell, and HP have a reputation in the industry for providing more extensive technical documentation than other manufacturers. To draw your own conclusions, follow these steps:

Manufacturer	Website
Acer	*us.acer.com* and *us.acer.com/ac/en/US/content/support*
Apple Computer	*apple.com* and *apple.com/support*
ASUS	*usa.asus.com* and *asus.com/us/support*
Dell Computer	*dell.com* and *support.dell.com*
Hewlett Packard (HP)	*hp.com* and *support.hp.com*
Lenovo	*lenovo.com* and *support.lenovo.com*
Microsoft	*microsoft.com*
Razer	*razer.com* and *support.razer.com*
Samsung	*samsung.com* and *samsung.com/support*
Sony (VAIO)	*store.sony.com* and *esupport.sony.com*
Toshiba America	*toshiba.com* and *support.toshiba.com*

Table 3-2　Laptop, netbook, and all-in-one manufacturers

1. Choose Lenovo, Dell, or HP to research. Then go to the Lenovo, Dell, or HP website and select a laptop model to research. Which manufacturer and model of laptop did you select?

   _____

2. Select a manufacturer other than Lenovo, Dell, HP, or Apple from Table 3-2. Go to that company's website and select one model to research. Which manufacturer and model did you select?

   _____

3. Go to the Apple website and select one laptop model to research. Which Apple laptop model did you select?

   _____

4. For each of the three models, go to the Support section of the manufacturer's website, search for documentation on the model, and follow the directions to download the documentation. Search for a user manual and a service manual. Also search for other types of technical support the sites might offer for this particular model. List the types of documentation you were able to find for each model. For each model, indicate if you were able to download or save the documentation locally, or if you could only view it on the company's website.

◢ Documentation for a Lenovo, Dell, or HP laptop:

_____

_____

_____

◢ Documentation for the second laptop you selected:

_____

_____

_____

_____

◢ Documentation for the Apple laptop:

_____

_____

_____

5. Using the documentation you found, answer questions *a* through *e* for each model in Table 3-3. If you can't answer a question because the information isn't included in the documentation, write "information unavailable."

   a. What type of processor does the laptop use?

   b. How much and what type of RAM is installed?

   c. What edition and type of operating system is currently installed on the laptop?

   d. What type of optical storage (CD, DVD, Blu-ray, and so forth) does the laptop offer, if any?

   e. What type of wired or wireless networking (for example, Ethernet, cellular, Wi-Fi, and Bluetooth) comes built in?

	Model 1	Model 2	Model 3 (Apple)
a.			
b.			
c.			
d.			
e.			

Table 3-3   Compare general documentation for three laptops

6. For each model, record your answers to the following questions in Table 3-4. These questions address information the three websites provide about servicing the laptop:

   a. Are instructions available for exchanging the hard drive?

   b. Are instructions available for upgrading RAM?

c. Can you obtain recovery media for the laptop in the event the hard drive needs replacing?

d. Are instructions available for replacing the optical drive, if one is included?

e. Are instructions available for replacing the processor?

f. Are BIOS/UEFI updates available for the laptop? Are instructions available to perform a BIOS/UEFI update?

g. Is a recovery partition available on the laptop? If so, how do you access the recovery tools and partition?

	Model 1	Model 2	Model 3 (Apple)
a.			
b.			
c.			
d.			
e.			
f.			
g.			

Table 3-4 Compare service documentation for three laptops

7. Answer the following questions about what you learned regarding manufacturer documentation:

   ◢ Of the three manufacturers you researched, which one provided the best documentation? Explain your answer.

   _____

   ◢ Which manufacturer's website was easiest to use? Why?

   _____

   ◢ Was any documentation missing that would be helpful when supporting a laptop?

   _____

REVIEW QUESTIONS

1. Other than documentation, what resources are available on a manufacturer's website to help you support a laptop?

   _____

   _____

2. Which manufacturer's site did you think was the most user friendly and, in general, offered the best support?

   _____

3. Besides the questions you researched in the lab, what other types of information are available in the manuals you reviewed?

_____

4. Of the laptops you researched, which one would you purchase? Explain your answer, listing the features that you liked best.

_____

LAB 3.6 TROUBLESHOOT MEMORY PROBLEMS

OBJECTIVES

The goal of this lab is for you to get hands-on experience in troubleshooting memory problems. After completing this lab, you will be able to:

◢ Identify some symptoms that indicate memory problems

◢ Identify a faulty module

◢ Use MemTest86 to test installed RAM

◢ Use Windows Memory Diagnostics to test installed RAM

MATERIALS REQUIRED

This lab requires the following:

◢ Internet access

◢ Windows 10/8/7 operating system

◢ A USB flash drive that can be fully erased

◢ A computer designated for disassembly

◢ A computer toolkit and ESD strap

LAB PREPARATION

Before the lab begins, the instructor or lab assistant needs to do the following:

◢ Verify that a computer designated for disassembly is available to each student or workgroup. The computer must be capable of booting from a USB flash drive.

◢ Verify that Internet access is available. For labs that don't have Internet access, download the latest image of MemTest86 from _memtest86.com_ to a file server or other storage media available to students in the lab.

ACTIVITY BACKGROUND

The symptoms of faulty RAM are many and varied. Faulty memory can cause a complete failure to boot, fatal exception errors while working with an application, or catastrophic data loss. However, faulty memory is sometimes noticeable only as annoying interruptions while you're working. RAM that's outright dead is fairly easy to identify. If the dead module is the only module installed, the system won't boot. If it's one of several modules, you'll notice that the system reports less memory than you expected.

A module might fail absolutely. More often, however, a module develops intermittent problems that cause data corruption, applications hanging at unexpected times, the system rebooting, or Windows hanging and displaying a stop error, also called the blue screen of death (which is an error message displayed on a blue background). In this lab, you learn how to detect and isolate faulty memory modules to prevent these problems.

ESTIMATED COMPLETION TIME: 60 MINUTES

 Activity

Reliable memory function is essential to system operation. Therefore, memory is checked when the system is booted. If memory isn't detected or if it has major problems, the startup BIOS/UEFI emits a beep code to define a general or particular memory problem. The memory testing on a computer is quite extensive. After POST startup does an initial test, the BIOS/UEFI does a more thorough test of physical memory, which is usually repeated three times before the system summary is displayed and booting continues. Then, while Windows is loading, Windows tests memory again.

These tests are all completed at startup, but partially corrupted modules often don't show a problem until they're running at certain temperatures. When problems do show up at certain temperatures, these problems are referred to as thermal intermittents. Although thermal intermittents are difficult to nail down and document, they are fairly easy to remedy if the fault is on the memory module instead of on the motherboard.

MemTest86 is a utility that allows you to test the memory from a bootable CD or flash drive. This kind of test is particularly useful in discovering a thermal intermittent fault.

In the following steps, you use MemTest86 to test installed RAM. First, you create a bootable flash drive with the MemTest86 software on it; you then use the USB flash drive to boot a computer and test memory on that computer. Follow these steps:

1. Open your browser and go to **memtest86.com**. Click the **Download now!** link. Scroll down, and click the link to download the latest version of MemTest86 for a bootable USB drive for Windows. At the time of this writing, you click **Image for creating bootable USB Drive for Windows/Linux/Mac system**.

2. Save the zipped file to your Downloads folder. What is the name of the downloaded file?

   _____

3. Extract the contents of the downloaded Zip file. The extracted folder contains the files that will be copied to your blank flash drive. One file has an .img file extension. What is the name of the IMG file in your Downloads folder? Close any open windows.

   _____

4. Next, you'll install the MemTest86 application on the flash drive using the imaging tool. Insert your USB flash drive, then double-click the **imageUSB.exe** file in the extracted folder. Respond to the UAC dialog box. The imageUSB window lists the installation steps. Under Step 1, select the correct USB flash drive in the list of drives. Leave the default settings for Steps 2 and 3. In Step 4, click **Write to USB** and follow the on-screen directions to create the bootable USB flash drive. All previous data on the flash drive will be erased.

5. Close the imageUSB window.

6. Use a felt-tip pen or write-on tape to label the flash drive **MemTest86**. Include the date on the flash drive.

7. The flash drive is now ready to be used on any computer. Reinsert the flash drive and boot the system to the flash drive. If necessary, go into BIOS/UEFI setup and change the boot device priority order to boot to the USB drive first.

8. The system boots into the MemTest86 utility. From the configuration menu, if necessary, select the option appropriate to your computer hardware. The utility displays the progress of the tests as it runs; see Figure 3-7.

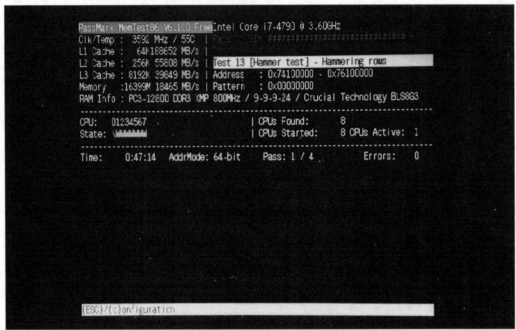

Source: Brady Tech, Inc.

Figure 3-7 The MemTest86 utility tests installed RAM

9. Allow the test to finish one pass, and then press **Esc** to exit and reboot to Windows. Did the test detect any errors?

_____

10. Return to the **memtest86.com** website, select **Technical Info,** and answer the following questions:

◢ What two options does MemTest86 have for reporting errors?

_____

◢ Besides memory, what other component(s) does MemTest86 test?

_____

◢ What is the first test (Test 0) that is performed by MemTest86?

_____

◢ Why does MemTest86 not require operating system support to run?

_____

Windows offers the Memory Diagnostics utility, which you can use to test memory. Follow these steps to launch the utility:

1. In the Windows 10/7 search box or the Windows 8 Run box, enter **mdsched.exe**. Click **Restart now and check for problems (recommended)**. The computer reboots, and the Windows Memory Diagnostics Tool screen appears. The memory test begins. How many times does the utility test memory?

   _____

2. Wait until the test completes. Did the test discover any memory problems?

   _____

Follow these steps to observe the effects of a faulty memory module and interpret beep codes:

1. Using skills you have learned in previous labs, determine the BIOS/UEFI manufacturer for your system, and record it here:

   _____

2. Search documentation or the web for a list of beep codes for that manufacturer.

3. Shut down the system and remove all external cabling. Press the power button for three seconds to drain residual power.

4. Put on your ESD strap, open the case, remove all memory modules, and set them aside in an antistatic bag.

5. Reassemble the system, leaving out the memory.

6. Power up the system and describe the outcome, including any beep codes:

   _____

7. If you heard beep codes, interpret their meaning using the information you found in Step 2:

   _____

8. Shut down the system, disassemble it, install the RAM, and reassemble.

9. Boot the system to verify that it is functional.

REVIEW QUESTIONS

1. What are some common symptoms of a thermal intermittent problem?

   _____

   _____

   _____

   _____

2. How many times does POST usually test memory?

   _____

3. Why must the MemTest86 software run from bootable media?

_____

_____

4. Describe the symptoms caused by a dead memory module.

_____

_____

5. Why would a continuous test be ideal for diagnosing a thermal intermittent?

_____

CHAPTER 4

Supporting the Power System and Troubleshooting Computers

Labs included in this chapter:

LAB 4.1 FIND DOCUMENTATION ON THE INTERNET ABOUT POWER RATINGS

OBJECTIVES

The goal of this lab is to determine how much power a component needs by locating documentation on the Internet. After completing this lab, you will be able to:

- Find the manufacturer and model of a component
- Locate a product's documentation or manual
- Download and view a product manual

MATERIALS REQUIRED

This lab requires the following:

- A computer designated for disassembly
- Internet access
- Adobe Acrobat Reader or a browser plug-in to view PDFs
- A computer toolkit with ESD strap
- A workgroup of two or three students or individual students
- Access to a printer (optional)

LAB PREPARATION

Before the lab begins, the instructor or lab assistant needs to do the following:

- Verify that a computer designated for disassembly is available for each student or workgroup
- Verify that Internet access is available

ACTIVITY BACKGROUND

Often the power specifications for a component aren't labeled on the component itself but are included in the documentation. When working with computers, it's common to encounter a component for which you have no documentation on hand. In this lab, you learn how to find a component's make and model and, if possible, find online documentation for it.

ESTIMATED COMPLETION TIME: 30 MINUTES

 Activity

1. Open the computer's case and locate the component your instructor assigned to you (or select a component randomly). If you're in a workgroup, each person should be assigned a different component.

> **Notes** The manufacturer and model aren't marked clearly on every component. If you're having trouble finding this information on a component, such as a video card, try researching based on the component's chipset. The information identifying the chip is usually stenciled on the chip. For a network card, look for an FCC number printed on the card, and use it for your search. If you need to find out how much power an unlabeled component uses, sometimes it's helpful to consult the documentation for similar components.

4

2. Examine the component until you find a sticker or stenciled label identifying its manufacturer and model number. Write down the identifiers.

_____

3. Take your notes to a computer that has Internet access.

4. If you already know the manufacturer's URL, go to that site and try to find documentation by searching in the Support, Download, or Customer Service section.

   If you're not sure of the manufacturer's URL, try searching the web for the manufacturer or model number. In fact, searching by model number often locates the information in the fewest steps. For example, if Z97I AC is imprinted on your motherboard, searching for "Z97I AC" can take you right to the documentation you need. Keep in mind that most documentation is in PDF format, which means you will need Adobe Acrobat Reader or a browser plug-in to view the documentation.

   ◢ What is the power consumption for the component expressed in watts?

_____

   If you are not able to find the power consumption for your component, search for the power consumption for similar components. For example, if you cannot find the power consumption for your network card that uses a PCIe ×4 slot, search for a PCIe ×4 network card from another manufacturer and record that information on the preceding line.

5. Print or save the documentation, and file it as a reference for when you need information about that component.

6. Now determine what CPU your system uses, and list that CPU here:

_____

7. Go to the manufacturer's website, and find and print the webpage showing the power consumption of your CPU expressed in watts.

REVIEW QUESTIONS

1. How is a computer component, such as a network card, commonly marked for identification?

_____

2. In what sections of a website are manuals commonly found?

_____

3. In what format are manuals usually provided?

_____

4. At what website can you download the technical product specification guide for an Intel DQ87PG motherboard? What is the name of the downloaded file?

_____

_____

5. Why would a computer repair technician need to know the power consumption of a peripheral component?

_____

LAB 4.2 MEASURE THE OUTPUT OF YOUR POWER SUPPLY

OBJECTIVES

The goal of this lab is to use a multimeter to measure the voltages provided by a power supply. After completing this lab, you will be able to:

▲ Use a multimeter

▲ Measure voltage provided by a power supply

MATERIALS REQUIRED

This lab requires the following:

▲ A computer designated for this lab

▲ A computer toolkit with ESD strap

▲ A laptop with its AC adapter

▲ A multimeter

▲ Access to the online content "Electricity and Multimeters," downloaded from the companion website at *cengage.com*. For more information, see the Preface.

▲ A workgroup of two to four students

LAB PREPARATION

Before the lab begins, the instructor or lab assistant needs to do the following:

▲ Announce to students that before they come to the lab, they should read the online content "Electricity and Multimeters." It is also suggested that students bring this content to class in printed form.

ACTIVITY BACKGROUND

In most situations, if you suspect a problem with a power supply, you simply exchange it for a known good one. In a few instances, however, you might want to measure your power supply's output using a multimeter.

A multimeter is an electrical tool that performs several tests. It can typically measure continuity, resistance, and voltage. It might have a digital or an analog meter that displays output. It also has two leads used to contact the component you're testing. The various models of multimeters each work slightly differently. Follow the correct procedure for your specific multimeter. In this lab, you measure the electrical voltage supplied to the motherboard and hard drives. Follow your computer lab's posted safety procedures when completing this lab.

ESTIMATED COMPLETION TIME: 30 MINUTES

 Activity

Using your multimeter, measure the power output to your system's motherboard and to an optical drive, and then fill in the following charts that apply to your system. Note that the column headings "Red Lead" and "Black Lead" refer to the colors of the probes.

4

> ⚡ **Caution** Be sure you have your multimeter set to measure voltage, not resistance (ohms) or current (amps). If the multimeter is set to measure current, you might damage the power supply, the motherboard, or both.

Again, detailed directions for using a multimeter can be found in the online content "Electricity and Multimeters." Be very careful as you work inside the computer case with the power on. Don't touch any components other than those described in the steps.

The following steps outline the basic procedure for using a multimeter:

1. Remove the cover from the computer case.
2. Set the multimeter to measure voltage of approximately 20 V, and set the AC/DC switch to DC. Insert the black probe into the meter's 2 jack and the red probe into the meter's 1 jack.
3. Turn on the multimeter, and then turn on the computer.
4. Measure each circuit by placing a red probe on the lead and a black probe on ground (see Figure 4-1).

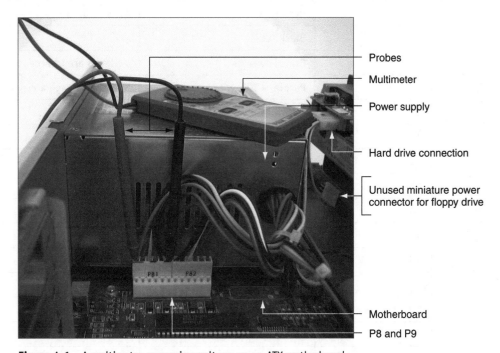

Figure 4-1 A multimeter measuring voltage on an ATX motherboard

5. An ATX Version 2.2 or higher motherboard and power supply use a 24-pin P1 connector. Figure 4-2 shows the 24-pin P1 power connector for an ATX motherboard, and the purposes of the pins are listed in Table 4-1. The colors listed are the colors of the wires on the P1 power connector to the power supply, which are shown in Figure 4-3.

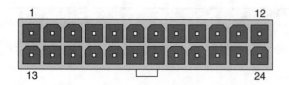

Figure 4-2   An ATX 24-pin P1 power connector on the motherboard

Lead or Pin	Description and Signal	Acceptable Range (Volts = V)
1	Orange, +3.3 V	3.2 to 3.5 V
2	Orange, +3.3 V	3.2 to 3.5 V
3	Black, COM	
4	Red, +5 V	4.75 to 5.25 V
5	Black, COM	
6	Red, +5 V	4.75 to 5.25 V
7	Black, COM	
8	Gray, Power OK	Voltages are in acceptable range
9	Purple, +5 V	Standby voltage always on
10	Yellow, +12 V	11.4 to 12.6 V
11	Yellow, +12 V	11.4 to 12.6 V
12	Orange, +3.3 V	3.2 to 3.5 V
13	Orange/Brown, +3.3 V	3.2 to 3.5 V
14	Blue, −12 V	−10.8 to −13.2 V
15	Black, COM	
16	Green, Signal	
17	Black, COM	
18	Black, COM	
19	Black, COM	
20	White, NC	
21	Red, +5 V	4.75 to 5.25 V
22	Red, +5 V	4.75 to 5.25 V
23	Red, +5 V	4.75 to 5.25 V
24	Black, COM	

Table 4-1   ATX 24-pin P1 power connector pinouts

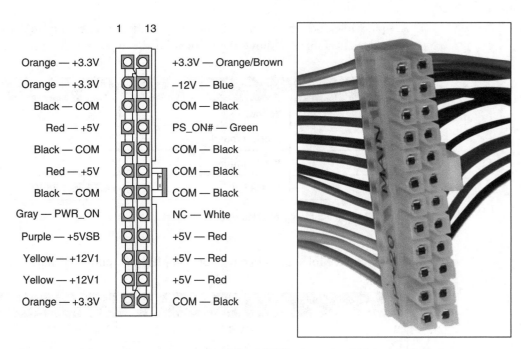

1   13

Orange — +3.3V   +3.3V — Orange/Brown
Orange — +3.3V   −12V — Blue
Black — COM   COM — Black
Red — +5V   PS_ON# — Green
Black — COM   COM — Black
Red — +5V   COM — Black
Black — COM   COM — Black
Gray — PWR_ON   NC — White
Purple — +5VSB   +5V — Red
Yellow — +12V1   +5V — Red
Yellow — +12V1   +5V — Red
Orange — +3.3V   COM — Black

Figure 4-3   A P1 24-pin power connection follows ATX Version 2.2 and higher standards

6. Working with a 24-pin P1 ATX motherboard, complete the following chart:

Red Lead (Positive)	Black Lead (Ground)	Voltage Measure
1	Ground	
2	Ground	
4	Ground	
6	Ground	
9	Ground	
10	Ground	
11	Ground	
12	Ground	
13	Ground	
14	Ground	
21	Ground	
22	Ground	
23	Ground	

7. A 4-pin Molex power connector is used to provide power to some older hard drives or other devices. Table 4-2 shows the pinouts for this type of connector.

Lead or Pin	Description and Signal	Acceptable Ranges (Volts = V)
1	Yellow, +12 V	11.4 to 12.6 V
2	Black, ground	
3	Black, ground	
4	Red, +5 V	4.75 to 5.25 V

Table 4-2 Pinouts for a 4-pin Molex power connector

8. Using a 4-pin Molex power connector, complete the following chart:

Red Lead	Black Lead	Voltage Measure
1	3	
4	2	

9. Turn off the computer and replace the cover.

If a laptop battery doesn't charge correctly, the problem might be the battery, the motherboard, or the AC adapter. The voltage output of an AC adapter can be tested using a multimeter. Do the following to learn more:

1. What is the brand and model of your laptop?

2. Search the web to find the online documentation for this laptop. How much voltage should the AC adapter provide to the laptop?

3. Unplug the AC adapter from the laptop. Plug the AC adapter into a wall outlet.

4. Using a multimeter, set the meter to measure voltage in the range the AC adapter is expected to provide the laptop. For most laptops, this range should be 1 to 20 V DC. However, some laptops receive more than 20 V DC; for these laptops, set the range from 1 to 200 V DC.

5. Place the red probe of the multimeter in the center of the DC connector of the AC adapter. Place the black probe on the outside cylinder of the DC connector.

◢ What is the DC voltage measurement?

◢ Is the value within 5 percent of the expected voltage according to the laptop documentation?

REVIEW QUESTIONS

1. What is the electrical voltage from a house outlet to a computer's power supply?

2. What voltages are supplied by the power supply on your system?

_____

3. What model of multimeter are you using?

_____

4. List the steps to set your multimeter to measure resistance.

_____

5. Besides voltage and resistance, what else can your multimeter measure?

_____

LAB 4.3 CHOOSE THE RIGHT POWER SUPPLY

OBJECTIVES

The goal of this lab is to locate documentation on the web so that you can determine how much power a system uses as a whole. You can use this information to decide the wattage rating of the power supply you need to purchase for a new or upgraded system. After completing this lab, you will be able to:

▲ Calculate the total wattage requirements for a system

▲ Choose the correct type and rating of a power supply

MATERIALS REQUIRED

This lab requires the following:

▲ A computer designated for disassembly

▲ A computer toolkit with ESD strap

▲ A workgroup of two or three students or individual students

▲ Access to a printer (optional)

▲ Internet access

LAB PREPARATION

Before the lab begins, the instructor or lab assistant needs to do the following:

▲ Verify that a computer designated for disassembly is available for each student or workgroup

▲ Verify that Internet access is available

ACTIVITY BACKGROUND

When selecting a power supply for a computer system, you must take many factors into account. It's important to look at the system's components as a whole and to consider how the system will be used. You might be tempted to simply purchase a power supply that has a very high wattage rating, but this choice isn't always the most economical. The typical efficiency rating of a power supply is 60 percent to 70 percent. Usually, this rating means

30 percent to 40 percent of the power is blowing out of the case as wasted heat. You want to keep waste to a minimum. On the other hand, if you intend to upgrade your system, buying an overrated power supply might be wise.

Running a system with an inadequate power supply can cause the power supply to wear out faster than normal. Also, an inadequate power supply can cause a system to reboot at odd times and experience other types of intermittent errors. It pays to install a correctly rated power supply for a system.

ESTIMATED COMPLETION TIME: 45 MINUTES

 Activity

1. Open your computer's case and locate each component listed in Table 4-3. Record how many components are present. Note that some entries will be zero.

Component	Number Present	Wattage Requirement	Total Wattage
Processor			
PCI Express video card			
PCI card			
Optical drive			
Hard drive			
Case fan or CPU fan			
Motherboard (without CPU or RAM)			
RAM module			
Other component 1			
Other component 2			
		Total Wattage	

Table 4-3   Calculate the wattage requirements for your system

2. Search the web for estimates of how much wattage each component uses, and fill in the last two columns in the table.

3. Add the wattage for all components to come up with the total wattage. Record the system's total wattage in the last row of the table.

4. Multiply the total wattage by 1.5 to reflect a 50 percent increase. This multiplier takes into account the overhead of the system, today's technology demands, and the goal of running a system at about 30 percent to 70 percent of its maximum capacity. What is your calculated total wattage, taking into account the required overhead?

5. Now look at the power supply to identify its connectors, which are shown in Table 4-4. Fill in Table 4-5 to identify the number and type of connectors in your system.

Connector	Description
	The 24-pin P1 connector, also called the 20+4-pin connector, is the main motherboard power connector used today.
	The 20+4-pin P1 connector has four pins removed so the connector can fit into an older 20-pin P1 motherboard connector.
	The 4-pin 12-V connector is an auxiliary motherboard connector, which is used for extra 12-V power to the processor.
	The 8-pin 12-V connector is an auxiliary motherboard connector, which is used for extra 12-V power to the processor, providing more power than the older 4-pin auxiliary connector.
	The 4-pin Molex connector is used for older IDE drives, some newer SATA drives, and to provide extra power to video cards. It can provide +5 V and +12 V to the device.
	The 15-pin SATA power connector is used for SATA (Serial ATA) drives. It can provide +3.3 V, +5 V, and +12 V, although +3.3 V is seldom used.
	The PCIe 6-pin connector provides an extra +12 V for high-end video cards using PCI Express.
	The PCIe 8-pin connector provides an extra +12 V for high-end video cards using PCI Express.
	The PCIe 6/8-pin connector is used by high-end video cards using PCIe ×16 slots to provide extra voltage to the card; it can accommodate a 6-hole or 8-hole port. To get the 8-pin connector, combine both the 6-pin and 2-pin connectors.

Table 4-4 Power supply connectors

Connector	Quantity	Quantity Currently Used
Molex connector		
Berg connector		
SATA connector		
ATX connector (24 pins)		
Auxiliary power (4, 6, or 8 pins)		
PCIe connector		

Table 4-5   Identify power connectors on your PSU (power supply unit)

6. Look on the power supply label for the peak load rating in watts. What is this value?

_____

7. Based on what you have learned in this lab, is the power supply adequate for the system? Why or why not?

_____

ESTIMATED COMPLETION TIME: 30 MINUTES

CHALLENGE ACTIVITY

1. Many power supply manufacturers offer a PSU wattage calculator on their websites that can save you time when deciding on the wattage requirements for a power supply. Here are two URLs that provide wattage calculators:

   ◢ outervision.com/power-supply-calculator

   ◢ coolermaster.com/power-supply-calculator

2. Using one of these wattage calculators or another on the web, determine the wattage requirements for your system. What is the minimum and recommended PSU wattage given by the calculator? How do these values compare with your own manual calculations?

   _____

   _____

3. Suppose your power supply stops working, and you must buy a replacement. Search the web for a comparable power supply. The cost of power supplies varies widely. For example, a 450 W power supply can cost from $40 to more than $200. The difference in quality can be judged partly by the weight of the power supply; in general, the heavier it is, the more transistors it has and the more heavy-duty the transistors are, which makes for a better power supply. Another factor to consider is noise level; quiet power supplies can be more expensive than noisy ones. Save or print two webpages showing a high-end and low-end power supply that would meet your system's needs. Which power supply would you recommend purchasing for your system, and why?

   _____

REVIEW QUESTIONS

1. What is the typical efficiency rating for a power supply?

   _____

2. Are there any connectors your system needs that the power supply doesn't have? If so, what are they?

   _____

3. Are there any connectors provided by the power supply that your system isn't using? If so, what are they?

   _____

4. Why is it important to buy a power supply that's close to the requirements for your system instead of buying a higher-wattage power supply? Under what circumstances might it be better to buy a higher-wattage power supply?

   _____

5. Some video cards require power provided directly by the power supply by way of a 6-pin or 8-pin PCIe power connector. How much wattage does a 6-pin PCIe connector provide? An 8-pin PCIe connector?

   _____

LAB 4.4 REPLACE A POWER SUPPLY

OBJECTIVES

The goal of this lab is to replace a power supply. After completing this lab, you will be able to:

◢ Identify the power supply

◢ Remove the power supply from the case

◢ Install a new power supply and new cabling

MATERIALS REQUIRED

This lab requires the following:

◢ A computer designated for this lab

◢ A computer toolkit with ESD strap

◢ A workgroup of two to four students

LAB PREPARATION

Before the lab begins, the instructor or lab assistant needs to do the following:

◢ Verify that a computer designated for disassembly is available for each workgroup

ACTIVITY BACKGROUND

This lab tests your ability to remove and replace a power supply. Power supplies, as a rule, are considered field replaceable units (FRUs). To save time and avoid the danger of working inside power supplies, IT technicians don't repair power supplies; they replace them. If you find that a power supply is faulty, replace it with a compatible power supply, and then send the original off to be reconditioned or recycled.

ESTIMATED COMPLETION TIME: 30 MINUTES

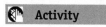 **Activity**

Follow these steps to examine and replace a power supply:

1. Turn the computer off and unplug the power cord. Press the power button for three seconds to drain any remaining power.

2. Disconnect all peripherals and remove the case cover.

3. Examine the label on the power supply. Answer the following questions:

   ▲ What is the peak load rating of the power supply? A system requiring more power than the power supply provides can contribute to an early failure of the power supply.

   _____

   ▲ How many and what type of power connectors does the power supply provide? (For example, it might provide six SATA connectors.)

   _____

   _____

   _____

   _____

   ▲ How many and what type of power connectors is the system currently using?

   _____

   _____

   _____

   ▲ What is the form factor of the power supply?

   _____

4. Remove the cabling and the power supply. Usually the power supply is held in place by four screws in the back of the case and perhaps a tab under the power supply. Some systems might use other methods of securing the power supply.

5. Examine the new power supply provided by your instructor, or swap your power supply with another workgroup. Answer the following questions:

   ▲ What is the form factor of this new power supply?

   _____

◢ What is the power rating of this new power supply?

_____

◢ Does the power supply provide all the power connectors the system needs?

_____

◢ Will this new power supply satisfy the needs of your system?

_____

6. Install the new power supply. Ask your instructor to check your work before you close the case. This check is crucial because some older power supplies must be connected correctly to ensure that they aren't damaged when they're turned on.

7. Close the case, reattach the peripherals, and test the system.

REVIEW QUESTIONS

1. How many connectors linked your original power supply to the motherboard?

_____

2. How many watts of peak power could the original power supply provide?

_____

3. Why is it important to calculate the peak power required for all components?

_____

4. What are two reasons that IT technicians don't usually repair a power supply?

_____

5. What term is used to refer to components that are commonly replaced but not repaired?

_____

6. What is the most efficient way to determine whether your power supply is bad?

_____

LAB 4.5 MEASURE TEMPERATURE AND ADJUST FAN SPEED

OBJECTIVES

The goal of this lab is to become familiar with thermal issues in your computer and how to adjust the system to compensate for them. After completing this lab, you will be able to:

◢ Access a system's temperature data

◢ Adjust the speed of the cooling fans

MATERIALS REQUIRED

This lab requires the following:

◢ A computer running Windows 10/8/7

◢ Internet access

◢ SpeedFan software downloaded from *filehippo.com/download_speedfan*

LAB PREPARATION

Before the lab begins, the instructor or lab assistant needs to do the following:

◢ Verify that Windows starts with no errors

◢ Verify that Internet access is available

ACTIVITY BACKGROUND

In the course of your career as a computer technician, you will become familiar with the problems that heat causes in a computer system. A computer's CPU is particularly susceptible to damage from excessive heat, but hard drives, RAM chips, video cards, and just about any other component you can think of are all susceptible to damage. If you suspect a computer is having a problem with overheating, you can install diagnostic software to monitor the temperatures from the Windows desktop. If the feature is enabled in BIOS/UEFI setup, you can also use this software to monitor and control the computer's fans.

In this lab, you use diagnostic software to look at the readouts from the computer's built-in temperature sensors and then adjust the temperature thresholds, which can be used to alter the behavior of the computer's fans in order to improve their efficiency.

ESTIMATED COMPLETION TIME: 45 MINUTES

 Activity

Follow these steps to install SpeedFan:

1. Go to **filehippo.com/download_speedfan**. At the time this lab was written, the latest version of SpeedFan was Version 4.52.

2. Click **Download Latest Version (2.94MB)** to start the download. Note that several other ad-supported download buttons are displayed on this webpage, and if clicked, they will download other files to your computer that are unrelated to this lab. Be careful to click the correct Download button for the SpeedFan freeware. At the time of this writing, the SpeedFan Download button includes the file size (2.94 MB). Save the file to your Downloads folder.

3. Double-click the downloaded file to install the software, using default settings for the installation.

4. Launch the SpeedFan utility. In the SpeedFan dialog box, select the **Readings** tab. See Figure 4-4. What are the current fan speeds and temperatures for your computer?

_____

_____

_____

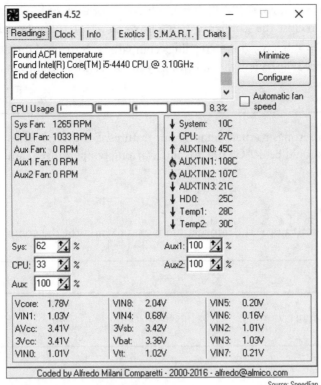

Figure 4-4   The Readings tab of SpeedFan displays current
fan speeds and temperatures

5. Take a screenshot of the SpeedFan dialog box displaying the Readings tab. Save the screenshot to your desktop to compare readings after changing settings.

Use the SpeedFan program to adjust the settings for the fans in your computer. You can raise the desired temperature to make a fan quieter or lower the desired temperature if your computer is overheating.

1. Click the **Configure** button to open the Configure dialog box.

2. Click the **Fan Control** tab, and check the **Advanced fan control** option.

3. To create a new fan controller, click **Add**. Enter the name **Test** and click **OK**. In this lab, you will not activate the fan controller. Some computers require alterations to be made in BIOS/UEFI in order for this feature to work. Also, it's easy to damage your computer equipment if the settings aren't carefully configured and monitored for a while. However, you can walk through the steps for creating a Test fan controller to see how it's done.

4. Click **Test** to view settings options for this fan controller.

5. Select **SUM of speeds** as your method. To add temperature sensors into your configuration, click **Add** under the Temperatures box.

6. Create a setting using the temperature of the processor. For multicore processors, there will be a temperature for each core. To begin, select the CPU from the list of available temperature sensors, and click **OK** to add it to this fan controller. Repeat this step for each of the cores of your processor.

7. Return to the **Temperatures** tab and click the CPU to view the settings options. Turn down the Desired temperature to about **20°C (68°F)**, and turn down the Warning

temperature to about **25°C (77°F)**. Repeat this step for each of the cores of your processor. Click **OK** to close the Configure dialog box and return to the SpeedFan main display.

8. On the **Readings** tab, how do the readings compare with the initial readings when you first opened SpeedFan? View the screenshot you took earlier in the lab to make the comparison.

_____

_____

9. Return the fan settings to their default temperatures. For the CPU and each core, Desired temperatures should be **40°C (104°F)**, and Warning temperatures should be **50°C (122°F)**.

REVIEW QUESTIONS

1. Where does SpeedFan get the information it uses to monitor the computer?

_____

_____

2. Why would you use a utility such as SpeedFan?

_____

_____

_____

3. In what situations would you want to adjust the speed of a fan on your computer?

_____

_____

4. Is it possible to damage a computer with a utility like SpeedFan? How?

_____

_____

LAB 4.6 CHOOSE A CPU COOLING SOLUTION

OBJECTIVES

Matching a CPU to an appropriate fan or other cooling system is a critical part of the process for replacing a CPU. The goal of this lab is to practice researching cooling options for a specific CPU. After completing this lab, you will be able to:

◢ Choose a heat sink and fan appropriate for your CPU

MATERIALS REQUIRED

This lab requires the following:

◢ A computer running Windows 10/8/7

◢ Internet access

LAB PREPARATION

Before the lab begins, the instructor or lab assistant needs to do the following:

◢ Verify that Windows starts with no errors

◢ Verify that Internet access is available

ACTIVITY BACKGROUND

A CPU handles a lot of information in its internal circuitry. Data processed in a CPU is represented by bits, which are 0s and 1s. Each transistor in a CPU can hold one bit, and today's CPUs contain several trillion transistors. Transistors can produce a large amount of heat, which needs to be dissipated in some way in order to keep the CPU operating temperature at an acceptable level. Most commonly, a heat sink and fan are used to reduce heat in a CPU. The heat sink is a metal unit that conducts heat away from the CPU and dissipates that heat into the air. A fan forces the hot air over the top or the side of the heat sink. Some fans are variable-speed fans that adjust their speeds according to the CPU's temperature.

The fan and heat sink are called a cooler or HSF (heat sink and fan). The most important factors to look for when choosing a cooling system for your CPU is that the cooler unit must fit the CPU and socket you are using. In addition, the cooler must provide adequate cooling at an acceptable noise level. Finally, the preferred unit should be easy to mount.

Gaming enthusiasts might overclock the CPU. Overclocking your CPU also means that more heat will be produced; in this case, upgrading your cooling system to a more efficient one might be necessary to protect your overclocked CPU.

ESTIMATED COMPLETION TIME: 45 MINUTES

 Activity

It's essential to choose a heat sink and fan made specifically for the processor you're using. Not only should the cooler fit, it should also cool the CPU sufficiently. Follow these steps to investigate coolers:

1. Go to **frozencpu.com**.

2. On the left side of the screen, under Shop by Category, click **CPU Heatsinks**. The CPU Heatsinks Categories screen is displayed.

3. Under CPU Heatsinks – Socket, click **Socket LGA 115x**.

4. Choose a heat sink and fan with a high star rating, and write down the following information:

    ◢ Brand and model: _____

    ◢ Price: _____

5. Read the product description, features information, and reviews, and then skim through the purchase options. List three features of this cooler:

    _____

    _____

    _____

6. Click the **Specifications** tab and use the information provided there to fill in the following chart. If the product specifications do not provide all of this information, find a different heat sink and fan with more complete information.

Feature	Specification
Socket type/compatibility	
Heat sink material	
Fan weight	
Fan speed	
Fan noise level	
Fan life expectancy	
Connector	

Complete the following steps to match a cooler to a processor used for gaming:

1. AMD makes processors popular in gaming computers. Go to the AMD website at **amd.com**. Explore the product menus, select a processor for gaming, and then answer these questions:

   ◢ Which processor did you select?

   _____

   ◢ Describe the processor specifications:

   _____

   _____

   ◢ Why did you select this processor?

   _____

   _____

2. Using other websites that sell or manufacture coolers, select the best cooler for the AMD processor that you selected in Step 1. Answer these questions:

   ◢ What is the cooler manufacturer and model?

   _____

   _____

   ◢ Why did you select this cooler?

   _____

   _____

   _____

Follow these steps to match a cooler for the socket and CPU installed in your system:

1. Using the skills you have learned so far in this course, determine the socket and processor installed in your lab computer.

   ◢ What processor is installed?

   _____

   ◢ What processor socket does the motherboard use?

   _____

2. Suppose the cooler on your processor has gone bad. Search the web for a cooler assembly that will work for the socket and processor your system uses.

   ◢ What is the cooler manufacturer and model?

   _____

   ◢ What is the price of the cooler?

   _____

REVIEW QUESTIONS

1. List three factors mentioned in this lab that you should consider when selecting a cooler.

   _____

   _____

   _____

2. What is the measurement unit for noise level when rating coolers? If you were in an office building and needed a very quiet system, what would be an acceptable noise level?

   _____

   _____

3. Suppose you have a CPU that gets very hot and will be used in a noisy industrial building. How would those factors affect your choice of coolers?

   _____

   _____

4. Why is it important to know the weight of a cooler when comparing coolers?

   _____

   _____

5. Why is it important to upgrade the CPU cooling system when overclocking the CPU?

   _____

   _____

   _____

LAB 4.7 DIAGNOSE SIMPLE HARDWARE BOOT PROBLEMS

OBJECTIVES

The goal of this lab is to practice diagnosing and repairing simple hardware problems. After completing this lab, you will be able to:

▲ Gather information useful in troubleshooting

▲ Diagnose a problem caused by someone else

▲ Record the troubleshooting process

MATERIALS REQUIRED

This lab requires the following:

▲ Computer designated for this lab

▲ Windows 10/8/7 operating system

▲ A computer toolkit, including screwdrivers and an ESD strap

▲ A pen and paper for taking notes

▲ The Computer Inventory and Maintenance form you first used in Chapter 1. You can download the form from *cengage.com*. For more information, see the Preface.

▲ A workgroup of two students

LAB PREPARATION

Before the lab begins, the instructor or lab assistant needs to do the following:

▲ Verify that Windows starts with no errors

ACTIVITY BACKGROUND

If you have worked in an IT service center that deals with the general public, you know that about half the problems you see are the result of an inexperienced person making a slight mistake when configuring a system and lacking the knowledge to diagnose and remedy the problem. Unless you're very skilled and lucky, you'll make similar mistakes from time to time. Your advantage is that you'll have the experience to narrow down and identify the problem and then fix it. This lab gives you experience troubleshooting and repairing simple problems. You also learn how good documentation can help you when troubleshooting a computer problem.

Before you begin, team up with another workgroup in your class. Your team works with this other group throughout the lab.

ESTIMATED COMPLETION TIME: 60–90 MINUTES

 Activity

Do the following to gather useful information about a system, and then troubleshoot a problem with the system that was created by another team:

1. To verify that your team's system is working correctly, shut down the system, start it up, and sign in to Windows. Did you encounter any errors during startup?

2. Skim over the Computer Inventory and Maintenance form, examine the system, and record any information on the form about your system that you think would be useful when troubleshooting a problem with this computer (for example, the user account name and password for an administrator account and the brand and model of the motherboard). Shut down the system.

▲ What type of information did you decide was important to record?

_____

_____

_____

3. Switch places with the other team. Make one of the following changes to the other team's system:

▲ Remove the power cable from the hard drive on which Windows is installed.

▲ Disconnect the P1 power cable from the motherboard.

▲ Remove or partially unseat the RAM. (Be sure to store all memory modules in an antistatic bag while they're outside the case. Store the RAM where the other team can't see it.)

▲ Disable SATA controllers in BIOS/UEFI setup.

▲ Remove the power-on wire from the motherboard header to the front of the computer case.

▲ Partially remove the data cable from the hard drive.

4. If you removed the case cover, replace the cover. Record the change you made to your team's system:

_____

_____

_____

5. Again switch places with the other team. Diagnose and remedy the problem on your system. Record the troubleshooting process in Section 7, Troubleshooting, on your Computer Inventory and Maintenance form. Make sure you answer the following questions here and on the form:

▲ Note the date, technician (your name), and symptoms. The symptoms are a description of the problem as a user would describe it to you if you were working at a help desk.

_____

_____

▲ What is your first guess as to the source of the problem?

_____

_____

▲ What did you do to solve the problem and return the system to good working order? Describe the actions taken and outcome here and on the Computer Inventory and Maintenance form:

_____

_____

_____

_____

◢ What information that you recorded earlier in the lab helped with the troubleshooting process?

_____

_____

◢ What information that you did not record would have been useful?

_____

6. Repeat Steps 2 through 4, choosing items at random from the list in Step 3. Continue until your team has made all the changes listed in Step 2 that are possible for your system.

ESTIMATED COMPLETION TIME: 30 MINUTES

CHALLENGE ACTIVITY

If time permits, try introducing two changes at a time. This approach can prove much more difficult.

REVIEW QUESTIONS

1. What problems resulted in a "No boot device available" error?

_____

_____

2. Typically, what's the first indication that RAM has been removed?

_____

3. What was the first indication of a problem with drive assignments?

_____

4. When a user calls to say his system is dead and nothing shows on his screen, what is one good suggestion you can offer for troubleshooting the problem?

_____

_____

5. In troubleshooting a boot problem, what would be the point of disabling the quick boot feature in BIOS/UEFI setup?

_____

6. If a user calls to say he sees a strange error message on the screen when he first turns on his computer, what should be your first question?

_____

LAB 4.8 TROUBLESHOOT GENERAL COMPUTER PROBLEMS

OBJECTIVES

The goal of this lab is to troubleshoot and remedy general computer problems. After completing this lab, you will be able to:

◢ Diagnose and solve problems with various hardware devices

◢ Document the troubleshooting process

MATERIALS REQUIRED

This lab requires the following:

◢ A computer designated for this lab

◢ Windows 10/8/7 operating system

◢ Windows installation DVD or flash drive, or installation files

◢ Drivers for all devices

◢ A pen and paper for taking notes

◢ A computer toolkit with ESD strap

◢ Internet access

◢ A workgroup partner

LAB PREPARATION

Before the lab begins, the instructor or lab assistant needs to do the following:

◢ Verify that Windows starts with no errors and can access the Internet

◢ Provide access to the Windows installation files

ACTIVITY BACKGROUND

In previous labs, you have learned to troubleshoot specific problems. This lab takes a comprehensive approach to troubleshooting an entire system, so the problem might relate to any subsystem. Troubleshooting a general problem is no different from troubleshooting a specific subsystem. You simply apply your troubleshooting techniques to a wider range of possibilities.

ESTIMATED COMPLETION TIME: 60–90 MINUTES

 Activity

Do the following to create a problem on your system, and then troubleshoot the problem your partner created on his or her system:

1. Verify that your computer and your partner's computer are working by checking that the systems both run smoothly and all drives are accessible. Browse the network and connect to a website.

2. Randomly pick one of the following hardware or software problems, and introduce it on your computer:

    ◢ Change the boot sequence to boot to the network.

⊿ If both the mouse and the keyboard have PS/2 connectors, switch the connectors at the case.

⊿ Using Control Panel, install a device that isn't actually available on the computer.

⊿ Remove the data cable from the hard drive that holds the Windows installation.

⊿ Change the display settings to two colors that are hard to read.

⊿ Remove the RAM from the system. (Be sure to store all memory modules in an antistatic bag while they're outside the case. Store the RAM where your partner can't see it.)

⊿ Unplug the monitor from the video adapter.

⊿ Use Control Panel to switch the primary and secondary buttons on the mouse.

⊿ Unplug the network cable from the wall or switch.

⊿ Use Control Panel to disable your current network connection.

3. If you removed the case cover, replace it. What problem did you introduce to your computer?

_____

4. Switch computers with your partner. Troubleshoot your partner's computer while your partner troubleshoots your computer. Verify that you can accomplish all the tasks you could before the computer was sabotaged.

5. On a separate sheet of paper, answer these questions:

⊿ What is the initial symptom of the problem as a user would describe it?

_____

_____

⊿ How did you discover the source of the problem?

_____

_____

⊿ How did you solve the problem?

_____

_____

⊿ If you were working at a help desk and someone called with this problem, could the problem have been solved over the phone, or would it have required a visit from a technician? Explain your answer:

_____

_____

6. Return to your computer and repeat Steps 2 through 5. Continue until you have solved all the problems listed in Step 2. For each problem, make sure to answer the questions in Step 5.

7. Which problem was the most difficult to solve? Why?

   _____

   _____

   _____

8. Of those problems that allowed the computer to boot, which problem was easiest to detect? Why?

   _____

   _____

   _____

9. Of those problems that prevented the computer from booting, which problem was easiest to detect? Why?

   _____

REVIEW QUESTIONS

1. Which problems caused the computer to halt during the boot process?

   _____

2. Was the solution to the problem usually obvious once you had discovered its source? Explain your answer:

   _____

3. What did you usually check first when you were troubleshooting? Why?

   _____

4. Now that you have been through this troubleshooting experience, what would you do differently the next time the same symptoms are exhibited?

   _____

5. What operating system utilities did you use or could you have used to solve a problem in this lab?

   _____

6. Is there any third-party software that might have been useful in solving the problems?

   _____

7. Which problem was the most difficult to solve? Why? In a real-life situation, what might happen that would cause this problem to occur?

   _____

LAB 4.9 USE LAPTOP DIAGNOSTIC SOFTWARE

OBJECTIVES

The goal of this lab is to research and use diagnostic software to troubleshoot problems with laptop computers. After completing this lab, you will be able to:

▲ Research and use diagnostic software on a laptop computer

▲ Research replacing a part on a laptop

MATERIALS REQUIRED

This lab requires the following:

▲ A working laptop computer

▲ Internet access

LAB PREPARATION

Before the lab begins, the instructor or lab assistant needs to do the following:

▲ Verify that a working laptop is available for each student or workgroup

▲ Verify that Internet access is available

ACTIVITY BACKGROUND

Servicing laptops is different from servicing desktop systems in many respects. One difference is that because laptops are more proprietary in design, you are more dependent on tools and manuals provided by the laptop manufacturer than you are when working with desktops. Some manufacturers provide excellent service manuals that you can download from their websites. On video-hosting sites such as *youtube.com*, you can also find good step-by-step tutorials.

Many laptop manufacturers offer diagnostic software on their websites and/or store diagnostic software on the laptop's hard drive, where it can be accessed at startup. This software can be used to test key hardware components and can be useful when troubleshooting a laptop. In this lab, you learn about laptop service manuals, diagnostic software, and other tools that are available, and you learn how to access and use them.

ESTIMATED COMPLETION TIME: 60 MINUTES

 Activity

You run a small IT service center, and Janice comes in with a laptop computer that has been dropped. The laptop is an HP Pavilion x360 (model number 11-n010dx) that is not under warranty. Janice tells you that she thinks the entire computer is useless because it appeared "dead" when she turned it on. She's especially upset over data on the hard drive that she believes has been lost. Do the following:

1. After you fill out the customer intake form, you are ready to tackle the problem. List the first three things you should do to try to save the data and troubleshoot the problem:

_____

_____

_____

4

_____

_____

2. After you plug in the AC adapter and turn on the laptop, you discover the lights on the computer are lit and you hear the fan running, but the LED touch screen is blank. When you connect an external monitor, you see the Windows sign-on screen. Janice breathes a sigh of relief. What do you do now?

_____

_____

You suspect that the LED touch screen is broken, but you decide it would be a good idea to run hardware diagnostic software to check for other hardware problems. Diagnostic software is written specifically for a particular brand of laptop and is often stored in a hidden utility partition on the hard drive or on the recovery disc that comes with the laptop. The software is accessed by pressing a key at startup or by booting from the recovery disc. For some laptops, the diagnostic software in the hidden partition is disabled by default and must be enabled in BIOS/UEFI setup before you can use it.

Do the following to find out about diagnostic software and how to use it:

1. Go to the HP website at **hp.com** and download the service guide for Janice's laptop. What is the name of the downloaded PDF file?

_____

2. Are there any recall alerts for this laptop? If so, which parts are included?

_____

3. What key do you press at startup to access the diagnostic software stored on this laptop?

_____

4. What types of tests can you run using the HP PC Hardware Diagnostics (UEFI) software?

_____

_____

5. If the hard drive is broken, what other method can you use to run the HP PC Hardware Diagnostics (UEFI) software?

_____

_____

6. Based on the information in the service guide, what is the part number of the LED touch screen?

_____

7. The laptop is fairly old, so HP might not still offer parts for sale. Are you able to buy the part from the HP website? What is the price of the LED touch screen if you buy it from the HP website?

_____

8. Do you think the laptop is worth the cost of the repair, including parts and labor? Explain your answer.

_____

_____

9. Research the service guide and list the high-level steps to replace the display assembly:

_____

_____

_____

_____

_____

_____

10. Before you commit to replacing an internal laptop component, you need to be confident that you have enough information and directions to open the laptop, access the part, and reassemble the laptop. Do you think you have enough information to do the repair? Why or why not?

_____

_____

11. If you don't think you have enough information, what is your next step?

_____

HP offers excellent diagnostic software, but not all laptop manufacturers do. Also, HP makes its laptop service manuals available on the web, but many laptop manufacturers release their service manuals only to authorized service centers. For these manufacturers, you can sometimes search the web to find alternative tutorials and advice. Using your lab laptop, available documentation for the laptop, and the web, answer these questions:

1. What is the brand and model of your laptop? What is the website of your laptop manufacturer?

_____

_____

2. Can you obtain the service manual for your laptop? If so, from where?

_____

_____

3. Does your laptop have diagnostic software? If so, how is it accessed? List all the methods:

_____

_____

_____

_____

4. If you have diagnostic software, how does this software compare with the HP PC Hardware Diagnostics (UEFI) software?

_____

_____

5. If you have diagnostic software, run it using the most thorough test that the software offers. List the results of the test:

_____

_____

REVIEW QUESTIONS

1. Why is it important to back up user data at the very first opportunity in the troubleshooting process?

_____

_____

2. What kinds of information can be found in a technical service manual?

_____

_____

3. Why would you want to run diagnostic software after you have repaired a laptop and verified that the repaired component works?

_____

4. Before you purchase an internal laptop part to replace a broken one, what should you verify?

_____

_____

5. List three troubleshooting situations in which diagnostic software might be useful:

_____

_____

_____

CHAPTER 5

Supporting Hard Drives and Other Storage Devices

Labs included in this chapter:

- **Lab 5.1:** Test Hard Drive Performance Using HD Tune
- **Lab 5.2:** Examine Your Hard Drive Using Four Methods
- **Lab 5.3:** Install a Second Hard Drive for Data Recovery
- **Lab 5.4:** Use Hard Drive Utilities
- **Lab 5.5:** Sabotage and Repair a System
- **Lab 5.6:** Replace a Laptop Hard Drive

LAB 5.1 TEST HARD DRIVE PERFORMANCE USING HD TUNE

OBJECTIVES

The goal of this lab is to use HD Tune to evaluate the performance of your system's hard drives against other hard drives. After completing this lab, you will be able to:

◢ Use HD Tune to test the performance of your hard drives

◢ Compare your system's drives with similar drives

MATERIALS REQUIRED

This lab requires the following:

◢ Windows 10/8/7 operating system

◢ An account with administrator privileges

◢ Internet access

LAB PREPARATION

Before the lab begins, the instructor or lab assistant needs to do the following:

◢ Verify that Windows starts with no errors

◢ Verify that each student has access to a user account with administrator privileges

◢ Verify that Internet access is available

ACTIVITY BACKGROUND

You can use HD Tune to run routine tests on your drive. This lab gives you an indication of how your drive is performing and whether another product is available that better meets your performance needs. Some tasks, such as video editing, make heavy demands on the drive where files are stored; a faster drive can increase productivity. When making an upgrade decision, it's helpful to compare results reported by HD Tune with information on other hard drives. In this lab, you use HD Tune to test your drive.

ESTIMATED COMPLETION TIME: 30 MINUTES

 Activity

Follow these steps to download and install HD Tune on your computer:

1. Sign in to Windows using an account with administrator privileges.

2. Using your browser, navigate to **hdtune.com**.

3. Click the **Download** tab. Scroll down to the HD Tune section, as shown in Figure 5-1, and click the file name to download. At the time of this writing, the file name was **hdtune_255.exe**.

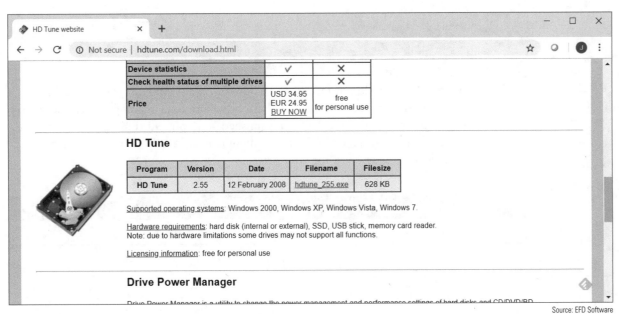

5

Figure 5-1 HD Tune is the free version of HD Tune Pro

4. Save the file to your hard drive. When the download is complete, open the folder where the file is saved. Do not close your web browser yet.

   ◢ What is the path and file name (including file extension) of the downloaded file? What is the size of the file?

   _____

   _____

5. To execute the downloaded file, double-click the file you just downloaded. Follow the on-screen directions to install the app, accepting all default settings. After the app installs, the HD Tune Hard Disk Utility dialog box appears.

Follow these steps to obtain benchmarks for your system's performance:

1. In the drop-down list of drives near the top of the dialog box, make sure the drive you want to scan is selected.

2. Record the following information for your drive. If the information is not included in the drop-down list, search the web using the details that *do* appear to find the missing information for the following list.

   ◢ Drive manufacturer: _____

   ◢ Model number: _____

   ◢ Capacity: _____

   ◢ Magnetic or SSD?: _____

   ◢ For magnetic drives, RPM: _____

   ◢ For magnetic drives, cache: _____

   ◢ Interface standard (for example, SATA2): _____

   ◢ Current drive temperature: _____

> **Notes** Some drives don't monitor temperature, so they won't be able to report that information to HD Tune.

3. While running the scan, do not move your mouse or do anything on your computer until the scan is complete, as this input will affect performance readings. Click the **Start** button to initiate the scan. After the scan is finished, a graph and summary are displayed. One example is shown in Figure 5-2, although yours may be different. Use the summary to complete the following chart for your drive:

Average Transfer Rate	Access Time

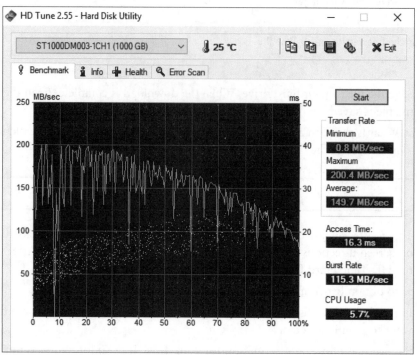

Figure 5-2 Results of HD Tune test for hard drive performance

Source: EFD Software

4. Click the **Info** tab.

◢ What are the drive's serial number and standard?

_____

_____

◢ How many partitions are on the drive?

_____

5. Click the **Health** tab and check the reported status for each attribute ID.

   ◢ Are there any attributes that are not OK? If so, list them here:

   _____

   _____

   _____

   ◢ What is the overall health status of the system?

   _____

6. Click the **Error Scan** tab. Select **Quick Scan** and then click **Start.** Watch as HD Tune scans the hard drive for damaged blocks. Did the utility find any damaged blocks?

   _____

When comparing the performance of hard drives, know that some manufacturers rate their drives by average access time and others use the maximum transfer rate. To compare the performance of your drive with other drives, do the following:

1. Search the web for your drive's manufacturer and model number. What is the advertised access time or maximum transfer rate for the drive? How does this value compare to the value you measured?

   _____

   _____

2. Suppose you decide to upgrade your hard drive to a faster model. What is one new feature you would select to best improve performance (for example, faster RPM or larger drive cache)?

   _____

3. Search the web for a new hard drive that has the feature you selected. Try to find a drive that is otherwise similar to your drive. What is the manufacturer and model of the new hard drive? What is the advertised access time or maximum transfer rate? What is the price of the drive?

   _____

   _____

   _____

4. Search the web for the fastest hard drive you can find that has the same capacity as your drive and uses the same drive interface to the motherboard. What is the manufacturer and model of the drive? What is the advertised access time or maximum transfer rate? What is the price of the drive?

   _____

   _____

   _____

HD Tune continues to monitor the system's operating temperature and reports this information in the taskbar while the program is open. You can view this data in the taskbar. (You might need to click the Show hidden icons arrow in the taskbar to see the temperature.) The temperature is displayed along with the hidden icons. By default, the temperature is shown in Celsius, but the unit can be changed to Fahrenheit in HD Tune's Options menu. Normal temperatures are shown in black and critical temperatures are shown in red. The critical threshold can also be set in the Options menu. The default critical threshold is 55°C.

◢ What is the current operating temperature?

_____

5. Exit HD Tune and close all open windows.

REVIEW QUESTIONS

1. Why might you want to test your drive with HD Tune?

_____

_____

2. Why is it important to monitor a drive's temperature?

_____

3. Based on your research, does a higher-capacity drive generally perform faster or slower than a lower-capacity drive?

_____

4. Suppose your current drive is a SATA2 drive. In what situation would a SATA3 drive perform no better than a SATA2 drive in your system?

_____

_____

5. If the HD Tune results indicated an obvious problem with a drive, such as a slow transfer rate, what is another feature of HD Tune you might use to get additional information about the drive?

_____

6. List four features of a hard drive that affect its overall performance.

_____

_____

_____

LAB 5.2 EXAMINE YOUR HARD DRIVE USING FOUR METHODS

OBJECTIVES

The purpose of this lab is to examine your hard drive and computer to find information about your hard drive. After completing this lab, you will be able to:

▲ Identify the manufacturer and model of your hard drive

▲ Determine the capacity of your hard drive

▲ Gather other information about your hard drive

MATERIALS REQUIRED

This lab requires the following:

▲ A computer running Windows 10/8/7

▲ Tools to open the computer case and examine the hard drive

▲ Internet access

LAB PREPARATION

Before the lab begins, the instructor or lab assistant needs to do the following:

▲ Verify that the Windows computer starts with no errors

▲ Verify that students have access to tools needed to open the computer case

▲ Verify that Internet access is available

ACTIVITY BACKGROUND

In the course of your career, you will frequently find yourself dealing with hard drives. You must be able to determine the vital statistics of a hard drive in order to resolve problems and upgrade a system. Information about a hard drive can be found in multiple locations. In this lab, you find this information using four different methods: physically inspecting the hard drive, looking in the BIOS/UEFI setup, using a third-party utility, and referring to the manufacturer's documentation.

ESTIMATED COMPLETION TIME: 30 MINUTES

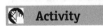 **Activity**

PART 1: GET INFORMATION BY PHYSICALLY INSPECTING THE DRIVE

Follow these steps to physically inspect your hard drive:

1. Open the computer's case and locate the hard drive seated in a bay.

> **Notes** Because computer cases come in many different configurations, you might need to consult the manual for your specific computer, and your experience may differ slightly from the instructions here.

2. If you can read the label on the hard drive, you may skip this step. If you cannot read the label on the hard drive, remove the cables (data and power), release the drive from its bay, and remove it for inspection.

3. Not all labels provide the same information. Using the label on the hard drive, write down the following information if available:

   ◢ Manufacturer:

   _____

   ◢ Model:

   _____

   ◢ Serial number:

   _____

   ◢ Part number:

   _____

   ◢ Capacity:

   _____

   ◢ SSD drive (yes or no):

   _____

4. Inspect the physical connection from the hard drive to the motherboard. What is the interface type?

   _____

5. Return the hard drive to its bay, plug it back in, and reassemble the computer.

PART 2: GET INFORMATION USING THE SYSTEM BIOS/UEFI

The BIOS/UEFI setup offers information about the hard drive(s) installed on a computer. Follow these steps to gather information about your computer using the system BIOS/UEFI:

1. Turn on your computer and enter the BIOS/UEFI setup.

2. Navigate to the drives section of BIOS/UEFI.

3. BIOS/UEFI uses a string of information to identify the hard drive. Write down this string exactly as it appears in BIOS/UEFI:

   _____

4. Use the information in this string to determine as much of the following information as possible:

   ◢ Manufacturer:

   _____

   ◢ Model:

   _____

◢ Capacity:

◢ Speed:

5. Using the speed of your hard drive, which version of SATA or PATA is your hard drive (SATA I, SATA II, SATA III or ATA 2, ATA 3, ATA 4, ATA 5, ATA 6, ATA 7)?

6. Is S.M.A.R.T. enabled on your system? What does S.M.A.R.T. stand for?

7. Exit the BIOS/UEFI setup without saving any changes and allow the computer to boot normally.

PART 3: GET INFORMATION USING THIRD-PARTY SOFTWARE

Using third-party software is another method to gather information about the hard drive(s) installed on a computer. Follow these steps to use Speccy to gather information about the hard drive installed on your computer:

1. Speccy might already be installed from a previous lab. If Speccy is not installed, download the Speccy utility by Ccleaner at **ccleaner.com/speccy**.

2. Open Speccy and go to the **Storage** section.

3. Using the information in the Storage section, write down the following information:

◢ Manufacturer:

◢ Device type:

◢ Interface:

◢ SATA type (including speed):

◢ ATA standard:

◢ Speed (expressed in revolutions per minute, or RPM):

◢ Transfer mode:

◢ Capacity:

◢ Form factor:

◢ S.M.A.R.T. temperature:

◢ S.M.A.R.T. status:

PART 4: GET INFORMATION FROM THE MANUFACTURER'S WEBSITE

The documentation for a hard drive offers any and all information about the hard drive that you might need. If you do not already have the printed documentation for your hard drive, research the web to find the documentation from the manufacturer's website. Complete the following steps:

1. Download the documentation and write down its file name:

2. Search through the documentation and determine the technology type of your hard drive. Is it a magnetic hard drive or an SSD drive?

REVIEW QUESTIONS

1. What important information can you consistently find on a hard drive's label?

2. What information about the hard drive can you *not* find on a hard drive's label?

3. What four methods do you have at your disposal to learn about a hard drive?

4. In this lab, you used a third-party utility to gather information about your hard drive. List two Windows utilities that can give you information about your hard drive.

5. What is the advantage of an SSD over a regular magnetic hard drive? What is the advantage of a magnetic hard drive over an SSD?

LAB 5.3 INSTALL A SECOND HARD DRIVE FOR DATA RECOVERY

OBJECTIVES

The goal of this lab is to install a second internal hard drive to recover data files. After completing this lab, you will be able to:

▲ Physically install a second hard drive

▲ Verify hard drive configuration in the BIOS/UEFI setup

▲ Use File Explorer/Windows Explorer to copy files

MATERIALS REQUIRED

This lab requires the following:

▲ Two computers that can be disassembled

▲ Cables necessary to attach the drive swapped between the computers

▲ A computer toolkit with ESD strap

▲ A workgroup of two to four students

LAB PREPARATION

Before the lab begins, the instructor or lab assistant needs to do the following:

▲ Verify that Windows starts with no errors on both computers

▲ Verify that both computers use compatible hard drives

ACTIVITY BACKGROUND

The precious thing about hard drives is the data they contain. Sometimes a hard drive may not boot properly, which could cause problems with access to the data stored on the drive or even prevent an operating system from booting properly. In this lab, we assume that your drive has failed to boot and you need to install the drive in another workstation so that you can recover the data files.

> **ESTIMATED COMPLETION TIME: 30 MINUTES**

 Activity

With your lab partner, decide which workstation has a drive that does not boot properly, and refer to this one as Workstation 1. The other workstation will be the data recovery workstation, Workstation 2.

On Workstation 1, follow these steps to create a folder that contains a couple of files you will recover:

1. Boot Workstation 1. Open File Explorer in Windows 10/8, or open Windows Explorer in Windows 7. Open the Documents library and create a folder named **Recovery**.

2. Copy and paste a couple of library document files into the Recovery folder. If no documents are available to copy, create two new document files.

3. Shut down Workstation 1.

Next, remove the hard drive from Workstation 1, and gather the information that you need to install the drive into Workstation 2. Follow these steps:

1. Using safety precautions and the ESD strap, remove the cover from Workstation 1, and then remove its hard drive. Be careful about disconnecting the cables from the hard drive so you don't bend or break connectors.

2. Examine the hard drive and record the following information:

   ◢ Manufacturer:

   _____

   ◢ Model:

   _____

   ◢ Capacity:

   _____

   ◢ Interface (SATA or PATA):

   _____

If your hard drive's interface is PATA, answer the following questions, and review the information to make sure you can properly install the hard drive into Workstation 2:

1. If the drive is a PATA drive, jumpers on the drive have been set for the PATA configuration in Workstation 1. These jumpers might need to be changed before you can install the drive in Workstation 2. Does the drive share a data cable with an existing drive, or is it the only drive installed on its data cable? Record the drive cable configuration here:

   _____

2. If the drive is a PATA drive, view the jumper settings on the drive. How are the jumpers set? Are they CS (cable select), device 0, or device 1? Record the jumper settings here:

   _____

If the PATA drive is sharing a data cable, the jumpers on both drives may need to be configured so that both drives are set to cable select (CS), or one drive is manually set as device 0 and the other is manually set as device 1. The original drive should be configured as device 0, and the second drive configured as device 1. If the jumpers are not set properly, BIOS/UEFI might not be able to detect the new drive. If you're unsure about how to set the jumpers, you can either consult the hard drive's documentation or ask your instructor. Most PATA drives are labeled with a diagram showing the proper jumper settings.

Complete the following steps to install and configure the hard drive from Workstation 1 into Workstation 2:

1. Go to Workstation 2. Remove the case cover and examine the hard drive configuration.

   ◢ Can you locate an unused power connector for the second drive? What type of power connector are you using?

   _____

2. If you are installing a PATA drive in a system that already has PATA drives installed, you must decide how the two PATA drives will be configured. Answer the following:

   ◢ How will you configure the PATA system?

   _____

   _____

◢ When installing a PATA drive, what jumper settings, if any, need to be changed on the PATA drive to be installed and/or on the PATA drives that are already installed? Be specific.

3. If your hard drive's interface is SATA, review the information to make sure you can properly install the hard drive into Workstation 2. If the drive is a SATA drive, it will not be sharing a data cable. The SATA system uses one drive per SATA connector on the motherboard. Your additional drive will need an additional SATA cable to attach to the motherboard connector. Depending on your motherboard, you may need to attach the cable to the next available connector, such as SATA 1, while your original drive is attached at SATA 0. Answer the following:

◢ Is there an extra SATA connector for the drive? Which SATA connector on the motherboard should you use? Verify the connector with your instructor.

4. Install the hard drive from Workstation 1 in a free bay, and attach both the data and power cables. Be careful to align the connectors correctly on the back of the drive. The connectors are keyed so that they will insert in only one direction. The same goes for attaching cables to the connector on the motherboard. Have your instructor verify your connections.

5. Boot the computer into the BIOS/UEFI setup screen, and ensure that BIOS/UEFI automatically detects the new hard drive in the storage section of the BIOS/UEFI information. Record the information that BIOS/UEFI gives about the hard drives:

◢ If there are PATA drives:

◢ IDE Primary:

◢ IDE Secondary:

◢ If there are SATA drives:

◢ SATA 0:

◢ SATA 1:

6. Boot the computer into Windows and use File Explorer/Windows Explorer to examine the files on the new drive.

◢ What is the drive letter designation for the added drive?

7. On the added drive, locate the Recovery folder you made earlier.

8. Copy the Recovery folder from the added drive to the Documents library of the C: drive, which will put the folder on the Workstation 2 original drive.

9. Open the Recovery folder on the C: drive. Do you see the files you saved into the folder from Workstation 1?

You have now recovered data files from a "damaged" system that you installed in another workstation. Complete the following steps to restore your computers to their original configurations:

1. Shut down Workstation 2, remove the drive you installed, and reinstall it in Workstation 1 in its original location. Be sure to use proper safety precautions, including using an ESD strap. Be mindful to restore the proper jumper and cable attachment configurations.

2. After the physical reinstallation, have your instructor verify your work. Reboot and enter the BIOS/UEFI setup of the workstation to verify that the drive is properly configured. Boot Workstation 1 to the Windows desktop, and verify that all is well.

3. Replace the cover on Workstation 2 and boot it up. Verify that you can boot it to the Windows desktop with no errors.

REVIEW QUESTIONS

1. If a hard drive fails to boot, why is it possible to recover data files by installing that drive in another system?

   _____

   _____

2. What is one way to determine how to set the jumpers on a PATA hard drive?

   _____

   _____

3. Was it necessary to install the second drive in Workstation 2 in order to recover the data? What are two reasons you might *not* want to install the drive during recovery?

   _____

   _____

4. If you had been unable to locate an available power connector in Workstation 2 for the recovered hard drive, what could you have done to power the hard drive?

   _____

   _____

5. If you installed a second hard drive in a workstation and BIOS/UEFI did not report it as being on the system, what is a possible cause?

   _____

   _____

   _____

LAB 5.4 USE HARD DRIVE UTILITIES

OBJECTIVES

The goal of this lab is to work with utilities from hard drive manufacturers to examine and diagnose hard drive problems. After completing this lab, you will be able to:

▲ Identify your hard drive manufacturer

▲ Evaluate utilities that hard drive manufacturers provide for their drives

▲ Test for hard drive problems

MATERIALS REQUIRED

This lab requires the following:

▲ Windows 10/8/7 operating system

▲ Internet access

LAB PREPARATION

Before the lab begins, the instructor or lab assistant needs to do the following:

▲ Verify that Windows starts with no errors

▲ Verify that Internet access is available

ACTIVITY BACKGROUND

Hard drive problems can manifest themselves in different ways. The drive might exhibit immediate and total failure so that it doesn't operate at all. If the failure is caused by a problem with the platters in the area where system files are stored, your computer might not be able to boot. If system files aren't affected, you might be able to boot and work normally, but you might have some file corruption or loss. Then again, you might not realize you have a hard drive problem if the drive has bad sectors in a physical area of the disk where data has not yet been saved. More often, however, when a disk begins to fail, Event Viewer in Windows reports errors. One tool you can use to diagnose hard drive problems is diagnostic software that your hard drive manufacturer supplies. In this lab, you identify your drive manufacturer and use its software to examine your drive.

ESTIMATED COMPLETION TIME: 60 MINUTES

 Activity

In order to use a hard drive diagnostic utility, you must first identify your hard drive's manufacturer and model number.

> **Notes** Hard drive manufacturers often abbreviate their names when providing information about their drives. Western Digital Corporation, for example, may be abbreviated as WDC, followed by a model number, or you might see ST for Seagate Technology, followed by a series of numbers and letters that provide further information.

1. Use the skills you've practiced in this chapter to find information about the hard drive you want to test. Record the following information:

   ◢ Hard drive manufacturer:

   _____

   ◢ Hard drive model:

   _____

Next, you find out about hard drive utilities supplied by two hard drive manufacturers, Seagate and Western Digital.

> 📓 **Notes** Websites change often. You might need to adjust the steps in this lab to account for changes to the websites used.

Follow these steps to find out about the Windows version of a Seagate software product called SeaTools for Windows, which works with Seagate and Maxtor hard drives as well as other brands of hard drives:

1. In your web browser, go to **seagate.com/support/downloads/seatools**. In the Downloads section, click **SeaTools for Windows**. The SeaTools program downloads. At the time of this writing, the name of the application file was SeaToolsforWindowsSetup.exe.

2. Double-click the downloaded file to start the installation, accepting all default settings. (You might be required to download and install .NET Framework software from Microsoft to complete the installation of SeaTools.)

3. SeaTools for Windows automatically places a shortcut icon on your desktop. Double-click the icon to open the application. The first time you run the software, the EULA may appear. If it does, click **I Accept**. The SeaTools for Windows window is displayed, as shown in Figure 5-3.

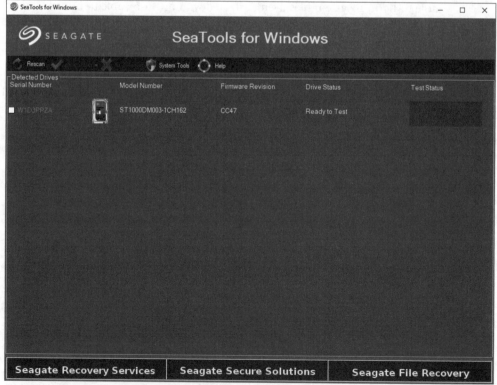

Source: Seagate Technology LLC

Figure 5-3 SeaTools for Windows is a useful diagnostic utility for hard drives

4. Select the drive on which you would like to run a test. On the toolbar, select **Basic Tests**. In the Basic Tests submenu, click **S.M.A.R.T Check**.

   ◢ What are the results of the S.M.A.R.T. test?

   _____

5. Select the drive again. In the Basic Tests submenu, click **Drive Information**, and record the following information:

   ◢ Serial number:

   _____

   ◢ Drive temperature:

   _____

   ◢ Power-on hours:

   _____

6. Using the Help feature on the SeaTools for Windows window, answer the following question:

   ◢ What is the difference between a fast test and a long test?

   _____

   _____

7. Browse through the Seagate website and answer these questions:

   ◢ Describe the purpose of SeaTools Bootable.

   _____

   _____

   ◢ What type of device does SeaTools Bootable install on?

   _____

Another very popular tool that Western Digital provides is the Data Lifeguard Diagnostic. Do the following to find out more about this software:

1. In your web browser, go to **support.wdc.com**. In the Downloads drop-down menu, select **WD Software**. Under Software for Windows, click **Data Lifeguard Diagnostic for Windows**. Then click **DOWNLOAD**. The zipped file downloads. At the time of this writing, the name of the file was WinDlg_v1_36.zip.

2. Install the Data Lifeguard program by double-clicking the file in the downloaded zip file. At the time of this writing, the file name was **WinDlg_v1_36.exe**. Accept all default settings to install the software. The application automatically launches when the installation completes. The Western Digital Data LifeGuard Diagnostics window is shown in Figure 5-4.

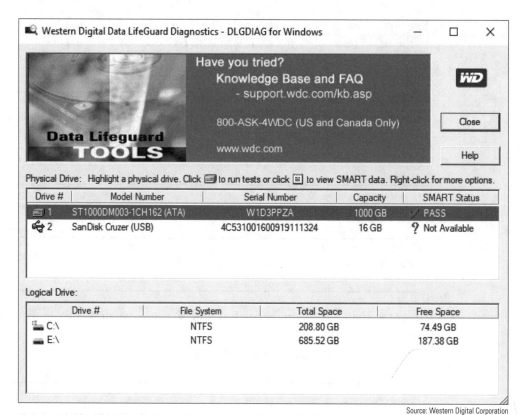

Figure 5-4 Data LifeGuard Diagnostics software reports information about a drive

3. Double-click the hard drive listed, and answer the following questions:

◢ What type of test does the QUICK TEST perform?

_____

◢ What type of test does the EXTENDED TEST perform? How long does the extended test take?

_____

_____

◢ Describe what the ERASE option does. What is one purpose of this option?

_____

_____

_____

Next, follow these steps to explore a manufacturer's utility to test your drive:

1. If your hard drive isn't made by Seagate, Maxtor, or Western Digital, go to your manufacturer's website and search for diagnostic software. If your hard drive manufacturer is Seagate, Maxtor, or Western Digital, do a quick search online to identify a different hard drive manufacturer, and then check its website for diagnostic software. What software did you find?

_____

2. Why do you think it's important to test a hard drive with software provided by the drive's manufacturer rather than that of another manufacturer?

_____

_____

REVIEW QUESTIONS

1. What are some symptoms of hard drive problems that might cause you to run the manufacturer's diagnostic software on the drive?

_____

_____

_____

2. Which hard drive manufacturer's website was the most informative and easiest to use? Explain your answer.

_____

_____

3. Which utility from a hard drive manufacturer seemed to be the most powerful? Explain your answer.

_____

_____

_____

4. Why is it useful to run hard drive diagnostics software from bootable media rather than from Windows?

_____

5. How do you determine that your system is set to boot from a CD or flash drive?

_____

LAB 5.5 SABOTAGE AND REPAIR A SYSTEM

OBJECTIVES

Having a seemingly unlimited number of possible causes for a computer's problems makes troubleshooting a bit more challenging. The goal of this lab is to troubleshoot a system by recovering from a sabotaged system. After completing this lab, you will be able to:

◢ Apply effective troubleshooting skills to identify and repair a computer problem

◢ Use appropriate tools to resolve computer problems

MATERIALS REQUIRED

This lab requires the following:

- ◢ A computer (containing no important data) that has been designated for sabotage
- ◢ The Computer Inventory and Maintenance form you first used in Chapter 1. You can download the form from *cengage.com*. For more information, see the Preface.
- ◢ Windows installation DVD or installation files
- ◢ A computer toolkit with ESD strap
- ◢ A workgroup of two to four students

LAB PREPARATION

Before the lab begins, the instructor or lab assistant needs to do the following:

- ◢ Verify that Windows starts with no errors
- ◢ Provide access to the Windows installation files
- ◢ Verify that students' computers contain no important data and can be sabotaged

ACTIVITY BACKGROUND

You have learned about several tools and methods you can use to troubleshoot and repair a failed system or failed hardware devices. This lab gives you the opportunity to use these skills in a simulated troubleshooting situation. Your group will work with another group to sabotage a system and then repair another failed system. This lab is more advanced than previous troubleshooting labs because you are not limited in what you do to sabotage the computer, as long as you don't cause physical damage.

Please don't introduce a problem on a computer in this lab that will cause permanent damage to a component!

ESTIMATED COMPLETION TIME: 60–90 MINUTES

 Activity

This lab works best and is more fun if you are troubleshooting a system that you have not worked on in previous labs. Do the following to gather information about the system, sabotage another team's computer, and then troubleshoot your system:

1. If possible, use a computer that you are not yet familiar with and have not used in previous labs. Examine the system. If the hard drive contains important data, back it up to another medium. Using your Computer Inventory and Maintenance form, record any information that you think might be useful when troubleshooting the system. Take note of anything else about the system you think might be useful, and record it here:

   _____

2. Trade systems with another group and sabotage the other group's system while that group sabotages your system. Do something that will cause the system to fail to work or give errors after booting.

   You can use any of the problems included in this lab manual, such as those used in Chapter 4. You can search the web or use your imagination to introduce a new nondestructive problem, such as turning down the brightness on the monitor or removing the CPU. Be creative and have fun. What did you do to sabotage the other team's system?

_____

_____

3. Return to your system and troubleshoot it. Record the symptoms and the troubleshooting process in Section 7 of your Computer Inventory and Maintenance form.

▲ Describe the problem as a user would describe it to you if you were working at a help desk:

_____

_____

▲ What was your first guess as to the source of the problem?

_____

▲ List the steps you took in the troubleshooting process:

_____

_____

_____

_____

_____

_____

▲ What did you do that finally solved the problem and returned the system to good working order?

_____

_____

4. Repeat Steps 2 and 3 so that each member of your group has an opportunity to create and solve several problems.

ESTIMATED COMPLETION TIME: 60–90 MINUTES

CHALLENGE ACTIVITY

Perform this lab again, but this time introduce two problems into the system at the same time.

1. What two problems did you introduce into the other team's computer?

_____

_____

2. How much more difficult was it to troubleshoot your computer with two problems compared with having only one problem to solve?

_____

_____

_____

3. Describe the troubleshooting process, and explain how you were able to distinguish between the two problems you needed to solve:

_____

_____

_____

_____

_____

REVIEW QUESTIONS

1. Think back on this troubleshooting experience to the problem that caused you the most difficulty. What would you do differently the next time you encounter the same symptoms?

_____

_____

2. Did you use any third-party software utilities or hardware devices to solve any of your problems? If so, what were they?

_____

3. Think of a computer problem you've experienced in the past. How did you handle the problem?

_____

_____

_____

4. Is there anything you could have done differently to diagnose the solution earlier or avoid the problem altogether?

_____

LAB 5.6 REPLACE A LAPTOP HARD DRIVE

OBJECTIVES

The goal of this lab is to practice replacing a hard drive in a laptop computer. After completing this lab, you will be able to:

▲ Locate the hard drive in a laptop computer

▲ Remove the hard drive from a laptop computer

▲ Replace the hard drive in a laptop computer

MATERIALS REQUIRED

This lab requires the following:

▲ A laptop computer or Internet access

▲ A computer toolkit with ESD strap

▲ Additional smaller screwdrivers, if necessary

LAB PREPARATION

Before the lab begins, the instructor or lab assistant needs to do the following:

▲ Verify that Internet access is available

ACTIVITY BACKGROUND

Hard disk drives are delicate devices. Dropping one even a few inches can cause permanent damage to the read/write heads, platter surfaces, or both. Laptop systems are, of course, often moved and commonly subjected to forces that most other hard drives never encounter. Although drives intended for laptop systems are designed to be resistant to movement and shock, they are still more likely to fail than any other laptop component. In this lab, you remove a hard drive from a laptop computer and then reinstall the same hard drive. If you don't have access to a laptop, skip to the alternate activity at the end of this lab.

Hard drives designed for laptop computers tend to be 50 percent to 75 percent more expensive than the standard 3.5-inch drives of comparable capacity for desktop computers. Also, although the majority of newer laptops support most 2.5-inch drives designed for laptops, some laptop computers require a proprietary hard drive. For these reasons, researching your replacement options before you purchase a new drive is important. Read the documentation that came with your laptop to determine what drives it supports. If this information isn't available in the documentation, search the manufacturer's website. In this lab, you remove the existing drive and then reinstall the same drive. The steps for your laptop might be slightly different from the procedures in this lab, so make sure you study the documentation before you begin.

ESTIMATED COMPLETION TIME: 30 MINUTES

Activity

Follow these steps to gather information about the laptop you are using in this lab:

1. What are the manufacturer and model of your laptop computer?

   _____

2. Using one or more of the methods you learned earlier in this chapter, gather the following information about your hard drive:
   - Manufacturer: _____
   - Model: _____
   - Capacity: _____
   - Speed: _____

3. Based on the laptop's documentation or information on the manufacturer's website, what type of hard drive can be used to replace the existing hard drive? Be as specific as you can:

   _____

   _____

4. Look for specific directions (in the documentation or on the website) for removing and replacing your laptop's hard drive. If you find any, summarize those directions here. (If you're using the website as your source of information, save or print any relevant webpages.)

   _____

   _____

   _____

   _____

Follow these general steps to remove the hard drive from a laptop computer. Note that these directions might not list every step necessary for your model. Refer to specific directions in the documentation or on the manufacturer's website, as needed.

1. Remove the main battery or batteries, and, if necessary, unplug the computer from the AC adapter. Close the lid and turn the computer so that the bottom is facing up.

   > **Notes** Some laptops have built-in batteries. For these devices, follow the manufacturer's instructions to disable the battery (often called Ship Mode), which prevents it from providing power to any component.

2. Locate and remove the access panel or component enclosing the drive bay. The hard drive might be located beneath the battery or behind a dedicated cover, as shown in Figure 5-5.

Figure 5-5   Remove a cover on the bottom of the laptop to exchange the hard drive, which is attached to a proprietary bracket

3. After you have accessed the drive, determine how it's secured in the system. It's commonly attached to a frame or "cradle" with small screws, and the cradle is often attached directly to the system chassis. This cradle helps locate and support the drive inside the drive bay. Remove the screws securing the cradle. In some systems, the hard drive is held in place by only a single screw. For these systems, remove the screw, then turn the laptop on its side and push the drive out of its bay.

4. In most laptops, data cables don't connect the hard drive to the motherboard, as is the case with desktop computers. Instead, a hard drive connects to the laptop's motherboard by way of an edge connector, similar to those on expansion cards in desktop computers. This type of direct connection has two advantages. First, it improves reliability because it reduces the total number of connection points; fewer connection points mean fewer connections that could shake loose as the laptop is moved around during daily use. The second advantage is that the lack of data cables reduces the laptop's overall size and weight. To remove the drive-cradle assembly, slide the cradle away from the connector. Slide the assembly back until all pins are clear of the connector. When the pins are clear, lift the assembly straight up out of the drive bay.

5. Note the orientation of the drive in the cradle so that when you reinstall the drive, you can mount it in the same direction. Remove the screws securing the drive in the cradle, and then remove the drive.

6. Examine the drive connections.

   ◢ Is the drive using a SATA interface or a PATA interface? How do you know?

   _____

   _____

   ◢ Is the drive a magnetic drive or an SSD drive? How do you know?

   _____

   _____

7. Using the information you have gathered about the drive—including its capacity, type (SSD or magnetic), speed (if a magnetic drive), brand, model, and interface—find a comparable hard drive on the web. Print or save the webpage showing the drive and its price. What is the drive brand, model, and price?

_____

Follow these general steps to reinstall the hard drive. Note that these directions might not list every step necessary for your model. Refer to specific directions in the documentation or on the manufacturer's website, as needed.

1. For a PATA drive, examine the jumper settings. What setting is currently used for the drive?

_____

2. Place the drive in the cradle so that the pins are oriented correctly, and then secure it with screws.

3. Set the drive-cradle assembly straight down into the drive bay. Gently slide the assembly to the connector, and verify that the pins are aligned correctly with the connector. Slide the assembly until the drive is fully seated in the connector. The cradle should now align with the holes in the chassis. If the holes don't align, you should remove the assembly, loosen the drive-retaining screws, and adjust the drive's position in the cradle. Repeat this process until the drive is fully seated so that there's no room for it to move after the cradle is secured. When the assembly is seated, secure it with screws.

4. Replace any components or access covers you removed to get at the hard drive.

5. Reinstall any batteries and reconnect to AC power, if necessary. As with any other hard drive, a new laptop drive must be correctly recognized by BIOS/UEFI and then partitioned and formatted before it can be used. This process isn't necessary in this lab because you haven't installed a new hard drive.

ESTIMATED COMPLETION TIME: 30 MINUTES

ALTERNATE ACTIVITY

If you don't have access to a laptop computer, follow these steps:

1. Using the documentation for one of the laptops you selected in Chapter 3 as your source, record the specific requirements for a replacement hard drive. Be as detailed as possible:

_____

_____

_____

2. Search the web for information on replacement hard drives, and print the webpage showing the correct specifications for a replacement hard drive. What is the cost of the drive? How much capacity does the drive have?

_____

3. Locate the steps for replacing the hard drive. To find this information, use the manuals you downloaded in Chapter 3, the manufacturers' websites, and other Internet resources

(such as websites for manufacturers of replacement laptop hard drives). How do the steps you found differ from the steps in this lab? Note the differences here:

_____

_____

_____

_____

_____

_____

_____

REVIEW QUESTIONS

1. Why should you research hard drives thoroughly when replacing one in a laptop computer?

_____

_____

2. What criteria should you consider when selecting a comparable hard drive to replace a hard drive in a laptop?

_____

_____

3. Why is hard drive cabling commonly not included in laptop systems?

_____

_____

4. How did the installation procedure for your laptop differ from the directions given in this lab?

_____

_____

_____

5. Suppose you need to install a hard drive in a laptop that doesn't include an access panel for the hard drive. Where should you look for the hard drive inside the laptop?

_____

_____

Supporting I/O Devices

Labs included in this chapter:

- **Lab 6.1:** Use Laptop Display Options
- **Lab 6.2:** Use Device Manager
- **Lab 6.3:** Update Drivers with Device Manager
- **Lab 6.4:** Use Diagnostics Software to Test I/O Devices
- **Lab 6.5:** Install a Sound Card
- **Lab 6.6:** Install Dual Displays in Windows
- **Lab 6.7:** Research High-End Video Cards
- **Lab 6.8:** Replace Laptop Components
- **Lab 6.9:** Compare Costs of Systems
- **Lab 6.10:** Plan a Customized System

LAB 6.1 USE LAPTOP DISPLAY OPTIONS

OBJECTIVES

The goal of this lab is to learn how to support laptop displays. IT technicians are often called on to support a variety of computers and peripherals; therefore, it's important to learn how to use more than one type of laptop. If possible, perform this lab using more than one type of laptop and with more than one operating system. After completing this lab, you will be able to:

▲ Change the display settings

▲ Use an external monitor or video projector

MATERIALS REQUIRED

This lab requires the following:

▲ Laptop computer running Windows

▲ Second laptop computer (optional)

▲ External monitor or projector

LAB PREPARATION

Before the lab begins, the instructor or lab assistant needs to do the following:

▲ Verify that the laptop computers start without errors

▲ Verify that the external video device is available and working

ACTIVITY BACKGROUND

IT support technicians often find themselves needing to respond to emergencies created by the lack of preparation by others. As you respond to these types of technical challenges, experience helps! Good communication skills and professional behavior are also needed to help calm nervous users in desperate situations.

ESTIMATED COMPLETION TIME: 45 MINUTES

 Activity

Sharon has worked for two weeks to put together a PowerPoint presentation to support her important speech to her company's top executives. The presentation is scheduled for 9:00 this Friday morning. On Monday, she requests that a projector be set up in the conference room by Thursday afternoon so that she'll have plenty of time to make sure all is working before people start to arrive around 8:45 on Friday morning. Late Thursday evening, she puts the finishing touches on the presentation and prints 25 handouts, more than enough for the expected 20 attendees. She arrives at work at 8:00 AM the next day and heads for the conference room to hook up her laptop to the video projector. So far, so good. But when she arrives in the conference room with handouts, laptop, and coffee in hand, she finds no projector! She calls technical support (that's you) to fix the problem.

You find a projector and bring it to the conference room. Sharon has powered up her Windows laptop and opened the PowerPoint presentation. The following steps explain how to connect the projector and set up the display so that the PowerPoint presentation is displayed on Sharon's laptop and on the projector. (In a lab environment where you don't have a projector, use an external monitor to practice these steps.) Follow these steps:

1. Physically attach the second display to the laptop. What kind of connector does it use?

   _____

2. On your particular laptop, what key do you use along with the Fn key to toggle the display between video devices?

   _____

> **Notes** A projector must support the screen resolution used by the laptop it is connected to. If the projector shows a blank screen, try a different screen resolution setting on the laptop. Make certain that the entire window displays on the projected screen.

6

3. If Sharon pauses too long during the presentation, the screen saver might activate and cause the screen to go blank, or the system might go into sleep mode. How do you set the power options and display settings on a laptop so that these potential interruptions to the presentation won't happen?

   _____

   _____

4. Sharon decides she needs her Windows desktop to be available on the laptop's screen at the same time the PowerPoint presentation is displayed on the projector, but she has no clue how to do this. List the steps to make this adjustment:

   _____

   _____

   _____

   _____

   _____

5. When the projector displays the presentation, you find that it's difficult to see the images clearly from the back of the room. List four things you can do to try to fix the problem.

   _____

   _____

   _____

   _____

REVIEW QUESTIONS

1. What display options are available on your laptop to help conserve battery power?

   _____

   _____

   _____

2. Laptops vary in the key combination used to toggle video. Without having a user manual available, describe how you would figure out which key combinations to use on a laptop:

   _____

3. List three types of ports a laptop might provide for an external monitor:

   _____

4. When using an external monitor with Windows 10, what is the name of the window in the Settings app that is used to switch between a duplicate desktop and an extended desktop?

   _____

5. When troubleshooting an LCD panel monitor that is malfunctioning or is blank, how can using an external monitor help you?

   _____

   _____

LAB 6.2 USE DEVICE MANAGER

OBJECTIVES

The goal of this lab is to use Device Manager to compile information on your system's devices and drivers, and to uninstall and reinstall a device. After completing this lab, you will be able to:

▲ Use Device Manager to investigate your system specifications

▲ Compile additional information for your Computer Inventory and Maintenance form

▲ Uninstall and reinstall a device

MATERIALS REQUIRED

This lab requires the following:

▲ Windows 10/8/7 operating system

▲ Computer Inventory and Maintenance form you first used in Chapter 1

LAB PREPARATION

Before the lab begins, the instructor or lab assistant needs to do the following:

◢ Verify that Windows starts with no errors

ACTIVITY BACKGROUND

Device Manager is an excellent tool for finding information about hardware specifications. As you continue to work with different kinds of computers, you'll find it extremely useful to maintain a report listing the components installed on each computer. This report is especially important if you're responsible for many computers.

When a device is malfunctioning, one thing you can do is uninstall and reinstall the device. Suppose, for example, that you cannot connect a computer to the network. After verifying network physical connections, confirming Windows network settings, and checking Device Manager for reported errors, you consider that the network adapter drivers might be corrupted. You can eliminate the drivers as the source of the problem by uninstalling and reinstalling the device.

When you first install a device, Windows stores a backup copy of the device drivers in a driver store. Later, if you uninstall and reinstall the device, Windows uses the drivers in the driver store rather than requesting that you provide the drivers again. This can be a convenience, but can also present a problem if the driver store is corrupted. To thoroughly eliminate the drivers as the source of a problem, take time to delete the driver store when you uninstall the drivers. Then you must provide a fresh copy of the device drivers when you reinstall the device.

In this lab, you use Device Manager to manage device drivers and to gather additional information for the Computer Inventory and Maintenance form that you started in Chapter 1.

ESTIMATED COMPLETION TIME: 30 MINUTES

 Activity

In earlier labs, you completed Sections 1 through 3, Section 5, and part of Section 4 on the Computer Inventory and Maintenance form. This lab continues under Section 4: Hardware Installed, in the Device Manager subsection.

1. To open Device Manager, right-click **Start**, and then click **Device Manager**. (In Windows 7, first open **Control Panel**, and then click **Device Manager**.) The Device Manager console opens, as shown in Figure 6-1.

Figure 6-1 Device Manager in Windows 10

2. Expand **Display adapters,** and record the name of the adapter(s) here and on the Computer Inventory and Maintenance form:

_____

3. Right-click the adapter name, and then click **Properties** to open the adapter's Properties dialog box. (If you have more than one display adapter, use the first adapter listed.)

4. Click the **Driver** tab, and record the driver version on the following line and on the Computer Inventory and Maintenance form:

_____

5. On the Driver tab, click **Driver Details** to view the driver file names and the paths to those files. Record that information for up to three files on the following lines and on the Computer Inventory and Maintenance form:

_____

_____

_____

6. Repeat the same procedure to collect similar information on your computer's wired and wireless network adapters and its sound controller. Record that information on the Computer Inventory and Maintenance form.

7. In Section 6 (Routine Maintenance) of the Computer Inventory and Maintenance form, add an activity titled "Additional inventory taken" along with your name and today's date.

When you first install a device and its drivers, Windows installs the drivers and keeps the driver package in a driver store. This driver store is available if you later uninstall and reinstall the device.

When you want to permanently remove a device from your system, you should uninstall it in Device Manager before you physically remove the device. If you don't, and you later install a similar device, you will end up with both devices installed under Device Manager, which can cause the new device not to work. When you uninstall a device, Windows gives you the option to also delete the driver store, which Windows calls the driver software. Follow these steps to learn more:

1. In Device Manager, open the Properties dialog box for a sound controller, and then click the **Driver** tab. What is the exact name of the adapter shown near the top of the Driver tab? What is the driver version?

   _____

   _____

2. Click **Driver Details**. Record the path and file name(s) of up to three driver files. Click **OK** to close the Driver File Details dialog box.

   _____

   _____

3. Click **Uninstall Device**. The Uninstall Device dialog box appears (see Figure 6-2).

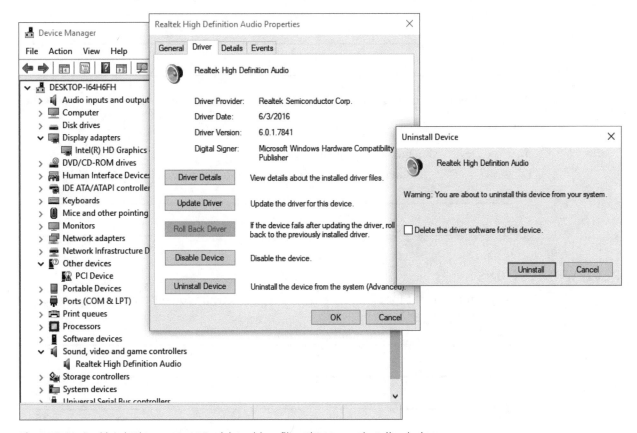

Figure 6-2   Decide whether you want to delete driver files when you uninstall a device

4. Notice that in the dialog box you can choose to delete the driver software, which deletes all driver files that are being used by this device (and that are *not* being used by other devices). This option also deletes the driver package in the driver store. Click **Cancel** to close the dialog box without uninstalling the sound controller.

Now let's uninstall and reinstall the optical drive. Before you uninstall a device, be sure to record information about the device and its drivers in case you need the information later. Follow these steps to uninstall and reinstall the optical drive in Device Manager:

1. In Device Manager, open the Properties box for your optical drive (for example, the DVD/CD-ROM drive), and then click the **Driver** tab. What is the exact name of the optical drive shown near the top of the Driver tab? What is the driver version? Write that information on the following lines and on the Computer Inventory and Maintenance form:

_____

_____

2. Click **Driver Details**. Record the path and file name(s) of up to three driver files on the following lines and on the Computer Inventory and Maintenance form. Click **OK** to close the Driver File Details dialog box.

_____

_____

3. Click **Uninstall Device**. The Uninstall Device box appears. Why do you think the option to delete the driver software for this device is missing?

_____

_____

4. Click **Uninstall** to uninstall the device. Is the device removed from the Device Manager listing?

_____

5. Close Device Manager and restart the computer.
6. Return to Device Manager. Did the optical drive you just uninstalled reappear? Why?

_____

_____

REVIEW QUESTIONS

1. Why is it important for IT technicians to keep documentation on computers for which they are responsible?

_____

_____

_____

2. What can happen if you don't uninstall a device before removing it from your system?

_____

_____

3. Why does Windows keep a driver package in the driver store?

_____

_____

_____

4. What are two reasons why you might want to delete the drivers and driver package when you uninstall a device?

_____

_____

5. List the steps to uninstall a device and delete the device driver files and the driver package in the driver store:

_____

_____

6. When Windows deletes the driver package and driver files, in what situation might it not delete driver files used by the device that is being uninstalled?

_____

LAB 6.3 UPDATE DRIVERS WITH DEVICE MANAGER

OBJECTIVES

The goal of this lab is to use Device Manager to update drivers. After completing this lab, you will be able to:

- Use Device Manager to find information about your display adapter and update the display adapter drivers
- Explore alternative methods to locate or update a driver

MATERIALS REQUIRED

This lab requires the following:

- Windows 10/8/7 operating system
- Updated driver files for the display adapter (optional)
- Internet access

LAB PREPARATION

Before the lab begins, the instructor or lab assistant needs to do the following:

- Verify that Windows starts with no errors
- Verify Internet access
- Locate or download updated driver files for the display adapter or video card if newer driver files are available

ACTIVITY BACKGROUND

With Device Manager, you can update device drivers as well as monitor resource use. If you find a new driver for a device, you can use Device Manager to select the device and update the driver. In this lab, you use Device Manager to update the driver for your display adapter.

ESTIMATED COMPLETION TIME: 30 MINUTES

 Activity

In this lab, you first use Device Manager to update a driver, and then you explore alternative ways to update drivers.

PART 1: USE DEVICE MANAGER TO UPDATE A DRIVER

1. To open Device Manager, open **Control Panel** in Classic view, and then click **Device Manager**.

2. Click the arrow next to **Display adapters** to expand this category, and then click your display adapter to select it. What is the name of your display adapter?

   _____

3. To open the Properties dialog box for your display adapter, right-click the adapter and select **Properties**. What is the manufacturer of your display adapter?

   _____

4. Click the **Driver** tab, and answer the following questions:

   ▲ What company is the provider for your driver?

   _____

   ▲ What is the driver date?

   _____

   ▲ What is the driver version?

   _____

5. Click the **Driver Details** button, and answer the following questions:

   ▲ Which folders contain the drivers used by your display adapter?

   _____

   _____

   _____

   ▲ What is the file version?

   _____

6. Click **OK** to return to the Driver tab in the display adapter's Properties dialog box. Click **Update Driver**. A dialog box appears asking where to find the drivers.

7. If your instructor has provided the updated drivers in a specific location on your computer, click **Browse my computer for driver software**. If your instructor has not

provided the drivers, you can allow Windows to search the web for the drivers. To do so, click **Search automatically for updated driver software**.

8. If you are using the web to update your drivers, follow the on-screen instructions to search for and install drivers. If your driver software is already up to date, Windows displays a message that the best driver software for your device is already installed. If Windows finds a newer version, it installs the update. When the update is finished, you might be asked to restart your computer. Then, proceed to Part 2 of this lab.

9. If your instructor has provided the drivers, type the location of the driver installation file, or click the **Browse** button to select the location your instructor has designated. After you have specified a location, click **Next**. Windows searches the location and reports its findings.

10. If the wizard indicates it has found a file for the display adapter, click **Next** to continue. If the wizard reports that it can't find the file, verify that you have entered the installation file's location correctly.

11. After Windows locates the drivers, it copies the driver files. If a file being copied is older than the file the system is currently using, you're prompted to confirm that you want to use the older file. Usually, newer drivers are better than older drivers. However, you might choose to use an older driver if you experience problems after updating drivers. In this case, you might want to reinstall the old driver that wasn't causing problems.

12. When the files have been copied, click **Finish** to complete the installation.

13. Close all open windows and restart the computer if prompted to do so.

PART 2: EXPLORE ALTERNATIVE WAYS TO UPDATE DRIVERS

1. Device Manager should now show updated driver information for your display adapter. Return to Device Manager. Record the new driver information on the following lines, and compare it with the information you collected earlier.

   ◢ Driver date:

   _____

   ◢ Driver version:

   _____

   ◢ File version:

   _____

Windows will not always have access to drivers through Device Manager, especially drivers for accessories or other aftermarket hardware. In these situations, you can do one of the following:

   ◢ Install a driver from a disk that comes with the new hardware. You can use the Browse option in Device Manager, as described earlier, or you can open File Explorer/Windows Explorer and double-click an installation program on the disk.

   ◢ Download a driver directly from the hardware manufacturer's website. To install a driver from a manufacturer's website, you need information about your system in order to search online for the correct driver. After the driver file is downloaded, you install the driver by double-clicking the downloaded file and following the on-screen directions.

To collect the information you need to find a driver online, follow these steps:

1. In the Run box, type **msinfo32** and press **Enter**.

2. Using the System Information dialog box, collect the following information:

  ◢ OS name: _____

  ◢ System manufacturer: _____

  ◢ System model: _____

  ◢ System type: _____

When downloading and running a program from the web, always download the file to your hard drive, and then use File Explorer/Windows Explorer to execute the downloaded file. To avoid accidentally installing malware, do not run the file from your browser. Also, always reboot your system after installing a new driver, even if not instructed to do so. This last precaution helps identify any problems with the boot process or with Windows that might be caused by a new device or driver.

PART 3: IDENTIFY AN UNKNOWN DEVICE

Sometimes Windows does not recognize a device and therefore is unable to locate drivers for it. For example, Figure 6-3 shows Device Manager in one system reporting that Windows cannot locate compatible drivers.

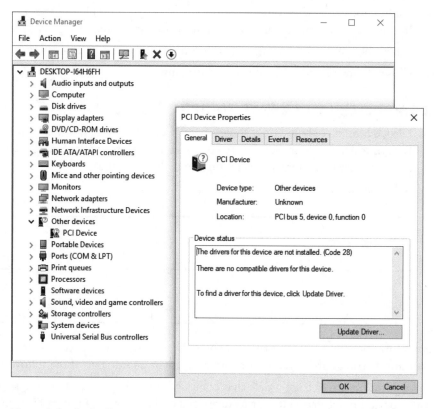

Figure 6-3 Device Manager reports an unknown device that is not installed correctly

Every device is assigned one or more hardware IDs, and you can search the web on these values to identify the manufacturer and device so that you can download and install its drivers. To practice identifying an unknown device, follow these steps:

1. In Device Manager, open the Properties dialog box of a device. Select the **Details** tab.

2. In the drop-down list under Properties, select **Hardware Ids**. A list of values appears.

3. Right-click a value, and select **Copy** from the shortcut menu.

4. Open a browser and paste the value in the search box, and then search on this value. Were you able to identify the manufacturer and device? If so, list the manufacturer and device.

_____

ESTIMATED COMPLETION TIME: 30 MINUTES

CHALLENGE ACTIVITY

Open Device Manager and select other devices to update. Device drivers that you might want to update include your motherboard and audio drivers. If an update does not work properly, you can use the Roll Back Driver button on the Driver tab of the device's Properties dialog box to return the device to a previously installed driver.

REVIEW QUESTIONS

1. In which situation would it be appropriate to update the motherboard drivers to fix a problem with video?

_____

2. What is the next step to solve a problem with video drivers after Windows reports it cannot find a driver that is better than the current driver?

_____

3. Why should you always restart a system after updating drivers or installing a new device?

_____

4. Why might you want to use an older driver for a device rather than the latest driver?

_____

LAB 6.4 USE DIAGNOSTICS SOFTWARE TO TEST I/O DEVICES

OBJECTIVES

The goal of this lab is to experiment with different diagnostic and performance tools to test and evaluate I/O devices. After completing this lab, you will be able to:

▴ Investigate the quality and performance of your monitor or LCD display using MonitorTest

▴ Use KeyboardTest to check that all your keyboard keys are working properly

MATERIALS REQUIRED

This lab requires the following:

▴ Windows 10/8/7 operating system

▴ Internet access

LAB PREPARATION

Before the lab begins, the instructor or lab assistant needs to do the following:

▲ Verify that Windows starts with no errors

▲ Verify that Internet access is available

ACTIVITY BACKGROUND

Intel has compiled a list of links to its own applications and other third-party applications that you can use to test and diagnose computer systems. Although the list of apps is compiled by Intel to test its motherboards, the apps work on most systems. You can find this list at *www.intel.com/content/www/us/en/support/articles/000005607/boards-and-kits/desktop-boards.html*. Many of these utilities will help you test the performance and functionality of I/O devices by emphasizing their features. In this lab, you explore some of these utilities. In Part 1, you test your monitor using MonitorTest. In Part 2, you check your keyboard for stuck or broken keys with KeyboardTest.

ESTIMATED COMPLETION TIME: 30 MINUTES

 Activity

PART 1: USE MONITORTEST

MonitorTest is a utility that allows you to test the performance and quality of your monitor or LCD display. To learn more, follow these steps:

1. Go to **passmark.com/products/monitortest.htm**.

2. Download MonitorTest and install it on your computer.

3. Run the test. Describe what happened during the test:

_____

_____

4. Use the help feature to answer the following questions:

▲ What should you look for when the solid-color test screen appears?

_____

▲ What should you look for when the contrast test screens appear?

_____

▲ How should you set the lighting in a room when the LCD Persistence test screen appears?

_____

PART 2: USE KEYBOARDTEST

Before you replace a suspected defective keyboard, you might want to run KeyboardTest to determine which key(s) is causing the problem. Follow these steps to learn more:

1. Open your browser and go to **passmark.com/products/keytest.htm**.

2. Download KeyboardTest and install it on your computer.

3. Run the test. Describe what happened during the test:

   _____

   _____

4. Using your test results, answer the following questions:

   ◢ What is the type of keyboard you are using?

   _____

   ◢ Which keys on your keyboard could not be tested?

   _____

   _____

   ◢ Were there any key failures on your keyboard? If so, which keys?

   _____

REVIEW QUESTIONS

1. In the list of utilities compiled by Intel, what other utilities (besides the ones used in this lab) test only I/O devices?

   _____

2. In the list of utilities compiled by Intel, what are three utilities that can monitor the temperatures of components?

   _____

3. For what purposes might you use KeyboardTest?

   _____

   _____

4. When using MonitorTest, what is the purpose of running the Fonts Test?

   _____

   _____

LAB 6.5 INSTALL A SOUND CARD

OBJECTIVES

The goal of this lab is to install, configure, and test a sound card. After completing this lab, you will be able to:

- Physically install a sound card
- Install device drivers
- Test the card and adjust the volume

MATERIALS REQUIRED

This lab requires the following:

- Windows 10/8/7 operating system
- An account with administrator privileges
- An empty expansion slot
- A compatible sound card with speakers or headphones
- Sound card device drivers
- Motherboard documentation, if your system uses embedded audio
- A computer toolkit with an ESD strap

LAB PREPARATION

Before the lab begins, the instructor or lab assistant needs to do the following:

- Verify that Windows starts with no errors
- Verify that each student has access to a user account with administrator privileges
- Verify availability of motherboard and sound card documentation

ACTIVITY BACKGROUND

Two of the most popular multimedia devices are the sound card and the embedded audio device. A sound card enables a computer to receive sound input, as when recording an interview, and to output sound, as when playing music. Many systems have audio embedded on the motherboard. As a computer technician, you need to know how to install a sound card, whether you're putting together a computer from scratch, repairing a failed device, or upgrading components on an existing system. In this lab, you disable, install, configure, and test a sound card.

ESTIMATED COMPLETION TIME: 45 MINUTES

 Activity

First, you need to find out whether your system has a sound card, an embedded audio device, or perhaps both or neither. Use the skills you have learned to discover and describe your system's audio configuration, and then work through the steps to complete the lab in the following general order:

- Disable any existing audio devices in Windows.
- Remove or disable the hardware device(s).
- Verify that the audio is disabled.

⊿ Physically install a sound card.

⊿ Install the drivers in Windows.

⊿ Verify the function of audio features.

⊿ Return the system to its original state (this is optional, per your instructor's directions).

Follow these steps to uninstall a sound card or embedded audio device in Windows:

1. After you have signed in as an administrator, open **Device Manager**.

2. Expand **Sound, video and game controllers**, and then select your audio device.

3. Right-click your device, and then click **Uninstall device**.

4. If necessary, check the **Delete the driver software for this device** box, as shown in Figure 6-4, and click **Uninstall**.

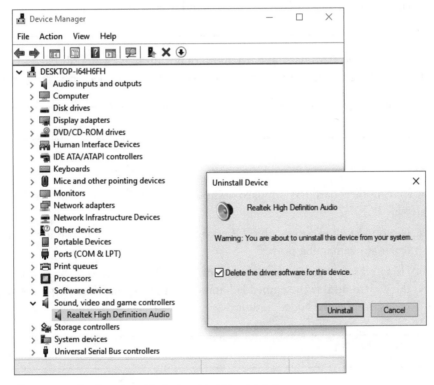

Figure 6-4 Confirm that this device should be deleted

5. Close any open windows, sign out, and shut down your computer.

Next, you either physically remove the sound card from your system or disable an audio device that's embedded in the motherboard.

Follow these steps to remove a sound card:

1. Disconnect all external cables and cords from the case. Press and hold the power button for three seconds to drain any remaining power in your computer.

2. Using all safety precautions, including an ESD strap, remove the case cover, and locate the sound card. Describe any cables connected to the sound card and the ports they are connected to:

_____

_____

_____

3. Disconnect any cables from the sound card. Remove the sound card, and put it in a safe place.

4. Reassemble the computer without the sound card, and boot to Windows to verify that the audio isn't functioning.

Your system's motherboard might have onboard (embedded) audio ports or headers. If so, you should disable these audio devices. For most computers, this is done using the BIOS/UEFI setup utility. Older computers used jumpers on the motherboard to enable or disable onboard audio. Follow these steps to disable the embedded audio device:

1. Examine the motherboard ports. Does the motherboard have onboard audio ports?

   _____

2. Consult the motherboard documentation to learn how to disable any embedded audio devices. How is onboard audio enabled and disabled?

   _____

3. If your motherboard has onboard audio that is disabled using BIOS/UEFI setup, enter BIOS/UEFI setup and disable the embedded audio device. Describe the steps you took:

   _____

   _____

   _____

4. If your motherboard has onboard audio that is disabled using jumpers, follow these steps:

   a. Disconnect all external cables. Press and hold the power button for three seconds to drain any remaining power.

   b. Using all safety precautions, including an ESD strap, remove the case cover, and locate the way to disable the embedded audio (if applicable). Write down the steps you took to disable the embedded audio:

   _____

   _____

   c. Remove any internal audio cables.

   d. Reassemble the system and boot to Windows to verify that the audio isn't functioning.

Now you are ready to physically install a new sound card. Follow these steps:

1. Shut down the computer, and disconnect all external cables from the case. Press and hold the power button for three seconds to drain any remaining power.

2. Using all safety precautions, including an ESD strap, remove the case cover.

3. Locate an empty expansion slot that you can use for the sound card. On some systems, expansion cards are attached to a riser card, which you might have to remove at this time. If necessary, remove the expansion slot faceplate on the case so that the sound card fits into the expansion slot. Some systems use a screw to hold a slot faceplate in place, while others use a clip or passive restraint system to hold the faceplate in place.

4. Insert the sound card into the expansion slot on the motherboard (or insert the sound card into the riser card and the riser card into the motherboard). Line up the sound card on the slot, and press it straight down, making sure the tab on the backplate (the metal plate on the rear of the card where sound ports are located) fits into the slot on the case. Normally, seating the card requires a little effort, but don't force it. If you can't insert the card with just a little effort, something is preventing it from seating. Check for obstructions and try again, removing components that are in the way, if needed. After you have inserted the sound card, verify that the gold "fingers" on the sound card are even across the length of the slot or that no gold is showing.

5. After the card is installed, secure it to the case with a screw or the passive restraint flange. The screw goes through a hole in the card's backplate, securing the backplate to the case.

6. Attach all cables required to carry an audio signal from other multimedia devices, such as an optical drive.

7. Replace any components you removed while installing the sound card, and replace and secure the cover on the case.

8. Reattach all cables from external devices to the correct ports. Attach speakers or headphones. (Some speakers receive power from the computer, and others have to be plugged into an external power source, such as a wall outlet.)

Next, you configure the drivers and other software for your sound card. If you have the documentation for your sound card, follow those instructions. Otherwise, follow these general steps to install software for most sound cards, keeping in mind that your sound card might require a slightly different procedure:

1. Start the computer and sign in as an administrator. If an "Installing device driver software" balloon pops up, wait for the drivers to install.

   ◢ If the installing device driver balloon has popped up, what does the system recognize this device as?

   _____

   ◢ Is this the full name of the sound card you are installing? If not, why?

   _____

   _____

2. If the drivers do not automatically install, install the drivers manually. You might need to insert a CD and execute the setup program on the CD. Alternately, you might need to download drivers from the web and execute the setup program you downloaded.

3. Typically, when you install sound card drivers, the installation asks about installing additional software for supporting the sound card's functionality. In this lab, you are just installing the device drivers. Select that option.

4. Follow the on-screen prompts to complete the installation. At the end of the process, the software might ask to reboot the system.

Follow these steps to test the sound card and adjust the volume in Windows:

1. Open **Control Panel** in Classic view, and then click **Sound**. The Sound dialog box opens, as shown in Figure 6-5.

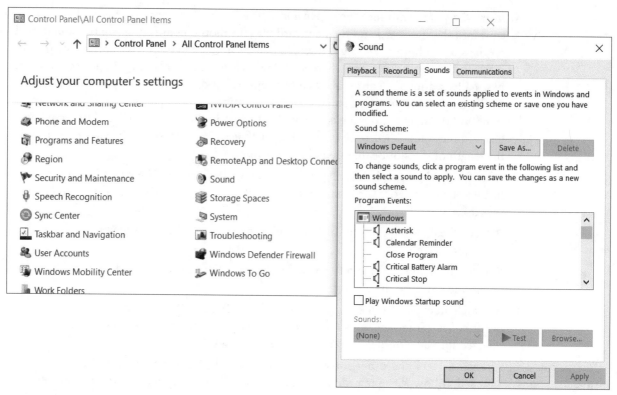

Figure 6-5   Check the settings on the Sounds tab

2. Click the **Sounds** tab. Scroll down and select **System Notification** in the Program Events section. Click the **Test** button; you should hear the system notification sound from your speakers/headphones. Click **OK** to close the dialog box, and then close Control Panel.

3. On the right side of the taskbar, the speaker volume setting—represented by a speaker icon—is displayed. Click the speaker icon. A pop-up tool opens with a mute button and a slider for adjusting speaker volume.

4. Drag the volume slider all the way to the highest volume, and then click somewhere on the desktop to close the pop-up tool.

5. Right-click the speaker icon, and then click **Open Volume Mixer**. The Volume Mixer window gives you more control than the pop-up tool you used in Step 4. On the following lines, list the volume controls that appear in the Volume Mixer window from left to right, and identify any settings (other than volume) that can be changed:

_____

_____

_____

_____

6. Set the Speakers volume slider to half volume, and then close the Volume Mixer window.

7. Next, to do a further test of your sound card, open your browser, find a video on **youtube.com** or a similar website, and play the video. Did you hear the video play?

_____

Follow your instructor's directions to return the system to its previous state if necessary.

REVIEW QUESTIONS

1. Was Windows able to find and install the drivers for your new device automatically? If not, what steps did you follow to install the drivers?

   _____

2. What other devices embedded on the sound card might Windows detect after the sound card installation is finished?

   _____

3. Why might you want to mute the Windows sounds but not mute the speakers?

   _____

   _____

4. Why might someone need to remove and then reinstall the drivers for his or her sound card?

   _____

   _____

5. Why might someone choose to disable an embedded sound device and then add a sound card instead?

   _____

   _____

LAB 6.6 INSTALL DUAL DISPLAYS IN WINDOWS

OBJECTIVES

The goal of this lab is to set up a second monitor on a system. After completing this lab, you will be able to:

- Install a second video card and its drivers
- Attach a second monitor or LCD projector
- Configure the system to use both monitors at the same time

MATERIALS REQUIRED

This lab requires the following:

- Windows 10/8/7 operating system
- An account with administrator privileges
- A computer toolkit with an ESD strap

▲ A second video card with drivers (if needed, borrow one from another computer and work with a partner)

▲ Optional dual-ported onboard video or video card installed

▲ Appropriate cables and adapters

▲ A second monitor or LCD projector

▲ Internet access (optional)

LAB PREPARATION

Before the lab begins, the instructor or lab assistant needs to do the following:

▲ Verify that Windows starts with no errors

▲ Verify that each student has access to a user account with administrator privileges

▲ Verify that all equipment is functioning

▲ Verify that Internet access is available

ACTIVITY BACKGROUND

Having two displays on a system is often quite handy. For instance, two monitors give you more desktop space and make it easier to work with multiple applications simultaneously. You might keep tabs on your email on one screen while surfing the Internet on the other. Alternatively, your second display could be something else, like an LCD display for presentations or a television for watching movies. In this lab, you install and configure a second display on a computer.

ESTIMATED COMPLETION TIME: 45 MINUTES

 Activity

It's important to verify that the original hardware is working correctly before you try to add a second monitor and video card (also called a graphics, display, or video adapter). That way, if a problem comes up after you install new hardware, you can be fairly sure something is wrong with the newly added components rather than the original equipment. Also, you should make sure the manufacturer of the new device offers drivers and specific instructions for use with your version of Windows.

In this lab, you explore two options to attach a second monitor. In Part 1 of this lab, you install a second video card. In Part 2, you install a second monitor using a dual-ported video adapter card or two onboard video ports.

PART 1: INSTALL A SECOND VIDEO CARD

If you are working with a system that has two onboard video ports, you might not need to install a second video card. In this situation, proceed to Part 2 to use and configure dual monitors.

Follow these steps to physically install a second video card:

> **Notes** You can borrow a video card from another computer in the lab and work with a partner, if needed.

1. Check to see if the original video card uses a PCI or PCIe standard, and decide whether it will be the primary or secondary display.

   ◢ What is the interface standard of the original video card?

   _____

   ◢ Will the monitor attached to the original video card be the primary or secondary display?

   _____

2. Determine which standard the new video card follows (PCI or PCIe), and install it as the second video card in the system.

   ◢ What is the interface standard of the new video card?

   _____

> **Notes** If you need additional guidance on installing an I/O card, use a process similar to the one you used to install the sound card in the previous lab.

3. Attach the second display to the port on the back of the new video card.

4. Boot your computer and enter BIOS/UEFI setup. If your setup has display settings for dual monitors, adjust them so that the card you've chosen as your primary video card is initialized first. If you don't see this setting, your BIOS/UEFI doesn't support this option, and your system will make the adjustment automatically. In that case, exit BIOS/UEFI setup, and wait for your system to finish booting.

Follow these steps to install device drivers and adjust Windows display settings:

1. When the system boots, sign in as an administrator. Windows recognizes the new video card and attempts to install the drivers automatically. Complete any steps displayed on the screen to install the new card. When the installation is complete, restart the system and verify that Windows restarts with no errors.

PART 2: USE A SECOND MONITOR

1. If you have not already done so, plug the second monitor into the second video port.

2. Restart the system and sign in to Windows as an administrator. When you restart the system, both screens might initially show a loading Windows display before one of the monitors goes black.

3. When you reach the Windows desktop, you can sometimes cause the second monitor to activate by right-clicking the desktop of the monitor screen that is activated. You should then see both monitors activated.

4. If only one monitor is activated, do one of the following:

   ◢ For Windows 10, open the **Settings** app, click **System**, click **Display**, and click **Identify**.

   ◢ For Windows 8/7, open **Control Panel** in Classic view, click **Display**, click **Adjust resolution**, and click **Identify**.

5. The two monitors are activated, and you can determine how the system is labeling your new monitor. Click the image of the monitor that is your new monitor.

6. Adjust the resolution to your preference by clicking the down arrow on the **Resolution** drop-down box.

7. Click the down arrow on the **Multiple displays** drop-down box, and then click **Extend these displays**.

8. Click **Apply** to apply the settings. The second monitor displays the desktop.

9. There is a shortcut to get to this Screen Resolution window by right-clicking the desktop. Write down the steps to access the Screen Resolution window more quickly:

_____

Follow these steps to test your dual-display configuration:

1. Open the Paint program, and then drag the Paint program window to the second display. Does your desktop extend to the second display as expected?

_____

2. Open File Explorer or Windows Explorer on the original display.

   ◢ Can you see your mouse move as expected from one display to the next?

   _____

   ◢ Does the mouse interact with applications on each display?

   _____

3. Close Paint and then reopen it. On which screen did the program open? What does this tell you about how Windows manages dual monitors?

_____

4. Return to the Screen Resolution window.

5. You can change the position of Screen #1 and Screen #2. Click and hold Screen #1, move the graphic to the other side of Screen #2, and release the mouse button. Apply the change. Move your mouse across the screens. What happens to the monitor display? How would you use this feature?

_____

_____

6. With the Screen Resolution window open, click the down arrow for the **Multiple displays** drop-down box.

7. Select **Show desktop only on X** (X being the number of your added monitor, 1 or 2). Apply your change. What changed as a result of this setting change?

_____

_____

8. Return to the Screen Resolution window, click the down arrow for **Multiple displays**, and then select **Duplicate these displays**. Apply your change. What changed as a result of this selection?

_____

_____

9. How does adjusting the settings of one display affect the settings of the other?

_____

If you are using a dual-ported video card or two onboard video ports, follow these steps:

1. Remove the second monitor.

2. Deactivate the second monitor in Windows to return to a single-monitor configuration.

If you installed a second video card, follow these steps to remove the second card and return to a single-monitor configuration:

1. Open Device Manager, find the second display adapter, and click it to select it. (Make sure you're choosing the second adapter, not the first.)

2. Right-click the display adapter, and then click **Uninstall**. If prompted, confirm that you want to remove the device. When asked if you want to restart the computer, click **No**.

3. Shut down the computer. Don't restart the computer at this time.

4. Remove the second display and video card. If necessary, reverse any BIOS/UEFI changes you made that affect the display initialization sequence, and then reboot the system to verify that it no longer recognizes the video card.

REVIEW QUESTIONS

1. What might be some advantages to using two video cards instead of one video card with two ports?

_____

_____

_____

2. Why do you think it is necessary to set the sequence in which the system initializes video cards so that the primary display is initialized first?

_____

_____

3. In a dual-monitor setup, why would it be better to open frequently used applications on one monitor rather than the other?

_____

_____

4. Why would the positioning of the primary (#1) and secondary (#2) monitors be important to a user?

_____

_____

5. Why might you want to install multiple monitors on a system?

_____

_____

LAB 6.7 RESEARCH HIGH-END VIDEO CARDS

OBJECTIVES

The goal of this lab is to gather information about new video cards. After completing this lab, you will be able to:

- ◢ Research GPUs and video cards on the manufacturer's website
- ◢ Match video cards to specifications and compare video cards based on third-party reviews

MATERIALS REQUIRED

This lab requires the following:

- ◢ Windows 10/8/7 operating system
- ◢ Internet access
- ◢ Adobe Acrobat Reader

LAB PREPARATION

Before the lab begins, the instructor or lab assistant needs to do the following:

- ◢ Verify that Windows starts with no errors
- ◢ Verify that Internet access is available
- ◢ Verify that Adobe Acrobat Reader works with no errors

ACTIVITY BACKGROUND

Your choice of video card can have a profound effect on your computer's performance, especially with applications that use 3-D effects, such as computer-aided design (CAD) software and games. To meet the ever-increasing requirements of new programs and operating systems, many people choose to upgrade their video card. In this lab, you research several new video cards on the web.

The two leading manufacturers of graphics processor units (GPUs) are AMD (*amd.com*) and Nvidia (*nvidia.com*). GPUs from both manufacturers are used by most video card manufacturers. Some leading manufacturers of video cards are Nvidia, AMD, Asus (*asus.com*), MSI (*us.msi.com*), Gigabyte (*gigabyte.com*), and EVGA (*evga.com*).

As you customize computers, you'll learn about the different lines of video cards and GPUs. For example, the Nvidia Tesla line of GPUs and video cards is designed for datacenter servers used for data streaming or powerful workstations for CAD software, while the Nvidia GeForce GPUs and cards are more suitable for gaming. Within each line, some cards are better than others. For example, the EVGA GeForce RTX 2060 is better than the EVGA GeForce RTX 1070. To find the best card for your situation, you need to compare features and read reviews.

ESTIMATED COMPLETION TIME: 30 MINUTES

 Activity

In this scenario, you are building a high-end gaming system. Your system has an available PCIe ×16, version 3 slot and a surplus of 500 watts of power that can be used for a video card. You are working within a limited budget. Follow these steps to research the Nvidia and AMD GPUs used in video cards:

1. Go to **amd.com** and search for graphics cards for desktop systems. At the time of this writing, you can see a list of products when you select **SHOP** on the home page and then click **GRAPHICS CARDS**. You can also find a list of graphics specifications at this link: *products.amd.com/en-us/search/desktop-graphics*. Alternately, you can look for other ways to compare AMD's GPU products on its website.

2. Select five graphics cards that are compatible with your new gaming system (keeping in mind the PCIe version and wattage needs) and fill in Table 6-1.

Card Manufacturer and AMD GPU Line	Output	Memory	Suggested Retail Price

Table 6-1 Compare graphics cards that use AMD GPUs

3. Now go to **nvidia.com** and use Table 6-2 to fill in similar information about five graphics cards that use Nvidia GPUs. To find cards, try clicking **SHOP** on the Nvidia home page. At the time of this writing, the following link takes you to the Compare and Buy GPUs page: *geforce.com/hardware/compare-buy-gpus*. If this link does not work or does not appear, look for another way to compare Nvidia GeForce GPU products on its website.

Card Manufacturer and Nvidia GPU Line	Output	Memory	Suggested Retail Price

Table 6-2 Compare graphics cards that use Nvidia GeForce GPUs

4. You're now ready to compare AMD and Nvidia GPUs. Search the web for comparisons and reviews of the lines of GPUs you selected, and answer the following questions:

▲ Which line of GPUs offers the best base clock and/or boost clock performances?

_____

▲ Which line of GPUs offers the highest bandwidth?

_____

▲ Which line of GPUs would you choose for a gaming machine? What criteria influenced your choice?

_____

_____

_____

5. Now that you know about GPUs, you're ready to research graphics cards. Search a computer components retail site such as *newegg.com* or *tigerdirect.com* to find the best graphics card based on each of the following criteria. Be sure to include the brand, model, and price of the card:

▲ A 256-bit, GDDR5 PCI Express 3.0 graphics card for under $600:

_____

▲ A card that supports 192-bit or more bandwidth and up to 6 GB of memory with at least one HDMI port for less than $400:

_____

▲ A PCI Express 3.0 card that incorporates DVI outputs for less than $250:

_____

▲ A pair of SLI (Nvidia) or CrossFire (AMD) cards for less than $800 total:

_____

▲ A 2 GB or better high-end gaming card with an Nvidia GPU for less than $300:

_____

6. Search the web and read at least one review about each video card you selected. Based on the reviews, which video card(s) you selected in Step 5 would you not purchase? Why?

_____

_____

_____

7. In summary, answer the following questions about your research:

▲ What information were you able to find on the retail website that was not available on the manufacturers' websites?

_____

_____

_____

▲ What information was available on the manufacturers' websites that was not available on the retail website?

_____

_____

_____

◢ What type of information did you find when searching for product reviews that was not available from manufacturers' websites or retail websites?

_____

_____

_____

REVIEW QUESTIONS

1. Why might you choose to upgrade your video card?

_____

_____

_____

2. Which manufacturer had the largest and most useful selection of video cards?

_____

3. Which website did you find to be the most informative? Why?

_____

4. When upgrading a video card, why might you also have to upgrade your power supply?

_____

_____

5. Suppose a video card requires a 6-pin PCIe power connector, but your power supply does not have this connector. What can you do to solve this problem without replacing the power supply?

_____

_____

LAB 6.8 REPLACE LAPTOP COMPONENTS

OBJECTIVES

The goal of this lab is to practice replacing components inside a laptop computer. After completing this lab, you will be able to:

◢ Evaluate the value of a laptop versus the cost of repair

◢ Replace laptop internal components

MATERIALS REQUIRED

This lab requires the following:

◢ A laptop computer that can be disassembled

◢ A toolkit designed for work on laptop computers, including small screwdrivers and a spudger

◢ The laptop's service manual that contains instructions for disassembly

◢ Internet access

LAB PREPARATION

Before the lab begins, the instructor or lab assistant needs to do the following:

- Provide each student or workgroup with a laptop computer that can be disassembled and its hardware service manual

- Assign each student or workgroup the component they will remove and replace in the laptop. Each workgroup can practice replacing different components or the same components.

- Verify that Internet access is available

ACTIVITY BACKGROUND

The A+ exams require that you know about replacing internal laptop components that are field replaceable units (FRUs). The internal FRUs for a laptop computer differ for each laptop and might include the hard drive, RAM, optical drive, LCD panel assembly, Mini PCIe card, CPU, keyboard, speaker, smart card readers, DC jack, embedded battery, and system board (motherboard).

Laptop computers vary drastically in the way they are assembled and disassembled. As an IT support technician, you are not required to know how to disassemble every brand and model of laptop. However, if you have a hardware service manual that includes the steps to disassemble a laptop and replace a component, you should be able to do the job. This lab gives you that information and experience. The instructions in this lab refer to a Lenovo IdeaPad 310. However, you will most likely use a different laptop, which will have its own service manual.

- What is the brand and model of laptop you are using in this lab?

_____

- What component will you remove and replace?

_____

ESTIMATED COMPLETION TIME: 3 HOURS

 Activity

PART 1: IS THE LAPTOP WORTH THE COST OF REPAIR?

Joseph brings you his laptop computer complaining that it is "dead," and asks you to repair it. Before you service any laptop, always ask these questions:

- Does it hold important data that is not backed up?

- Is the laptop under warranty?

- What recently happened to the computer before the problem appeared (such as installing new programs, loaning the computer to a friend, or losing power during a thunderstorm)?

- What do I need to do to reproduce the problem?

In asking these four questions, you find out that the laptop does hold important data and that it is not under warranty. You also find out that Joseph allowed a coworker to carry his laptop from one building to another along with a bunch of other computers and components. Joseph suspects the coworker was not careful when handling the laptop. The first time Joseph turned on the laptop after this move, he found it "dead."

You're now ready to investigate the problem. You plug in the laptop, turn it on, and make these observations: The LCD panel appears blank, but the laptop is running. The keyboard lights are lit, and you hear the sound of the fan when you first turn on the computer. You look very carefully at the LCD panel and notice a faint display that you cannot read. You next try to use the keys to increase the LCD panel brightness. Even when you have increased the brightness as much as possible, you still can't read what's on the screen. Next, you plug in an external monitor and use the appropriate keys to direct video output to this device. You can now read the display on the external monitor. What is the next (very important) thing you should do?

_____

_____

_____

Before you discuss repair options with Joseph, you need to know the cost of the repairs and the value of his laptop. The laptop does not use a video card, so the FRU that applies to video in this case is the LCD panel assembly. Will replacing the LCD panel cost more than the laptop is worth?

Research and answer these questions about the laptop you are using in this lab:

1. What is the brand and model of the laptop?

_____

2. Search the service manual for information about the LCD panel assembly. What are the part numbers you must purchase to replace the entire assembly?

_____

_____

3. Search the manufacturer's website or other online sources to find information about the cost of replacing the LCD panel assembly on your laptop.

   ◢ What is the total price of all parts? Save or print webpages supporting your answer.

_____

   ◢ What is the value of the laptop? Determining the value of a laptop can be a little difficult and is usually a best guess. Try searching auction sites such as *eBay.com* for a match or near match.

_____

   ◢ What sources of information did you use to determine the value of the laptop?

_____

_____

PART 2: PRACTICE REPLACING A COMPONENT

You're now ready to practice replacing a component in your laptop. Follow these steps:

1. Power down the laptop, unplug it, and remove the battery. If the battery is embedded, follow the service manual instructions to disable the battery (often called Ship Mode).

2. Carefully read through the service manual to determine which components must be removed and in what order they are removed. For example, to remove the LCD panel assembly from the Lenovo IdeaPad 310, you must first remove the hard drive, memory, Mini PCIe card compartment, optical drive, keyboard bezel, system board, and fan and heat sink assembly. Only then can you remove the LCD panel assembly.

   ◢ What is the component you are replacing?

_____

◢ List the components that you must remove to get to the component you want to replace. List components in the order they are removed.

_____

_____

_____

_____

_____

3. Most likely, you can remove the hard drive, memory, Mini PCIe cards, and perhaps even the optical drive or an embedded battery without cracking the case. Of the components listed, which ones should be removed before you crack the case?

_____

_____

_____

4. Using all the safety guidelines you have learned about in this course, follow instructions in your service manual to remove all components listed in Step 3. For example, to remove the optical drive from the IdeaPad 310 laptop, you remove one screw and then slide the drive out of the case (see Figure 6-6).

Figure 6-6   Slide the optical drive out of the case after removing the screw securing the optical drive to the laptop

5. You're now ready to remove screws that hold the case together. Locate and remove all screws as directed in your service manual. For example, Figure 6-7 shows the 13 screws that must be removed on the bottom of the IdeaPad 310. How many screws must you remove on your laptop before you can crack the case?

_____

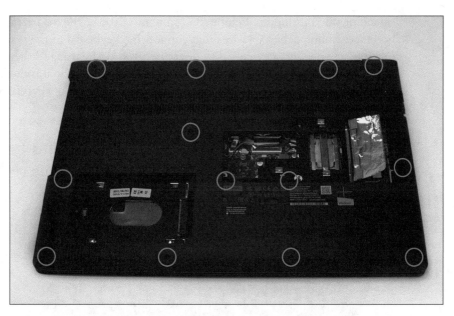

Figure 6-7 Remove 13 screws on the bottom of the laptop before opening the case

> **Notes** Be sure to keep the removed screws well organized and labeled so you will be able to put the right screws in the right holes when you reassemble the laptop.

6. Now crack the case, which separates the top and bottom of the case so you can see internal components. As you work, be careful to use a spudger to pry open the case so that you don't scar or scratch it. See Figure 6-8. (You don't want to replace a component but still have a dissatisfied customer because of a damaged case.)

Figure 6-8 Using a spudger helps prevent harming the casing when prying it open

7. Depending on your laptop, before you can remove the keyboard bezel, you might need to disconnect ribbon cables or wires that connect the keyboard to the system board. Follow directions in your service manual to disconnect the keyboard, and then lift it out and put it aside. For example, for the IdeaPad 310, you turn the laptop upside down to disconnect the ribbon cable from the keyboard. Then you can lift the keyboard bezel out of the case (see Figure 6-9).

Figure 6-9   Lift the keyboard bezel up and out of the case

> **Notes** Be careful as you work. Many laptop parts are plastic and are fragile. If you force them, they might break. Also, don't stack components as you remove them.

8. Follow directions in your service manual to remove the next component in your list. For some laptops, you can reach the LCD panel assembly without removing the system board. For others, you must first remove the system board. For the IdeaPad 310, the system board must be removed first. To do that, you remove five screws holding the system board to the case and then disconnect several ribbon cables. Next, shift the system board away from the jacks on the side of the case to detach the board from the jacks, and then carefully lift the board up and out of the case (see Figure 6-10).

Figure 6-10 Detach the system board from jacks on the left side of the case and then lift the system board up and out of the case

9. Follow directions in your service manual to continue removing components until you have removed the one you plan to replace.

10. You are now ready to reassemble the laptop. As you work, replace components in the reverse order you disassembled the laptop. Be sure to use every screw in its position and tighten it securely.

11. Replace the battery. Pick up the laptop and shake it. If you hear a loose screw, disassemble the laptop and fix the problem.

12. Plug in the AC adapter, and then power up the laptop.

REVIEW QUESTIONS

1. A customer asks how much you would charge to upgrade the processor in his laptop. He gives you the brand and model of the laptop. List three questions you should research before you discuss the upgrade with the customer.

   _____

   _____

   _____

2. Why would you pry open a case with a spudger rather than a flat-head screwdriver?

   _____

3. Why is it important to remove the battery or deactivate an embedded battery before working on a laptop?

   _____

4. To protect the user's investments in time and money, what two very important questions should a technician always ask the user before disassembling a laptop?

_____

_____

5. Generally, when is it a good idea to advise a customer that the laptop should not be repaired?

_____

LAB 6.9 COMPARE COSTS OF SYSTEMS

OBJECTIVES

The goal of this lab is to compare a preassembled system with the components that could be assembled to build a comparable system. After completing this lab, you will be able to:

▲ Identify the key components of a preassembled system

▲ Locate prices for components needed to assemble a comparable system

▲ Compare the costs of a preassembled system and a self-assembled system

MATERIALS REQUIRED

This lab requires the following:

▲ Internet access

LAB PREPARATION

Before the lab begins, the instructor or lab assistant needs to do the following:

▲ Verify that Internet access is available

ACTIVITY BACKGROUND

In this lab, you compare the cost of a brand-name system with the cost of a system having similar specifications but assembled from separate components. Brand-name manufacturers typically build their systems from parts that only they market; these parts are called proprietary parts. Therefore, it's unlikely that you'll be able to find exact matches for brand-name components. However, you can find comparable components. For example, if a Dell computer has a 1 TB, 7200 RPM hard drive installed, find another 1 TB, 7200 RPM hard drive for your list of parts. The idea is to find a close match for each major component so that you can compare the total cost of a brand-name system and that of a similar system built from parts. Use the Internet and available computer-related publications as your sources for information.

ESTIMATED COMPLETION TIME: 45 MINUTES

 Activity

First you research a preassembled system and record information about its components.

1. Find an advertisement for a complete preassembled system similar to the one in Figure 6-11. Some manufacturers you might want to check out are Lenovo (*lenovo.com*), Acer (*acer.com*), Dell (*dell.com*), HP (*hp.com*), Asus (*asus.com*), and Gateway (*gateway.com*).

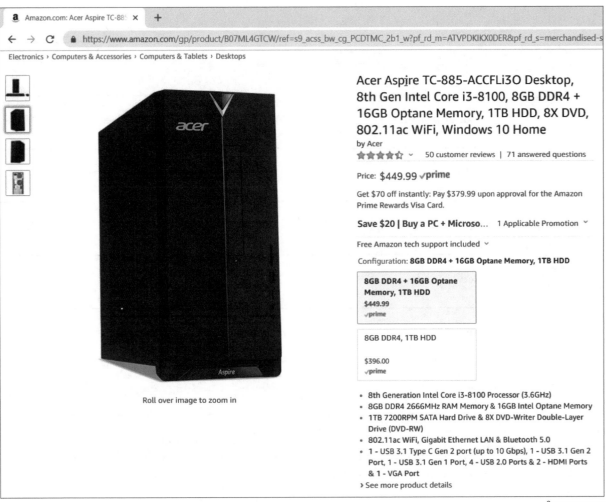

Figure 6-11 The Amazon website explains the product features of a complete preassembled system

2. Study the advertisement you found and list the following specifications:

   ◢ Processor brand, model, and speed:

   _____

   ◢ Processor cores and cache:

   _____

   ◢ RAM type, speed, and amount:

   _____

   ◢ OS type and edition:

   _____

   ◢ HDD (magnetic/SSD/hybrid, SAS or SATA details), capacity, speed, and buffer size
   (if present):

   _____

◢ Monitor:

_____

◢ Video card:

_____

◢ Sound/speakers:

_____

◢ Other drives:

_____

◢ Removable device ports:

_____

◢ Network adapter:

_____

◢ Bundled software:

_____

◢ Total price:

_____

3. Research websites that sell computer parts, such as *tigerdirect.com*, *newegg.com*, or *microcenter.com*, and find advertisements similar to those shown in Figure 6-12. Notice that items are grouped by component type.

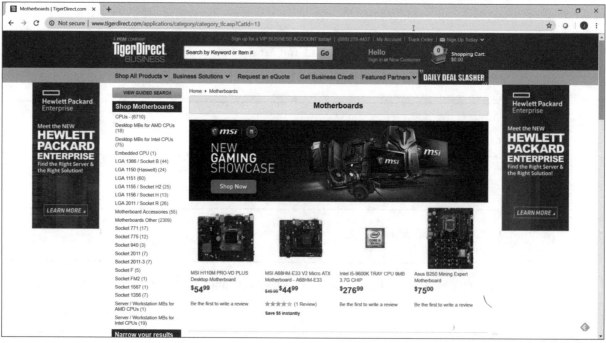

Figure 6-12   Components for sale

4. Using Table 6-3, list and describe the comparable components, their prices, and the source of your information. You might want to check several sources to find the best price.

> **Notes** Remember, most mail-order or online purchases have shipping costs. If you can determine an exact shipping price for each component, include this information as part of the component's price. If you can't find the exact shipping price, include a 10 percent fee as part of the price for each shipped component. Also include sales tax in the price.

Component	Description	Source	Price
Processor/cores/GHz			
Motherboard			
RAM			
Case and power supply			
HDD type and capacity			
Optical drive			
Other drives			
Removable device ports			
Monitor			
Video adapter			
Sound/speakers			
Bonus items			
Operating system			
Bundled software			
TOTAL SYSTEM PRICE			

Table 6-3   Components for assembling a system

5. When you select computer parts for a system, you need to make sure the parts are compatible. Answer the following questions:

   ◢ The motherboard must support the selected processor. Is the processor you selected listed in the motherboard advertisement as a compatible processor?

   ◢ What is the maximum amount of RAM the board can support? Is the type and amount of RAM compatible with the motherboard?

◢ What form factors do the case and motherboard use? Is the case compatible with the motherboard?

_____

◢ What is the wattage rating of the power supply? Does this rating meet the requirements for the system?

_____

◢ What interface does the hard drive use? Does the motherboard have this type of interface?

_____

◢ What interface does the optical drive use? Does the motherboard have this type of interface?

_____

◢ What type of slot does the video adapter use? Does the motherboard have this type of slot?

_____

REVIEW QUESTIONS

1. Which approach to acquiring a system seems to be less expensive?

_____

2. Which single component determines the compatibility of other components in a system?

_____

3. What is the single most expensive component of a system built from separate components?

_____

4. What was the estimated cost of shipping (if any) for the component-built system?

_____

5. What are some potential pitfalls of building your own computer? What are some rewards?

_____

_____

_____

_____

_____

_____

LAB 6.10 PLAN A CUSTOMIZED SYSTEM

OBJECTIVES

The goal of this lab is to plan and price a computer system to fit custom needs for function and performance. After completing this lab, you will be able to:

▲ Describe what you want your system to be able to do

▲ Pick components that best meet the design goals

MATERIALS REQUIRED

This lab requires the following:

▲ Internet access

▲ A workgroup of four students

LAB PREPARATION

Before the lab begins, the instructor or lab assistant needs to do the following:

▲ Verify Internet access

ACTIVITY BACKGROUND

As an IT technician, you might be in a position to build a system from separate components for a customer to meet particular specifications. Systems are often built to meet specific needs with components that will deliver certain performance values. Generally, systems fall within the following groups:

▲ *Gaming computer.* Powerful processor, large amount of RAM, high-end video adapter, high-end sound, and high-end cooling

▲ *Multimedia editing workstation.* Powerful processor, high-end video, maximum RAM, specialized sound, large and fast hard drive, and dual monitors

▲ *Thick or thin client.* Meets basic processor and RAM requirements for running Windows, meets needs of basic applications, affordable video adapter and sound card, and low-demand business uses

▲ *Home or small-office computer.* Medium to high-end processor, media streaming and file sharing capabilities, Gigabit NIC, and ability to use RAID arrays

In this lab, you research and propose a customized system for a machine that has been assigned to your team. Your team members will act as customers, so prepare to justify your selection.

ESTIMATED COMPLETION TIME: 45 MINUTES

 Activity

Choose and research a custom computer:

1. Each team member selects a different system group from the computer groups listed earlier. Which system type did you select?

2. As a team, determine three questions that a customer might ask a technician about the recommendations for a customized system.

Question 1:

_____

_____

Question 2:

_____

_____

Question 3:

_____

_____

Do research on the web for all components needed to build your custom system. Use Table 6-4 to list the components you would like to include in your custom system, the features and cost of each component, and your justification for purchasing it. Use a separate piece of paper if you need more writing space.

1. When selecting parts, begin by selecting the motherboard and processor at the same time.

    ▲ Which motherboard and processor brands and models did you select?

    _____

    _____

    ▲ Which processor socket do they use?

    _____

    ▲ Does the board have onboard video? If so, what type of video port(s) does the board have?

    _____

2. If your system uses a video card, select the card next. Which video card did you select?

    _____

3. Next, select the computer case. Make sure the case uses the form factor of the motherboard and has the room you need for all internal components. Consider where and how the case will be used. Which case did you select?

    _____

4. You can now select the other components for your system. Be sure you include RAM, at least one hard drive, an optical drive, an OS, and a monitor. Fill in all details in Table 6-4.

Component Category	Features	Cost	Justification
Processor GHz/cores			
RAM			
Motherboard			
Hard drives			
Optical drives			
Removable device ports			
Video adapter			
Monitor			
Network adapter			
Sound adapters			
Case and power supply			
Additional components			
Operating system			
TOTAL COST			

Table 6-4 Customized system components

After you have completed Table 6-4, join your team members to discuss your findings.

1. With your team together, have each member present the customized system he or she selected, with other team members playing the role of the customer by asking questions about the system.

   ◢ Which questions were you unable to answer?

   _____

   _____

   ◢ Which questions could you confidently answer?

   _____

   _____

2. Have team members play the role of your technical associates. Have them ask questions about your system to make sure the parts are compatible.

   ◢ List three questions team members asked about your system to determine if parts were compatible:

   _____

   _____

   _____

◢ Which parts, if any, did team members discover were not compatible?

_____

_____

3. If you discovered that some parts were not compatible, go back and select new parts for your system.

4. Have team members decide if your proposal is a good one and make recommendations for improvements. What assessment and recommendations for improvements did the team make?

_____

_____

REVIEW QUESTIONS

1. When investigating the components for your particular customized system, what was your greatest challenge?

_____

2. If you were given a budget for the system, what components would receive the largest share of the budget?

_____

3. What changes would you make if you had to reduce the costs because of budget restrictions while still meeting the customized needs of your system?

_____

4. What would be the expected life cycle of your customized system before it needs to be upgraded? At the end of the life cycle, what components would need to be upgraded?

_____

Setting Up a Local Network

Labs included in this chapter:

- **Lab 7.1:** Network Two Computers
- **Lab 7.2:** Set Up a Wireless Router
- **Lab 7.3:** Secure a Wireless LAN
- **Lab 7.4:** Practice Troubleshooting using TCP/IP Utilities
- **Lab 7.5:** Analyze a System with Event Viewer
- **Lab 7.6:** Set Up a VPN
- **Lab 7.7:** Create a Network in Packet Tracer

LAB 7.1 NETWORK TWO COMPUTERS

OBJECTIVES

The goal of this lab is to install and configure a network interface card (NIC) and configure the TCP/IP settings to connect two computers. After completing this lab, you will be able to:

▲ Uninstall and install a NIC

▲ Configure TCP/IPv4 settings

▲ Share files and folders between two computers

▲ Configure IP addressing

MATERIALS REQUIRED

This lab requires the following:

▲ Windows 10/8/7 operating system

▲ An account with administrator privileges

▲ A wireless NIC and the associated drivers

▲ Wi-Fi network access

▲ A workgroup partner

LAB PREPARATION

Before the lab begins, the instructor or lab assistant needs to do the following:

▲ Verify that Windows starts with no errors

▲ Verify that each student has access to a user account with administrator privileges

▲ Verify that drivers for the NIC and wireless equipment to connect two computers are available

ACTIVITY BACKGROUND

Computers on a network have the ability to communicate with one another and share resources, such as files and devices. A computer connects to a network through a network interface card (NIC). In this lab, you install a NIC, configure necessary network settings, and verify that the NIC is functioning correctly. Working with a partner, you create a simple network of two computers and work through the basics of networking.

ESTIMATED COMPLETION TIME: 45 MINUTES

 Activity

A NIC allows its computer to communicate on the network. Follow these steps to learn to uninstall and reinstall a wireless NIC:

1. Power on your computer, and then sign in to Windows.

2. Disconnect any network cable, and then disable Wi-Fi.

3. Open **Device Manager**. Expand the **Network adapters** listing. What are the names of the network adapters installed on your system?

_____

_____

4. Right-click the **Wi-Fi network adapter,** and then click **Uninstall device** in the shortcut menu. Click **OK** at the confirmation prompt.

5. Restart the computer and install the NIC. The installation process might take a few minutes because there might be several layers to the drivers.

6. After the installation is complete, return to **Device Manager**. Verify that your NIC has been reinstalled and that Device Manager reports no problems with the device.

Now that the network adapter is working, you need to configure the computer to gain access to shared resources on the network. It is important for you to know where to locate and how to modify settings that control network communication. These settings make your computer unique on the network and easily identified by other computers. Let's explore how to configure network settings.

To verify and configure the current TCP/IP settings, follow these steps:

1. Open **Control Panel** in Classic view and click **Network and Sharing Center** (see the left side of Figure 7-1). In the left panel, click **Change adapter settings**. Right-click the **Wi-Fi** network connection and click **Properties** in the shortcut menu. The Wi-Fi Properties dialog box opens.

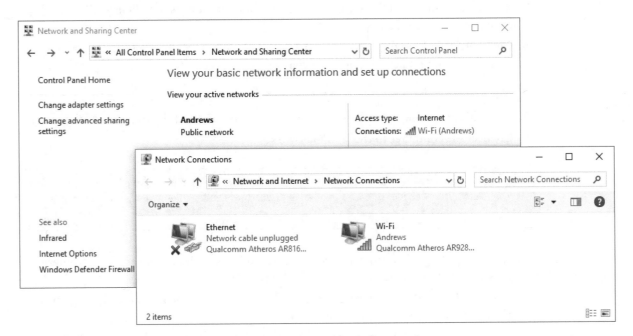

Figure 7-1 The Network and Sharing Center reports the status of network connections

2. In the list of connection items, click **Internet Protocol Version 4 (TCP/IPv4),** and then click **Properties**. The Properties dialog box that opens can be used to configure the IP settings for the connection.

3. For this part of the lab, you use static IP addressing. With your lab partner, determine who will use the Partner 1 information in the following grid and who will use the Partner 2 information:

	Partner 1	Partner 2
IP address	192.168.1.1	192.168.1.2
Computer name	Lab1	Lab2
Workgroup name	WORKGROUP	WORKGROUP

4. Select the **Use the following IP address** option, and then enter your chosen IP address.

5. Use the **Tab** key to move to the Subnet mask box. If Windows doesn't automatically populate the subnet mask, enter a subnet mask of 255.255.255.0.

6. Click **OK**, and then close all windows.

Now that your computer has a unique IP address on the network, it is time to assign a name to your computer. A computer name gives the computer an identity on the network. Follow these steps:

1. Open **Control Panel** in Classic view and click **System**. The System window opens. In the Computer name, domain, and workgroup settings area, click **Change settings**. The System Properties dialog box opens.

2. Click **Change**. The Computer Name/Domain Changes dialog box opens.

3. Enter the computer name for your machine from the chart. The Windows default name for a workgroup is WORKGROUP. If the workgroup name is not WORKGROUP, change it to WORKGROUP.

4. Click **OK**. Windows displays a message with instructions about applying the change. What must you do next to apply the change?

_____

5. Click **OK** and close all windows. Restart your computer, and then sign in to Windows.

6. Connect the computer to the Wi-Fi network.

> **Notes** Earlier versions of Windows relied on workgroups and network security profiles to secure a Windows network connection. These methods are not recommended for current versions of Windows and are not used in this lab.

Next, you configure security settings that control how the computer's resources can be accessed from the network. Follow these steps to allow access to the computer's resources:

1. Open the **Network and Sharing Center** and then click **Change advanced sharing settings**. The Advanced sharing settings window opens.

2. If necessary, expand the profile that is designated the **current profile**. (It doesn't matter if that profile is the Guest, Public, Private, or Home profile.)

3. Under Network discovery, select **Turn on network discovery**.

4. Under File and printer sharing, select **Turn on file and printer sharing**.

5. Expand the **All Networks** profile. Under Public folder sharing, select **Turn on sharing so anyone with network access can read and write files in the Public folders**.

6. Under Password protected sharing, select **Turn off password protected sharing**.

7. Click **Save changes**.

8. Open File Explorer or Windows Explorer. In the left pane, scroll down and then click **Network**.

   ◢ What machines show up in the Computer section?

   _____

9. Close all windows.

Now let's see what happens when there is a conflict in IP addresses on your small network. Follow these steps:

1. Partner 1: Return to the Internet Protocol Version 4 (TCP/IPv4) Properties dialog box and change the IP address of your machine to **192.168.1.2**.

2. Partner 1: Click **OK** and close all windows. (If you are using a Windows 7 computer, you can dismiss the error message that appears.)

3. Partner 1: Open a command prompt window, type **ipconfig**, and then press **Enter**. What is the IPv4 address for your computer? What does this information tell you?

   _____

   _____

4. Partners 1 and 2: Close all windows, reboot your computers, and sign in. If necessary, connect to the network. Wait for the Network icon in the taskbar to finish processing network discovery.

5. Partners 1 and 2: Open File Explorer or Windows Explorer, and drill down into the **Network** group.

   ◢ What computers have been discovered? (You might need to refresh this screen a couple of times. To refresh a selected window, press **F5**.)

   _____

   ◢ Explain the importance of using correct IP addressing when networking computers.

   _____

   _____

6. Partner 1: Return your IP address to 192.168.1.1, reboot your computer, and sign in. If necessary, connect to the network.

With the computers communicating with each other on the network, you and your partner can now view shared resources on each other's computer through the network. Follow these steps:

1. Open File Explorer or Windows Explorer, and drill down into the **Network** group. What computers are identified in the right pane?

   _____

2. Double-click your partner's computer icon to open that computer. What folder is presented to you?

   _____

3. Open the folder from Step 2. What folders are now presented to you?

   _____

4. Open the **Public** folder, and then open **Public Documents**.

   ◢ What files or folders do you find inside?

   _____

◢ What files or folders do you find in the Public Pictures folder?

_____

5. Close all windows.

6. To open WordPad, type **WordPad** in the search box, and then press **Enter**. Using WordPad, create a document with a single line of text, and save this document in your **Documents** library with a name of **Test Document**. What file extension did WordPad automatically assign the file?

_____

7. Display your partner's computer in the Network listing of the Computer window.

8. Explore your partner's computer.

◢ Are you able to see your partner's WordPad document?

_____

◢ What theory do you have as to why you can or cannot see the document?

_____

Follow these steps to find out what changes are made to shared resources when you turn off Public folder sharing:

1. Return to the **Network and Sharing Center,** and access **Advanced sharing settings.**

2. Under Public folder sharing, select **Turn off Public folder sharing,** and save your changes.

3. Using File Explorer or Windows Explorer, look in the **Network** group for your partner's computer. Explore the user profile folders for your partner's user account. What has changed?

Now let's configure each computer to use dynamic IP addressing. If there is no DHCP server available to provide an IP address to your computer and Windows is set for dynamic IP addressing, Windows will use Automatic Private IP Addressing (APIPA). Follow these steps to investigate this situation:

1. Open an elevated command prompt window. List the exact steps you took to do so:

_____

_____

_____

2. At the command prompt, enter **ipconfig /all** and press **Enter**. What are the following values for your network connection?

◢ IPv4 address: _____

◢ Subnet mask: _____

◢ Default gateway: _____

◢ DNS server: _____

3. Close the command prompt window.

4. Open the Internet Protocol Version 4 (TCP/IPv4) Properties dialog box.

5. Select **Obtain an IP address automatically** and **Obtain DNS server address automatically**. Click **OK** and close all windows.

6. Reboot the computer and launch a command prompt window. Enter the **ipconfig /all** command, and record the results here:

   ◢ IPv4 address: _____

   ◢ Subnet mask: _____

   ◢ Default gateway: _____

   ◢ DNS server: _____

7. Compare these results with those recorded in Step 2. What are your conclusions about the TCP/IP values assigned to your computer?

   _____

   _____

REVIEW QUESTIONS

1. What dialog box do you use to configure TCP/IPv4 settings for the network adapter?

   _____

2. What are the two types of addresses or names used in this lab that can uniquely identify a computer on the network?

   _____

3. If there is no DHCP server to provide a computer a unique IP address, how is a computer able to acquire an IP address?

   _____

   _____

4. What is the exact path to the Windows 10 Documents folder for a user named John Smith?

   _____

   _____

5. What is the exact path to the Public Documents folder?

   _____

6. What is the name of the window you can use to configure the network discovery and file sharing settings?

   _____

LAB 7.2 SET UP A WIRELESS ROUTER

OBJECTIVES

The goal of this lab is to install and configure a wireless router. After completing this lab, you will be able to:

◢ Install and configure a wireless router

◢ Configure computers to connect to a wireless router

MATERIALS REQUIRED

This lab requires the following:

◢ Windows 10/8/7 computer designated for this lab

◢ An account with administrator privileges

◢ A wireless router with setup CD or user's manual

◢ A USB wireless NIC (recommended)

LAB PREPARATION

Before the lab begins, the instructor or lab assistant needs to do the following:

◢ Verify that Windows starts with no errors

◢ Verify that each student has access to a user account with administrator privileges

◢ Verify that a network connection is available

ACTIVITY BACKGROUND

A small office/home office (SOHO) router, such as the one shown in Figure 7-2, is the best device to use to set up a small network. A router can provide these basic functions on the network:

◢ It can serve as a gateway to the Internet. The router stands between the networked computers and a DSL, cable modem, or other type of connection to an ISP and to the Internet.

◢ The router can add more security by providing a hardware firewall and limiting access to the Internet.

◢ A router can provide wired and wireless access to the network.

◢ The router can serve other purposes, such as functioning as a DHCP server.

Source: amazon.com

Figure 7-2 The NETGEAR Nighthawk AC1900 dual band Wi-Fi Gigabit router

In this lab, you set up and configure a wireless router, and then connect to it from a remote computer.

Activity

Follow these steps to set up your router:

1. If your router comes with a setup CD, run the setup program on one of your wired computers on the network (it doesn't matter which one). Follow the instructions on the setup screen or in the accompanying user's manual to use network cables to physically connect the computer to the router, plug in the router, and turn it on either before or after you run the setup CD. A computer can connect directly to a network port (Ethernet port) on the router (see Figure 7-3), or you can connect through a switch or hub to the router.

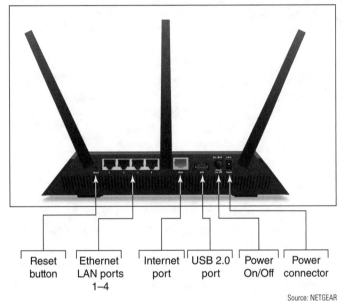

| Reset button | Ethernet LAN ports 1–4 | Internet port | USB 2.0 port | Power On/Off | Power connector |

Source: NETGEAR

Figure 7-3 Connectors and ports on the back of the NETGEAR router

2. Connect the other wired computers on your network to the router.

3. Firmware on a router (which can be flashed for updates) contains a configuration program that you can access using a web browser from anywhere on the network. In your browser address box, enter the IP address of the router (for many routers, that address is 192.168.0.1 or 192.168.1.1), and then press **Enter**. What is the name and IP address for your router?

_____

4. You'll probably be required to sign in to the router firmware utility using a default password. The first thing you want to do is reset this password so that others cannot change your router setup. What is your new router password?

_____

5. After you change the password, a basic setup window appears, as shown in Figure 7-4. For most situations, the default settings on this and other screens should work without any changes required. The setup program will take you through the process of configuring the router. After you've configured the router, you might have to turn your

cable or DSL modem off and back on so that it correctly syncs up with the router. What basic steps did the setup program have you follow to configure the router?

_____

_____

_____

_____

Source: NETGEAR

Figure 7-4 The main screen for router firmware setup

6. Spend some time examining the various features of your router. What security features does it have?

_____

_____

_____

7. What is the IP address of the router on the ISP network?

_____

8. Why is it necessary for the router to have two IP addresses?

_____

_____

Follow these steps to create a wireless connection to your wireless router from another computer:

1. Make sure you are signed in to Windows as an administrator. If you are using a USB wireless NIC, plug it into an available USB port. If necessary, install the drivers.

2. After the NIC has finished installing, click the **Network** icon in your taskbar. (If you don't see the Network icon, click the up arrow on the right side of the taskbar, and then click the **Network** icon, as shown in Figure 7-5A.)

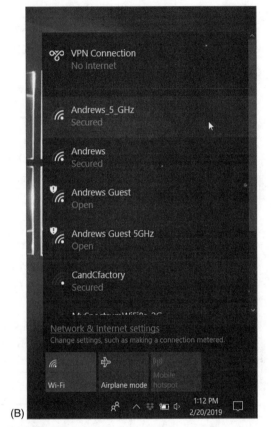

(A)   (B)

Figure 7-5   Use the Network icon to make a network connection

3. Windows displays a list of wireless networks that are broadcasting availability (see Figure 7-5B for Windows 10). List all the networks that are available on your computer:

_____

4. Select the name of the network you would like to connect to. If you are comfortable with Windows automatically connecting to this network in the future, check **Connect automatically,** and then click **Connect.** If you are attempting to connect to a secured network, Windows will prompt you for the security key.

5. Windows reports the connection is being made. To see the network to which you are connected, click the **Network** icon in the taskbar or in the hidden icons box.

> **Notes** To add the Network icon to the taskbar, right-click the taskbar. For Windows 10, click **Taskbar settings** and then click **Select which icons appear on the taskbar**. For Windows 8/7, click **Properties** and then click **Customize**.

6. Open the **Network and Sharing Center**. Click **Change advanced sharing settings** in the left pane. The Advanced sharing settings window appears.

7. Verify that Network discovery, File and printer sharing, and Public folder sharing settings are all turned off.

8. To see the status of your wireless connection, click the **Back** arrow to return to the Network and Sharing Center. In the View your active networks section, click the wireless network connection.

    ◢ What speed is your wireless connection?

    _____

    ◢ Fast Ethernet runs at 100 Mbps, and Gigabit Ethernet runs at 1000 Mbps. How does your wireless network speed compare with these two types of wired networks?

    _____

    _____

9. Open your browser to test the connection.

10. When you're finished, reset and uninstall the wireless router and NIC.

REVIEW QUESTIONS

1. What additional features on your router would you implement if you were setting up a small wired and wireless network?

    _____

    _____

2. Name two ways your router can limit Internet access.

    _____

    _____

3. Name one advantage and one disadvantage of a wireless connection compared with a wired connection.

    _____

    _____

4. Most wireless routers have a reset switch. Give an example of when this might be useful.

    _____

    _____

LAB 7.3 SECURE A WIRELESS LAN

OBJECTIVES

Your goal in this lab is to learn how to set up and configure security options on a wireless router. After completing this lab, you will be able to:

▲ Download a manual for a wireless router

▲ Explain how to improve wireless security

▲ Describe a few methods for securing a wireless LAN

MATERIALS REQUIRED

This lab requires the following:

▲ Windows 10/8/7 operating system

▲ Internet access

▲ Adobe Acrobat Reader installed for viewing PDF files

▲ Wireless router (optional)

▲ Laptop or desktop computer with compatible wireless access (optional)

LAB PREPARATION

Before the lab begins, the instructor or lab assistant needs to do the following:

▲ Verify that Windows starts with no errors

▲ Verify that Internet access is available

ACTIVITY BACKGROUND

Wireless networks are a simple way to include computers in a home or small office network. Without adequate security, however, you can open up your network to a wide range of threats. In this lab, you learn how to enable and configure some security features of a wireless router.

If you have a router, use it in this lab. If you don't have a router to do this lab, you can still complete the lab. To do so, assume that your router is the Linksys WRT1900ACS dual-band Wi-Fi router shown in Figure 7-6.

Source: linksys.com

Figure 7-6 A Linksys WRT1900ACS dual-band Wi-Fi router

If you are not using the Linksys WRT1900ACS router, what router brand and model are you using?

 Activity

1. Open your web browser and locate the support page for your router provided by the router manufacturer. For the Linksys WRT1900ACS router, go to the Linksys site at **linksys.com/us/support/**, and then search on the router model number.

   Follow links to view or download the user guide for your router. You might also find the user guide on the setup CD for your router. If you cannot find a user guide, then search the support documentation provided for the router on the manufacturer's website. Using any of these sources, answer the following questions:

   ▲ Most wireless routers can be configured with a web-based utility by entering the router's IP address in the browser address box. What's the default IP address of this router?

   ▲ Describe how you would sign in to the router for the first time:

Most routers are easily configured with a setup utility that asks a series of questions about your network and your Internet service provider. The default settings, however, might not enable all your router's security features. Here are the four most important steps in securing your LAN:

   ▲ Update the router's firmware from the manufacturer's website so that any known security flaws are fixed.

   ▲ Set a password on the router itself so that other people can't change its configuration.

   ▲ Disable remote configuration of the router.

   ▲ Use some kind of wireless encryption. (WEP is better than nothing; WPA is better; and WPA2 is better still.)

Here are two more ways to secure a router. They are not considered strong security measures because they are easily hacked:

   ▲ Change the wireless network's name (called a service set identifier, or SSID) and turn off the SSID broadcast to anyone who's listening.

   ▲ Enable MAC filtering so that only the computers whose MAC addresses are listed in your router table can access the network.

Continue to use the manual to answer the following additional questions:

   ▲ Which window in the router's web-based utility do you use to change the password needed to configure the router?

◢ List the steps for changing the router's SSID:

_____

_____

_____

_____

◢ Does the router support Wi-Fi Protected Setup? If so, on which screen can it be enabled?

_____

◢ Describe the steps to allow access through MAC filtering only to the computer you are now using:

_____

_____

_____

ESTIMATED COMPLETION TIME: 30 MINUTES

CHALLENGE ACTIVITY

If you have access to a wireless router, set up a secure wireless connection by following these steps:

1. Set up a nonsecure wireless connection with the router, as covered in the previous lab.

2. Go to the router manufacturer's website and update the router's firmware (if necessary) to the latest version. Did your router require an update? What version of the firmware is it now running?

_____

3. Set a strong password for the router. What password did you use?

_____

4. Disable remote configuration for the router so it cannot be configured wirelessly. List the steps you went through to complete this task:

_____

_____

_____

_____

5. Change the router's name (SSID). What was the router's default name, and what is the new name?

_____

6. Disable the broadcast of the new SSID.

7. Set up some kind of wireless encryption on the router. What form of encryption did you use?

_____

8. Enable MAC filtering so that only the computer you are using can connect. How did you determine the MAC address of your computer?

_____

_____

9. Test your network connection by opening your browser and surfing the web.

10. When you're finished, reset the router to undo any changes you made to it.

REVIEW QUESTIONS

1. What client application on your computer is used to configure a home router?

_____

2. Why should you update your router's firmware before making any other security changes?

_____

_____

3. How could not changing your router's password compromise all of your other security changes?

_____

4. Why wouldn't "password" or "Linksys" make a good password for your router?

_____

5. How can you configure your router once you've disabled remote configuration?

_____

LAB 7.4 PRACTICE TROUBLESHOOTING USING TCP/IP UTILITIES

OBJECTIVES

The goal of this lab is to use Windows TCP/IP utilities that you might need when you are troubleshooting network connectivity problems. After completing this lab, you will be able to:

▴ Use the ipconfig utility

▴ Use the ping utility

▴ Use the tracert utility

▴ Use the nslookup utility

▴ Use the netstat utility

MATERIALS REQUIRED

This lab requires the following:

- Windows 10/8/7 operating system
- An account with administrator privileges
- A DHCP server
- Internet access

LAB PREPARATION

Before the lab begins, the instructor or lab assistant needs to do the following:

- Verify that Windows starts with no errors
- Verify that Internet access is available
- Verify that students can sign in to their computers with administrator privileges

ACTIVITY BACKGROUND

Loss of network connectivity can be frustrating to users and can be costly to a business. As an IT technician, you might be asked to restore these connections, and sometimes you have to deal with several failed connections at one time. When troubleshooting network connections, it helps to know whether many users in one area of a network are having the same connection problem. That information can help you narrow down the source of the problem. After you have an idea of which machine is causing the problem, you can use a few TCP/IP utilities to test your theory without physically checking the machine. In this lab, you learn to use TCP/IP utilities to isolate connection problems.

ESTIMATED COMPLETION TIME: 30 MINUTES

 Activity

Follow these steps to display IP settings in Windows:

1. Open the Network and Sharing Center.
2. In the left pane, click **Change adapter settings**. Right-click the active network connection (whether Ethernet or Wi-Fi), and select **Properties** in the shortcut menu. The connection's properties dialog box opens.
3. Click **Internet Protocol Version 4 (TCP/IPv4)**, and then click the **Properties** button. The Internet Protocol Version 4 (TCP/IPv4) Properties dialog box opens. Notice the different options. In what two ways can you set up the IP configuration?

_____

_____

4. Select **Obtain an IP address automatically** if it is not already selected.
5. Click **OK** to close the Internet Protocol Version 4 (TCP/IPv4) Properties dialog box, and then close any open windows.

Adjusting the size and colors of the command prompt window can make it easier to read command output. Although Windows 10 allows you to resize the command prompt window, the default state of Windows 8/7 does not. Follow these steps to see how to customize the Windows 10/8/7 command prompt window:

1. Open a command prompt window.

2. Right-click the title bar of the command prompt window and select **Properties** in the shortcut menu. The Command Prompt Properties dialog box opens.

3. For Windows 8/7, on the Layout tab in the Screen Buffer Size section (see Figure 7-7), enter **150** for width and **300** for height. These settings enable you to scroll in the command prompt window and view 300 lines and 150 characters per line.

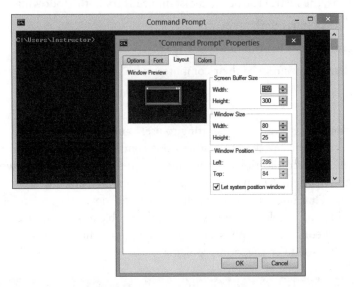

Figure 7-7 Adjust the command prompt window display settings

4. Select the **Colors** tab. Change the screen background to gray and the screen text to black. Click **OK** to save your changes. If you like, return the screen background to black and the screen text to white.

> **Notes** You might want to further customize the command prompt window and make these changes permanent, even after you restart your computer. To do so, right-click the title bar of the window, and click **Defaults**. Changes you make are retained and can include the screen buffer size, font color, and background color of the command prompt window.

Follow these steps to learn how to display IP information from the command line:

1. At the command prompt, type **ipconfig /?** and press **Enter**. List five parameters and their descriptions for ipconfig.

_____

_____

_____

_____

_____

2. Type **ipconfig** and press **Enter**. What is the IP address and subnet mask for the active network connection?

_____

3. To get more information about your IP settings, type **ipconfig /all** and press **Enter**. Answer these questions:

   ◢ What is the physical address (MAC)?

   _____

   ◢ What is the address of the default gateway?

   _____

   ◢ What is the address of the DHCP server?

   _____

   ◢ What is the address of the DNS server?

   _____

4. Because your system is using DHCP to obtain an IP address, you can ask DHCP to renew the IP address. To do so, first release the existing IP address lease. Type **ipconfig /release** and press **Enter**. Then request a new IP address lease; type **ipconfig /renew** and press **Enter**. The command prompt window again displays IP information.

5. Again, type **ipconfig /all** and press **Enter**. Compare the earlier IP address lease information to the information on the screen. What information changed?

_____

6. Once again, type **ipconfig /release** and press **Enter**. Note that your adapter has no IP address and no subnet mask. These two parameters are necessary to communicate with TCP/IP. How do you predict this command will affect connectivity?

_____

_____

7. The ping command tests if an IP address is accessible by sending four packets to the IP address and recording the time required for the round trip. To use the ping command, type **ping cengage.com** at the command prompt. Press **Enter**. What message is displayed?

_____

8. Attempt to ping the DHCP server and DNS server IP addresses you recorded in Step 3. What are the results?

_____

9. Type **ipconfig** and press **Enter**. What IPv4 address is listed for the active network adapter now? How did your computer obtain this IP address? How do you know?

_____

_____

10. To get an IP address lease from the DHCP server again, type **ipconfig /renew** and press **Enter**. New IP information, which might be the same address as before, is assigned.

11. Find your new IP address lease information (the time obtained and the time it will expire). List the command you used to find this information and the lease information:

_____

_____

Follow these steps to determine what route your packets take to reach an Internet address:

1. If necessary, open a command prompt window.

2. Type **tracert** followed by a single space and then a domain name on the Internet (for example, type **tracert cengage.com**). Press **Enter**.

3. The DNS server resolves the domain name to an IP address. When the tracert command reports the name of a DNS server, you know your packets traveled at least as far as this server. Also, each hop (or router your packet passes through) is listed with the time in milliseconds that the packet took to reach its destination. How many hops did the packets take to reach the domain you specified?

_____

4. Now use the tracert command with an illegitimate domain name (for example, type **tracert mydomain.c**). What are the results of this command?

_____

5. When you're finished, close any open windows.

When you first type the URL _cengage.com_ into your browser, your computer does not know the actual IP address of that website. Without the IP address, your computer cannot create packets at the Network layer because all packets must contain a source IP address and a final destination IP address. To find the destination IP address, your computer requests it from a Domain Name Service (DNS) server. The job of the DNS server is to resolve IP addresses to domain names. The nslookup command gives information about DNS and can run in interactive mode or noninteractive mode. To learn more, follow these steps:

1. Open an elevated command prompt window.

2. At the command prompt, type **nslookup** and then press **Enter**. The name and IP address of the default DNS server appear, and nslookup starts in interactive mode.

   ◢ What new command prompt appears?

   _____

   ◢ What is the name of the DNS server?

   _____

   ◢ What is the IP address of the DNS server?

   _____

3. At the nslookup command prompt, type **help** and then press **Enter**. A list of nslookup commands appears.

4. To find out the IP address of the web server for _cengage.com_, type **cengage.com** and press **Enter**. What is the IP address?

   _____

5. To exit nslookup interactive mode, type **exit** and then press **Enter**. The normal command prompt appears.

6. To use nslookup in noninteractive mode, type **nslookup cengage.com** and then press **Enter**. Describe any output differences between nslookup in interactive mode and nslookup in noninteractive mode:

_____

_____

The local computer does not need to go back to the DNS server to resolve an IP address every time you request the same webpage. Instead, your local computer stores a list of previously resolved IP addresses in a local cache. To display the cached list of previously resolved domain names to IP addresses, follow these steps:

1. Open your browser and go to **cengage.com**. Then go to **course.com**. Close your browser. To access these webpages, the computer needed to resolve the domain names and IP addresses; it then stored this information in the local cache.

2. At the command prompt, type **ipconfig /displaydns** and then press **Enter**.

3. Browse through the results and observe any cached results for *course.com* or *cengage.com*.

4. Close all open windows.

At the Transport layer, segments are commonly labeled as TCP data packets when a delivery confirmation is required or as UDP datagrams when a delivery confirmation is not required. As an IT technician, you might have to monitor TCP and UDP traffic. The netstat command can help. To learn more about this command, follow these steps:

1. Open an elevated command prompt window.

2. Type **netstat** and then press **Enter**. A list of active connections appears. The protocol for each connection (for example, TCP or UDP) appears in the first column of this list. Answer the following questions:

   ◢ What protocol is used for the first connection in the list?

   _____

   ◢ What is the foreign address of this connection and the state of the connection?

   _____

3. To stop the netstat command from reporting active connections, press **Ctrl+C**. The command prompt appears.

4. At the command prompt, type **netstat –s** and then press **Enter**. Answer the following questions:

   ◢ What is the purpose of the –s parameter used with the netstat command?

   _____

   ◢ In the TCP Statistics for IPv4 section, what is the number of current connections?

   _____

   ◢ In the UDP Statistics for IPv4 section, what is the number of datagrams sent?

   _____

5. At the command prompt, type **netstat –a** and then press **Enter**. Describe the difference in the output when using the –s parameter with the netstat command versus using the –a parameter with the netstat command:

   _____

   _____

6. To stop the netstat command, press **Ctrl+C**.

7. Close all open windows.

REVIEW QUESTIONS

1. List four additional types of information that the ipconfig command with the /all parameter provides over entering the ipconfig command without the parameter.

_____

_____

2. What type of server resolves a domain name to an IP address?

_____

3. What command discards the IP address for a connection?

_____

4. What command do you use to determine whether you can reach another computer on the local network? Would this command work if the default gateway were down?

_____

5. When troubleshooting problems with resolving domain names to IP addresses, flushing the DNS cache can sometimes help because the local computer must build the cache again. What is the command to flush the DNS cache?

_____

LAB 7.5 ANALYZE A SYSTEM WITH EVENT VIEWER

OBJECTIVES

Your goal in this lab is to learn to work with Windows Event Viewer. After completing this lab, you will be able to use Event Viewer to:

▲ View Windows events

▲ Save events

▲ View event logs

▲ Compare recent events with logged events

MATERIALS REQUIRED

This lab requires the following:

▲ Windows 10/8/7 operating system

▲ Network access

▲ An account with administrator privileges

LAB PREPARATION

Before the lab begins, the instructor or lab assistant needs to do the following:

▲ Verify that Windows starts with no errors

▲ Verify that each student has access to a user account with administrator privileges

ACTIVITY BACKGROUND

Windows records many events or activities of your computer in logs, which can be helpful to understand the source of a networking, application, hardware, or Windows problem. In this lab, you will take a look at the Event Viewer tool, which allows you to examine these Windows logs of events. Event Viewer notes the occurrence of various events, lists them chronologically, and gives you the option of saving the list so you can view it later or compare it with a future list. You can use Event Viewer to find out how healthy your system is and to troubleshoot problems in Windows.

ESTIMATED COMPLETION TIME: 30 MINUTES

 Activity

Follow these steps to begin using Event Viewer:

1. Sign in as an administrator.

2. Open **Control Panel** in Classic view, and click **Administrative Tools**. The Administrative Tools window opens.

3. Double-click **Event Viewer** to open the Event Viewer window. The console tree is shown in the left pane, with Event Viewer (Local) listed at the top. A list of events is shown in the center pane, with available Actions in the right pane (see Figure 7-8). When you select an event in the upper-center pane, details about the event appear in the lower-center pane. Maximize the Event Viewer window to see more information in the middle pane.

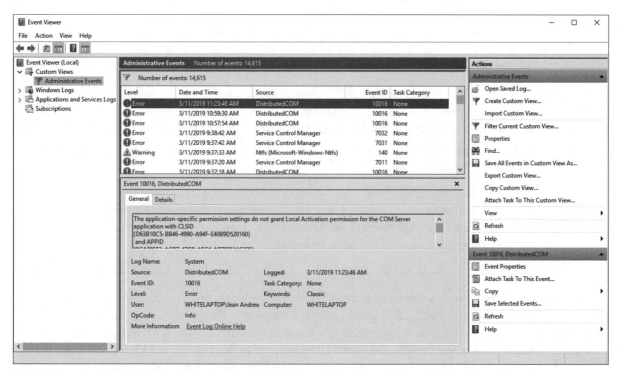

Figure 7-8 Event Viewer tracks failed and successful events

4. You can drag the lines separating the panes to widen or narrow each pane. Widen the center pane because it contains the most useful information.

5. In the console tree, expand **Windows Logs**, and then click **System** in the Windows Logs group. The System log appears in the center pane. In the center pane, if necessary, you can drag the bar between the boxes down so you can see more of the list of events in the top box. The symbols to the left of each event indicate important information about the event. For example, a lowercase *i* in a white circle indicates an event that provides information about the system, and an exclamation mark in a yellow triangle indicates a warning event, such as a disk being near its capacity. An exclamation mark in a red circle is an error, and an *X* in a red circle is a critical event. Each event entry includes the time and date it occurred. Click on several events to see what information changes in various parts of the Event Viewer window when selecting different events.

◢ For each of the four most recent events, list the source (what triggered the event), the time, and the date:

_____

_____

_____

_____

6. Double-click the top (most recent) event. The Event Properties dialog box opens. What additional information does this dialog box provide?

_____

_____

_____

7. Close the Event Properties dialog box.

Because Event Viewer provides so much information, it can be difficult to find what you need; however, events can be sorted by clicking the column headings. Do the following to find the most important events:

1. To sort by Level, click **Level**. Events are listed in the following order: Critical, Error, Warning, and Information.

2. To sort events by Date and Time, click **Date and Time**.

3. To see a list of only Critical, Error, and Warning events, expand **Custom Views** in the console tree, and then select **Administrative Events**. How many Critical, Error, and Warning events are recorded on your system?

_____

You can save the list of events shown in Event Viewer to a log file. When naming a log file, it's helpful to use the following format: *Typelog*EV*mm-dd-yy*.evtx, where *mm* = month, *dd* = day, and *yy* = year. For example, you would name a log file of System events saved on January 27, 2019, as SystemEV01-27-19. evtx. After you create a log file, you can delete the current list of events from Event Viewer, allowing the utility to begin creating an entirely new list of events. A short log and resulting log file is easier to view and easier to send to other support technicians when you need help.

Follow these steps to save the currently displayed events as a log file, and then clear the current events:

1. Open File Explorer/Windows Explorer, and create a folder called **Logs** in the root directory of drive C:.

2. Leaving File Explorer/Windows Explorer open, return to Event Viewer, and then click **System** in the console tree in the left pane. The System log is selected, but no particular event is selected. How many events are there in this log?

_____

3. To save the System log to a log file, open the menu bar, click **Action**, and then click **Save All Events As**.

4. Navigate to the **Logs** folder you created in Step 1. Name the file **SystemEV*mm-dd-yy*** (replace the italicized portion with today's date), click **Save**, and then click **OK**. What is the name of your log file, including the file extension?

_____

5. Now you're ready to clear the current list of events from Event Viewer. With the System log still selected, click **Action**, and then click **Clear Log**.

6. When asked if you want to save the System log, click **Clear**. The Event Viewer window now displays only one event. What is this event?

_____

7. Close Event Viewer.

It can be useful to save a log that shows the events of a successful, clean boot so you can use it as a reference when you have a problem with a boot. You can compare the two logs to help you identify a problem. To save a log of a boot, follow these steps:

1. With your System events log recently cleared, reboot your computer.

2. Return to Event Viewer. How many events are now recorded in your System log?

_____

3. Does this list of events include any Warning or Error events? If so, describe these events here:

_____

4. Save a new file of System events to your Logs folder, and name the file **SystemBootEV*mm-dd-yy***. What is the name of the log file, including the file extension?

_____

5. With the System log still selected, clear the System log.

6. Close Event Viewer.

Next, you intentionally create a problem by disconnecting the network cable from your computer. Then, you observe how the resulting errors are recorded in Event Viewer. Do the following:

1. Carefully disconnect the network cable from the network port on the back of your computer.

2. Open Internet Explorer and try to surf the web.

3. Close Internet Explorer, and then open Event Viewer. How many new events are displayed?

_____

4. List the source, date, and time for any Error or Warning events you see:

_____

5. Click each Error or Warning event and read the details. How does Event Viewer describe what happened when you unplugged the network cable?

_____

To restore the network connection and verify that the connection is working, follow these steps:

1. Reconnect the network cable to the network port on the back of your computer. Open Internet Explorer. Can you surf the web?

_____

2. In the center pane of the Event Viewer window, the System log reports that new events are available. To see these events, open the menu bar, click **Action**, and then click **Refresh**. How many events are now listed?

_____

When troubleshooting a system, comparing current events with a list of events you previously stored in a log file is often helpful because you can spot the time when a particular problem occurred. Follow these steps to compare the current list of events with the log you saved earlier:

1. Use File Explorer or Windows Explorer to locate the System log files in the C:\Logs folder you created earlier in this lab. Double-click one of these log files. A second instance of Event Viewer opens and displays the log file. Notice in this new window that the saved log file is listed in the console tree under Saved Logs.

   ◢ List all the saved logs that are displayed:

   _____

   ◢ What happens when you click on a saved log?

   _____

2. To compare two logs, you can position the two Event Viewer windows side by side. Snap one Event Viewer window to the right of your screen by dragging the window to the right edge of the screen, and then snap the other Event Viewer window to the left of your screen.

3. Widen or narrow the panes in each window so you can see the events listed in each window. In a troubleshooting situation, you would look for differences in the two logs to help you find the source of a problem.

4. Close both Event Viewer windows.

REVIEW QUESTIONS

1. Judging by its location in Control Panel, what type of tool is Event Viewer?

_____

2. What is the file extension that Event Viewer assigns to its log files?

_____

3. How can you examine events after you have cleared them from Event Viewer?

   _____

4. Explain how to compare a log file with the current set of listed events:

   _____

   _____

5. Why might you like to keep a log file of events that occurred when your computer started correctly?

   _____

   _____

   _____

LAB 7.6 SET UP A VPN

OBJECTIVES

The goal of this lab is to set up a secure VPN. Technicians in the field are often called on to help clients connect to the corporate network using a VPN when they are traveling or working from home. After completing this lab, you will be able to:

- Set up a VPN in Windows
- Use third-party software to securely access the Internet from a public network

MATERIALS REQUIRED

This lab requires the following:

- Two Windows 10/8/7 computers
- An account with administrator privileges
- Internet access
- VPN server (optional)
- Workgroup of two students

LAB PREPARATION

Before the lab begins, the instructor or lab assistant needs to do the following:

- Verify that Windows starts with no errors
- Verify that each student has access to a user account with administrator privileges
- Verify that Internet access is available
- Set up a VPN server, and record the server's IP address (optional)
- Set up a user account on the VPN server, and record the user name and password (optional)

ACTIVITY BACKGROUND

A virtual private network (VPN) offers a secure connection between two computers. It uses a process called tunneling to form a private connection that encrypts communications independently of the type of network being used. VPNs are often used when a user has to connect to a private network over a nonsecure public network such as a wireless hotspot.

This lab presents three options for setting up a VPN connection. In Part 1, you set up a VPN connection between two Windows computers. In Part 2, you set up a VPN connection from a computer to a VPN server. In Part 3, you use browser software to set up a VPN connection using a third-party server.

ESTIMATED COMPLETION TIME: 60 MINUTES

 Activity

PART 1: CREATE A VPN CONNECTION BETWEEN TWO WINDOWS COMPUTERS

In this part of the lab, you create a VPN connection between two computers connected to the Internet. To do this, you must first set up one computer to host or serve up a VPN connection and then allow specific user names to access this connection. Follow these steps to configure an incoming VPN connection to your computer, which acts as a VPN server:

1. Sign in using an account with administrator privileges.

2. Create a standard user account with a password. Name the standard account **Newuser** and make the password **newuser**.

3. To configure your computer as a VPN server, open the **Network and Sharing Center**. In the left pane, click **Change adapter settings**.

4. Select your connection, and then press the **Alt** key to display the menu. Click **File** on the menu bar, and then click **New Incoming Connection** to open the "Allow connections to this computer" dialog box.

> **Notes** If you don't see the menu bar with the File option, click **Organize** in the toolbar, select **Layout**, and then click **Menu bar**. The menu bar is now displaced above the toolbar.

5. Select the **Newuser (Newuser)** check box, and then click **Next**.

6. Make sure **Through the Internet** is selected and click **Next**.

7. Leave the networking software settings at their defaults to use Internet Protocol Version 4 (TCP/IPv4), and click **Allow access**.

8. The final screen of this setup gives the computer name, which is used to establish the VPN connection. Write down the computer name and give it to your partner, who will use this VPN connection to your computer. Click **Close**. Close any open windows.

Now that you have configured the VPN server and granted permission for your partner to use the Newuser account to connect to your computer through this VPN connection, you are ready for your partner to test the connection from his or her computer to yours. Then you can try to connect to your partner's computer using his or her VPN connection. You are only able to do this one at a time. Designate one partner as Partner 1 and the other partner as Partner 2.

▲ Who is Partner 1?

_____

▲ Who is Partner 2?

_____

CREATE AN OUTGOING CONNECTION

Partner 1 follows these steps to make an outgoing VPN connection as Partner 2 observes:

1. If necessary, sign in using an account with administrator privileges.
2. Open the **Network and Sharing Center** and click **Set up a new connection or network**.
3. Select **Connect to a workplace**, and then click **Next**, as shown in Figure 7-9.

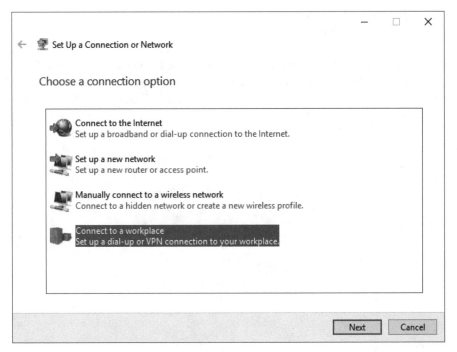

Figure 7-9 Beginning a Windows VPN setup

4. Click **Use my Internet connection (VPN)**.
5. In the Internet address field, enter the computer name provided by your partner in the previous Step 8. What is the name your partner gave you? In Windows 10/8, click **Create**. In Windows 7, click **Next**.

_____

6. To establish the VPN connection, click the **Network** icon in the taskbar, click **VPN Connection**, and click **Connect**. In the Windows Security box (see Figure 7-10), enter the user name **Newuser**, enter a password, and click **OK**. The connection is made, and you can use it to communicate with your partner's computer.

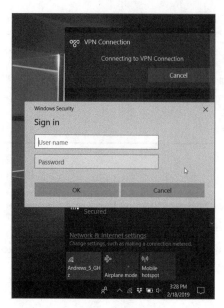

Figure 7-10 Authenticate to use the VPN connection

7. To view the VPN connection status, open the **Network and Sharing Center,** and click **Change adapter settings** in the left pane. Notice the new connections listed on the host machine, as shown in Figure 7-11A. On the client computer, the connections are slightly different, as shown in Figure 7-11B.

Figure 7-11 (A) The host computer and (B) the client computer report an active VPN connection

Follow these steps to disconnect and delete the outgoing VPN connection:

1. To disconnect, click the network connection icon in the notification area of the taskbar. Click **VPN Connection**, and then click **Disconnect**.

2. To delete the VPN connection, open the **Network and Sharing Center**.

3. Click **Change adapter settings** in the left pane. Right-click the **VPN Connection** icon, and select **Delete** in the shortcut menu. Click **Yes** to confirm.

Now Partner 2 makes an outgoing connection while Partner 1 observes. Partner 2 should go back to the "Create an Outgoing Connection" heading and follow the steps back to this point in the lab.

PART 2: CREATE A VPN CONNECTION USING A VPN SERVER (OPTIONAL)

This part of the lab is optional. If your instructor has provided a VPN server, you can follow these steps to connect to it. If a VPN server is not available, please proceed to Part 3 of this lab. To connect to a VPN server in Windows, follow these steps:

1. Log on using an account with administrator privileges.

2. Open the **Network and Sharing Center**, and click **Set up a new connection or network**.

3. Select **Connect to a workplace**, and then click **Next**.

4. Click **Use my Internet connection (VPN)**.

5. Enter the Internet address of the VPN server provided by your instructor. What is the address you used?

   _____

6. Click **Next**. Enter the user name and password provided by your instructor. What user name and password did you use?

   _____

7. Click **Connect**. A message confirms that you are connected. Click **Close**.

8. If a Set Network Location window appears, click **Work network**, and then click **Close**.

9. Disconnect and delete this VPN connection the same way you did the last VPN connection.

PART 3: USE A BROWSER WITH A BUILT-IN VPN SERVICE

Third-party VPN software, such as Hotspot Shield (*hotspotshield.com*), can be purchased and installed on your computer, smartphone, or other mobile device to protect your communication on the Internet when using a browser, email client, or other software that uses the Internet. However, Opera is a free browser that has a built-in VPN connection it uses for all communication within the browser. To set up a secure connection using Opera, follow these steps:

1. Sign in using an account with administrator privileges.

2. Go to **opera.com**. Click the download button and follow the on-screen directions to install the Opera browser, accepting all default settings.

3. Launch the browser. Browse the web to verify that you have Internet connectivity.

4. Click the red **O** in the upper-left corner of the browser window. In the drop-down menu, click **Settings**.

5. On the Settings page, expand the **Advanced** settings. Click **Privacy & security**.

6. Turn on the switch to Enable VPN (see Figure 7-12). Know that when the VPN is enabled, response time will be slower.

   ◢ What do you look for in the Opera window to know that the VPN connection is active?

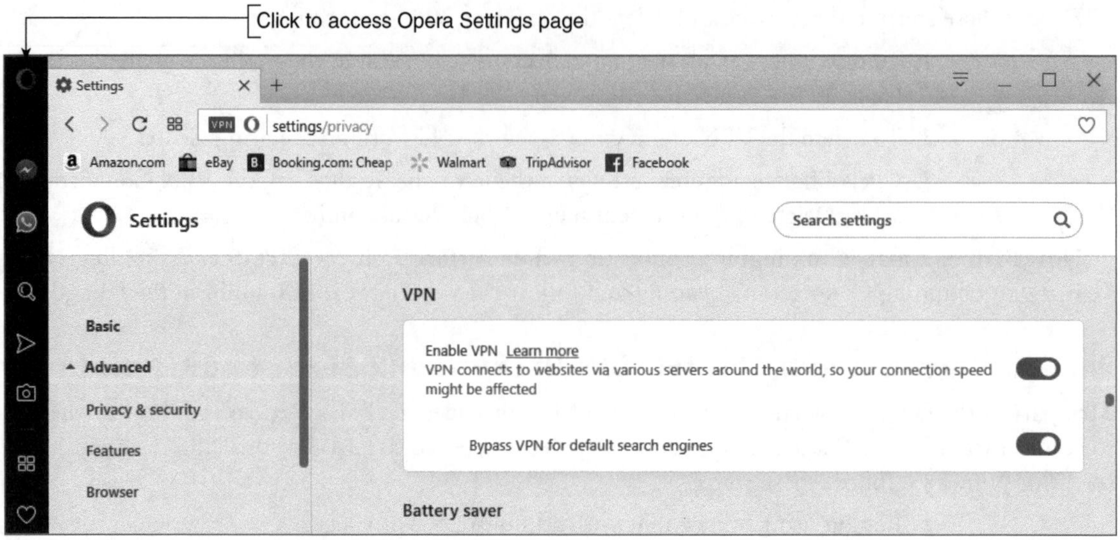

Click to access Opera Settings page

Source: Opera Software

Figure 7-12 Enable the embedded VPN in the Opera browser

REVIEW QUESTIONS

1. Will VPNs work on both wired and wireless networks?

2. What process do VPNs use to form a private connection between computers?

3. Why might it be dangerous to do online banking transactions through a public Internet hotspot without using a VPN connection?

4. What type of secure connection does an online banking site usually offer its customers?

5. How does a VPN connection differ from using Remote Desktop? Is a Remote Desktop connection a secured connection?

6. Why is a VPN more secure than other forms of wireless encryption such as WPA2?

7. Why do you think using Opera for secured VPN connections slows down response time when surfing the web?

LAB 7.7 CREATE A NETWORK IN PACKET TRACER

OBJECTIVES

The goal of this lab is to implement a wired and wireless network with a SOHO router in Packet Tracer. After completing this lab, you will be able to:

◢ Set up a small network in Cisco Packet Tracer

MATERIALS REQUIRED

This lab requires the following:

◢ Computer with Windows 10/8/7

◢ Internet access

LAB PREPARATION

Before the lab begins, the instructor or lab assistant needs to do the following:

◢ Verify that the computer works with no errors

◢ Verify Internet access

ACTIVITY BACKGROUND

Cisco Packet Tracer simulates many functions of a network and can be useful to help you learn and practice networking skills. In this lab, you install Packet Tracer and use it to build and configure a small wired and wireless network that uses a SOHO router and cable modem for Internet connectivity.

ESTIMATED COMPLETION TIME: 50 MINUTES

 Activity

PART 1: DOWNLOAD AND INSTALL PACKET TRACER

Follow these steps to download and install Packet Tracer:

1. Go to **netacad.com/courses/packet-tracer**.

2. Click **Enroll to download Packet Tracer**. Hover over **Sign up today!**, click **English**, and then follow instructions to sign up for the Introduction to Packet Tracer course. (It is not necessary that you take the course, although it teaches you a lot about Packet Tracer.)

3. Open your email app and click the link in the message from the Networking Academy Team to confirm your account. Sign in to the course and look in the Student Resources area to find the link to download Packet Tracer. Select the latest version of Packet Tracer for your operating system.

4. Decompress the zipped files and install Packet Tracer. When you first launch Packet Tracer, you are required to sign in to Cisco Networking Academy using the email address and password you used to set up the account. The Cisco Packet Tracer window appears. See Figure 7-13.

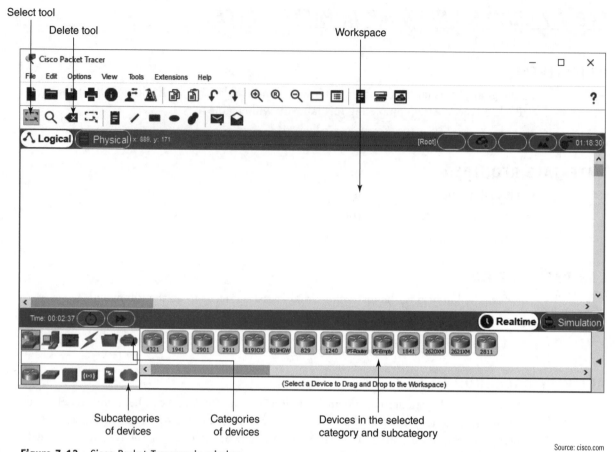

Figure 7-13 Cisco Packet Tracer main window

Source: cisco.com

5. Take a few moments to explore the Packet Tracer menus and features.

> **Notes** The web is an excellent source of information about Packet Tracer. For example, you can search *youtube.com* on "how to use packet tracer" for a quick tutorial.

PART 2: BUILD A NETWORK IN PACKET TRACER

Follow these steps to build a network in Packet Tracer:

1. To add a device to your network, select a category of devices in the bottom-left portion of the window, and then press and drag a device to the workspace. Follow these steps to add devices to your network, arranging the devices as shown in Figure 7-14. Do not worry about configuring any of the devices yet.

   a. Select **End Devices**, and then press and drag a PC to the workspace.

   b. Press and drag a laptop to the workspace.

   c. Press and drag a printer to the workspace.

   d. Select **Miscellaneous** (the folder icon), and then press and drag a wireless PC to the workspace.

   e. Select **Network Devices**, select **Switches**, and then press and drag the first switch in the list to the workspace.

f. With Network Devices selected, select **Wireless Devices**, and then press and drag the **WRT300N** wireless router to the workspace.

g. With Network Devices selected, select **WAN Emulation**, and then press and drag a cable modem to the workspace.

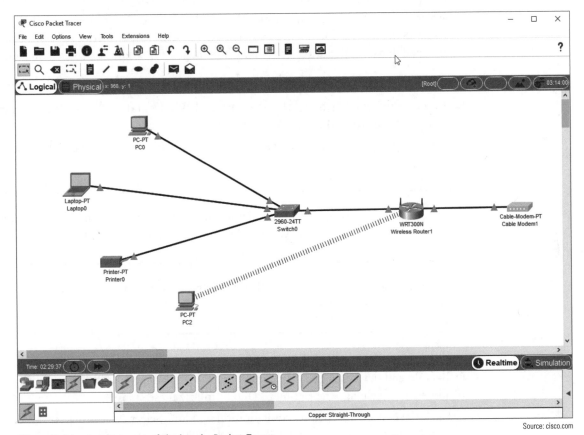

Source: cisco.com

Figure 7-14 Arrangement of devices in Packet Tracer

> **Notes** To delete a device from the workspace, select the **Delete** icon in the menu bar. Your pointer changes to an ×. Then click the device you want to delete. To return to the Select function, click the **Select** icon in the menu bar.

2. You're now ready to use Ethernet cable to connect devices in your network. To connect a cable, you first select the type of cable you want. Then click the first device in the connection and select its port. Next, click the second device and select its port. The cable connects the two devices. If both devices are turned on, they will attempt to automatically establish connectivity.

3. In the categories of devices in the bottom-left portion of the window, select **Connections** (the lightning bolt icon). In the list of cable types, press and drag a Copper Straight-Through cable (a black solid line) to the switch. Select the first port on the switch, then click the first PC and select the FastEthernet port. The Ethernet cable connects the switch and PC. In the same manner, make the following connections, as shown in Figure 7-14:

◢ Connect the switch to the laptop.

◢ Connect the switch to the printer.

◢ Connect the switch to the Ethernet 1 port on the wireless router.

◢ Connect the Internet port on the wireless router to Port 1 on the cable modem.

4. To configure the router, click the router to open its configuration window. Click **GUI** to see the web-based utility the WRT300N wireless router provides. You can use this GUI interface or the Config tab to configure the router. To use the GUI interface, follow these steps:

a. Select the GUI **Setup** tab, and notice that the local IP address of the router is 192.168.0.1. Also notice that DHCP is enabled, so devices on your network can be assigned dynamic IP addresses. What is the range of IP addresses to be assigned?

_____

b. To secure the wireless network, select the GUI **Wireless** tab, select **Wireless Security**, and set the Security Mode to **WPA2 Personal**.

c. Create a passphrase for the wireless security key. What is the passphrase? Save your settings.

_____

d. To rename the SSID of the router, click **Basic Wireless Settings**. The name of the SSID is Default. Change the SSID. What is the new SSID? Save your settings.

_____

e. To secure the router, select the GUI **Administration** tab. Change the Router Password. What is the Router Password? Save your settings.

_____

f. Close the router configuration window.

5. By default, end devices are set for static IP addresses and have not yet been assigned IP addresses. To change the setting to DHCP, follow these steps:

a. Click the first PC to open its configuration window. Select the **Config** tab. Under Gateway/DNS IPv4, select **DHCP**. Close the configuration window.

b. In the same manner, open the laptop configuration window, and set the laptop to receive dynamic IPv4 addresses.

c. Configure the printer to receive dynamic IPv4 addresses.

d. Configure the wireless PC to receive dynamic IPv4 addresses.

6. Now let's connect the wireless PC to the network. Click the wireless PC to open its configuration window. Click **Desktop**, click **PC Wireless**, and then click **Connect**. To refresh the list of available wireless access points, click **Refresh**. Select your SSID and click **Connect**. Enter the security key to your wireless network that you created earlier. Click **Connect**. The wireless connection is made. Close the PC's configuration window.

7. To test connectivity from the first PC to your router, open the PC's configuration window, click **Desktop**, and then click **Command Prompt**.

◢ What is the command to determine the IP address of the PC?

_____

◢ What is the command to test connectivity to the router? Do you have connectivity?

_____

8. Click **File**, click **Save as**, and save the Packet Tracer file in a safe place for future labs.

REVIEW QUESTIONS

1. How are IP addresses in end devices configured in Packet Tracer by default?

_____

2. Does an end device require an IP address in order to establish network connectivity with a switch? When is connectivity with the switch established?

_____

3. What TCP/IP command is used to test for connectivity between a device with an IP address of 192.168.1.101 and another device that has an IP address of 192.168.1.102?

_____

4. In the Packet Tracer workspace, why does the wireless PC show connectivity with the router, but not with the switch?

_____

7

Network Infrastructure and Troubleshooting

Labs included in this chapter:

- **Lab 8.1:** Inspect Cables
- **Lab 8.2:** Compare Options for a Small Office or Home Office LAN
- **Lab 8.3:** Create a Straight-Through Cable
- **Lab 8.4:** Create a Crossover Cable
- **Lab 8.5:** Set Up Advanced IP Scanner and Wake-on-LAN
- **Lab 8.6:** Sabotage and Repair a Network Connection
- **Lab 8.7:** Understand the OSI Model
- **Lab 8.8:** Convert Binary and Hexadecimal Numbers

LAB 8.1 INSPECT CABLES

OBJECTIVES

The goal of this lab is to visually inspect a set of cables and use a multimeter to test them. After completing this lab, you will be able to:

- Identify two CAT-5e or CAT-6 wiring systems
- Test cables with a multimeter
- Draw pinouts for cable connectors
- Determine whether a cable is a patch cable (also known as a straight-through cable) or a crossover cable
- Visually inspect cables and connectors

MATERIALS REQUIRED

This lab requires the following:

- A variety of cables, including a patch cable and a crossover cable
- A multimeter
- Internet access
- Access to a printer (optional)

LAB PREPARATION

Before the lab begins, the instructor or lab assistant needs to do the following:

- Verify that Internet access is available

ACTIVITY BACKGROUND

For a network connection to function properly, the cables must be wired correctly and have no defects. In this lab, you physically inspect cables and the connector and then test the cable's pinouts and continuity using a multimeter.

ESTIMATED COMPLETION TIME: 45 MINUTES

 Activity

1. The two wiring standards for a patch cable or crossover cable are T568A and T568B. Go to **lanshack.com** or other websites and search for CAT-5e or CAT-6 wiring diagrams for each standard. Which website did you use?

   _____

2. For both wiring schemes, use separate sheets of paper to print or draw a pinout diagram for a patch cable and a crossover cable.

Follow these steps to visually inspect cables:

1. Examine the length of the cable for obvious damage, such as a cut or abrasion in the outer sleeve with further damage to the twisted pairs inside. A completely cut strand is an obvious problem, but the conductor inside the cable might be broken even if the insulator is intact. Any visible copper is an indication you need a new cable.

2. Inspect the RJ-45 connectors. In particular, look for exposed twisted pairs between the clear plastic connector and the cable sleeve or jacket. This indicates that the cable was assembled improperly or excessive force was used when pulling on the cable. The cable sleeve should be crimped inside the RJ-45 connector. Sometimes you can identify a nonconforming wiring scheme by noting the color of the insulation through the clear connector, but you should check the cable with a multimeter to verify its condition.

3. Next, verify that the retaining clip on the connector is present. When an assembled cable is pulled, this clip often snags on carpet or other cables and breaks off. This results in a connector that's likely to become loose or fall out of the jack. Worse still, this connection might be intermittent. Some cables have boots to prevent the clip from snagging when pulled, but these boots can cause problems when seating the connector in the jack if the boot has slid too far toward the end of the cable.

4. Test your cables with a multimeter, and fill in Table 8-1. For each cable, you need to identify which pin at one end of a cable connects to which pin at the other end of the cable. To do so, you use the multimeter to systematically determine continuity between pins. For example, start with pin 1 of cable 1. First record the insulator color for this pin. Then check for continuity between it and each of the pins at the other end of the cable. Which pin connects to pin 1? Record that information (insulator color and pin position) in the first row of the table. Then continue to the other pins and cables until the table is completed. What settings on the multimeter did you use when testing the cables?

		End A		End B		Questions About the Cable
	Pin #	Insulator Color	Pin Tied to Pin at End B	Insulator Color	Pin Tied to Pin at End A	Is the cable good or bad?
Cable 1	1					
	2					Wired with what scheme?
	3					
	4					
	5					Is the cable a crossover or patch cable?
	6					
	7					
	8					

Table 8-1 Pin connections for selected cables (continues)

	End A		End B		Questions About the Cable
Pin #	**Insulator Color**	**Pin Tied to Pin at End B**	**Insulator Color**	**Pin Tied to Pin at End A**	**Is the cable good or bad?**
1					
2					**Wired with what scheme?**
3					
4					
5					**Is the cable a crossover or patch cable?**
6					
7					
8					
Pin #	**Insulator Color**	**Pin Tied to Pin at End B**	**Insulator Color**	**Pin Tied to Pin at End A**	**Is the cable good or bad?**
1					
2					**Wired with what scheme?**
3					
4					
5					**Is the cable a crossover or patch cable?**
6					
7					
8					

Cable 2 (rows 1–8, top section) · *Cable 3* (rows 1–8, bottom section)

Table 8-1 Pin connections for selected cables

REVIEW QUESTIONS

1. If you can see a copper conductor in a cable, what should you do with the cable?

2. What type of connector is used with CAT-5e and CAT-6 cables?

3. Based on your research, which cabling scheme is more common: straight-through or crossover?

4. On a patch cable, pin 3 on one end connects to pin _____ on the other end of the cable.

5. On a crossover cable, pin 2 on one end connects to pin _____ on the other end of the cable.

LAB 8.2 COMPARE OPTIONS FOR A SMALL OFFICE OR HOME OFFICE LAN

OBJECTIVES

The goal of this lab is to research the costs and capabilities of upgrading wired and wireless home local area networks (LANs). After completing this lab, you will be able to:

▲ Research wired and wireless Ethernet

▲ Research 802.11 standards

▲ Identify components to build the network

MATERIALS REQUIRED

This lab requires the following:

▲ Internet access

LAB PREPARATION

Before the lab begins, the instructor or lab assistant needs to do the following:

▲ Verify that Internet access is available

ACTIVITY BACKGROUND

As the prices of equipment and computers fall, installing a home LAN has become increasingly popular. SOHO (small office or home office) is a term that often refers to a virtual office, which has many of the same components as a brick-and-mortar office, such as computer and communication equipment to provide data storage and support device sharing. Even though a SOHO tends to be relatively small in scope, it still demands sophisticated software and networking hardware to support a variety of office applications and functions. In this lab, you research wireless and wired Ethernet and determine which option is better in a SOHO environment.

ESTIMATED COMPLETION TIME: 30 MINUTES

 Activity

Search the web to investigate and answer the following questions about wireless LAN standards:

1. The current Wi-Fi wireless standard is 802.11ac. Answer the following questions about this standard compared with Ethernet wired standards:

   ▲ What is the theoretical throughput of 802.11ac?

   _____

   ▲ What is the theoretical range of 802.11ac?

   _____

   ▲ What frequency does 802.11ac use?

   _____

◢ What is an advantage of the frequency used by 802.11ac on a network?

_____

_____

◢ Why might a wireless router have two or more antennas rather than just one?

_____

_____

◢ What is the speed of 802.11n wireless?

_____

◢ What is the speed of Fast Ethernet?

_____

◢ What is the speed of Gigabit Ethernet?

_____

◢ How does the speed of 802.11ac compare with the speed of 802.11n?

_____

◢ How does the speed of 802.11ac compare with the speed of Fast Ethernet?

_____

◢ How does the speed of 802.11ac compare with the speed of Gigabit Ethernet?

_____

2. In a small office, there are five computers, a network printer, and a broadband connection to the Internet. What devices are needed to set up a wired network for these five computers, the network printer, and the broadband connection?

_____

_____

_____

_____

3. Which device connects wireless users to a wired network?

_____

4. What is the function of a router?

_____

_____

_____

5. Search the web to find two routers that could be used to build your SOHO Gigabit Ethernet network, and list their distinguishing characteristics and prices:

Router #1:

_____

_____

Router #2:

_____

_____

6. If a computer in the home office doesn't have Gigabit Ethernet, how would you add that feature?

_____

7. Research and find two Gigabit Ethernet network adapter interface cards that you could add to a workstation. Include key features and prices:

Adapter # 1:

_____

_____

Adapter # 2:

_____

_____

8. Research and find two USB wireless Wi-Fi adapters that you could add to a workstation. List the key features and prices:

Adapter # 1:

_____

_____

Adapter # 2:

_____

_____

9. If you were to include in a home office setup a laptop that has an onboard Fast Ethernet port, how could you upgrade to Gigabit Ethernet?

_____

_____

10. Research and find two Gigabit Ethernet upgrades for your laptop. List key characteristics and prices:

   Adapter # 1:

   _____

   _____

   Adapter # 2:

   _____

   _____

11. What happens to the connection speed if you connect your laptop or workstation with Fast Ethernet to a Gigabit Ethernet router?

   _____

12. Based on the previous question, in order to get the fastest connection speed between routers and computers, how must the devices be set up?

   _____

13. In a wired network, you will need cables to connect the devices. What cabling standard is needed to upgrade to a Gigabit Ethernet network?

   _____

14. Does this cabling standard require different RJ-45 connectors? Why?

   _____

15. Research and find Gigabit Ethernet 25-foot network cables. Record the source and price:

   _____

16. A home office in a medium-sized room has the following setup:
    ◢ One desktop computer with a Fast Ethernet NIC
    ◢ One desktop computer with a Gigabit Ethernet NIC
    ◢ One laptop with a Fast Ethernet NIC
    ◢ Gigabit router with four ports; compliant with the 802.11n standard
    ◢ All-in-one wireless printer that has a USB connection and an onboard Fast Ethernet NIC

   Your mission is to upgrade the setup to Gigabit Ethernet for the fastest network connection speed (without using fiber optics). From your research in the preceding steps, list the components you would use along with an approximate total price of the upgrade:

   _____

   _____

   _____

   _____

   Total price: _____

REVIEW QUESTIONS

1. What is the least expensive way to connect five computers using a wired network to a router that has only four network ports?

   _____

2. Theoretically, which is faster: the current Wi-Fi standard or Gigabit Ethernet (1000BaseT)? What real-world issues might affect actual speeds for each technology?

   _____

   _____

   _____

3. What is the name for a cable that connects a computer to another computer to create a two-node network?

   _____

4. What determines the speed of devices on a LAN that consists of both 100-Mbps and 1000-Mbps devices?

   _____

5. Could you combine a wireless and wired LAN in the same home? Why would you?

   _____

   _____

   _____

8

LAB 8.3 CREATE A STRAIGHT-THROUGH CABLE

OBJECTIVES

The goal of this lab is to create a straight-through cable (also called a patch cable). After completing this lab, you will be able to:

⬢ Identify the color scheme for T568A and T568B wiring

⬢ Understand the process of crimping cables

⬢ Identify the tools needed to create a straight-through cable

⬢ Create a cable and test it using a cable tester

MATERIALS REQUIRED

This lab requires the following:

⬢ One meter of CAT-5 cable

⬢ Up to eight RJ-45 connectors

⬢ Wire cutter or electrician snips

◢ Wire-stripping tool

◢ Crimping tool

◢ Cable tester

LAB PREPARATION

Before the lab begins, the instructor or lab assistant needs to do the following:

◢ Verify that CAT-5 cable is available

◢ Verify that RJ-45 connectors are available

◢ Verify that wire cutters or electrician snips are available

◢ Verify that a wire-stripping tool is available

◢ Verify that a wire crimper is available

◢ Verify that a cable tester is available

ACTIVITY BACKGROUND

Industry standards have been established to make sure that everyone who deals with the same type of technology can ensure interconnectivity. You can think of standards as agreements by which everyone abides. The Electronics Industries Alliance (EIA) began the work of developing standards for telecommunications cabling and later turned the job over to the Telecommunications Industry Association (TIA), which currently develops voluntary, consensus-based industry standards for a variety of situations used in communication and information technology (IT) applications. (The areas of IT that apply to communication are sometimes called the information and communication technology [ICT] segment of IT.) One set of TIA standards applies to network and telecommunications cabling standards for commercial buildings. The wiring standards that govern wiring category (CAT) cable or patch cable are referred to as EIA/TIA-568. There are two types of wiring standards: T568A and T568B. These standards outline the wiring scheme for RJ-45 connectors and wall jacks. For commercial applications, the most common wiring scheme is T568B. In government buildings, the most common wiring scheme is T568A.

As an IT support technician, you need to know how to create, repair, and test the different types of cables used to connect computers, switches, routers, and other network devices using both the T568B and T568A standards.

ESTIMATED COMPLETION TIME: 40 MINUTES

 Activity

Having the right cable for the job is essential. A straight-through cable is used to connect a computer to a switch, hub, or router, or to connect a printer, switch, or hub to a router. Both ends of a straight-through cable are terminated the same way, in agreement with either the T568A or T568B standard. Table 8-2 shows the T568A standard, and Table 8-3 shows the T568B standard.

RJ-45 Pin Number	Wire Color (T568A)
1	White/green
2	Green
3	White/orange
4	Blue
5	White/blue
6	Orange
7	White/brown
8	Brown

Table 8-2   T568A wiring standard for a network cable

RJ-45 Pin Number	Wire Color (T568B)
1	White/orange
2	Orange
3	White/green
4	Blue
5	White/blue
6	Green
7	White/brown
8	Brown

Table 8-3   T568B wiring standard for a network cable

> **Notes** To make this lab easier, go to *youtube.com* and then search for and watch a video on "how to make a network patch cable."

To create a straight-through cable using the T568B standard, follow these steps:

1. Cut the desired length of the CAT-5 cable plus six or eight extra inches (needed for trimming).

2. Use wire strippers to strip away about two inches of the plastic jacket from one end of the cable. The four twisted pairs of the cable are exposed.

3. Use wire cutters to start a cut into the jacket. Then pull the rip cord up into the cut, and rip back about two inches of the jacket (see Figure 8-1). Cut off this extra jacket and the rip cord. You take this extra precaution in case you nicked the insulation around a wire when you were using the wire strippers.

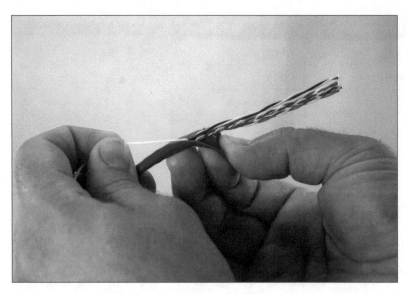

Figure 8-1   Rip back the jacket, and then cut off the extra jacket and rip cord

4. Separate each wire from its pair, and extend the wires away from each other.

5. Straighten each wire as much as possible by stretching it out and smoothing it between your fingers.

6. Grip the base of the white/orange wire with your left thumb and index finger (reverse if you are left-handed), and use your right hand to extend the wire, stretching it out until it is perfectly straight.

7. Continue to hold the white/orange wire from the base, and bring the orange wire into your grip.

8. Continue to hold the previous two wires, and bring the white/green wire into your grip. Wiggle the three wires up and down and side to side to get them as close together as possible.

9. Continue to hold the previous three wires, and bring the blue wire into your grip. Wiggle the wires up and down and side to side to get them as close together as possible.

10. Continue to hold the previous four wires, and bring the white/blue wire into your grip, wiggling the wires up and down and side to side to get them as close together as possible.

11. Continue to hold the previous five wires, and bring the green wire into your grip, wiggling the wires up and down and side to side to get them as close together as possible.

12. Continue to hold the previous six wires, and bring the white/brown wire into your grip. Wiggle the seven wires up and down and side to side to get them as close together as possible.

13. Continue to hold the previous seven wires, and bring the brown wire into your grip, wiggling the wires up and down and side to side to get them as close together as possible.

14. Holding the wires in a flat and straight position, cut the wires about half an inch away from the insulation. You can judge the exact length by holding the RJ-45 connector up to the wires. You want to leave enough jacket to go inside the connector. See Figure 8-2.

Figure 8-2   Evenly cut off wires measured to fit in the RJ-45 connector with the
jacket protruding into the connector

8

15. Hold the RJ-45 connector with the clip toward the bottom, and insert the wires into the connector. Push the wires all the way to the front of the connector, making sure that you can see the ends of the wires touch the plastic at the front of the connector. Also make sure the cable jacket goes into the back of the connector far enough so that when you crimp it, the plastic wedge can put pressure on the jacket to help hold the cable in place.

16. Insert the RJ-45 connector into the RJ-45 hole on the crimping tool. Use one hand to push the cable into the hole while you use the other hand to crimp the connector. See Figure 8-3. After the cable is partially crimped, you can use both hands to apply more force and completely crimp the connector.

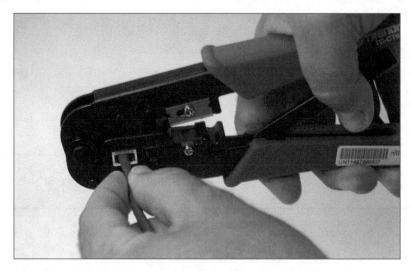

Figure 8-3   Use the crimper to crimp the connector to the cable

17. Remove the cable from the crimper. Use moderate (not too strong) force to try to pull the connector off the cable, and make sure it is solidly crimped. If the connector comes off the cable, throw it away and try again.

18. Examine the connector, which should look like the one in Figure 8-4.

▲ Do you see the crimp holding the cable jacket securely?

_____

▲ Do you see the eight wires pierced through with eight blades near the front of the connector?

_____

▲ Do you see the eight wires each in their correct positions at the end of the connector?

_____

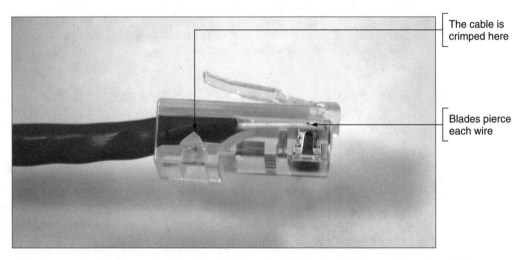

The cable is crimped here

Blades pierce each wire

Figure 8-4   The crimper crimps the cable, and the eight blades pierce the jacket of each individual copper wire

19. Repeat the process on the other end of the cable.

20. Test the cable using a cable tester. If the cable does not pass the test, carefully examine each connector to decide which one is bad. Cut the bad connector off the cable, and try again with a new connector.

▲ Did the cable tester show that the cable was made correctly?

_____

▲ What indicator did the tool use to let you know the cable was correctly wired?

_____

21. Wiring jobs can create a mess. Take a few minutes to clean up. Be sure to save your first network cable as a souvenir!

Suppose a client requires 20 network cables that are each 10 feet long. Follow these steps to compare the prices of making the network cables versus buying ready-made cables:

1. Don't forget to include extra wiring and connectors, which are needed when making cables. Using the web, search for these prices:

▲ The price of 220 feet of CAT-5e network cabling:

_____

◢ The price of 40 or more RJ-45 connectors and boots:

_____

◢ The price of 20 straight-through cables that are each 10 feet long:

_____

2. Calculate and compare the prices:
   ◢ For one handmade 10-foot cable:

_____

   ◢ For one ready-made 10-foot cable:

_____

   ◢ For this cable job, which is less expensive: handmade network cables or ready-made cables?

_____

REVIEW QUESTIONS

1. What is the difference in typical usage between T568A and T568B standards?

_____

_____

2. What is TIA, and what is it responsible for?

_____

_____

3. Which devices can be connected using a straight-through cable?

_____

_____

4. What is the color scheme for T568B wiring?

_____

5. Why is it advisable to rip back the jacket and cut it from the cable even after you have already stripped the jacket?

_____

6. What was the most difficult part of this lab as you created a straight-through cable?

_____

LAB 8.4 CREATE A CROSSOVER CABLE

OBJECTIVES

The goal of this lab is to create a crossover cable. After completing this lab, you will be able to:

▲ Identify the color scheme for T568A and T568B wiring

▲ Understand the process of crimping cables

▲ Create a crossover cable

▲ Test a cable

MATERIALS REQUIRED

This lab requires the following:

▲ One meter of CAT-5 cable

▲ Up to eight RJ-45 connectors

▲ Wire cutter or electrician snips

▲ Wire-stripping tool

▲ Crimping tool

▲ Cable tester

LAB PREPARATION

Before the lab begins, the instructor or lab assistant needs to do the following:

▲ Verify that CAT-5 cable is available

▲ Verify that RJ-45 connectors are available

▲ Verify that wire cutters or electrician snips are available

▲ Verify that wire strippers are available

▲ Verify that a wire crimper is available

▲ Verify that a cable tester is available

ACTIVITY BACKGROUND

As with straight-through CAT cable, industry standards exist for crossover cables. A crossover cable is wired differently than a straight-through cable, and its transmit and receive lines are reversed so that one device receives from the line to which the other device transmits. Crossover cables were once required when using Fast Ethernet to connect a hub to a hub or a switch to a switch. Using Gigabit Ethernet, straight-through cables can be used for these connections because Gigabit switches use auto-uplinking. With auto-uplinking, a device automatically switches between transmit and receive on the same wire as needed to communicate with the other device. Today, a crossover cable is mostly used when you want to connect two computers in the simplest network of all. A crossover cable for Fast Ethernet is wired differently than a crossover cable for Gigabit Ethernet.

For Fast Ethernet, if you use T568A wiring on one end of the cable and T568B on the other end of the cable, you have a crossover cable (see Figure 8-5A). For Gigabit Ethernet that transmits data on all four pairs, you must cross not only the green and orange pairs, but also the blue and brown pairs to make a crossover cable (see Figure 8-5B).

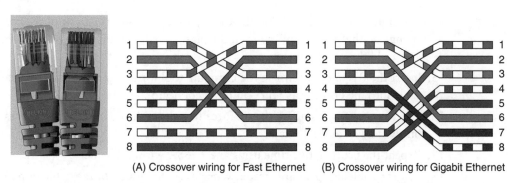

(A) Crossover wiring for Fast Ethernet   (B) Crossover wiring for Gigabit Ethernet

Figure 8-5 (A) Two crossed pairs in a crossover cable compatible with Fast Ethernet; (B) four crossed pairs in a crossover cable compatible with Gigabit Ethernet

It will be useful to you to know how to create, repair, and test the different types of cables used to connect computers, switches, routers, and other network devices.

ESTIMATED COMPLETION TIME: 40 MINUTES

 Activity

A crossover cable for Fast Ethernet has a T568A termination on one end and a T568B termination on the other. Refer to Tables 8-2 and 8-3 for the T568A and T568B wiring standards, respectively.

> **Notes** To make this lab easier, go to *youtube.com* and then search for and watch a video on "how to make a network crossover cable."

To create a Fast Ethernet crossover cable, first wire one end using the T568B standard as follows:

1. Cut the desired length of the CAT-5 cable, plus a few inches.

2. Choose one end of the cable, and strip away about two inches of the jacket to expose the four pairs of cables.

3. Start a cut into the jacket, and use the rip cord to pull back about two inches of the jacket. Cut off the extra jacket and rip cord.

4. Separate each wire from its pair and extend the wires away from each other. Extend the wires straight by stretching them out as much as possible.

5. Using the method you learned in the previous lab, grip the white/orange wire from the base with your left thumb and index finger (reverse if you are left-handed), and use your right hand to extend the wire straight.

6. Continue to hold the white/orange wire from the base, and bring the orange wire into your grip.

7. Bring the white/green wire into your grip.

8. Bring the blue wire into your grip.

9. Bring the white/blue wire into your grip.

10. Bring the green wire into your grip.

11. Bring the white/brown wire into your grip.

12. Bring the brown wire into your grip.

13. Holding the wires in a straight position, cut the wires about half an inch away from the end of the insulation.

14. Hold the RJ-45 connector with the clip toward the bottom, and insert the wires into the connector, making sure that you can see the copper touch the plastic inside the front of

the connector. Make sure that the cable jacket goes into the back of the connector far enough so that when you crimp it, the plastic wedge can put pressure on the jacket to help hold the cable in place.

15. Insert the RJ-45 connector in the crimping tool for the appropriate connector. Push the cable into the crimper as you crimp the connector.

16. Test the crimp by using moderate force to pull on the connector. If it comes off the cable, throw it away and try again.

17. Repeat the process, this time using the T568A wiring scheme.

18. Test the cable using a cable tester. What were the results of the cable tester?

_____

A Gigabit Ethernet crossover cable has four pairs of wires crossed. Do the following to create a Gigabit Ethernet crossover cable:

1. Fill in the following chart to show the color for each pin on each end of this type of cable:

Pin	Color for End 1	Color for End 2
1		
2		
3		
4		
5		
6		
7		
8		

2. Create the Gigabit Ethernet crossover cable.

3. Test the cable with a cable tester.

   ◢ What indicator did the tool use to let you know the cable was correctly wired?

_____

4. Wiring jobs can create a mess. Take a few minutes to clean up.

REVIEW QUESTIONS

1. Which wires get switched by wiring one end as T68A and the other end as T568B? What type of crossover cable is created using this wiring scheme?

_____

_____

2. How many pairs of wires get switched when making a Gigabit Ethernet crossover cable? Which wires are switched?

_____

_____

_____

3. Which devices can be connected using a crossover cable?

   _____

4. Which step was the most difficult when creating a crossover cable?

   _____

5. What is the wiring scheme for the T568A standard?

   _____

LAB 8.5 SET UP ADVANCED IP SCANNER AND WAKE-ON-LAN

OBJECTIVES

The goal of this lab is to set up and use Advanced IP Scanner to remotely power on a computer. After completing this lab, you will be able to:

- Set up Wake-on-LAN
- Remotely power on a computer

MATERIALS REQUIRED

This lab requires the following:

- Windows 10/8/7 workstation with Wake-on-LAN feature
- Internet access
- Two or more computers on the same wired network (not wireless)

LAB PREPARATION

Before the lab begins, the instructor or lab assistant needs to do the following:

- Set up a simple network with two or more computers
- Provide Internet access in the lab, or provide students with the Advanced IP Scanner utility
- Verify that the Wake-on-LAN feature can be enabled on one or more machines

ACTIVITY BACKGROUND

Often, a technician needs to be able to identify and control machines on a network. Modern motherboards often have a Wake-on-LAN feature, which enables a technician to control a machine without having to be at the machine. This increases the efficiency of managing machines and decreases the time needed to complete support activities.

ESTIMATED COMPLETION TIME: 30 MINUTES

 Activity

Follow these steps to set up Wake-on-LAN:

1. Select one of the lab machines to use as a test for the Wake-on-LAN feature.

2. Boot the machine and enter its BIOS/UEFI setup.

3. In BIOS/UEFI, locate and enable the Wake-on-LAN feature. Save the setting change and reboot the machine.

4. Record the IP address of the machine by opening a command prompt window and issuing the **ipconfig /all** command.

Write down the IP address: _____

5. Close the command prompt window.

6. Next, you enable Wake-on-LAN in Windows. Open **Control Panel** in Classic view, and click **Network and Sharing Center**.

7. In the left pane, click **Change adapter settings**.

8. Right-click the network adapter for the wired connection, and then click **Properties**.

9. Click **Configure**, and then select the **Power Management** tab.

10. Make sure that the **Allow the computer to turn off this device to save power** option is selected. This enables power management in Windows.

11. Check **Allow this device to wake the computer**.

12. Click **OK**.

Go to another workstation and install the Advanced IP Scanner utility. Follow these steps:

1. Using your web browser, go to **advanced-ip-scanner.com**. Download and install the software utility, **Advanced IP Scanner**.

2. Launch Advanced IP Scanner.

3. After Advanced IP Scanner loads, click the **Scan** button to scan your network. As the scanning progresses, the lower pane shows network devices and machines that the utility discovers. See Figure 8-6.

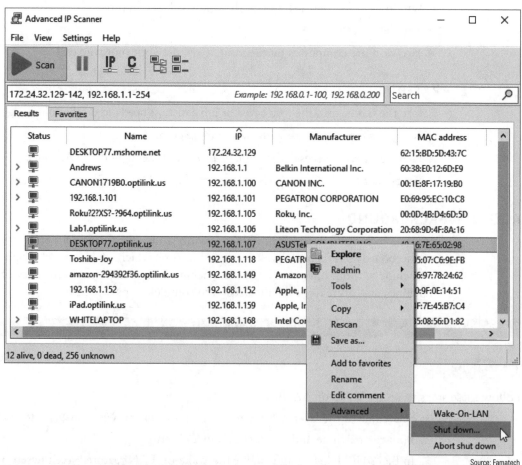

Figure 8-6   Advanced IP Scanner detects devices on a network

4. In the Status column, select one of the machines listed, and expand it to view the contents. You can access shared folders and devices by double-clicking items listed under a machine.

5. Use the IP address information to find and select the machine on which you enabled the Wake-on-LAN feature.

6. Right-click the selected machine, and point to **Advanced** in the shortcut menu. Then click **Shut down**, as shown in Figure 8-6. If needed, provide a user name and password for the remote machine.

   ◢ Did the machine shut down?

   _____

7. Right-click the selected machine again, and point to **Advanced**. Then click **Wake-on-LAN** to send Wake-on-LAN packets.

   ◢ Did the machine boot up?

   _____

8

REVIEW QUESTIONS

1. If you want to turn on a machine remotely, what motherboard feature must be enabled?

   _____

2. When using the scan feature of Advanced IP Scanner, what information does it provide about the network?

   _____

3. As an IT technician in the field, how might you use this utility?

   _____

   _____

4. The Advanced IP Scanner utility has a print function. How can this be useful?

   _____

   _____

LAB 8.6 SABOTAGE AND REPAIR A NETWORK CONNECTION

OBJECTIVES

The goal of this lab is to troubleshoot and remedy common network connectivity problems. After completing this lab, you will be able to:

◢ Diagnose and solve connectivity problems

◢ Document the troubleshooting process

MATERIALS REQUIRED

This lab requires the following:

- Windows 10/8/7 operating system
- A computer connected to a network and to the Internet
- Windows installation DVD or flash drive or installation files
- A computer toolkit with ESD strap
- A workgroup partner

LAB PREPARATION

Before the lab begins, the instructor or lab assistant needs to do the following:

- Verify that Windows starts with no errors
- Provide each student with access to the Windows installation files in case a student needs to repair the Windows installation during the lab

ACTIVITY BACKGROUND

To a casual user, Internet and network connections can be confusing. When users have a connectivity problem, they usually have no idea how to remedy the situation. In this lab, you introduce and solve common connectivity problems.

ESTIMATED COMPLETION TIME: 60 MINUTES

 Activity

1. Verify that your network is working correctly by browsing the network and connecting to a website.
2. Do one of the following:
   - Change your computer's IP address.
   - Change your computer's subnet mask.
   - Remove your computer's network cable.
   - Uninstall TCP/IP from your computer.
   - Uninstall your computer's network adapter in the active connection's properties dialog box.
   - Unseat or remove your computer's NIC, but leave it installed in the active connection's properties dialog box.
   - Disable your computer's NIC in Device Manager.
   - Release your computer's IP address (if DHCP is enabled).
3. Swap computers with your partner, and troubleshoot the network connection on your partner's computer.
4. Answer these questions about the problem you solved (additional paper might be needed):
   - What was the initial symptom of the problem as a user might describe it?

◢ What steps did you take to discover the source of the problem?

_____

_____

◢ What steps did you take to solve the problem?

_____

5. Repeat Steps 1 through 4 until you and your partner have used all the options listed in Step 2. Be sure to answer the questions in Step 4 for each troubleshooting situation.

REVIEW QUESTIONS

1. What type of network connectivity problem can be solved using Device Manager?

_____

_____

2. Which problem (or problems) might require you to reboot the computer after repairing it?

_____

_____

3. When configuring TCP/IP, what two values are necessary for using static IP addressing?

_____

4. What TCP/IP utility was the most useful, in your opinion, for troubleshooting the problems in this lab? Why?

_____

5. Why should you always check for physical problems like unplugged network cables before considering logical problems like missing drivers?

_____

_____

LAB 8.7 UNDERSTAND THE OSI MODEL

OBJECTIVES

The goal of this lab is to understand some of the concepts and principles of networking technology. After completing this lab, you will be able to:

◢ Describe the OSI layers

◢ Apply OSI layer principles to networking

MATERIALS REQUIRED

This lab requires the following:

- ▲ Windows 10/8/7 operating system
- ▲ Internet access

LAB PREPARATION

Before the lab begins, the instructor or lab assistant needs to do the following:

- ▲ Verify that Windows starts with no errors
- ▲ Verify that Internet access is available

ACTIVITY BACKGROUND

Network architects use a variety of principles and concepts for communication when designing and implementing networks. Collectively, this architectural model is called the OSI (Open Systems Interconnection) model. The OSI model consists of seven layers. As an IT support technician, you do not need to understand network architecture. However, you might find it interesting to know a little about these fundamental concepts, which can help you better understand how the TCP/IP protocols work. Understanding these concepts will also help you better communicate with network specialists.

> **ESTIMATED COMPLETION TIME: 30 MINUTES**

 Activity

Using the Internet for your research, answer the following questions:

1. What are the seven OSI layers? Enter their names in the empty boxes on the left side of Table 8-4.

OSI Layer	TCP/IP Protocol Stack Layer
7	**Application layer** (For example, email using SMTP and IMAP protocols)
6	
5	
4	**Transport layer** (TCP protocol)
3	**Internet layer** (IP protocol)
2	**Network interface layer** (Network card using Ethernet protocol)
1	

Table 8-4   Describing the OSI model and the TCP/IP model

2. The OSI model is easier to understand if you memorize the seven layers. You can use a phrase mnemonic, in which the beginning letter of each layer is used to create a memorable phrase, to help you with this task. Research online for a mnemonic to help you memorize the OSI layers, and record it here:

   _____

3. TCP/IP is a suite of protocols that follow the concepts of the OSI model. The four layers of the TCP/IP model are shown on the right side of Table 8-4. Email is one example of a TCP/IP application that works at the Application layer. What are two more examples of applications that work at this layer?

   _____

4. The TCP protocol works at the Transport layer of TCP/IP. Briefly describe the function of the TCP protocol as used in Internet communications:

   _____

   _____

5. The IP protocol, working at the Internet layer, is responsible for locating the network and host for a data packet being transmitted by TCP. What type of address does the IP protocol use to identify a unique network and host?

   _____

6. Other than a network card (NIC), what is an example of a device that works at the Network layer of the TCP/IP stack?

   _____

7. Other than IP, what is an example of a protocol that works at the Internet layer of TCP/IP?

   _____

8. At which TCP/IP layer does a MAC address function?

   _____

9. At which TCP/IP layer does the TLS protocol work?

   _____

10. At which TCP/IP layer does the SNMP protocol work?

    _____

11. Why do you think TCP/IP is often called a protocol stack rather than a protocol suite?

    _____

    _____

8

REVIEW QUESTIONS

1. What mnemonic can you use to help you remember the seven OSI layers?

_____

2. List all of the OSI layers used when an email client requests email over the Internet.

_____

3. What protocol does a web browser normally use? At which OSI layer does this protocol work?

_____

4. When more than one application is running on a server, how does IP know which service should be presented an incoming data packet?

_____

5. When configuring a network connection to the Internet, you might need to enter the IP address of the computer, the DNS server, the subnet mask, and the default gateway. Of these four items, which are used to determine whether a remote computer is on the same network or a remote network?

_____

6. Of the four items listed in Question 5, which is used to relate a domain name to an IP address?

_____

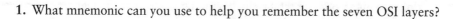

LAB 8.8 CONVERT BINARY AND HEXADECIMAL NUMBERS

OBJECTIVES

The goal of this lab is to practice converting numbers between decimal, binary, and hexadecimal forms. After completing this lab, you will be able to:

▲ Convert decimal numbers (base 10) to hexadecimal and binary form

▲ Convert hexadecimal numbers (base 16) to binary and decimal form

▲ Convert binary numbers (base 2) to decimal and hexadecimal form

MATERIALS REQUIRED

This lab requires the following:

▲ A pencil and paper and/or Windows Calculator

▲ Access to the online content "The Hexadecimal Number System" that accompanies this lab manual; for instructions on how to access this content at *cengage.com*, see the Preface.

▲ Windows 10/8/7 computer

LAB PREPARATION

Before the lab begins, the instructor or lab assistant needs to do the following:

▲ Announce to students that, before they come to the lab, they should read the online content "The Hexadecimal Number System." It is also suggested that students bring this content to class in printed form.

ACTIVITY BACKGROUND

IPv4 addresses are displayed and written in decimal and often need to be converted to binary. In addition, IPv6 addresses are written and displayed in hex, and you often need to write them in binary or decimal. It's also interesting to know that MAC addresses are displayed in hex.

As an IT support technician, you are likely to encounter the need to convert numbers from one number system to another, such as when you are comparing an IP address with a subnet mask in order to decide if the IP address is in a particular subnet. This lab gives you that practice.

ESTIMATED COMPLETION TIME: 60 MINUTES

8

 Activity

Follow these steps to practice converting numbers from one number system to another:

1. Convert the following decimal numbers to binary numbers using a calculator or by following the instructions in the online content "The Hexadecimal Number System." (To access Windows Calculator, enter **calculator** in the Windows 10/7 search box or the Windows 8 Run box. If necessary, click **View** on the Calculator menu bar, and then click **Programmer** to access the function you need to perform the conversions in these steps.)

   ▲ 14 = _____

   ▲ 77 = _____

   ▲ 128 = _____

   ▲ 223 = _____

   ▲ 255 = _____

2. Convert the following decimal numbers to hexadecimal notation:

   ▲ 13 = _____

   ▲ 240 = _____

   ▲ 255 = _____

   ▲ 58880 = _____

   ▲ 65535 = _____

3. Convert the following binary numbers to hexadecimal notation:

   ▲ 100 = _____

   ▲ 1011 = _____

   ▲ 0011 1101 = _____

   ▲ 1111 1000 = _____

   ▲ 1011 0011 = _____

   ▲ 0000 0001 = _____

4. Hexadecimal numbers are often preceded by "0x." However, when converting a hexadecimal number, do not include the "0x" in the entry on the calculator. Convert the following hexadecimal numbers to binary numbers:

◢ 0x0016 = _____

◢ 0x00F8 = _____

◢ 0x00B2B = _____

◢ 0x005A = _____

◢ 0x1234 = _____

5. Convert the following hexadecimal numbers to decimal:

◢ 0x0013 = _____

◢ 0x00AB = _____

◢ 0x01CE = _____

◢ 0x812A = _____

6. Convert the following binary numbers to decimal:

◢ 1011 = _____

◢ 0001 1011 = _____

◢ 1010 1010 = _____

◢ 0001 1111 0100 = _____

◢ 0101 1101 1101 = _____

◢ 0011 1110 0000 1111 = _____

A network card, also called a network adapter or NIC, is assigned a MAC address (or physical address) at the factory. Windows assigns to a network connection an IPv4 address, a subnet mask, and possibly an IPv6 address each time the connection is created. In the following steps, you find these assigned values for your computer and then convert them to binary numbers:

1. Open a command prompt window, and enter the **ipconfig /all** command.

2. Write down the following information for your system's active network connection (most likely either Ethernet or Wi-Fi):

◢ What is the physical address in paired hexadecimal form?

_____

◢ Convert the physical address to binary pairs:

_____

◢ What is the IPv4 address in decimal form?

_____

◢ Convert the IPv4 address to four octets in binary form:

_____

◢ What is the subnet mask in decimal form?

_____

◢ Convert the subnet mask to four octets in binary form:

_____

◢ What is the IPv6 address expressed as eight blocks of hexadecimal numbers (some of these blocks might contain a zero)?

_____

◢ Convert the IPv6 address in hex to eight blocks of binary numbers:

_____

_____

Memory addresses are displayed in hexadecimal form. Do the following to find out the memory address range assigned to the NIC on your computer, and then convert this range to decimal:

1. Open **Device Manager**, and then open the **Properties** dialog box for the network adapter. Click the **Resources** tab. What are the memory address ranges for the NIC?

_____

_____

2. Convert the numbers in the network adapter's memory ranges, and determine how many bytes, expressed as a decimal number, are in each memory address range:

_____

_____

ESTIMATED COMPLETION TIME: 15 MINUTES

CHALLENGE ACTIVITY

1. A typical video card uses a color depth of 8 bits to define the screen color in Safe Mode in Windows. Eight bits can form 256 different numbers from 00000000 to 11111111 in binary (0 to 255 in decimal), so 256 different colors are possible. How many colors are available with a 16-bit color depth? How many are available with a 24-bit or a 32-bit depth?

_____

_____

_____

REVIEW QUESTIONS

1. How long, in bits, is a typical MAC address?

_____

2. Computers often express numbers in _____ format, which is a base 16 number system.

3. Most people are more comfortable working with a(n) _____, or base 10, number system.

4. In the hexadecimal system, what decimal value does the letter A represent?

_____

5. Hexadecimal numbers are often preceded by _____ so that a value containing only numerals is not mistaken for a decimal number.

6. Write the following IPv6 address using a shorthand method:
   2001:0:4147:0:0:1c32:0:fe99

   _____

7. The IP address of Computer 1 is 192.168.200.10, and it has a subnet mask of 255.255.240.0. The IP address of Computer 2 is 192.168.195.200, and the IP address of Computer 3 is 192.168.230.40.

   a. How many bits of the IP address for Computer 1 are used to define its subnet?

   _____

   b. Are Computer 1 and Computer 2 part of the same subnet? Explain your answer.

   _____

   _____

   _____

   c. Are Computer 1 and Computer 3 part of the same subnet? Explain your answer.

   _____

   _____

   _____

CHAPTER 9

Supporting Mobile Devices

Labs included in this chapter:

- **Lab 9.1:** Research the Latest Smartphones

- **Lab 9.2:** Research Android Apps and Use Dropbox

- **Lab 9.3:** Explore How Android Apps Are Developed and Tested

- **Lab 9.4:** Configure Email and Dropbox on Mobile Devices

- **Lab 9.5:** Research Xcode and the iOS Simulator

- **Lab 9.6:** Create a Smart Home IoT Network in Packet Tracer

LAB 9.1 RESEARCH THE LATEST SMARTPHONES

OBJECTIVES

The goal of this lab is to explore the similarities and differences among iOS, Android, and Windows smartphones. Understanding the characteristics of different smartphones can help you make wise purchasing decisions for yourself or on behalf of a client. After completing this lab, you will be able to:

▲ Research different types of smartphones

▲ Summarize and compare the major features and capabilities of an Android, iOS, and Windows smartphone

MATERIALS REQUIRED

This lab requires the following:

▲ Windows 10/8/7 computer

▲ Internet access

LAB PREPARATION

Before the lab begins, the instructor or lab assistant needs to do the following:

▲ Verify that Windows starts with no errors

▲ Verify that Internet access is available

ACTIVITY BACKGROUND

Smartphones are becoming more available and more accessibly priced every day. New smartphones are constantly being released, so when you are ready to upgrade your phone, you need to do research to find the best option available to meet your needs. In addition, as a support technician, you will likely be called on to help a client decide which technology to purchase. Therefore, you need to be familiar with the technologies and options a client might want or need.

Deciding factors to consider when selecting your own smartphone or presenting options to a client are brand, capabilities, features, support provided by a manufacturer or apps vendor, and price. In this lab, you research iOS, Android, and Windows smartphones.

ESTIMATED COMPLETION TIME: 30 MINUTES

 Activity

In this lab, you research specifications for three different smartphones for comparison:

1. Use the Internet to research one example of a smartphone for each of the mobile operating systems named at the top of Table 9-1. You might find these phones on the manufacturers' websites or on service provider websites. Use the table to record the specifications for each of the smartphones.

Specification	Android	iOS	Windows
Brand or manufacturer			
Model			
Price			
Version of OS installed			
Processor			
Types of network connections			
Storage capacity			
Screen size			
Screen resolution			
Camera pixels			
Website for cloud storage and app purchases			
Amount of free cloud storage			
Unique features			

Table 9-1   Fill in the specifications for three smartphones

2. Use the Internet to research reviews for each of the phones that you selected in Step 1. Record the highlights of those reviews, as detailed in the following list:

◢ Android advantages:

_____

_____

◢ Android disadvantages:

_____

_____

◢ iOS advantages:

_____

_____

◢ iOS disadvantages:

_____

_____

9

◢ Windows advantages:

_____

_____

◢ Windows disadvantages:

_____

_____

3. Close all open windows.

REVIEW QUESTIONS

1. Assume that you are in the market to buy a new smartphone. Which of the smartphones you researched would you purchase? Why would you choose this smartphone over the other two?

_____

2. What are some methods service providers use to offer lower prices on the devices they sell?

_____

_____

3. Some smartphones provide more flexible options for updating hardware than others. Of the smartphones you researched, which (if any) allow for the battery to be replaced?

_____

4. Other than the criteria given in this lab, what criteria might influence which smartphone you would purchase?

_____

_____

5. Give two reasons why you should research information about related apps and app stores when deciding which smartphone to buy:

_____

_____

LAB 9.2 RESEARCH ANDROID APPS AND USE DROPBOX

OBJECTIVES

The goals of this lab are to research and compare Android apps and to explore how to sync data between two sources using an Android app. This exploration is useful because, as an A+-certified technician, you will be expected to know how to service Android mobile devices and the apps installed on them. This service includes knowing how to sync data between two sources and back up data on an Android device. Android offers many data sync options to choose from, including the very popular Dropbox app. After completing this lab, you will be able to:

- Use the Google Play Store to research apps for Android devices
- Find additional information on apps using other resources
- Install Dropbox, an Android-compatible app, on your computer
- Sync data between two sources using Dropbox

MATERIALS REQUIRED

This lab requires the following:

- Windows 10/8/7 computer
- An account with administrator privileges
- Internet access
- Email account
- Email addresses for your instructor and a classmate

LAB PREPARATION

Before the lab begins, the instructor or lab assistant needs to do the following:

- Verify that Windows starts with no errors
- Verify that each student has access to a user account with administrator privileges
- Verify that Internet access is working
- Verify that Dropbox is not already installed

ACTIVITY BACKGROUND

Because Android is open source software, Android-compatible apps are available from many different developers. It's not unusual to find several apps that do essentially the same tasks. Some developers produce excellent apps, and some produce only mediocre ones. Therefore, research is important in finding the best app for the job.

Most Android apps are available through the Google Play Store (*play.google.com/store/apps*), as shown in Figure 9-1, and this is a central location for information about those apps. Each app listed contains information on what access privileges the app needs, who the developer is, how much memory the app requires, and what other users think of the app. The five-star rating system and the user reviews provide a wealth of feedback on the functionality and performance of apps, including how to address problems with the app features or installation.

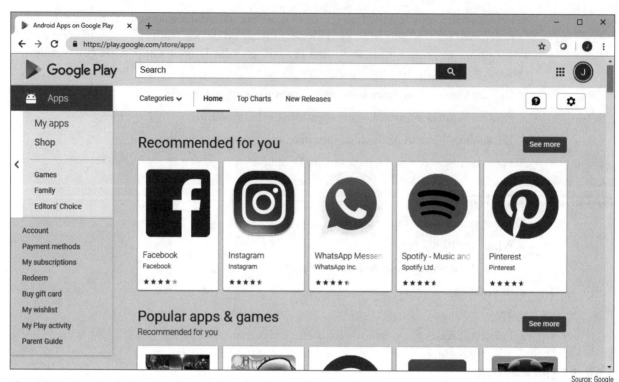

Figure 9-1   The Google Play Store is one of the many sources for Android apps

Source: Google

One widely used file-sharing program available for Android is Dropbox. You can install Dropbox on nearly any current Windows, macOS, Linux, or Android device, and share files between all those devices. Files saved in your Dropbox account are stored in the cloud, and Dropbox automatically syncs these files with all of your Dropbox-enabled devices. Your Dropbox folders can be managed directly from any of these devices or through your online dashboard using a personal computer.

In this lab, you investigate some Android apps, and then you install and use the Dropbox software on your personal computer. If you have access to an Android device, you can also install and use the Dropbox app to sync data on your device with your other devices and computers, and with other users.

ESTIMATED COMPLETION TIME: 45 MINUTES

 Activity

The flashlight app can turn your smartphone or tablet into a flashlight. To collect information on flashlight apps, follow these steps:

1. Using a browser, go to Google Play at **play.google.com/store/apps**.

2. Click the **Categories** tab, and then click **Tools**.

3. Find three different flashlight apps, and collect the following information about them, as detailed in Table 9-2:

Specification	App 1	App 2	App 3
App name			
Rating			
Number of reviews			
Date last updated			
Three key features			
One negative issue raised by reviewers			

Table 9-2 Fill in the specifications for three apps available at Google Play

4. If you were to choose one of these flashlight apps, which one would you choose and why?

_____

_____

5. Third-party websites can be an excellent source of information on apps you're researching. Do a quick search on **google.com** for the flashlight app you chose in Step 4; be sure to select **Past year** in the Search tools menu to ensure that you find the latest information on the app. Is your selected app also available in the App Store at *itunes.apple.com* for iOS devices?

_____

6. Next, research a different kind of app. A chromatic tuner is a device used by musicians to tune instruments. Do a Google search for chromatic tuner apps for Android, and answer the following questions:

   ◢ Based on your Google search results, what are three apps that can be used to tune a musical instrument?

_____

_____

   ◢ Besides Google Play, what is another source for one of the tuner apps you listed?

_____

> **Notes** Different apps work with different devices. App listings online include a list of which devices are compatible with that app. However, when you surf the Play Store directly from your Android phone, only device-compatible apps show up in your search.

To install Dropbox on a mobile device, you download the Dropbox app from the device's primary application source (Google Play Store for an Android device or the App Store for an iOS device). To install Dropbox on your computer, do the following:

1. Go to **dropbox.com** and click **Download** to download the app. What is the name of the downloaded file?

_____

2. Locate the downloaded file and install Dropbox.

3. In the Set Up Dropbox dialog box, click **Sign up**, and enter the requested information to create an account. Write down the email address and password for your account:

---

4. Complete the installation process and open Dropbox. Dropbox opens automatically in File Explorer or Windows Explorer and puts an icon in the notification area of the Windows taskbar. What file is included in your Dropbox folder by default? In the left pane of Explorer, where is the Dropbox shortcut located?

You can share Dropbox files and folders with other people. Anyone who has the link to a particular file or folder can view it in a browser, even without using a Dropbox account. It's important to note that you have no control over who can use the link, so be sure you don't put private information in a shared folder. To practice sharing a file, do the following:

1. Create a text file using Notepad, and type a couple of lines of text. Click **File**, and then click **Save**. In the left pane of the Save As window, click **Dropbox**. Name the file **MeetingNotes**, and then click **Save**.

2. Close the file. Using File Explorer or Windows Explorer, find your file in the Dropbox folder.

3. Now verify that the file is stored in the cloud. One way to open your Dropbox home page is to click the Dropbox icon in the notification area of the taskbar. Then click the globe icon (see Figure 9-2). Your Dropbox home page opens. Verify that the MeetingNotes file is present. If not, it has not yet synced. Wait a moment for it to sync; a small green circle indicates an item has synced. Figure 9-3 shows the MeetingNotes file in your Dropbox account in the cloud and the MeetingNotes file in Explorer on the computer.

4. To share a link to the file, right-click the **MeetingNotes** file in Explorer, and click **Copy Dropbox link**, as shown in Figure 9-3. The link is copied to your Clipboard.

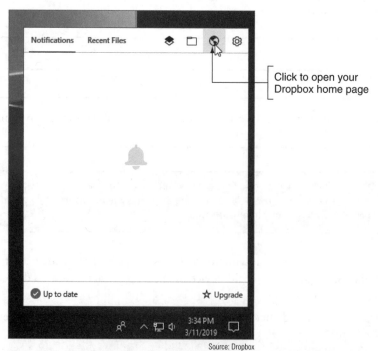

Source: Dropbox

Figure 9-2 Dropbox notifications accessed through the Windows taskbar icon

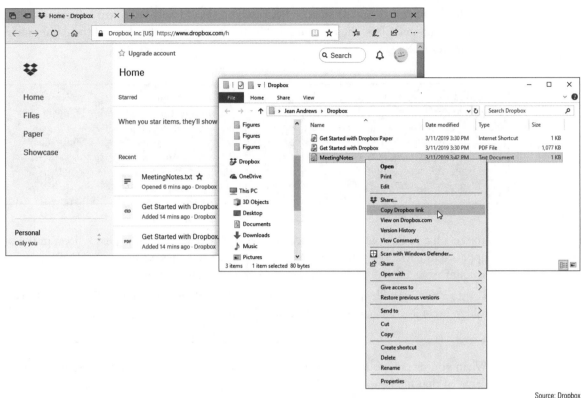

Source: Dropbox

Figure 9-3 Files in Dropbox are synced between the computer and the cloud

5. Paste the link into an email message to your instructor and to a classmate, and then send the email. When you receive your classmate's email, click the link. The file opens in your browser. Notice that you cannot change the text of your classmate's file, but you can copy the file to your computer and edit it there. You can also make comments on the file and subscribe to notifications of future changes to the file.

Files placed in your Dropbox are automatically synced with your Dropbox on other devices linked to your account. To share files in your Dropbox with other people, it is not necessary to share your Dropbox account information. When you invite other Dropbox users to one of your folders, the folder and all of its files and subfolders are synced in their accounts and in your account (however, other folders in your Dropbox remain private unless you share them). To invite a classmate to one of your Dropbox folders, do the following:

1. Return to your Dropbox folder in File Explorer or Windows Explorer. Click **New folder** and name the folder **Computer Class**.

2. On your Dropbox home page, click **Share** next to Computer Class. The first time you associate your email address with Dropbox, Dropbox requests verification of your email address in order to share folders. To verify your email address, click **Send email**.

3. Open the email sent by Dropbox (be sure to check your junk folder if you don't see the Dropbox email in your inbox), and click the link to verify your email. Now that your email address is verified, repeat Step 2 to share the Computer Class folder.

4. In the Computer Class dialog box, enter a classmate's email address. In the drop-down list, select **Can view** and then click **Share**. An invitation email is sent to your classmate. When your classmate accepts your invitation, you should receive a confirmation email.

5. To accept a Dropbox folder shared by your classmate, click the **Go to folder** link in the invitation email that you receive. Sign in if necessary, and then click **Add to Dropbox**

to add the folder to your Dropbox. Because you should now have two folders with the name Computer Class, the new one will have a version number behind the name, such as Computer Class (1).

> **Notes** Be aware that shared folders count toward a user's storage quota. Also, once a folder is shared, you cannot change the name or location of that folder, as it is listed in another Dropbox. However, you can change the name or location of the folder in your own Dropbox.
>
> To unshare a folder, sign in on the Dropbox website. Locate the folder and then click **Share**. Click the status of the person with whom you have shared the folder (Can view or Can edit). Change the status of the person to **Remove**. You can choose whether to allow the person to keep a copy of the shared folder, and then click **Remove**. The person is removed from the folder share.

---

6. To see a list of devices that have accessed your Dropbox, click the person icon in the upper-right corner of your Dropbox home page. Then click **Settings**. On the Personal account page, click **Security** and scroll down to the Devices section.

7. Create a new text file using Notepad, and save the file to your shared Computer Class folder. Include your name as part of the file name. What is the file name?

_____

8. When you receive your classmate's file in his or her shared Dropbox folder, write the name of that file here:

_____

9. Close any open windows.

If you want to use your Dropbox on a computer that has already been linked to another user's Dropbox, you can unlink the computer and add your own account. Follow these steps to set up your Dropbox account on another computer:

1. Go to another computer in the lab that has Dropbox installed. Click the **Dropbox** icon in the taskbar, click the cog settings icon, and then select **Preferences**.

2. From the Dropbox Preferences box, select **Account**. The email address currently linked to Dropbox on this computer appears. Click **Unlink This Dropbox** and click **OK**.

3. The Set Up Dropbox dialog box opens; you used it earlier to create your account. You can use this setup box to create a new Dropbox account or set up an existing Dropbox account on the computer. Follow directions on the screen to set up your existing Dropbox account on this computer. Verify that your Dropbox folders and files are present.

4. If you're working on a lab computer or public computer, go to the Windows 10/8 **Apps & Features** window or the Windows 7 **Programs and Features** window, and uninstall Dropbox.

5. Close any open windows.

REVIEW QUESTIONS

1. Besides apps and games, what other kinds of files can you download from Google Play?

_____

2. Downloading apps on a mobile device can drain a user's cellular data allotment quickly. What is one way to avoid data charges when downloading apps?

_____

3. Suppose you have many folders and files in Dropbox and you want to sync some folders to your computer, but not all of them. How can you select which Dropbox folders get synced to your computer?

_____

_____

_____

4. A file placed in a shared Dropbox folder is accessible by anyone with a link to that folder, no matter how they obtained the link. How can you remove the file from public access?

_____

_____

5. Do a quick Google search for an app other than Dropbox that can sync files between a mobile device and a personal computer. Which app did you find?

_____

LAB 9.3 EXPLORE HOW ANDROID APPS ARE DEVELOPED AND TESTED

OBJECTIVES

Your goal in this lab is to learn how Android apps are developed and tested using the Android Software Development Kit (SDK) and an Android virtual device (AVD). If you have never used an Android device, this is your chance to learn about Android using an Android emulator. After completing this lab, you will be able to:

◢ Describe the tools and procedures used to develop and test Android apps

◢ Install and use an Android virtual device

MATERIALS REQUIRED

This lab requires the following:

◢ Windows 10/8/7 computer

◢ Internet access

LAB PREPARATION

Before the lab begins, the instructor or lab assistant needs to do the following:

◢ Verify that Windows starts with no errors

◢ Verify that Internet access is available

ACTIVITY BACKGROUND

The Android website at *android.com* by Google offers tools to develop and test Android apps. The process can be fun to learn, but it does require you to download and install multiple pieces of software. In this lab, you won't actually write an Android app, but you will learn about the tools used and how the process works.

ESTIMATED COMPLETION TIME: 60 MINUTES

 Activity

PART 1: RESEARCH ANDROID APP DEVELOPMENT AND ANDROID VIRTUAL DEVICES

How do you prefer to learn a new computer skill? You might prefer to watch a video, read a book, search for online discussions or tutorials, or discuss and investigate the topic with your friends. The following steps will help you explore online videos and websites related to developing Android apps:

1. Go to **youtube.com** and search for tutorial videos. Possible search strings are "android application development," "make your first android app," and "android application tutorials."

2. Search the web for additional information and tutorials. Good search strings to use are "android app tutorial for beginners" and "how to develop android apps."

3. Explore websites that might help you with your research. Try researching on these useful websites: *techradar.com* and *androidcommunity.com*.

   ◢ What is Android Studio, and where can you get it?

   _____

   _____

   ◢ What is the AVD Manager, and how would you use it when developing an Android app?

   _____

   _____

   ◢ What programming language does Android Studio include by default to write Android apps?

   _____

PART 2: TURN ON CPU VIRTUALIZATION

To run the Android emulator on your computer, CPU virtualization technology must be enabled in BIOS/UEFI, and Microsoft Hyper-V must be disabled. If your computer has already been used to run a virtual machine (VM), you can assume CPU virtualization has already been turned on. Also, Microsoft Hyper-V is disabled by default. Do the following to verify or change these settings:

1. Shut down and boot up your computer. As it boots, enter BIOS/UEFI setup. Recall that you press a key, such as Del or F2, at the beginning of the boot to enter BIOS/UEFI setup.

2. Search for the option to enable virtualization, also known as Intel VT with Intel processors or AMD-V with AMD processors. (Most likely, the option is on a chipset or processor screen.) If necessary, turn on all the options in the virtualization category.

3. Save your changes and restart the system to the Windows desktop.

4. Open **Control Panel** in Classic view, and click **Programs and Features**. In the left pane of the Programs and Features window, click **Turn Windows features on or off**. If necessary, uncheck **Hyper-V**. Click **OK**. Close all windows. If you made a change, restart your computer.

PART 3: INSTALL AND RUN ANDROID STUDIO AND AN ANDROID EMULATOR

Follow these steps to download and install Android Studio:

1. Go to **developer.android.com/studio** and download Android Studio for Windows. Install the downloaded software, accepting all default settings.

2. Android Studio automatically launches and opens to the Android Studio Setup Wizard (see Figure 9-4). If it does not launch, you can launch it from the Windows start menu.

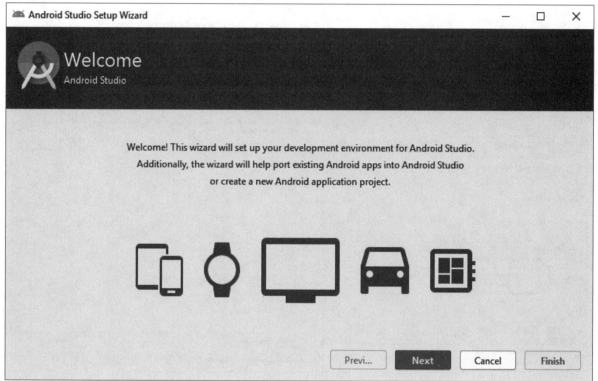

Source: Android Studio

Figure 9-4 Configure the Android Studio installation through the Android Studio Setup Wizard

3. To complete setup, click **Next** three times to accept default settings in three windows until you get to the SDK Components Setup window. In the list of components, check **Android Virtual Device**. What is the Android SDK Location path where the virtual devices will be stored? Click **Next**.

4. In the next window, click **Finish**. The selected components are downloaded and installed.

For Intel processors, the Hardware Accelerated Execution Manager (HAXM) is included as a component in Android Studio and is the last component to install. If the installation hangs when it attempts to install the HAXM software, most likely Hyper-V has not been disabled. In this situation, follow these steps:

1. Go back to Part 2, make sure virtualization is turned on in BIOS/UEFI, and make sure Hyper-V is disabled.

2. Rather than starting over with the Android Studio installation, you can manually install just the HAXM software. Open Explorer and navigate to C:\Users*username*\AppData\Local\Android\sdk\extras\intel\Hardware_Accelerated_Execution_Manager. Then double-click **intelhaxm-android.exe** and follow the on-screen instructions.

The AVD Manager is used to create and manage an Android virtual device (AVD) and is included in the Android SDK. Android app developers test an app on several AVDs, one for each type of Android device they expect the app to use. To access the AVD Manager, you first create a new project and then configure the virtual device. Follow these steps to use the AVD Manager program to set up an Android Virtual Device (AVD):

1. Open Android Studio, close the Tip of the Day box, and click **Start a new Android Studio project**. Follow the on-screen directions, accepting all default settings for your new app called My Application. Once your project is created, the My Application window shows a plethora of development tools used to build your app (see the left side of Figure 9-5).

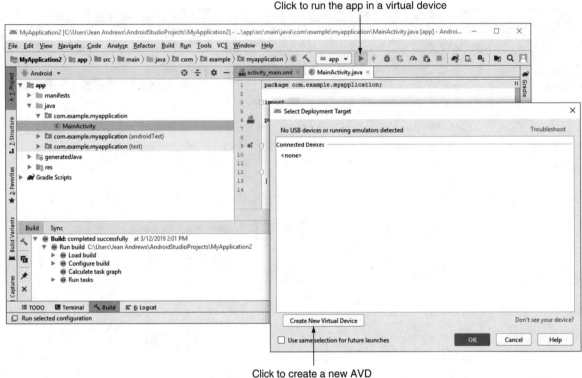

Click to run the app in a virtual device

Click to create a new AVD

Source: Android Studio

Figure 9-5   Android Studio shows the new application and tools used to build it

2. Click the green run button in the toolbar. The Select Deployment Target box appears (see the right side of Figure 9-5).

3. Click **Create New Virtual Device**. To create the virtual device, you first select the device and then the Android release. Select the **Phone** category, and select a device in this category, such as the **Pixel**. Click **Next**.

4. For the system image, select the latest Android release, which is the first item listed. Click **Download** beside the release name, and follow directions on the screen to complete the download.

5. When the system image installation completes, you are returned to the System Image window. Click **Next**.

6. The Android Virtual Device window appears. Click **Finish**.

7. In the Select Deployment Target box, with the virtual device you just created still selected, click **OK**. The emulator launches with the application installed in it. The application displays "Hello World!" on the virtual device screen (see Figure 9-6).

Source: Android Studio

Figure 9-6 An Android virtual device with an app installed

For actual development and testing of Android apps, you would create several virtual devices, each using a different version of Android so that you could test your apps on several Android platforms.

Let's see how a virtual Android device works. To find out, do the following:

1. Use the emulator as you would an Android device. What happens when you try to use it to surf the web?

_____

2. Scroll up to use the App Launcher to view the installed apps. See Figure 9-7. List six apps installed on the AVD.

_____

_____

_____

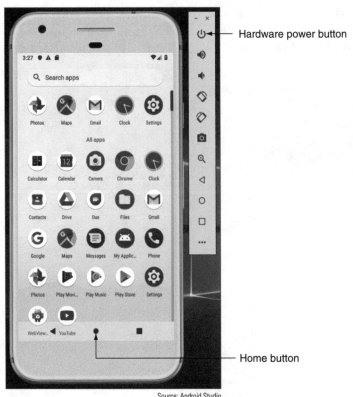

Source: Android Studio

Figure 9-7   The AVD showing installed apps

3. Check out the Settings app. List three settings you can adjust on the AVD.

_____

_____

_____

4. Open the Camera app and take a picture. Open the Photos app and verify that the picture is present.

5. Close any open windows.

REVIEW QUESTIONS

1. Why might an app developer want to test apps on an AVD rather than on actual Android devices?

_____

_____

2. List four programming languages that can be used to write Android apps.

_____

3. Why must virtualization be turned on in BIOS/UEFI setup before you can use the Android emulator?

_____

4. Which program is used to create an Android virtual device?

_____

5. What would be the advantage of creating several AVDs when testing Android apps?

_____

LAB 9.4 CONFIGURE EMAIL AND DROPBOX ON MOBILE DEVICES

OBJECTIVES

The goal of this lab is to practice configuring various accounts, such as for email and Dropbox, on an Android device. After completing this lab, you will be able to:

▲ Create a new email account through the Email app on an Android virtual device

▲ Install Dropbox on a smartphone or tablet

▲ Sync Dropbox files from a smartphone or tablet

MATERIALS REQUIRED

This lab requires the following:

▲ Windows 10/8/7 computer

▲ Internet access

▲ Email account with password

▲ Email address for your instructor

▲ Dropbox account with sign-in information (created earlier in this chapter)

▲ Android Studio, as installed in the previous lab

▲ Android, iOS, or Windows Phone mobile device (optional)

LAB PREPARATION

Before the lab begins, the instructor or lab assistant needs to do the following:

▲ Verify that Windows starts with no errors

▲ Verify that Internet access is available

▲ Verify that Android Studio is correctly installed

ACTIVITY BACKGROUND

Email, files, and other data stored on mobile devices can be automatically synced over either Wi-Fi or cellular connections for any current Android, iOS, or Windows Phone mobile device.

In this lab, you add an email account to the Email app on your Android virtual device. Next, you install the Dropbox app on an Android, iOS, or Windows Phone mobile device that belongs to you or a classmate. Then you sync a file to Dropbox on your computer.

ESTIMATED COMPLETION TIME: 30 MINUTES

 Activity

To add an email account on an Android virtual device, complete the following steps:

1. Open **Android Studio**. In the menu bar, click **Tools** and click **AVD Manager**. In the Android Virtual Device Manager window, double-click the virtual device you created in the previous lab.

2. After the device boots up, scroll down to and open the **Settings** app. Click **Accounts**. Click **Add account**.

3. Click **Personal (IMAP)**, and then follow the on-screen directions to enter your email account information, keeping other default settings.

4. Click the **Home** button, as shown earlier in Figure 9-7.

5. Open the Email app and complete any setup steps required. How far back in time did your email account sync on the virtual device?

_____

6. Compose a new email and send it to your instructor.

7. To view settings for this email account, click the **Menu** icon, scroll down, and then click **Settings**. Click the name of the email account.

8. If you are using an email address other than Gmail, you can view the Server settings. To do so, click **Incoming settings** and answer the following questions:

   ◢ What is the name of the incoming server?

_____

   ◢ What port is the server using?

_____

   ◢ What is the security type?

_____

9. To protect your privacy, be sure to remove your email account from any virtual devices. The most secure way to do this is to delete the AVD. Describe the steps to do this. Be sure to complete the deletion process so your information is protected.

_____

_____

_____

Dropbox is compatible with many operating systems, including Android, iOS, and Windows Phone. Use your own smartphone or tablet for this portion of the lab, or team up with one or more classmates to use their mobile device(s). Alternatively, pair up with a classmate whose mobile device uses a different OS from your own, and install Dropbox on both devices so you both can see how the app works on multiple mobile operating systems.

Complete the following steps:

1. Download Dropbox from your phone's primary app provider.

2. Sign in using the Dropbox account you created earlier in this chapter.

3. Take a screenshot of your phone's display that shows your Dropbox folders on your phone.

4. Open the screenshot, click the **Share** icon, and add the screenshot file to Dropbox. Save it to the Computer Class folder you created in the Dropbox lab earlier in this chapter.

5. Open Dropbox on your computer. (If you're using a lab computer and Dropbox is not installed, use the online Dropbox dashboard at **dropbox.com**.) Sign in if necessary.

6. Open the **Computer Class** folder. Click on the screenshot file to view it, and then click **Share**. Enter your instructor's email address to send the link, and then click **Send**.

REVIEW QUESTIONS

1. What port number is used by default to receive IMAP email? POP3 email?

2. What port numbers are used to receive email by IMAP and POP3 servers when using SSL?

3. Why do you think Android Gmail does not allow a user to edit the server names and port numbers it uses for Gmail email accounts but does allow editing these values for other email accounts?

4. Why should you delete the AVD at the end of the lab?

LAB 9.5 RESEARCH XCODE AND THE iOS SIMULATOR

OBJECTIVES

The goal of this lab is to explore the features and requirements of Xcode. After completing this lab, you will be able to:

◢ Describe the purpose of Xcode

◢ Explain the use of the Simulator tool in Xcode

MATERIALS REQUIRED

This lab requires the following:

◢ Internet access

LAB PREPARATION

Before the lab begins, the instructor or lab assistant needs to do the following:

◢ Verify that Internet access is available

ACTIVITY BACKGROUND

When app developers create apps for iOS devices, they use Apple's Xcode application. The program is available only for macOS computers; however, you can learn about the application without downloading it by going to the iOS Developer website (*developer.apple.com*), which contains a wealth of useful information, resources, and community support. In this lab, you explore some of Apple's app developer tools contained within Xcode.

> **ESTIMATED COMPLETION TIME: 45 MINUTES**

 Activity

Do the following to find out more about Xcode:

1. In your web browser, go to **developer.apple.com**, and explore the resources on the main page. If necessary, use a search engine as you answer the following questions, and add the **site:developer.apple.com** tag to limit your search to Apple's website:

   a. How much does an individual membership cost for the Apple Developer Program?

   _____

   > **Notes** Some schools qualify for the free iOS Developer University Program, which provides a suite of tools for student development projects and collaboration between students and instructors. Learn more at *developer.apple.com/programs/ios/university*.

   b. What is Xcode? What is the current version of Xcode?

   _____

   _____

   c. What equipment and OS do you need to get Xcode from the App Store for free?

   _____

   d. What is Simulator?

   _____

   _____

   e. What is Swift?

   _____

   _____

   f. How can you access iOS Simulator in Xcode?

   _____

   g. How are gestures simulated on a virtual device in Simulator?

   _____

h. What is the playground?

_____

i. What is a storyboard?

_____

2. Do a general web search to find out whether it is possible to develop iOS apps on a Windows computer. Describe one solution that you find.

_____

_____

_____

REVIEW QUESTIONS

1. What programming language does Apple currently use for iOS apps?

_____

2. What OS is used on Apple Watch devices?

_____

3. Xcode is a free app from the App Store, so why might you need to pay for an Apple Developer Program membership?

_____

4. If you were to begin developing apps, which OS would you prefer to work with? Why?

_____

LAB 9.6 CREATE A SMART HOME IoT NETWORK IN PACKET TRACER

OBJECTIVES

Your goal in this lab is to use Packet Tracer to explore the basics of setting up a smart home with IoT devices and controlling these devices with a smartphone. After completing this lab, you will be able to:

- Describe the components of a smart home network
- Use Packet Tracer to practice setting up a smart home with IoT devices

MATERIALS REQUIRED

This lab requires the following:

- Windows 10/8/7 computer
- Internet access (optional)

LAB PREPARATION

Before the lab begins, the instructor or lab assistant needs to do the following:

◢ Verify that the computer works with no errors

◢ Verify that Packet Tracer is installed and working or that Internet access is available to download and install Packet Tracer

ACTIVITY BACKGROUND

As an IT support technician, you can expect that your career will lead you into learning many new technologies. The world of IoT and smart homes is one example of the changing landscape of knowledge and skills expected of a technician. In this lab, you get the chance to practice setting up a smart home without the investment of buying IoT devices. You use Packet Tracer to control a garage door and lamp from a smartphone.

ESTIMATED COMPLETION TIME: 35 MINUTES

 Activity

1. If you have not already installed Packet Tracer on your computer, follow the steps given in Lab 7.7 in Chapter 7 to download, install, and launch Packet Tracer.

2. Next, you place devices on the Packet Tracer workspace. A smart home needs a gateway device to connect all IoT devices. Select the **Network Devices** category, select the **Wireless Devices** subcategory, and press and drag a home gateway to your workspace. Position all devices as shown in Figure 9-8.

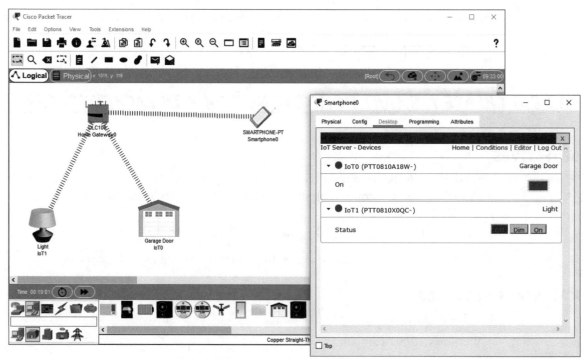

Figure 9-8 IoT devices in the smart home network controlled by a smartphone

3. Select the **End Devices** category, select the **End Devices** subcategory, and press and drag a smart device to the workspace. A smartphone is added to the workspace.

4. In the End Devices category, select the **Home** subcategory, and press and drag a light to the workspace.

5. Press and drag a garage door to the workspace.

6. Click the home gateway to open its configuration window. Select the **Config** tab. Click **LAN**. What is the IP address of the home gateway?

_____

7. Click **Wireless**. What is the SSID of the wireless network that the home gateway provides?

_____

8. The light and garage door, by default, have an Ethernet port for a wired connection. In our smart home, we want to use wireless. To install a wireless adapter, click the light to open its configuration window. Click **Advanced**, and then click the **I/O Config** tab. To the right of Network Adapter, in the drop-down list, select **PT-IOT-NM-1W-AC**, which is a Wi-Fi wireless adapter. Close the configuration window. A wireless connection from the light to the home gateway appears.

9. In the same manner, change the network adapter in the garage door from an Ethernet adapter to the Wi-Fi adapter.

10. Now that the IoT devices are connected to the gateway, you register them with the IoT server embedded in the gateway. Click the light and click the **Config** tab. Select **Home Gateway**. Close the configuration window. Do the same for the garage door.

11. Now let's connect the smartphone to the home gateway and configure an app on the phone to manage the devices connected to the home gateway. To connect to Wi-Fi, click the smartphone and click **Config**. Click **Wireless0**. Change the SSID to the SSID of the home gateway. Close the configuration window and verify that the wireless connection is made.

12. To use the phone to manage the IoT devices, click the smartphone and click **Desktop**. Click **IoT Monitor**. Notice the IP address of the IoT server is correct. Click **Login** to sign in to the server. You should now be able to control the light and the garage door from the IoT Monitor app on the smartphone, as shown earlier in Figure 9-8.

REVIEW QUESTIONS

1. In this Packet Tracer lab, which component (hardware or software) is similar in concept to the Amazon Alexa app?

_____

2. In this Packet Tracer lab, which component (hardware or software) is similar in concept to a SOHO router?

_____

3. Define an IoT gateway. Which Packet Tracer component (hardware or software) in this lab acted as your IoT gateway?

_____

4. When setting up the Amazon Echo Dot, you communicate with it through your smartphone and configure the Dot to connect to the home Wi-Fi network. Then you must register IoT devices with the Dot by adding these devices to your Alexa account. In this Packet Tracer lab, which action is equivalent to registering IoT devices in your Alexa account?

_____

5. In this Packet Tracer lab, you installed Wi-Fi network adapters in the light and garage door controllers. Many IoT devices use a different wireless standard than Wi-Fi. What device is required so that these non-Wi-Fi devices can connect to the Wi-Fi network?

_____

Virtualization, Cloud Computing, and Printers

Labs included in this chapter:

- **Lab 10.1:** Create a VM in Oracle VirtualBox

- **Lab 10.2:** Use a Microsoft Account and OneDrive

- **Lab 10.3:** Install and Share a Local Printer

- **Lab 10.4:** Install a Network Printer

- **Lab 10.5:** Update Printer Drivers

- **Lab 10.6:** Maintain and Troubleshoot a Printer

- **Lab 10.7:** Manage Print Jobs

- **Lab 10.8:** Sabotage and Repair a Printer

LAB 10.1 CREATE A VM IN ORACLE VIRTUALBOX

OBJECTIVES

The goal of this lab is to install and use VirtualBox to create a Windows 10 VM. After completing this lab, you will be able to:

▲ Install Oracle VirtualBox

▲ Use VirtualBox to create a new VM

▲ Install Windows 10 in the VM

MATERIALS REQUIRED

This lab requires the following:

▲ Windows 10 operating system, any edition and any architecture (32-bit or 64-bit), with current updates installed

▲ A minimum of 4 GB of RAM

▲ A minimum of 20 GB of available hard drive space

▲ Windows 10 installation media

▲ Windows 10 product key

▲ Internet access

> **Notes** Virtual machine software and virtual machines tend to require heavy system resources. Don't forget that any memory a VM uses will not be available to the host operating system while the VM is open.

LAB PREPARATION

Before the lab begins, the instructor or lab assistant needs to do the following:

▲ Verify that Windows 10 starts with no errors

▲ Verify that Internet access is available

▲ Create or download an ISO file of a Windows 10 operating system and make this file available to students

ACTIVITY BACKGROUND

Oracle's VirtualBox is a Type 2 hypervisor that can be installed in Windows and used to create VMs. This lab walks you through that process. In Part 1, you determine if virtualization must be enabled in BIOS/UEFI and, if needed, you enable virtualization. Microsoft Client Hyper-V is a Type 2 hypervisor embedded in professional and business editions of Windows.

Because VirtualBox and Hyper-V are not compatible, you need to disable Hyper-V before you install VirtualBox. In Part 2, you install VirtualBox, and then in Part 3, you create a new VM and install Windows 10 in it.

ESTIMATED COMPLETION TIME: 60 MINUTES

 Activity

PART 1: ENABLE VIRTUALIZATION IN BIOS/UEFI

To install a 64-bit OS in a VM that is hosted by a 64-bit machine, you must enable virtualization in BIOS/UEFI. However, this setting is not necessary for a 32-bit installation. To determine whether you need to enable virtualization in BIOS/UEFI, complete the following steps:

1. Open **Control Panel** in Classic view and click **System**.

   ◢ What is the System type you are using?

   _____

   ◢ Are you using a 32-bit or 64-bit installation of the OS?

   _____

2. Check with your instructor to determine which type of ISO you've been given. Does the ISO contain a 32-bit or 64-bit OS?

   _____

   Know that a 32-bit OS can be installed in a VM on a computer using a 32-bit or 64-bit OS, but you cannot install a 64-bit OS in a VM that is on a computer using a 32-bit version of Windows.

If you are using a computer that has a 64-bit OS installed, complete the following steps to enable virtualization in BIOS/UEFI:

1. Reboot the computer. Press a key, such as Del or F2, during startup to access BIOS/UEFI setup.

2. Search for a setting that references virtualization technology and make sure that it is set to Enabled. For some systems, the CPU Configuration screen shown in Figure 10-1 provides access to that setting, but on your computer, it may be located on a different screen. Also make sure that any subcategory items under HAV are enabled. What is the exact name of the virtualization setting(s) you found?

   _____

   _____

10

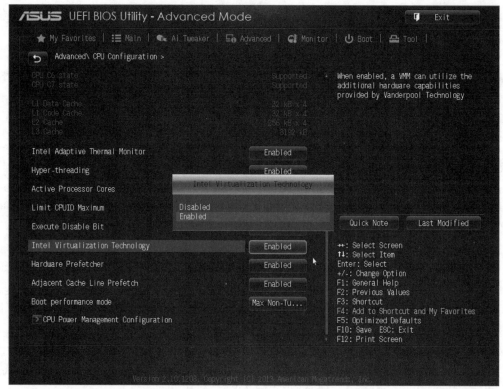

Source: American Megatrends, Inc.

Figure 10-1   Virtualization must be enabled in UEFI setup

3. Save your changes, exit BIOS/UEFI setup, and allow the system to restart into Windows.

4. Open **Control Panel** in Classic view, and click **Programs and Features**. In the left pane of the Programs and Features window, click **Turn Windows features on or off**. If necessary, uncheck **Hyper-V**. Click **OK**. Close all windows. If you made a change, restart your computer.

PART 2: INSTALL ORACLE VIRTUALBOX

Complete the following steps to download and install Oracle VirtualBox:

1. Open a browser and go to **virtualbox.org/wiki/Downloads**.

2. Download the **VirtualBox platform package** for Windows hosts to your desktop or another folder on your hard drive. What is the name of the downloaded file?

3. Launch the downloaded program file, and follow on-screen instructions to install the software, accepting all default settings during the installation. When the installation is complete, the Oracle VM VirtualBox Manager window opens (see Figure 10-2).

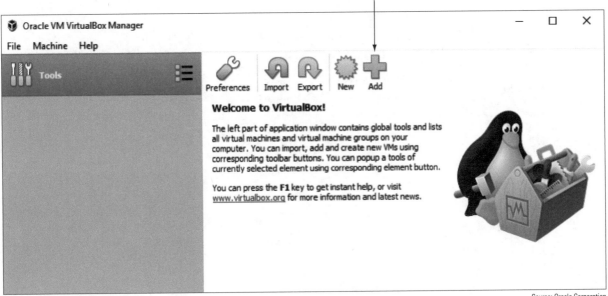

Figure 10-2 Use the VirtualBox Manager to create and manage virtual machines

10

PART 3: CREATE A NEW VM AND INSTALL WINDOWS 10 IN IT

Complete the following steps to create a new VM and install Windows 10:

1. Click **Add** in the toolbar and follow the wizard to create a VM. Select a name for your VM—for example, VM1 or VM_Lab1—and select the Windows OS you will install in it. You can accept all default settings for the VM unless directed otherwise by your instructor.

> **Notes** If you want to install a 64-bit OS but only 32-bit OSs are listed, most likely Hyper-V has not yet been disabled. In this situation, close the VirtualBox Manager, disable Hyper-V, and restart the system. You should then see 64-bit OSs listed for the new VM.

2. With the VM selected, click **Settings** in the toolbar. In the VM's Settings box, click **Storage** in the left pane.

3. In the Storage Devices area, to the right of Controller: SATA, click **Add optical drive**, which is represented by a CD icon with a plus (+) symbol, as shown on the left side of Figure 10-3.

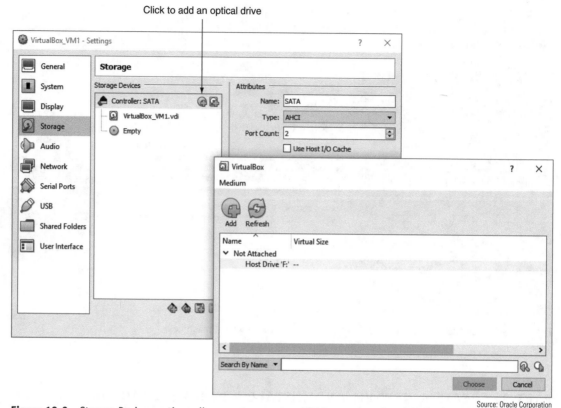

Click to add an optical drive

Source: Oracle Corporation

Figure 10-3   Storage Devices options allow you to mount an ISO image as a virtual CD in the VM

4. In the Question dialog box, click **Choose disk**. In the VirtualBox dialog box that appears, click **Add** to add a disk image (see the right side of Figure 10-3). Browse to the location of the ISO file that contains the Windows operating system setup files made available by your instructor, select the ISO file, and click **Open**. With the ISO file selected, click **Choose**.

5. Verify in the Storage Devices area that you have two devices: a virtual hard drive and a virtual optical drive with the Windows ISO image mounted. Then click **OK** to return to the VirtualBox Manager window.

6. Click **Start** on the toolbar. Your VM starts up and begins the process of installing the operating system. Complete the Windows installation.

> **Notes** If you have trouble booting to the ISO file, consider increasing the VM's available memory in the Settings menu. For example, 64-bit Windows installs more easily with 4 GB of RAM rather than the minimum 2 GB.

7. With the Oracle VM VirtualBox Manager window still open, answer the following questions:

   ◢ Which key do you press to release your mouse and keyboard from the VM? In VirtualBox, what is this key called?

◢ How many network cards can VirtualBox emulate?

REVIEW QUESTIONS

1. What is the purpose of a hypervisor?

2. An ISO file contains the image of the contents of what device?

3. What kind of controller does VirtualBox use to communicate with the VM's virtual drives?

4. What company currently develops and supports the VirtualBox hypervisor?

LAB 10.2 USE A MICROSOFT ACCOUNT AND ONEDRIVE

OBJECTIVES

The goal of this lab is to set up and use a Microsoft account and OneDrive in Windows 10. After completing this lab, you will be able to:

◢ Use a local account, a Microsoft account, and OneDrive in Windows 10

◢ Switch between a Microsoft account and a local account

MATERIALS REQUIRED

This lab requires the following:

◢ Windows 10 operating system

◢ Internet access

LAB PREPARATION

Before the lab begins, the instructor or lab assistant needs to do the following:

◢ Verify that Windows starts with no errors

◢ Verify that Internet access is available

ACTIVITY BACKGROUND

Windows 10 and Windows 8 give users the option to log in with a Microsoft account, local account, or network ID to a Windows domain. When you sign in with a Microsoft account, you automatically have access to OneDrive, which is storage in the Microsoft cloud that syncs to your computer. Windows 8 required you to sign in to Windows with a Microsoft account to get access to OneDrive, but Windows 10 allows you to sign in with a non-Microsoft account and still get access to OneDrive. In this lab, you learn how this works in Windows 10.

ESTIMATED COMPLETION TIME: 45–60 MINUTES

 Activity

PART 1: IDENTIFY OR CREATE A MICROSOFT ACCOUNT

1. What is the local account user name for your Windows 10 computer?

   _____

2. Do you have an existing Microsoft account with an @outlook.com, @hotmail.com, @live.com, @msn.com, or other email address? If so, what is the email address associated with your Microsoft account?

   _____

3. If you don't have a Microsoft account, follow these steps to create one:

   a. Go to **onedrive.com** and click **Sign up for free**. Then click **Create a Microsoft account**.

   b. If you want to use an existing email address other than a Microsoft email address, enter the address, click **Next**, and follow directions on the screen to set up the Microsoft account. Do not set up OneDrive at this time.

   c. If you want a new email address, click **Get a new email address**, click **Next**, and follow directions on the screen to create a new email address that is also your Microsoft account. Do not set up OneDrive at this time.

PART 2: USE ONEDRIVE

1. Sign in with a local account.

2. To create a test file, right-click the desktop, point to **New** in the shortcut menu, and click **Text Document**. Create a text document on your desktop named **MyTest**. Open the document and type some text in it. Then close the document.

3. In the taskbar, click the OneDrive icon. The first time you sign in to OneDrive, the dialog box shown in Figure 10-4 appears. Click **Sign in**.

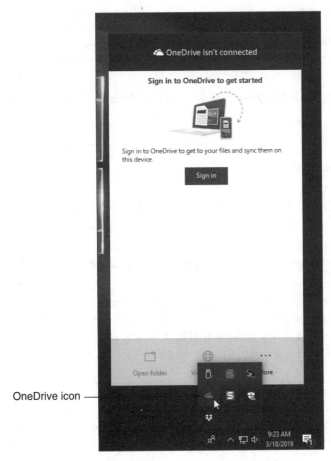

OneDrive icon —

Figure 10-4   Set up OneDrive

4. Enter your Microsoft account email address and click **Sign in**. In the next box, enter your password and click **Sign in**. OneDrive reports the folder location on your computer. What is the path to your OneDrive folder? Click **Next**.

_____

5. Click **Not now** to skip the option to purchase additional OneDrive storage and follow the steps through the brief tutorial about OneDrive. Then close the tutorial box. What are two facts about OneDrive described in the tutorial?

_____

6. Open **File Explorer**. Notice the OneDrive folder is listed in the left pane. Expand the folder. How many subfolders does the OneDrive folder contain?

_____

7. Hold down the Ctrl key as you drag and drop the MyTest file from your desktop into the OneDrive folder. The file is copied (not moved) to the folder.

8. To see your OneDrive contents online, click the OneDrive icon in the taskbar. In the OneDrive dialog box, click **More** and click **View online**. Your browser opens to the OneDrive page. Click **Sign up for free**. Under OneDrive, click **sign in** and follow directions to sign in to your OneDrive online account. Do you see the MyTest file online?

> 📄 **Notes** To protect your privacy on the computer you are using, don't allow the browser or Microsoft to save your passwords or to keep you logged on to OneDrive.

9. Right-click the **Correspondence** folder and click **Share**. What are two ways you can share the folder?

   _____

10. Close all open windows.

PART 3: SWITCH BETWEEN A MICROSOFT ACCOUNT AND A LOCAL ACCOUNT

1. You can sign in to Windows with your Microsoft account, which can make online resources such as OneDrive more accessible. To change how you sign in to Windows, open the **Settings** app and click **Accounts**. Click **Your info**.

2. On the Your info page, click **Sign in with a Microsoft account instead**. Follow directions on the screen to enter your Microsoft account and password and your local password. You are also required to create a four-digit PIN that can be used in place of your password when you sign in to Windows. (The PIN will not work on other devices that use the same Microsoft account.) What is your PIN?

   _____

3. Your local account has been switched to a Microsoft account on the computer. Now, when you sign in to your computer, you will use your Microsoft account information and *not* the local account sign-in information. Close all windows and restart your computer.

4. Sign in to Windows using your PIN.

5. Check your OneDrive to verify that it is accessible in File Explorer.

Next, you'll disconnect the Microsoft account. Follow these steps to disconnect your Microsoft account from Windows:

1. Open the **Settings** app and click **Accounts**. On the Your info page, click **Sign in with a local account instead**, and follow directions on the screen to return to using a local account. Windows signs you off. Sign in again, this time using your local account. Notice that when you sign back in, you have the option to use the PIN or your local password.

2. Open **File Explorer** and verify that you can still access your OneDrive. Close **File Explorer**.

3. To unlink your computer from your OneDrive, click the OneDrive icon in the taskbar, click **More**, and click **Settings**. Select the **Account** tab on the Microsoft OneDrive dialog box. Click **Unlink this PC**. Click **Unlink account**.

4. Close the box that asks you to set up OneDrive again.

5. Open **File Explorer**. Does OneDrive still appear in the left pane?

   _____

6. Drill down to the OneDrive folder. (You recorded the path earlier in this lab.) Are the MyTest file and subfolders present? Delete all contents of the OneDrive folder.

   _____

7. Earlier in the lab, OneDrive was already set up when you switched to a Microsoft account. If OneDrive is not already set up and you switch from a local account to a

Microsoft account, do you think OneDrive will automatically sync to your computer? List the steps to verify your answer.

_____

_____

_____

_____

REVIEW QUESTIONS

1. What are the domain name endings offered when creating a new Microsoft account?

_____

2. What are the two ways you can share a folder in OneDrive?

_____

3. Why might you want to save files to OneDrive instead of just saving to your local hard drive?

_____

_____

4. Describe how Microsoft Office integrates with OneDrive.

_____

5. When you unlink a computer from OneDrive, does Windows automatically delete the contents of the OneDrive folder? When you switch from a local account to a Microsoft account to sign in to Windows, does Windows automatically set up OneDrive?

_____

10

LAB 10.3 INSTALL AND SHARE A LOCAL PRINTER

OBJECTIVES

The goal of this lab is to install and share a printer. After completing this lab, you will be able to:

◢ Install a local printer on a computer

◢ Share a local printer with other users on the network

◢ Using another computer on the network, install and use a shared network printer

MATERIALS REQUIRED

This lab requires the following:

◢ A USB printer and its printer drivers

◢ Two or more Windows 10/8/7 computers connected to a network

◢ Access to the printer manual

LAB PREPARATION

Before the lab begins, the instructor or lab assistant needs to do the following:

▲ Verify that Windows starts with no errors

▲ Verify that one or more USB printers with printer drivers are available

▲ Verify that the printer manual is available or that students have Internet access so they can locate the manual on the web

> 📄 **Notes** You can install drivers for a printer even when the printer is not available. If you are working in a computer lab that has no printer, most of this lab can still be done. You just won't be able to print a test page.

ACTIVITY BACKGROUND

A network printer connects directly to a wired or wireless network, and any computer on the network can access it. A local printer connects directly to a computer by way of a USB port, wireless Bluetooth, or other type of connection, and can be shared with other computers on a network. In order for the printer to appear as a network printer on the network, the computer with the printer physically connected to it must have file and printer sharing turned on.

In this lab, you install and share a printer, and then another computer on the network uses the shared printer.

ESTIMATED COMPLETION TIME: 45 MINUTES

 Activity

First, follow these steps to install a USB printer on one computer:

1. If the USB printer is connected to the computer, disconnect it.

2. To make sure the printer is not already installed in Windows, open **Control Panel**, and then click **Devices and Printers**. (In Windows 7, you can click **Devices and Printers** directly in the Start menu.) The Devices and Printers window opens.

   ▲ What make and model of printer are you using?

   _____

   _____

   ▲ Is the printer already installed in Windows?

   _____

3. If the printer is already listed as an installed printer, right-click the printer icon, and select **Remove device** in the shortcut menu. Click **Yes** to remove the device.

4. With the printer turned off, connect the printer to the USB port on your computer. Next, turn on the printer. Windows has embedded USB printer drivers and automatically begins the process of installing the printer.

   ▲ Describe the messages that appear in Windows as the printer installs:

   _____

   _____

5. In the Devices and Printers window, a green check mark indicates the printer is the default printer. If it is not the default printer, make it the default printer.

◢ If a printer is not the default printer, how do you make it the default printer?

_____

_____

6. To verify the installation, print a Windows test page.

◢ List the steps you took to print the test page:

_____

_____

◢ Describe the type of information that prints on the Windows test page:

_____

_____

7. Close any open windows.

If you are troubleshooting a printing problem and the Windows test page does not print, the next step in the troubleshooting process is to print a test page at the printer. If the printer test page prints successfully, you have proven the problem is not with the printer itself. Do the following:

1. Disconnect the printer from the USB port.

2. List the steps you must take to print a test page at the printer. If you need help printing the test page, see the printer manual. If the manual is not available, search the web for the printer manufacturer and model to find directions on how to use the printer. Table 10-1 can help you find the correct website.

_____

_____

Printer Manufacturer	Website
Brother	brother.com
Canon	canon.com
Epson	epson.com
Hewlett-Packard	hp.com
Lexmark	lexmark.com
OKI Data	oki.com
Samsung	samsung.com
SATO	satoamerica.com
TallyGenicom	tallygenicom.com
Xerox	xerox.com

Table 10-1 Printer manufacturers and their websites

10

3. Print a printer test page.

4. What type of information prints on the printer test page that does not print on the Windows test page?

_____

_____

5. Reconnect the printer to the computer.

If you are working in a lab that does not have a printer, follow these steps to install drivers for a printer:

1. Open the **Devices and Printers** window. Click **Add a printer**. In the Add Printer dialog box on a Windows 10/8 system, click **The printer that I want isn't listed** (you don't have to wait for the search to finish). Select the option **Add a local printer or network printer with manual settings**, and then click **Next**. On a Windows 7 computer, in the Add Printer box, click **Add a local printer**.

2. Select **Create a new port**, and if necessary, select **Local Port** from the drop-down menu. Click **Next**.

3. For the port name, type **VirtualUSB**, and then click **OK**.

4. Select a printer manufacturer and printer model, and then click **Next**. Click **Next** again.

5. Select **Do not share this printer**, and then click **Next**.

6. If available, check **Set as the default printer**, and then click **Finish**.

After the printer is installed, you need to make it possible for other computers in the network to access it. Follow these directions to share the printer with other computers on the network:

1. Using the computer with the locally installed printer, open the **Devices and Printers** window. Right-click the printer, and click **Printer properties** in the shortcut menu.

2. Click the **Sharing** tab. Check **Share this printer**, and type a share name for the printer. Usually the share name is the name of the printer or the physical location of the printer. Make sure **Render print jobs on client computers** is selected.

   ◢ What is the share name?

   _____

   ◢ Describe what happens to print jobs when the "Render print jobs on client computers" option is not selected:

   _____

   _____

3. Click **Additional Drivers**. Answer these questions:

   ◢ In the Additional Drivers dialog box (see Figure 10-5), which type of processor is selected?

   _____

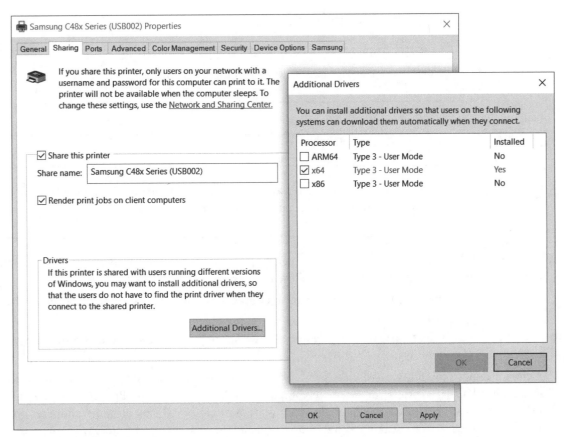

Figure 10-5 Decide which printer drivers Windows can make available to other computers that use the shared printer

10

◢ What is the advantage of selecting both x64 and x86 processors?

_____

_____

◢ Which option should be selected in the Additional Drivers dialog box if other computers on the network that have a 32-bit version of Windows installed will require the printer drivers?

_____

4. Click **OK** to close the Additional Drivers dialog box. Close the printer properties dialog box, saving your changes.

◢ Using the Devices and Printers window, describe how you can tell that the printer is shared:

_____

◢ What is the computer name?

_____

◢ List the steps you took to find the computer name:

_____

_____

_____

◢ What is the exact name of the shared printer on the network, including the computer name (include backslashes in your answer)?

_____

The next step in ensuring that the printer appears as a network printer on the network is to configure Windows to allow file and printer sharing. Follow these steps:

1. Open the **Network and Sharing Center** window and click **Change advanced sharing settings**.

2. If necessary, turn on file and printer sharing. Save your changes and close all windows.

Before a remote computer can use the printer, printer drivers must be installed on the remote computer. You can install a shared printer on a remote computer using the Devices and Printers window in Control Panel or the Network window in File Explorer or Windows Explorer. Using another computer on the network, follow these steps to install the shared printer using the Devices and Printers window:

1. Make sure the shared printer is turned on and not in sleep mode.

2. Open the **Devices and Printers** window, and then click **Add a printer**. On a Windows 10/8 computer, wait for Windows to complete its search. On a Windows 7 computer, in the Add Printer box, click **Add a network, wireless or Bluetooth printer**, and wait for Windows to complete its search.

3. If the shared printer appears in the list of available printers, select the shared printer, and then click **Next**. (If you don't see the shared printer, skip to Step 4.) If a warning box appears and asks if you trust this printer, click **Install driver**. The printer is installed. Click **Next**. In the next dialog box, you are given the opportunity to print a Windows test page. Print the test page and close all windows.

4. If the printer is not listed among available printers, click **The printer that I want isn't listed** (see the middle of Figure 10-6). On the next screen (see the right side of Figure 10-6), select **Select a shared printer by name**, and then click **Browse**. Drill down to the computer that is sharing the printer, and then select the printer. Click **Select**, and then click **Next** to continue the printer installation. Be sure to print a Windows test page.

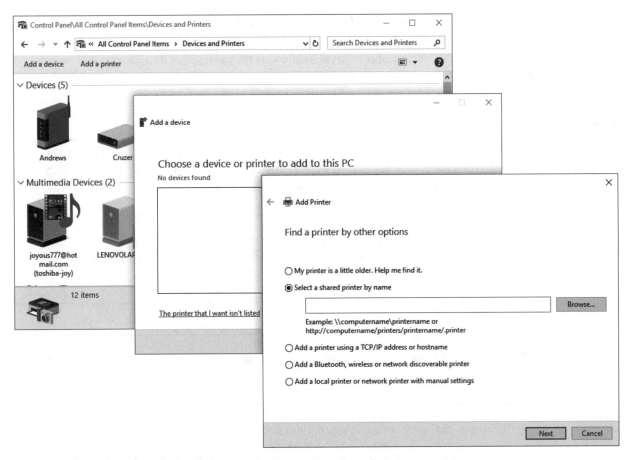

Figure 10-6 Browse to find a printer shared by a computer on the network

5. Verify that the printer is listed in the Devices and Printers window.

◢ Did the Windows test page print successfully?

_____

◢ On the Windows test page, what is the computer name?

_____

◢ What is the complete printer name listed on the test page?

_____

◢ Does the test page identify which remote computer printed the test page?

_____

To see how you can use the Network window to install a shared printer, follow these steps using the same remote computer on the network:

1. First, use the Devices and Printers window to remove the printer.

2. On the same computer or another remote computer on the network, open **File Explorer** or **Windows Explorer** and examine the **Network** window.

3. In the group of computers on the network, drill down to the computer that is sharing the printer. Right-click the shared printer and click **Connect**.

4. Return to the Devices and Printers window. Is the printer listed as an installed printer?

_____

REVIEW QUESTIONS

1. Where would a 32-bit installation of Windows find drivers for a shared USB printer when the printer is being shared by a computer that has a 64-bit installation of Windows installed? Will these drivers be 32-bit drivers or 64-bit drivers?

_____

2. When troubleshooting a printing problem, what advantages does printing a Windows test page from the printer properties dialog box in Windows have over printing a test page using buttons on the printer?

_____

_____

3. Can you still print on a shared printer from a remote computer when the host computer is shut down?

_____

4. What two characters precede a computer name on the network?

_____

5. What two windows can be used to install a shared printer?

_____

_____

LAB 10.4 INSTALL A NETWORK PRINTER

OBJECTIVES

The goal of this lab is to install a network printer and then print to it from a remote computer on the network. After completing this lab, you will be able to:

◢ Install a network printer

◢ Test the printer across the network

MATERIALS REQUIRED

This lab requires the following:

◢ Windows 10/8/7 operating system

◢ Network printer, patch cable, printer driver files, and documentation

◢ A functioning network

◢ A workgroup of two to four students

LAB PREPARATION

Before the lab begins, the instructor or lab assistant needs to do the following:

◢ Verify that Windows starts with no errors

◢ Verify that the network printer, patch cable, printer drivers, and printer documentation are present and working

◢ Verify that the network is working

ACTIVITY BACKGROUND

A network printer connects directly to the network and doesn't require a host computer. After you connect a network printer directly to the network, any computer on the network can install it if the computer has the printer drivers. In this setup, each computer is responsible for managing the printer and its print queue.

In a large organization where many users share a network printer, a network administrator might want more control over the network printer. She can set up one computer on the network as the print server. This computer installs the network printer and shares the printer. Then other computers on the network install the printer by connecting to the shared printer. The result is that all print jobs must flow through the print server computer. The network administrator can monitor and manage the use of the printer from this central location.

In this lab, you learn to install a network printer and connect to it from other computers on the network. In this lab, it is assumed that the network printer and all the networked computers belong to the same subnet. Printing across subnets is not covered in this lab.

10

> **ESTIMATED COMPLETION TIME: 30 MINUTES**

 Activity

The following steps describe the default method for installing a network printer. However, printer manufacturers often provide specialized steps and/or software for installing their devices. In that case, you should follow the steps your printer manufacturer prescribes rather than the steps listed here.

A network printer can be identified on the network by its IP address or printer name. Follow these steps to install a network printer using its IP address:

1. Attach your printer to the network using a network patch cable. Turn the printer on. The printer should indicate in some way that it is connected to the network. For example, many network printers have a control panel that displays "Ready" or "Online."

   ◢ How does your printer indicate that it is connected to the network?

   _____

   ◢ Most printers can print a status page telling you their IP address or can display the IP address in the control panel. Consult the printer's documentation or the web to figure out how to determine the IP address of your printer. How did you determine the IP address for your printer, and what is it?

   _____

   _____

   _____

Go to a computer on the network, and follow these steps to install the network printer using Windows 10/8/7:

1. Open the **Devices and Printers** window, and click **Add a printer**, as you did in the previous lab. In Windows 7 only, click **Add a network, wireless or Bluetooth printer**, and then click **Next** if necessary.

2. Notice that Windows will begin to search the network for available printers. If your printer is displayed, select it, and then click **Next**. Follow the on-screen directions to install the network printer and print a Windows test page to confirm the installation.

3. If the printer is not listed, click **The printer that I want isn't listed**. The dialog box shown earlier in Figure 10-6 appears. If another computer, such as a print server, were sharing the printer, you could browse to find the shared printer or identify the shared printer by name. Because your printer is connected directly to the network, select **Add a printer using a TCP/IP address or hostname**, and click **Next**.

4. Enter the IP address assigned to your printer, and then click **Next**. Follow the on-screen instructions to complete the installation.

5. When the installation is complete, print a test page to test your printer.

When installing a network printer using its IP address, the printer must use the same IP address each time it connects to the network. Follow these steps to learn more:

1. Turn off the printer, and then turn it back on. What is the new IP address of the printer? Did the IP address change?

_____

2. Using controls at the printer, determine if the printer is set to use static IP addressing or dynamic IP addressing, and make note of the address configuration below:

_____

3. Most network printers can use static IP addressing or dynamic IP addressing. If the printer is using dynamic IP addressing, the DHCP server (for example, a router that provides this service) might be serving up the same reserved IP address to this printer each time it connects to the network. For that to happen, the DHCP server must know the MAC address of the printer. Using controls at the printer, find the MAC address of the printer, and list the MAC address here:

_____

Notes For easier printer installations, a network printer and all the computers that use it should be on the same subnet.

Some network printers serve up a browser-based utility that can be used to configure and manage the printer. Follow these steps to learn more:

1. Open a browser and enter the IP address of the printer in the address box of the browser. Did the printer serve up a printer utility?

2. If the printer provides the utility, log on to the printer, and answer the following questions:

   ◢ Can you configure the IP address of the printer using the utility? If so, how is the IP address currently configured?

_____

◢ Outdated firmware on a network printer can sometimes cause problems. The printer's browser-based utility might provide a way to update the firmware. Search the utility for this feature. Did you find the ability to update the printer firmware? What is the version number of the current firmware?

◢ List three other functions available in the utility. For each function, describe one way the function might be useful when managing the printer:

Sometimes when you are having a problem installing a network printer, the solution is to use the setup program provided by the printer manufacturer. Follow these steps to learn more:

1. Using the Devices and Printers window, remove the network printer.

2. If you have the CD that contains the printer drivers, use this CD to install the printer.

3. If you don't have the CD that contains the printer drivers, use the web to search for the printer drivers on the printer manufacturer's website. Use Table 10-1 to help find the correct website.

   ◢ What is the network printer brand and model?

   ◢ What is the website of the printer manufacturer?

   ◢ What is the name of the file(s) you downloaded and used to install the printer?

   ◢ Describe how the installation using the printer setup program differed from the installation using the Devices and Printers window:

REVIEW QUESTIONS

1. A printer is connected locally on Computer1 and is shared on the network. Computer2 installs the shared printer and connects to it. Computer1 considers the printer to be a(n) _____ printer, and Computer2 considers the printer to be a(n) _____ printer.

2. Why should you use the manufacturer's prescribed method for installing its printer even if it differs from the default Windows method?

3. Is it possible for a single printer to be both a local and a network printer? Why or why not?

10

4. How can you determine the IP address of a network printer?

_____

_____

_____

5. What would be the advantage of connecting a printer to a network server locally rather than having users connect to it directly through the network?

_____

LAB 10.5 UPDATE PRINTER DRIVERS

OBJECTIVES

The goal of this lab is to practice updating printer drivers. After completing this lab, you will be able to:

▲ Identify driver information

▲ Locate new drivers

▲ Install new drivers

▲ Test printer drivers for functionality

MATERIALS REQUIRED

This lab requires the following:

▲ Windows 10/8/7 operating system

▲ Internet access

▲ A local printer

LAB PREPARATION

Before the lab begins, the instructor or lab assistant needs to do the following:

▲ Verify that Windows starts with no errors

▲ Verify that Internet access is available

ACTIVITY BACKGROUND

Printer manufacturers often release new drivers for their existing printers to fix problems with earlier drivers, add new functions, support new applications, and accommodate new operating system features. An IT support technician needs to know how to update printer drivers as they become available. The process of updating printer drivers is similar to that for other devices. You must gather information about the device and the currently installed drivers, download the new drivers, and install them. As with other devices, after printer drivers are installed, you should test the printer to be certain it is functioning correctly before turning it over to end users. The process of updating printer drivers is similar across different Windows platforms and printer manufacturers.

This lab gives you general instructions for updating printer drivers. Modify these instructions to fit your situation and printer.

Activity

The first step in updating printer drivers is to gather information about your current printer and drivers. Use the Devices and Printers window and any other resources at your disposal to research and answer the following questions:

1. How is your printer generally used (for example, for text, photographs, or graphics)?

   _____

2. What operating system are you using? Are you using a 32-bit or 64-bit installation?

   _____

3. Who is the printer manufacturer?

   _____

4. What is the model of the printer?

   _____

5. What is the printer interface (USB, parallel, network, other)?

   _____

6. Printers typically have many setup options that deal with print quality and paper handling. Open the **Devices and Printers** window, right-click the printer, and click **Printer properties** in the shortcut menu. Note any customized printer settings; you'll probably need to reapply them after the driver is updated. (Tabs on the properties dialog box might differ from one printer to another.)

   _____

   _____

7. To identify the printer drivers, click the **Advanced** tab of the printer properties dialog box. What's the name of the driver listed in the Driver drop-down list?

   _____

8. When you're finished, close any open windows.

Follow these general directions to locate available driver updates:

1. Go to the printer manufacturer's website, and locate the driver download section. Use Table 10-1 to help find the website. What's the URL of the driver download page?

   _____

2. When you search for the correct driver on the website, you might find more than one driver that will work for your printer, operating system, or application. Generally, you should select the most recent version that matches your printer and operating system. There are exceptions, however. For instance, if a driver is listed as beta, it's still in development and has been released for evaluation. Usually, but not always, the manufacturer has most of the kinks worked out. To be on the safe side, don't download

a beta release driver. List up to three drivers, with brief descriptions, for your printer and operating system:

_____

_____

3. What driver did you select to download?

_____

4. Find and list any special installation instructions the manufacturer recommends:

_____

_____

5. Create a folder named **Downloads** on your C drive, if necessary. Then create a subfolder, such as C:\Downloads\Lexmark, named for the manufacturer. What's your folder name?

_____

6. Download the driver you intend to install to that folder.

With any device, it's best to follow the manufacturer's recommended method of installation instead of the Windows method. A good manufacturer tests the driver as well as the installation process. Do the following to install the new driver using the manufacturer's installation process:

1. Print an example—a document or a digital picture—of the printer's main use. This printout verifies that your printer is working before you make any changes and is later used for comparison to verify that the new drivers are working.

2. In File Explorer or Windows Explorer, double-click the file you downloaded. If it's a compressed file, it self-extracts the files or uses file compression software on your computer to extract the files. If an installation wizard starts after the files are extracted, exit it.

3. Were any files extracted? List the first three files here:

_____

4. Locate any Readme.txt files for late-breaking information about the installation.

5. Double-click the setup or installation program. Document the process you used to install the new drivers:

_____

_____

_____

Do the following to test the printer and new drivers:

1. Open the **Devices and Printers** window, and then print a Windows test page. Did the page print successfully?

_____

2. Apply any customized printer settings you recorded at the beginning of this lab.

3. Reprint the typical document or photograph, and compare it with the one printed before the driver update. List any differences you see:

_____

ESTIMATED COMPLETION TIME: 15 MINUTES

CHALLENGE ACTIVITY

Suppose you have shared a printer with other computers on the network. The host computer is using a 32-bit version of Windows 8, and you have made available 32-bit printer drivers to be used by other computers on the network when they install the shared printer. List the steps to make available 64-bit printer drivers for other computers on the network that use 64-bit installations of Windows:

_____

_____

_____

_____

10

REVIEW QUESTIONS

1. List four reasons you might want to update a printer's drivers.

_____

_____

_____

_____

2. List four facts you should know about your printer before you start searching the web for updated drivers.

_____

_____

_____

_____

3. What does the label "beta release" indicate about a driver?

_____

4. Will 32-bit printer drivers work in a 64-bit installation of Windows?

_____

5. List the steps to print a test page in Windows.

_____

_____

LAB 10.6 MAINTAIN AND TROUBLESHOOT A PRINTER

OBJECTIVES

The goal of this lab is to practice supporting printers. After completing this lab, you will be able to:

▲ Use the web to help with printer maintenance

▲ Correct common printer problems

MATERIALS REQUIRED

This lab requires the following:

▲ Internet access

▲ A printer

LAB PREPARATION

Before the lab begins, the instructor or lab assistant needs to do the following:

▲ Verify that Internet access is available

ACTIVITY BACKGROUND

Printers require more maintenance than most other peripheral devices. Paper gets jammed, ink cartridges and toner run out, and image or document quality can degrade due to dust and misalignment. Most manufacturers and many models have specific instructions for maintaining ink and toner cartridges, and these instructions apply exclusively to the targeted printers; thus, you must rely on the printer manufacturer for instructions when maintaining a printer. In this lab, you investigate maintenance and troubleshooting instructions for several types of printers.

ESTIMATED COMPLETION TIME: 30 MINUTES

 Activity

Use the web to research how to solve the following problems. The first printer you'll research is a high-end, color laser printer, the LaserJet Enterprise M750n printer, by Hewlett-Packard (_hp.com_). Answer these questions about routine maintenance for this printer:

1. What is the average number of pages that prints from one black toner cartridge? From one color toner cartridge? You'll need part numbers when ordering toner cartridges. What are the part numbers of the cartridges?

_____

_____

2. Besides toner cartridges, other replaceable printer parts include the paper tray, the fuser, and the parts used in the transfer portion of the printing process, which come as an assembled unit called a transfer kit. Find and list the part numbers for these items that are compatible with the LaserJet Enterprise M750n:

_____

_____

3. What items are included in the transfer kit assembly?

_____

_____

The next printer is an inkjet printer, the HP DeskJet 1010 printer. Answer these questions:

1. Printouts from your printer contain no black ink but do include the three colors. You know that you replaced the black cartridge recently. Search the HP website, and locate the troubleshooting steps to solve the problem.

2. What is the first thing HP suggests you do when you experience this type of problem?

_____

3. If the ink level is low, HP instructs the user to replace the ink cartridge. What is the last step in replacing the ink cartridge, which might be easy for a user to forget to do?

_____

4. One troubleshooting step that HP suggests is that you clean the cartridge contacts. List the steps to do this on a Windows computer:

_____

_____

_____

5. If the problem isn't fixed, what does HP suggest that you check next?

_____

Next, follow these steps to learn how to perform routine maintenance or troubleshoot problems on your local printer:

1. List the following information to identify your local printer:

◢ Printer manufacturer:

_____

◢ Printer model:

_____

◢ Printer interface (USB, Bluetooth, other):

_____

10

2. Search the manufacturer's website for troubleshooting and maintenance procedures, and answer the following questions:

◢ What types of problems are addressed for your printer?

_____

_____

◢ Does the manufacturer offer a printer maintenance kit? If so, what components are included, and how much does the kit cost?

_____

_____

◢ What maintenance tips for your printer can you find on the website?

_____

_____

REVIEW QUESTIONS

1. When a printer isn't working correctly, what are two ways the problem is communicated to users?

_____

2. Why do printers require more maintenance than other peripherals?

_____

3. Besides toner cartridges, what are three replaceable parts in a laser printer?

_____

4. When replacing an ink cartridge in an inkjet printer, what is the final step, which must be completed through Windows?

_____

LAB 10.7 MANAGE PRINT JOBS

OBJECTIVES

Your goal in this lab is to learn how to use the printer queue to manage print jobs. After completing this lab, you will be able to:

◢ Use the printer queue to troubleshoot printing problems

◢ Stop and restart the Print Spooler service

MATERIALS REQUIRED

This lab requires the following:

◢ Two or more Windows 10/8/7 computers connected to a network and belonging to the same Windows workgroup

◢ A local or network printer

◢ A workgroup of two to four students

LAB PREPARATION

Before the lab begins, the instructor or lab assistant needs to do the following:

◢ Verify that Windows starts with no errors

◢ Verify that a printer is available for each student workgroup

ACTIVITY BACKGROUND

A network administrator is typically responsible for a printer and any problems that might arise with print jobs not printing. One way to make this job easier is to use one computer as a print server, which manages print jobs for all users. In this lab, you can practice managing a printer from a centralized print server.

ESTIMATED COMPLETION TIME: 30 MINUTES

 Activity

For your workgroup of two or more computers, do the following to make sure the printer is available to all computers in your workgroup:

1. Using the knowledge that you've gained from previous labs, install a local or network printer on one computer, and designate this computer as the host computer or print server.

2. Install the printer on other computers in the workgroup. The installation should use the shared printer provided by the host computer.

3. On the host computer, in the Devices and Printers window, double-click the shared printer. For Windows 10, click **See what's printing**. The printer queue appears but shows no documents listed. See Figure 10-7.

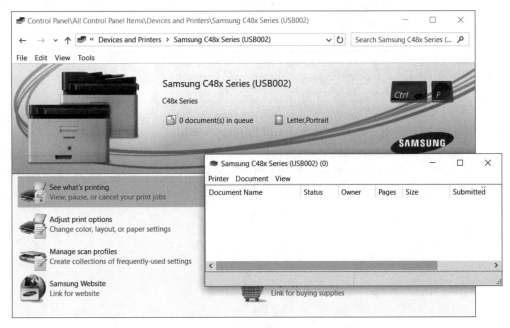

Figure 10-7 Use the printer queue window to manage print jobs waiting to print or in the process

> **📝 Notes** When you double-click a printer in the Devices and Printers window, the printer window—where you can manage the print queue and other printer features—should appear. If the printer is not properly installed, a properties dialog box appears instead. The dialog box has only two tabs: the General tab and the Hardware tab. If you see this type of dialog box, go back and troubleshoot the printer installation. Try removing and reinstalling the printer.

4. Print a Windows test page from each computer in your workgroup. As the documents print, observe the printer queue on the host computer. Does every print job sent to the printer appear in the queue?

_____

5. Turn off the printer. On the remote computers, send new print jobs until three jobs are backed up in the queue. How can you tell which print job belongs to which computer or user?

_____

6. In what order are print jobs listed? Delete the first print job queued that has not yet printed.

_____

7. Turn on the printer. Did the other two print jobs print successfully?

_____

8. Remove the paper from the printer and print a test page from each computer in your workgroup.

   ◢ What does the printer queue window report on the host computer about the problem?

   _____

   ◢ What does the printer queue window on a remote user's computer report about the problem?

   _____

The Windows Print Spooler service is responsible for managing the printer queue. If the queue gets stuck, one thing you can do is stop and restart the Print Spooler service. Do the following to learn more:

1. Verify that you still have jobs waiting in the printer queue. Close any open windows, including the Devices and Printers window.

2. Enter **services.msc** in the Windows 10/7 search box or the Windows 8 Run box. The Services console window opens. Make sure the **Extended** tab is selected near the bottom of the window (see Figure 10-8).

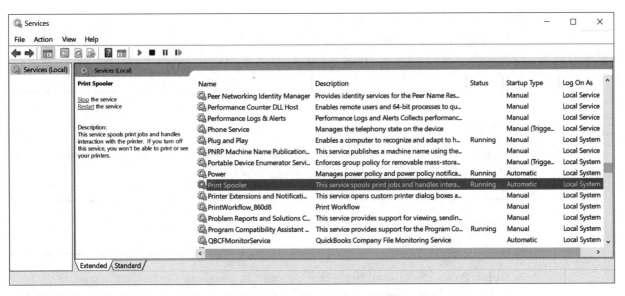

Figure 10-8 Use the Services console to stop and start the Print Spooler service

10

3. Scroll down to and select **Print Spooler**.

   ◢ What is the Status of the service?

   _____

   ◢ What is the Startup Type of the service?

   _____

4. With the Print Spooler service selected, click **Stop**.

5. Open the **Devices and Printers** window. Double-click the printer. Can you view the printer queue? Why or why not? Close the window.

   _____

6. Return to the Services console, and again select **Print Spooler**. Click **Start**. The spooler starts again.

7. Open the **Devices and Printers** window and double-click the printer. Are the print jobs still in the print queue?

   _____

8. Close the window.

Stopping and starting the Print Spooler can sometimes solve a printing problem. In addition, you can manually delete all jobs in the queue while the service is stopped, which can solve a problem when a print job is corrupted. Follow these steps to learn more:

1. Return to the Services console, and stop the **Print Spooler**.

2. Windows stores queued print jobs in the C:\Windows\System32\spool\PRINTERS folder. Open **File Explorer** or **Windows Explorer**, and drill down to this folder. How many files are in the folder?

   _____

3. Delete all files in this folder.

4. Use the Services console to start the **Print Spooler**.

5. Return to the Devices and Printers window. Are all jobs removed from the print queue?

_____

REVIEW QUESTIONS

1. If you are responsible for managing and maintaining a network printer, why might you want all print jobs routed through a print server?

_____

2. What are the steps to delete a single print job in the printer queue?

_____

3. Group Policy can be used to prevent a user from installing a network printer and bypassing a host computer serving up the printer. What advantage does this group policy provide?

_____

_____

4. If a network administrator does not want to be called upon frequently to refill the paper in a printer, what can he do to make it easier for users to handle this chore?

_____

_____

5. How do you permanently remove print jobs from the print queue when the Print Spooler service is not running?

_____

LAB 10.8 SABOTAGE AND REPAIR A PRINTER

OBJECTIVES

Your goal in this lab is to learn how to troubleshoot problems with a printer. After completing this lab, you will be able to:

▲ Identify symptoms of common printer problems

▲ Troubleshoot printing issues

MATERIALS REQUIRED

This lab requires the following:

▲ Two or more computers connected to a network and belonging to the same Windows workgroup, including one computer that shares a printer with other computers on the network

▲ A workgroup of two to four students

LAB PREPARATION

Before the lab begins, the instructor or lab assistant needs to do the following:

◢ Verify that Windows starts with no errors

◢ Verify that a printer is available for each student workgroup

ACTIVITY BACKGROUND

Problems with a network printer are common, and an IT support technician is often called on to solve them. This lab gives you practice solving these types of problems.

ESTIMATED COMPLETION TIME: 45 MINUTES

 Activity

For your workgroup of two or more computers, do the following to make sure the printer is available to all computers in your workgroup:

1. Using the knowledge that you've gained from previous labs, install a local or network printer on one computer and designate this computer as the host computer.

2. Install the printer on other computers in the workgroup. The installation should use the shared printer provided by the host computer.

3. Trade systems with another group, and sabotage the other group's system while that group sabotages your system. The following list has some suggestions for preventing a computer from using the printer. Do something in this list, or think of another option:

   ◢ On the host computer, remove the sharing option for the printer.

   ◢ Uninstall the printer on a remote computer.

   ◢ Pause printing on one or more computers.

   ◢ Turn the printer off, or turn it offline.

   ◢ Disconnect the printer cable from the host computer (for a local printer) or from the network (for a network printer).

   ◢ Remove paper from the printer.

   ◢ Introduce an error in the printer configuration on the host computer or a remote computer.

4. What did you do to sabotage the other team's system?

_____

Return to your system and troubleshoot it. Complete the following:

1. Describe the problem as a user would describe it to you if you were working at a help desk:

_____

_____

2. What is your first guess as to the source of the problem?

_____

10

3. List the steps you took in the troubleshooting process:

_____

_____

_____

4. How did you solve the problem and return the printing system to working order?

_____

_____

5. What might cause this problem to happen again?

_____

_____

REVIEW QUESTIONS

1. How did you initially test the printer to see if it was working?

_____

2. What should you do to make sure the printer itself is printing properly?

_____

3. For a network printer, what TCP/IP command can you enter at a command prompt to verify that Windows can communicate with the printer?

_____

4. What would you do differently the next time you encounter the same indications of a printing problem?

_____

Windows Versions and Customer Service

Labs included in this chapter:

- **Lab 11.1:** Create and Manage Multiple Desktops
- **Lab 11.2:** Use Windows Keyboard Shortcuts
- **Lab 11.3:** Use the Problem Steps Recorder
- **Lab 11.4:** Record Apps with Game DVR
- **Lab 11.5:** Understand IT Codes of Ethics
- **Lab 11.6:** Provide Customer Service
- **Lab 11.7:** Practice Help-Desk Skills
- **Lab 11.8:** Practice Good Communication Skills
- **Lab 11.9:** Understand How to Create a Help-Desk Procedure

LAB 11.1 CREATE AND MANAGE MULTIPLE DESKTOPS

OBJECTIVES

Your goal in this lab is to familiarize yourself with Task View and manage app windows on multiple desktops. After completing this lab, you will be able to:

◢ Use Task View

◢ Create and use multiple desktops

◢ Move apps between desktops

◢ Use keyboard shortcuts to manage multiple desktops

MATERIALS REQUIRED

This lab requires the following:

◢ Windows 10 operating system

LAB PREPARATION

Before the lab begins, the instructor or lab assistant needs to do the following:

◢ Verify that Windows starts with no errors

ACTIVITY BACKGROUND

A convenient new feature of Windows 10 is Task View, which enables multiple desktops to hold different groups of apps as you manage your workload. The key to getting the most out of a convenience feature such as multiple desktops is becoming comfortable with how to use it and learning what it can do.

ESTIMATED COMPLETION TIME: 30 MINUTES

 Activity

Complete the following steps to practice using multiple desktops in Task View:

1. Open File Explorer, Control Panel, Paint, and Edge on your desktop.

2. Click the **Task View** icon in the taskbar. Drag one app and drop it in the New desktop area, as shown in Figure 11-1. Two desktop thumbnails appear in the top pane (see Figure 11-2).

3. Click the **Desktop 2** thumbnail. Which app is open on this desktop?

_____

4. Close the app in Desktop 2, and click the **Task View** icon in the taskbar. Notice that Desktop 2 still exists even though no apps are currently open on it. Click **New desktop** to create a third desktop, which also has no open apps.

5. Float the mouse pointer over the Desktop 1 thumbnail without clicking on it. What happens?

_____

_____

Paint app is dropped
in New desktop area

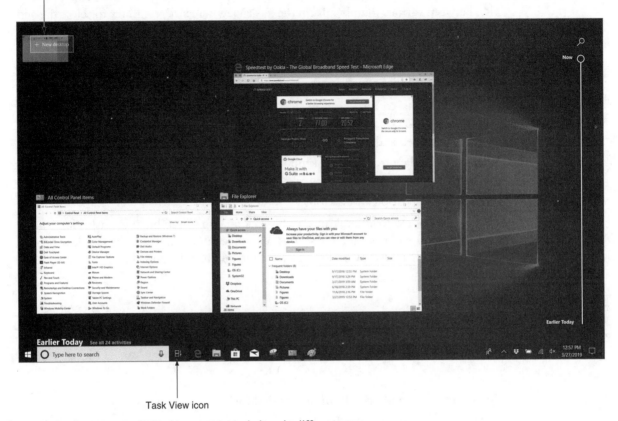

Task View icon

Figure 11-1 Create a new desktop to group app windows in different areas

> **Notes** If the Task View icon is missing in the Windows taskbar, right-click the taskbar and check Show Task View.

Figure 11-2 Create as many desktops as you need to organize your workspace

6. Drag the app thumbnails to place at least one open app on each of the three desktops. Float the mouse pointer over each desktop thumbnail, and notice how the app icons in the taskbar change depending on which apps are open for each desktop. What graphic indicates open apps on a desktop?

It's easy to access Task View and move among the desktops by using some handy keyboard shortcuts.

11

1. Press **Win+Tab** on your keyboard to view the active desktop. Press **Win+Tab** again to return to Task View. Use the **Tab** and **Left** or **Right** arrow keys to move the active selection between various thumbnails on the Task View screen. Press **Enter** to select the active thumbnail.

2. Return to Task View. Press **Ctrl+Win+Left** or **Ctrl+Win+Right** to select a different desktop in Task View. This also works when you're viewing a desktop. Click a desktop to view it, and then press **Ctrl+Win+Left** or **Ctrl+Win+Right** to switch between desktops.

3. Press **Ctrl+Win+D** to create a new desktop. Return to Task View to see how many desktops are open and which apps are shown in each desktop.

4. To move a window from one desktop to another, open **Task View** and drag a window to a new desktop.

You can make a single window appear on all desktops.

1. To pin the window to all desktops, right-click an app's thumbnail in Task View and click **Show this window on all desktops**. View each desktop to see the window on each one. To unpin the window, right-click the thumbnail again, and click to deselect the same setting.

> **Notes** If you have multiple windows open for a single app, click **Show windows from this app on all desktops** to see all of that app's windows on every desktop.

2. Go to Desktop 3 and open **Paint** on this desktop.

3. In Task View, close Desktop 3 as follows: Float the mouse pointer over the desktop thumbnail, and then click the **X** that appears above the thumbnail, as shown in Figure 11-3. What happens to the Paint app that was open on that desktop? Where is it now?

_____

_____

_____

Active desktop thumbnail

Figure 11-3 Open windows on a desktop are not lost when the desktop is closed

REVIEW QUESTIONS

1. Which taskbar icon shows you all existing desktops on your Windows 10 computer?

   _____

2. Which keyboard shortcut toggles between the active desktop and Task View?

   _____

3. Which two keyboard shortcuts switch between desktops without using Task View?

   _____

4. Why might you want one window pinned to all desktops?

   _____

   _____

5. How do you think you might be able to use multiple desktops?

   _____

   _____

   _____

   _____

11

LAB 11.2 USE WINDOWS KEYBOARD SHORTCUTS

OBJECTIVES

Your goal in this lab is to learn some keyboard shortcuts. After completing this lab, you will be able to use the keyboard to:

▲ Display the Start menu

▲ Launch Help and Support

▲ Switch between open applications

▲ Launch utilities with the Windows logo key

MATERIALS REQUIRED

This lab requires the following:

▲ Windows 10/8/7 operating system

▲ Internet access

▲ A keyboard with the Windows logo key

LAB PREPARATION

Before the lab begins, the instructor or lab assistant needs to do the following:

◢ Verify that Windows starts with no errors

◢ Verify that Internet access is available

ACTIVITY BACKGROUND

You can use certain keys or key combinations (called keyboard shortcuts) to perform repetitive tasks more efficiently. These shortcuts are also useful if your mouse is not working. In this lab, you learn to use some common keyboard shortcuts. You can find a full list of keyboard shortcuts by searching for "keyboard shortcuts" in the Windows Help and Support Center.

ESTIMATED COMPLETION TIME: 30 MINUTES

 Activity

The F1 key is the universal keyboard shortcut for launching Help. To learn more, follow these steps:

1. Click the desktop, and then press **F1**. Windows Help and Support opens.

2. Close Windows Help and Support.

3. Open File Explorer in Windows 10/8 or Windows Explorer in Windows 7.

4. With the File Explorer/Windows Explorer window as the active window, press **F1**.

5. Explore the Help options available for File Explorer/Windows Explorer.

6. Open Notepad.

7. With the Notepad window as the active window, press **F1**.

8. Explore the Help options available for Notepad.

   ◢ How are the Windows Help and Support options different if you press F1 when the desktop is active as opposed to when the File Explorer/Windows Explorer window or Notepad window is active?

   _____

   _____

   _____

9. Use Windows Help and Support to find a list of general keyboard shortcuts. What key can you press to activate the menu in an application window? Close all windows.

   _____

10. You can activate many shortcuts by pressing the Windows logo key in combination with other keys. An enhanced keyboard has two Windows logo keys, usually located between the Ctrl and Alt keys on either side of the Spacebar. Try the combinations listed in Table 11-1, and record the result of each key combination in the Result column. (Close each window you open before proceeding to the next key combination.)

Key or Key Combination	Result
Windows logo	
Windows logo + E	
Windows logo + F	
Windows logo + R	
Windows logo + Pause	
Windows logo + M	

Table 11-1 Key combinations using the Windows logo key

To become more efficient and productive with your work by using shortcut keystrokes, follow these steps:

1. Press the Windows logo on your keyboard; the Start menu or screen opens. In Windows 10/8, type **notepad** and press **Enter**. In Windows 7, type **notepad** in the Search programs and files box, and press **Enter**. The Notepad app opens.

2. Press the Windows logo on your keyboard; the Start screen or menu opens. In Windows 10/8, type **paint** and press **Enter**. In Windows 7, type **mspaint** in the Search programs and files box, and press **Enter**. Microsoft Paint opens.

3. Press the Windows logo on your keyboard; the Start screen or menu opens. In Windows 10/8, type **calc** and press **Enter**. In Windows 7, type **calc** in the Search programs and files box, and press **Enter**. The Calculator opens.

4. With all those applications open, try the following key combinations:

   a. Press the **Alt+Tab** keys.

   b. Continue to hold down the **Alt** key, and repeatedly tap the **Tab** key.

   ◢ How can these key combinations assist you in being more efficient with your work?

   _____

   _____

ESTIMATED COMPLETION TIME: 15 MINUTES

CHALLENGE ACTIVITY

Using the keyboard skills you have learned in this lab, complete the following steps without using the mouse, and answer the respective questions:

1. Where online can you find a more complete list of keyboard shortcuts for Windows operating systems? Record the URL for this list:

   _____

   _____

2. Using the Windows Help and Support utility, what key combination can be used for printing a document?

   _____

11

3. Using the Windows Help and Support utility, what key combination can be used to save your work in a document in progress?

_____

4. What key combination can you use with Internet Explorer that may help you when browsing?

_____

REVIEW QUESTIONS

1. What key is universally used to launch Help?

_____

2. How many Windows logo keys are usually included on an enhanced keyboard?

_____

3. What keyboard shortcut combinations can be used to copy and paste a block of text?

_____

4. Which key can you press to open the Start menu?

_____

5. What is the result of pressing the ▦ Windows logo + P key combination? Describe a situation in which a user might find this menu helpful:

_____

_____

LAB 11.3 USE THE PROBLEM STEPS RECORDER

OBJECTIVES

Your goal in this lab is to use the Windows Steps Recorder. After completing this lab, you will be able to:

◢ Record steps using Steps Recorder

◢ Review steps recorded

MATERIALS REQUIRED

This lab requires the following:

◢ Windows 10/8/7 operating system

LAB PREPARATION

Before the lab begins, the instructor or lab assistant needs to do the following:

◢ Verify that Windows starts with no errors

ACTIVITY BACKGROUND

When you're troubleshooting a problem in Windows, recording the steps you take can be crucial to proper documentation. Recording steps is also helpful when you're documenting how to do something or when a user needs to show you what he or she is doing. Fortunately, Microsoft provides Steps Recorder to record steps and generate a report with all actions recorded.

ESTIMATED COMPLETION TIME: 20 MINUTES

 Activity

Follow these steps to use Steps Recorder:

1. Open the Steps Recorder app. To open the app in Windows 10, click **Start,** click **Windows Accessories,** and click **Steps Recorder**. For Windows 8/7, click **Start,** click **Accessories,** and click **Problem Steps Recorder.**

2. Click **Start Record**. The Steps Recorder begins recording all actions taken on the computer.

3. Open the Paint app. Note that as you click, a red dot appears. This indicates that the action was recorded.

4. Draw a mark or shape on the Paint window.

5. In the Steps Recorder program, click **Stop Record**. Steps Recorder automatically opens a file containing all the steps and information that was recorded. See Figure 11-4. Scroll down the window to review the scripted steps and images that were recorded while you opened the Paint program and drew an image in the Paint window.

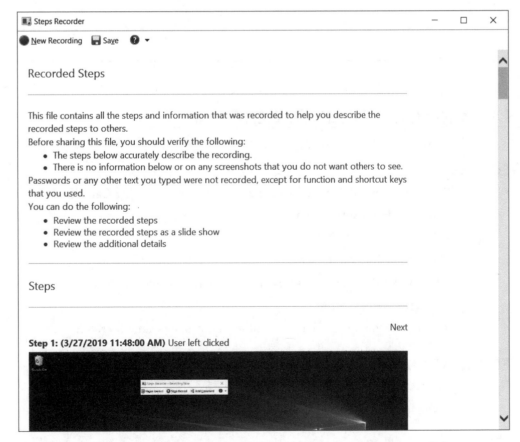

Figure 11-4 The Steps Recorder records screen captures and detailed steps of user activity

6. In the Steps Recorder window showing the file of recorded steps, click **Save**.

7. Save this report to your computer, and name it **UsingPaint.zip**. Close the Steps Recorder and Paint windows (no need to save changes in Paint).

8. Open the UsingPaint.zip file, and then open the recording file. Review your recording, and close the file.

REVIEW QUESTIONS

1. In Steps Recorder, how do you know that an action using the mouse is recorded?

_____

2. What type of folder contains the file of recorded steps?

_____

3. What type of file contains the recorded steps? By default, which program is used to view the file?

_____

4. Does Steps Recorder record a script of the actions taken or images of the actions taken?

_____

5. Imagine you have a job working on a help desk. In what situation might you use Steps Recorder?

_____

_____

_____

LAB 11.4 RECORD APPS WITH GAME DVR

OBJECTIVES

The goal of this lab is to record activity on your screen using Game DVR.

After completing this lab, you will be able to:

◢ Activate the Game Bar

◢ Record actions on the screen

◢ Use background recording to capture actions already completed

◢ Locate saved captures

◢ Change keyboard shortcuts and other settings for Game DVR

MATERIALS REQUIRED

This lab requires the following:

◢ Windows 10 operating system

LAB PREPARATION

Before the lab begins, the instructor or lab assistant needs to do the following:

◢ Verify that Windows starts with no errors

ACTIVITY BACKGROUND

You used Steps Recorder in the preceding lab. This helpful tool captures screenshots with each click on the screen and generates a report of all actions taken. The tool is available in Windows 10, but you might find a different Windows 10 tool, Game DVR, even more useful. Game DVR captures video and audio of on-screen activity. It is designed for sharing gaming activities, but it can also be used to capture user activity in other apps. This can be helpful when you're documenting how to do something or when a user needs to show you what he or she is doing.

ESTIMATED COMPLETION TIME: 15 MINUTES

 Activity

Complete the following steps to record on-screen activity using Game DVR:

1. Open the app you want to record, and make sure it's the active window. For this example, we used the Paint app. Press **Win+G** on your keyboard. If you're not playing a game, the notification in Figure 11-5 asks if you want to open the Game Bar. To use Game DVR, check the box next to **Yes, this is a game**.

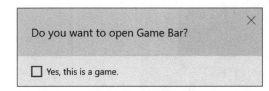

Do you want to open Game Bar?

☐ Yes, this is a game.

Figure 11-5   You don't actually have to be playing a game to use Game DVR

2. The Game Bar shown in Figure 11-6 contains tools that allow you to access Xbox, take a screenshot, capture a video of previous actions (provided you turn on background recording first), begin recording new actions, broadcast a recording, or change settings. Experiment by taking several screenshots and recording several videos.

> **Notes** The Game Bar display times out quickly and disappears if you're not interacting with it frequently. At any time, you can press Win+G on your keyboard to display the Game Bar again.

Figure 11-6   The screenshot, recording, and broadcast tools can all be accessed with keyboard shortcuts

11

3. Each screenshot or video capture is saved automatically in the user's Videos\Captures folder. Each file is named according to the app that was recorded and the time and date of the recording. What file type is used for videos? What file type is used for screenshots?

4. Click the **Settings** gear icon in the Game Bar. On the General tab (see Figure 11-7), you can change settings for background recording and choose whether or not to remember the current app as a game.

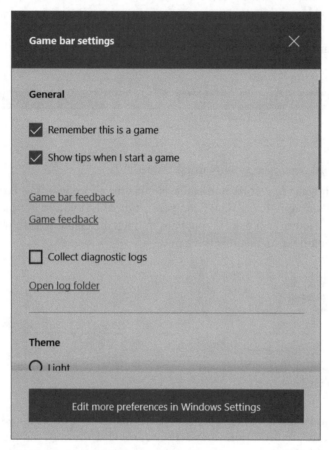

Figure 11-7   Make changes to the general settings in the Game Bar settings

5. Scroll down to explore the options for broadcasting and to change audio recording settings.

REVIEW QUESTIONS

1. What app is similar to Game DVR but captures screenshots and generates a report of all actions taken?

2. Which keyboard shortcut opens the Game Bar?

3. Why do you have to tell Windows that an app is a game in order to use Game DVR?

_____

_____

_____

4. Where are Game DVR screenshots and video captures automatically saved?

_____

_____

5. What information is automatically included in a video's file name?

_____

_____

_____

6. Describe the steps for disabling background recording after it's been enabled.

_____

_____

_____

_____

LAB 11.5 UNDERSTAND IT CODES OF ETHICS

OBJECTIVES

Your goal in this lab is to become familiar with the concept of a code of ethics for IT professionals. After completing this lab, you will be able to:

▲ Examine a code of ethics for IT professionals

▲ Consider different values when making an ethical decision

MATERIALS REQUIRED

This lab requires the following:

▲ A Windows 10/8/7 workstation

▲ Internet access

▲ A workgroup of two to four students

LAB PREPARATION

Before the lab begins, the instructor or lab assistant needs to do the following:

▲ Read through the IEEE code of ethics and be prepared to discuss it with each group

▲ Verify that Windows starts with no errors

▲ Verify that Internet access is available

ACTIVITY BACKGROUND

Most companies and professional organizations have a code of ethics or a code of conduct that they expect their employees or members to uphold. The code typically outlines the rights and responsibilities of employees and members as well as their customers. Certain practices, such as respecting confidentiality and avoiding conflicts of interest, are common to most codes, while other behaviors are industry specific. In addition, many businesses publish a Statement of Values that outlines the values or qualities that guide their actions. In this lab, you examine a code of ethics developed by the Institute of Electrical and Electronics Engineers (IEEE) and consider the values it represents.

ESTIMATED COMPLETION TIME: 60 MINUTES

 Activity

To develop your own code of ethics that you think professionals in the computer industry should follow, complete these steps:

1. In your opinion, what are the three most important ethical issues that professionals in the computer industry regularly face?

   _____

   _____

   _____

2. Develop an ethical standard that professionals in the computer industry should use when faced with each of the three issues you identified in the preceding step:

   _____

   _____

   _____

3. Discuss your ideas in your workgroup, and, as a group, create a code of ethics using the five ethical standards your group thinks are most important for professionals in the computer industry:

   _____

   _____

   _____

   _____

   _____

To learn more about computer industry ethics and values, follow these steps:

1. To begin, go to the IEEE website (**ieee.org**), and search for the IEEE code of ethics. Review the code, and then do the following:

   ◢ Discuss this code with your group. What do you, as a group, consider to be the most important guideline in the list?

   _____

   ◢ Describe any significant similarities or differences between the IEEE code and the code of ethics your workgroup created:

   _____

   _____

   _____

   ◢ Find at least one other technological organization or company that posts a code of ethics on its website. Write down the name of the organization and its URL on the following lines:

   _____

   _____

   ◢ Describe any significant similarities or differences between the IEEE code and the code from the other technological organization:

   _____

   _____

   _____

Ethical decisions are often constructed around a set of priorities or values, such as fairness, equality, and honesty. Further evaluate values by following these steps:

1. On your own, write down as many unique values as you can in 10 minutes. You might want to research "ethical values" on the Internet for inspiration.

   _____

   _____

   _____

   _____

   _____

2. When you're finished, share your list of values with your group, and try to agree on what you consider the seven most important values for aiding ethical decision making. Remember that there are no right or wrong answers; you're just trying to determine what's most important to the members in your group.

   ◢ List the values on the following lines:

   1. _____

   2. _____

   3. _____

11

4. _____

5. _____

6. _____

7. _____

3. What values from your group's list are also represented by the IEEE code of ethics?

_____

_____

_____

_____

Case study: You are working in the IT department of a large company. Your employer has asked you to monitor the email and Internet activity of select individuals in the company and to submit a report on those activities at the end of the week. Answer the following questions:

1. Does your employer have the right to monitor this information? Does it have a responsibility to do so? Explain your answer:

_____

_____

_____

2. Does your employer have a responsibility to inform its employees that their email and Internet activity are being monitored? Explain your answer:

_____

_____

3. What should you do if you discover an illegal activity during your investigation? What if your employer doesn't agree with your decision?

_____

_____

_____

4. What would you do if you discovered that your employer was engaged in illegal activity, such as using pirated software?

_____

_____

_____

5. If a coworker who is a close friend is found to be using the Internet while at work for job hunting, would you mention it in your report? Explain your answer:

_____

_____

_____

REVIEW QUESTIONS

1. Did your group have any trouble agreeing on the seven most important values? Why did you agree or disagree?

   _____

   _____

2. Do you think having a company code of ethics makes ethical decisions any easier? Why?

   _____

   _____

3. Do you think most people share a fundamental set of values? Why?

   _____

   _____

4. What can you do in cases where your personal values conflict with the values of your employer?

   _____

   _____

LAB 11.6 PROVIDE CUSTOMER SERVICE

OBJECTIVES

The goal of this lab is to develop an understanding of some of the issues involved in providing excellent customer service. After completing this lab, you will be able to:

▲ Evaluate the service needs of your customers

▲ Plan for good customer service

▲ Respond to customer complaints

MATERIALS REQUIRED

This lab requires the following:

▲ A workgroup of two to four students

LAB PREPARATION

Before the lab begins, the instructor or lab assistant needs to do the following:

▲ Read through the customer service scenarios and be prepared to discuss them with each group

ACTIVITY BACKGROUND

An IT technician needs to be not only technically competent, but also skilled at providing excellent customer service. Acting in a helpful, dependable, and, above all, professional manner is a must—whether the technician deals directly with customers or works with other employees as part of a team.

To complete this lab, work through the following customer service scenarios. When you are finished, compare your answers with those from the rest of your group, and see whether you can arrive at a consensus. Keep in mind that there might not be a single right answer to each question.

ESTIMATED COMPLETION TIME: 60 MINUTES

 Activity

Working with a group, review the following customer service scenarios, and answer the accompanying questions:

1. A customer returns to your store, complaining that the upgraded computer he just picked up doesn't boot. You remember testing the computer yourself before the pickup, and everything was fine.

   ◢ What can you do to remedy the situation?

   _____

   _____

   ◢ How can you avoid this kind of problem in the future?

   _____

   _____

2. You're working in a call center that provides support to customers who are trying to install your company's product at home. While working with an inexperienced customer over the telephone, you realize that she's having trouble following your directions.

   ◢ What are some ways you can help customers even when they can't see you face-to-face?

   _____

   _____

   _____

   _____

   _____

   ◢ How can you communicate clearly with your customers while avoiding the impression that you're talking down to them?

   _____

   _____

   _____

3. You arrive on a service call, and the overly confident office supervisor shows you the malfunctioning computer. She begins to explain what she thinks is the problem, but you can tell from the computer's operation that it's something else. You suspect that the office supervisor might have caused the malfunction.

◢ How can you troubleshoot the problem without offending your customer?

_____

_____

_____

◢ Would it be a mistake to accuse the customer of causing the problem? Why?

_____

_____

4. An irate customer calls to complain that he's not satisfied with service he has received from your company, and he tells you he plans to take his future business elsewhere.

◢ Should you apologize even if you don't think your company acted improperly?

_____

_____

◢ How can you give the customer the impression that you and your company are listening to his complaints?

_____

_____

REVIEW QUESTIONS

1. What viewpoints about the preceding scenarios did other members of your group have that you hadn't considered?

_____

_____

_____

2. Did you have any trouble coming to a consensus about how to deal with each situation? Explain your answer:

_____

_____

3. Why is an understanding of good customer service important for a technician who doesn't work directly with customers?

_____

_____

4. How can you improve your listening skills when working with customers?

_____

_____

_____

LAB 11.7 PRACTICE HELP-DESK SKILLS

OBJECTIVES

Your goal in this lab is to learn how to work with a customer via a chat session and a telephone conversation. After completing this lab, you will be able to:

◢ Use help-desk skills in a chat session and on the phone to solve customer problems

MATERIALS REQUIRED

This lab requires the following:

◢ Two or more Windows 10/8/7 operating systems

◢ Internet access

◢ Access to instant messaging software such as Skype

◢ A phone (or cell phone) for each student

LAB PREPARATION

Before the lab begins, the instructor or lab assistant needs to do the following:

◢ Verify that Windows starts with no errors

◢ Verify that Internet access is available

◢ Verify that messaging software is available

◢ Instruct students to bring their cell phones to the lab, or provide telephones in the lab

ACTIVITY BACKGROUND

In the past, help-desk support was provided solely by telephone; however, most hardware and software companies now also offer technical support for their products through chat sessions with the company's help-desk staff. Help-desk personnel need to know how to ask questions, connect with customers in a friendly and personal tone, and solve problems via a telephone conversation or a chat session. Typically, a customer can initiate a chat session by clicking a link on a company's website. For example, in Figure 11-8, you can see where to click to start a live chat session with NETGEAR support.

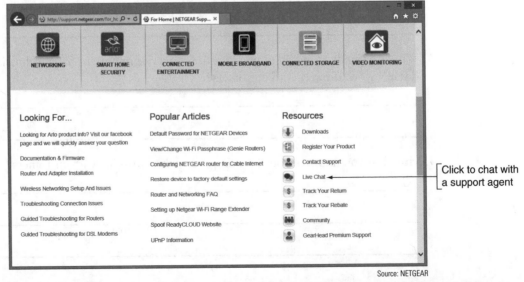

Source: NETGEAR

Figure 11-8   Chat sessions for technical support are often available through manufacturer websites

Activity

Imagine that Jesse is having problems securing his home wireless network. The router that serves as his wireless access point was not working, so he pressed the Reset button on the router. The router began working, but Jesse then discovered he had reset the router back to the factory default settings, undoing all his wireless security settings. When Jesse tried to reconfigure the router, he could not find the router documentation, which included the user name and password to the router firmware utility. After giving up his search for the documentation, he has decided to contact NETGEAR for help.

Jesse goes to the NETGEAR website and clicks the Support link, which opens the page shown earlier in Figure 11-8. He clicks the Live Chat link and, on the next page, enters his name, phone number, and email address, as well as the product name. After he submits this information, a chat window opens, similar to the one in Figure 11-9. Farly is working the help desk at NETGEAR and responds to Jesse.

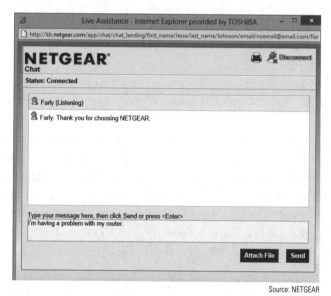

Source: NETGEAR

Figure 11-9   A sample technical support chat window

Working with a partner in your workgroup, use network and chat software such as Skype, and complete the following steps:

1. Select one person in your workgroup to play the role of Jesse, the customer. Select another person to play the role of Farly, the help-desk technician.

2. Jesse initiates a chat session with Farly. What is the first thing Farly says to Jesse in the chat session?

_____

3. In your chat session between Jesse and Farly, communicate the following:

   ◢ Farly asks Jesse for the serial number of the router. This number is embedded on the bottom of the router.

   ◢ Farly knows that the default user name for this router is a blank entry with "admin" for the password. Farly wants Jesse to know it would have been better for him to have reset the router by unplugging it and then plugging it back in rather than using the Reset button. Farly also tells Jesse that, for security reasons, he needs to enter a new user name and password for the router.

4. Print the chat session. If your chat software does not have a print option, then copy and paste the chat session text into a document and print the document. As a courtesy, many companies send the customer a transcription of the chat session via email.

5. Critique the chat session with others in your workgroup. Make suggestions that might help Farly to be more effective, friendly, and helpful.

Use telephones to simulate a help-desk conversation. Use the same troubleshooting scenario, but this time, switch players between Jesse and Farly. Do the following:

1. Jesse calls Farly, and Farly answers, "Hello, this is Farly Jackson with the NETGEAR help desk. May I please have your name, the product you need help with, your phone number, and email address?"

2. After the necessary information is collected, Farly allows Jesse to describe the problem and then steps him through the solution.

3. When the problem is solved, Farly ends the call politely and positively.

4. Ask your workgroup to make suggestions that might help Farly to be more effective, friendly, and helpful.

In the next help-desk session, Joy contacts technical support for her company, complaining of too many pop-up ads on her desktop. Do the following:

1. Select someone to play the role of Joy and another person to play the role of Sam, the help-desk technician. Assume that Joy is a novice user who needs a little extra help with keystrokes.

2. Using chat software, Joy starts a chat session with Sam, and Sam solves the problem.

3. Sam decides to have Joy turn on the Internet Explorer pop-up blocker, use previously installed anti-malware software to scan for viruses, and run Windows Defender if she has Windows 10/8. (If Joy has Windows 7, she should download, install, and run Microsoft Security Essentials software from the Microsoft website.)

4. Print the chat session and discuss it with your workgroup. Do you have any suggestions for Sam to improve his help-desk skills?

_____

_____

5. Using telephones, switch players for Joy and Sam, and solve the same problem. Do you have any suggestions for Sam to improve his help-desk skills?

_____

_____

ESTIMATED COMPLETION TIME: 30 MINUTES

CHALLENGE ACTIVITY

Do the following to get more practice supporting users on the phone:

1. Think of a computer problem you or a friend has encountered that you or your friend could not quickly solve. Describe the problem as a user would describe it when he first calls a help desk:

_____

_____

2. Working with a partner, the partner plays the role of a help-desk technician, and you play the role of the user. Call the "help desk," and describe your problem. Work with your partner toward a solution. Answer the following questions:

   ▲ Was your partner able to help you solve the problem?

   _____

   ▲ Assess how well your partner handled the call. How would you assess the service you received?

   _____

   _____

3. Switch roles with your partner, and repeat Steps 1 and 2. You become the help-desk technician as your partner gets help with a problem she or a friend has encountered in real life.

REVIEW QUESTIONS

1. After doing your best but finding you cannot solve a customer's problem, what is the appropriate next step?

   _____

   _____

2. Your cell phone rings while you're working with a customer. You look at the incoming number and realize it's your sister calling. How do you handle the call?

   _____

   _____

   _____

3. Why is it not a good idea to tell a customer about the time you were able to solve the computer problem of a very important person?

   _____

   _____

4. A customer is angry and tells you he will never buy another product from your company again. How do you respond?

   _____

   _____

LAB 11.8 PRACTICE GOOD COMMUNICATION SKILLS

OBJECTIVES

The goal of this lab is to help you learn how to be a better communicator. After completing this lab, you will be able to:

▲ Listen better

▲ Work with a customer who is angry

▲ Act with integrity toward customers

MATERIALS REQUIRED

This lab requires the following:

▲ Paper and pencil or pen

▲ A workgroup of two or more students

LAB PREPARATION

No lab preparation is necessary.

ACTIVITY BACKGROUND

IT support technicians are expected to be good communicators; however, technical people often find this to be a difficult skill to master, so practice and training are very important. In this lab, you discover some ways to be an active listener and a better communicator.

ESTIMATED COMPLETION TIME: 60 MINUTES

 Activity

Work with a partner to learn to be a better listener. Do the following:

1. Sit with paper and a pencil in front of another student who will play the role of a customer. As the customer describes a certain computer problem he or she is having, take notes as necessary.

2. Describe the problem back to the customer. Were you able to describe the problem accurately, without missing any details? Have the customer rate you from one to ten, with ten being the highest rating, for good listening skills. What rating did you receive?

_____

3. Switch roles as you, the customer, describe a problem to the support technician. Then have the technician repeat the problem and its details. Rate the technician for good listening skills on a scale of one to ten.

4. Choose a somewhat more difficult problem with more details, and describe it to the support technician. Rate the technician on a scale of one to ten for good listening skills.

5. Switch roles and listen as the customer describes a more detailed and difficult problem. Then repeat the problem and its details back to the customer and have the customer rate your listening skills. What rating did you receive?

_____

Being a good communicator requires being able to deal with people who may be angry and difficult. Make suggestions as to the best way to handle these situations:

1. An angry customer calls to tell you that she has left you numerous phone messages that you have not answered. She is not aware that you receive about 25 voice messages each day and are trying hard to keep up with the workload. What do you say?

_____

_____

2. A customer who is frustrated and angry begins to use abusive language. What do you say?

_____

_____

3. You have tried for more than two hours, but you cannot fix the customer's boot problem. You think the motherboard has failed, but you are not sure. Before you make your conclusions, you want to try a POST diagnostic card. The customer demands that you fix the problem immediately, before she leaves the office at 4:45 p.m.—about 10 minutes from now. What do you say to her?

_____

_____

Discuss in your workgroup the ethical thing to do in each of the following situations. Write down the group consensus to addressing each problem:

1. You work on commission in a computer retail store. One day, you spend more than an hour working with a very difficult customer who then leaves without buying anything. As he walks out the door, you notice he dropped a 20-dollar bill near where you were talking. What do you do?

_____

_____

2. A customer is yelling at a coworker in a retail store. You can see that your coworker does not know how to handle the situation. What do you do?

_____

_____

3. You are working in a corporate office as a technical support person, trying to fix a scanner problem at an employee's workstation. You notice the employee has left payroll database information displayed on the screen. You know this employee is not authorized to view this information. What do you do?

_____

_____

4. Your supervisor has asked you to install a game on his computer. The game is on a CD-R and is obviously a pirated copy. What do you do?

_____

_____

11

5. You work for a retail store that sells a particular brand of computers. A customer asks your opinion of another brand of computer. What do you say?

_____

_____

6. You are asked to make a house call to fix a computer problem. When you arrive at the appointed time, a teenage girl answers the door and tells you her mother is not at home but will return in a half hour. What do you do?

_____

_____

Have a little fun with this one! Working in a group of three, one member of the team plays the role of tech support. A second team member writes down a brief description of a difficult customer and passes the description to a third team member. (The tech support person cannot see this description.) The third team member plays out the described customer role. Use the following scenarios or make one up:

1. A customer calls to say his notebook will not start. The LCD panel was broken when the customer dropped the notebook, but he does not willingly disclose the fact that the notebook was dropped.

2. A customer complains that her CD drive does not work. The CD is in the drive upside down, and it is clear that the customer sees herself as a techie and does not want the tech to ask her about such a simple issue.

REVIEW QUESTIONS

1. When working at a retail store that also fixes computers, what five pieces of information should you request when a customer first brings a computer to your counter?

_____

_____

_____

_____

_____

2. List three things you should not do while at a customer's site:

_____

_____

_____

3. When is it acceptable to ask a customer to refrain from venting about a problem?

_____

_____

_____

4. When is it appropriate to answer a cell phone call while working with a customer?

_____

_____

5. When is it appropriate to install pirated software on a computer?

_____

LAB 11.9 UNDERSTAND HOW TO CREATE A HELP-DESK PROCEDURE

OBJECTIVES

The goal of this lab is to explore the process of creating help-desk procedures. After completing this lab, you will be able to:

- Identify problems that would prevent users from browsing the network
- Determine which types of problems can be solved over the telephone
- Decide which types of problems require administrative intervention
- Create a help-desk procedure that includes a support matrix for telephone instruction

MATERIALS REQUIRED

This lab requires the following:

- Windows 10/8/7 operating system
- A network connection
- Paper and pencil or pen
- Internet access (optional)
- Two workgroups, with two to four students in each group

LAB PREPARATION

Before the lab begins, the instructor or lab assistant needs to do the following:

- Verify that Windows starts with no errors
- Verify that the network connection is available
- Verify that Internet access is available (optional)

ACTIVITY BACKGROUND

When a company sets up a help desk for computer users, it establishes a set of procedures to address common troubleshooting situations. Well-written help-desk procedures ensure that help-desk workers know each and every step to perform in a given situation, which means they can solve problems more quickly and confidently. These procedures should include instructions that the average user can be expected to carry out with telephone support from help-desk staff. In this lab, you create help-desk procedures for resolving a common problem: the inability to connect to a network. Assume you're working at a company help desk. If you can't solve the problem, you escalate it to the network administrator or an on-site technician who actually goes to the computer to fix the problem.

11

ESTIMATED COMPLETION TIME: 60 MINUTES

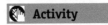 **Activity**

Work with a group to better understand how to create help-desk procedures. Do the following:

1. Assume that your company network is designed according to the following parameters. (Note that your instructor might alter these parameters so that they more closely resemble your network's parameters.)

   ◢ Ethernet LAN is using only a single subnet.

   ◢ TCP/IP is the only protocol.

   ◢ The workgroup name is ZEBRA.

   ◢ The DHCP server assigns IP information.

2. Assume that all users on your company network use computers with the following parameters. (Note that your instructor might alter these parameters so that they more closely resemble your computer.)

   ◢ Core i7 2.9 GHz

   ◢ Windows 10 operating system

   ◢ Internal NIC

   ◢ Category 5e cabling with RJ-45 connectors

3. As a group, discuss the reasons a user might not be able to connect to the network, and then make a list of the four most common reasons. In your list, include at least one problem that would be difficult to solve over the phone and would require the network administrator or another technician to go to the computer to solve the problem. Order the four problems from the least difficult to solve to the most difficult to solve. The one problem that requires administrator intervention should be Problem 4. If your group has trouble completing the list, ask your instructor or search the web for ideas. List the source of these problems, both hardware and software, on the following lines:

   ◢ Source of Problem 1:

   _____

   ◢ Source of Problem 2:

   _____

   ◢ Source of Problem 3:

   _____

   ◢ Source of Problem 4:

   _____

For each problem, describe the symptoms as a user would describe them:

   ◢ Symptoms of Problem 1:

   _____

   _____

◢ Symptoms of Problem 2:

_____

_____

◢ Symptoms of Problem 3:

_____

_____

◢ Symptoms of Problem 4:

_____

_____

As a group, decide how to solve each problem by following these steps:

1. On separate sheets of paper, list the steps to verify and solve each problem. (This list of steps is sometimes referred to as a procedure, support matrix, or job aid.)

2. Double-check the steps by testing them on your computer. (In real life, you would test the steps using a computer attached to the network you're supporting.) When making your list of steps, allow for alternatives, based on how the user responds to certain questions. For example, you might include one list of steps for situations in which the user says others on the network are visible in the Network window and another list of steps for situations in which the user says no remote computers can be seen in the Network window.

3. For any problem that can't be solved by the procedure, the last step should be for help-desk personnel to escalate the problem. In your procedure, include questions to the user when appropriate. As you work, you might find it helpful to use a diagram or flowchart of the questions asked and decisions made. Here's an example of one step that involves a question:

    ◢ Question: Is your computer on?

    ◢ Answer: Yes, go to Step 3; no, go to Step 2.

Now it is time to test your help-desk procedures by using them on another workgroup. Follow these steps:

1. Introduce one of your four problems on a computer connected to a network.

2. Have someone from another workgroup sit at your computer. The remaining steps in this sequence refer to this person as "the user."

3. Sit with your back to the user so that you can't see what he or she is doing. Place your step-by-step procedures in front of you, either on paper or on the screen. (It's helpful if you can sit at a computer connected to the network so that you can perform the same steps you ask the user to perform. However, make sure you can't see the other computer screen or see what the user is doing.)

4. The user should attempt to access the network and then "call" your help desk for assistance.

5. Follow your procedure to solve the problem.

6. Revise your procedure as necessary.

7. Test all four help-desk procedures.

11

REVIEW QUESTIONS

1. Can all users' computer problems be solved with remote help-desk support? Why or why not?

_____

_____

2. After you design and write your help-desk procedures to solve problems, what should you do next?

_____

3. How should help-desk procedures address complex problems that require administrative intervention?

_____

_____

_____

4. How should you write your procedures based on your users' technical experience?

_____

5. Why do you need to consider the network and computer configuration when creating your procedures?

_____

_____

6. What has been your experience when calling a help desk? How well did the technician walk you through the process of solving your problem?

_____

_____

Installing Windows

Labs included in this chapter:

- **Lab 12.1:** Create a Bootable Windows 10 Setup DVD

- **Lab 12.2:** Use Client Hyper-V to Manage a Virtual Machine (VM)

- **Lab 12.3:** Perform a Clean Installation of Windows 10

- **Lab 12.4:** Perform a Clean Installation of Windows 8.1

- **Lab 12.5:** Upgrade to Windows 10

- **Lab 12.6:** Install Windows 7 in a Hyper-V VM

- **Lab 12.7:** Install and Remove a Windows Dual Boot Configuration

- **Lab 12.8:** Partition a Hard Drive Using GPT before a Windows Installation

> **Notes** The instructions in these labs assume that you are using a mouse and a keyboard. If you're using a touch screen, simply tap instead of click, press and hold instead of right-click, double-tap instead of double-click, and swipe to scroll the screen to the right or left.

LAB 12.1 CREATE A BOOTABLE WINDOWS 10 SETUP DVD

OBJECTIVES

The goal of this lab is to download an ISO file and use it to create a bootable Windows 10 setup DVD. After completing this lab, you will be able to:

- Download the Windows 10 ISO installation file
- Create a bootable Windows 10 setup DVD
- Create a bootable Windows 10 USB flash drive (optional)

MATERIALS REQUIRED

This lab requires the following:

- Windows 10/8/7 computer with ability to burn a DVD
- Blank writable DVD
- 8-GB USB flash drive (optional)
- Internet access

LAB PREPARATION

Before the lab begins, the instructor or lab assistant needs to do the following:

- Verify that Windows starts with no errors
- Verify that Internet access is available

ACTIVITY BACKGROUND

Windows can be installed in a variety of ways. If the hard drive is new or will not boot, you can boot the computer from a bootable DVD or flash drive and use it to install Windows. An ISO file is an image of a DVD, and you can mount the ISO file in Windows as a virtual DVD. You can then use the mounted virtual DVD to access Windows setup files or to upgrade Windows. An ISO file is also handy when installing Windows in a virtual machine (VM). In this lab, you download the Windows 10 ISO setup file and use it to create a bootable Windows 10 setup DVD. You also learn how to create a bootable Windows 10 setup USB flash drive, which can be handy when you need to install Windows on a computer that does not have an optical drive.

Activity

To create the installation media, you'll need a blank DVD and at least 5 GB of free space on your hard drive. To use the Media Creation Tool to download the Windows ISO file and create a bootable DVD, follow these steps:

1. To download and install the Media Creation Tool, go to the website **microsoft.com/en-us/software-download/windows10**, and click **Download tool now**. Download the program file and then execute it. If necessary, respond to the UAC box.

2. Accept the license terms. In the next window, select **Create installation media (USB flash drive, DVD, or ISO file) for another PC**, and click **Next**.

3. Use the default options to download a 64-bit version of Windows 10. Click **Next**.

4. Navigate to the location to save the file, such as your Windows desktop or the Downloads folder, and click **Save**. Follow the on-screen instructions to complete the download.

5. Insert a blank DVD-R disc in the optical drive, right-click the ISO file, and click **Burn disc image**. After the disc is burned, remove it from the drive, and label it "Windows 10 64-bit setup" with the date.

6. To see the contents of the ISO disc image, open File Explorer or Windows Explorer, right-click the Windows.iso file, and click **Mount**. The ISO file is assigned a drive letter. Drill down into its contents and get familiar with the folder structure on the disc image. If you were to use the disc image to perform an upgrade to Windows 10, what is the path to the program to start the upgrade?

_____

7. Close all open windows. Save the disc and ISO file because you'll need them in later labs.

If you want to create a bootable Windows setup USB flash drive, follow these steps:

1. Insert an 8-GB or larger USB flash drive in a USB port. Use a blank flash drive because any data on it will be lost. For best performance, insert the flash drive in a USB 3.0 port, which is a blue port.

2. Enter **MediaCreationTool** in the Windows 10/7 search box or the Windows 8 Run box to execute the Media Creation Tool program you previously downloaded. Respond to the UAC box, and accept the license terms.

3. In the next window, select **Create installation media (USB flash drive, DVD, or ISO file) for another PC** and click **Next**. Click **Next** again.

4. Select **USB flash drive** and click **Next**. The tool searches for the drive. Point to the flash drive, and follow directions on the screen to create the bootable Windows 10 setup flash drive.

5. Close all open windows. Use a paper tag or peel-off label to label the flash drive "Windows 10 64-bit setup" with the date.

REVIEW QUESTIONS

1. What are two advantages of using a 64-bit installation of Windows rather than a 32-bit installation of Windows?

_____

_____

12

2. Which standards organization defines the standards for an ISO disc image?

_____

3. What are three purposes of the Media Creation Tool application?

_____

_____

4. When might you need to install a 32-bit version of Windows 10 rather than a 64-bit version?

_____

LAB 12.2 USE CLIENT HYPER-V TO MANAGE A VIRTUAL MACHINE

OBJECTIVES

The goal of this lab is to install and use virtual machines with Client Hyper-V in Windows 10 Pro. After completing this lab, you will be able to:

▲ Turn on Hyper-V in Windows 10 Pro

▲ Set up Hyper-V to allow a VM to connect to the network

▲ Create a VM using Hyper-V

▲ Use the VM in Hyper-V

MATERIALS REQUIRED

This lab requires the following:

▲ Windows 10 Pro 64-bit operating system

▲ Internet access

> **Notes** If you have not already installed Windows 10 Pro on your computer and plan to do so, complete your installation of Windows 10 Pro and then return to this lab. The details of installing Windows 10 are covered in Lab 12.3 (clean installation) and Lab 12.5 (upgrade).

LAB PREPARATION

Before the lab begins, the instructor or lab assistant needs to do the following:

▲ Verify that Windows starts with no errors

▲ Provide each student with access to the Windows 10 ISO disc image file (this file was downloaded from the Microsoft website in Lab 12.1)

ACTIVITY BACKGROUND

If you need quick and easy access to more than one operating system or to different configurations of the same operating system, a virtual machine is a handy tool to have. The virtual machine creates a computer within a computer; it's almost as if you can remotely control a computer in a different location from a window on your desktop. Virtual machines are heavily used by IT support to replicate and resolve issues, test software, and learn about new operating systems.

> **Notes** Hyper-V will not work in Windows 10 Pro when it is installed in a virtual machine. In other words, you can't use Hyper-V to create a VM within a VM. You must have the 64-bit version of Windows 10 Pro installed to use Hyper-V. Also, Hyper-V does not play well with other virtual machine management software; therefore, if you need to install VMware Workstation or another hypervisor, you must first disable Hyper-V.

ESTIMATED COMPLETION TIME: 45 MINUTES

 Activity

The steps to set up a VM using Windows 10 Pro are presented in three parts in this lab. In Part 1, you prepare Hyper-V to create a VM, and then you create the VM in Part 2. In Part 3, you manage and use the VM.

PART 1: PREPARE HYPER-V USING WINDOWS 10 PRO

To configure Hyper-V in Windows 10 Pro, follow these steps:

1. For Hyper-V to work, hardware-assisted virtualization (HAV) must be enabled in BIOS/UEFI setup. If you are not sure it is enabled, power down your computer, turn it back on, go into BIOS/UEFI setup, and make sure hardware-assisted virtualization is enabled. Also make sure that all subcategory items under HAV are enabled. Save your changes, exit BIOS/UEFI setup, and allow the system to restart to Windows 10.

> **Notes** HAV might have a different name in the BIOS/UEFI setup screens, depending on your motherboard. Intel BIOS/UEFI refers to HAV as Intel Virtualization Technology. AMD calls it AMD-V.

2. Right-click **Start** and click **System**. The About window appears, which provides information about the current Windows installation. Which edition and version of Windows 10 is installed? If 64-bit Windows 10 Pro is not installed, don't continue with this lab.

3. Hyper-V is disabled in Windows 10 Pro by default. To turn it on, open **Control Panel** in Classic view and click **Programs and Features**.

4. Click **Turn Windows features on or off**. Place a check mark next to Hyper-V and click **OK**.

5. Windows applies the changes. Click **Restart now**. After the system restarts a couple of times, sign in to Windows.

> **Notes** If another hypervisor, such as Oracle VirtualBox, was installed in Windows before you enable Hyper-V, Hyper-V might not install correctly. In this situation, you must first uninstall the hypervisor interfering with Hyper-V.

12

6. To launch the Hyper-V Manager, go to the Start screen, start typing **Hyper-V**, and then click **Hyper-V Manager**. The Hyper-V Manager window appears on the desktop.

7. In the left pane of the Hyper-V Manager, select the host computer.

8. To make sure your VMs have access to the network or the Internet, you need to first install a virtual switch in Hyper-V. To create a virtual switch, click **Virtual Switch Manager** in the Actions pane on the right.

9. The Virtual Switch Manager dialog box appears. In the left pane, make sure **New virtual network switch** is selected. To bind the virtual switch to the physical network adapter so the VMs can access the physical network, select **External** in the left pane, and click **Create Virtual Switch**.

10. In the Virtual Switch Properties pane that appears, make sure **Allow management operating system to share this network adapter** is checked, and then click **Apply**. Click **Yes** to create the virtual switch. Click **OK** to close the Virtual Switch Manager.

PART 2: CREATE A VM USING HYPER-V

To create a VM, follow these steps:

1. In the Actions pane of the Hyper-V Manager window, click **New**, and then click **Virtual Machine**. The New Virtual Machine Wizard launches. Click **Next**.

2. In the next dialog box, assign a name to the VM. What is the name you assigned the VM?

_____

3. If you want the VM files to be stored in a different location than the default, check **Store the virtual machine in a different location**, and browse to that location. After you've selected the location, click **Next**.

4. In the Specify Generation dialog box, Generation 1 is selected. Click **Next**.

5. In the next dialog box, set the amount of RAM for the VM at **4096 MB**. Check **Use Dynamic Memory for this virtual machine**. Click **Next** to continue.

6. In the drop-down options of the Configure Networking dialog box, select the new virtual switch you created earlier, and click **Next**.

7. In the Connect Virtual Hard Disk dialog box, make sure **Create a virtual hard disk** is selected, and leave the default settings. Click **Next**.

8. In the Installation Options box, select **Install an operating system from a bootable CD/DVD-ROM**. Then select **Image file (.iso)** and browse to the location of the Windows ISO file. Select the file and click **Open**. Click **Next**.

9. The last dialog box shows a summary of your selections. Click **Finish** to create the VM. The new VM is listed in the Virtual Machines pane of the Hyper-V Manager window.

PART 3: MANAGE AND USE THE VM

Follow these steps to configure and use the VM:

1. To manage the VM's virtual hardware, select the VM, and click **Settings** near the bottom of the Actions pane. The Settings dialog box for the VM appears.

2. Explore the hardware listed in the left pane, and apply your settings in the right pane. Note that you can use the right pane to mount a physical CD or DVD to the drive, or you can mount a different ISO file.

3. To boot to the optical drive, select **BIOS** and verify the correct boot priority order. The first device listed should be CD. Note that you also have the option to boot from the network to perform a network-based installation of the guest OS.

4. Click **OK** to close the Settings dialog box. To start the VM, select it and click **Start** in the Actions pane. The VM boots from the optical drive, and Windows setup is launched to begin the process of installing Windows 10. (You will learn the details of installing Windows 10 in the next lab.)

5. A thumbnail of the VM appears in the bottom-middle pane of the Hyper-V Manager window. To see the VM in its own window, double-click the thumbnail, as shown in Figure 12-1.

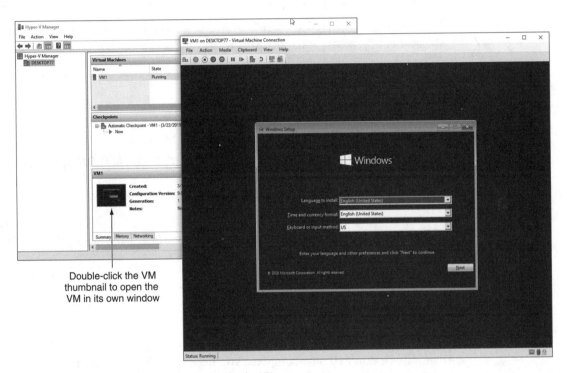

Double-click the VM
thumbnail to open the
VM in its own window

Figure 12-1   Windows 10 setup is running in the VM

6. Hyper-V allows you to close the application without shutting down virtual machines that are running in it. Close the VM window. Notice the state of the VM is listed as Running. How much memory is currently assigned to the VM?

_____

7. Close the Hyper-V Manager window and any other open windows. Restart Windows.

8. After you have signed back in to Windows, launch the **Hyper-V Manager**. What is the state of the VM you created? How much memory is currently assigned to the VM?

_____

9. Close all open windows.

REVIEW QUESTIONS

1. Why did you create a virtual switch in Hyper-V?

_____

_____

_____

12

2. Why would you use dynamic memory with a virtual machine?

_____

_____

3. Why might it be important to limit the number of VMs you run concurrently in Hyper-V?

_____

4. When you close the Hyper-V application and have VMs running in it, what happens to the states of the VMs? What happens to the VM states when you open Hyper-V?

_____

_____

LAB 12.3 PERFORM A CLEAN INSTALLATION OF WINDOWS 10

OBJECTIVES

The goal of this lab is to install Windows 10 without already having an OS installed on your computer. After completing this lab, you will be able to:

▲ Perform a clean installation of Windows 10

MATERIALS REQUIRED

This lab requires the following:

▲ To install Windows 10 on a computer, you need the Windows 10 setup DVD or installation files on another medium, such as a USB flash drive

▲ To install Windows 10 on a VM, you need the Windows 10 setup ISO file

▲ Product key from Windows 10 package or downloaded from the web (optional)

> **Notes** This lab provides steps for performing a clean installation of Windows 10. You can install Windows 10 on a computer or in a VM. Also, you have the option of not entering a product key during the installation.
> You might consider performing this lab twice: once in a VM and once on a computer.

LAB PREPARATION

Before the lab begins, the instructor or lab assistant needs to do the following:

▲ Verify that the computer powers up properly

▲ Provide each student with access to the Windows 10 installation files and product key

▲ Verify that any necessary Windows 10 drivers are available

ACTIVITY BACKGROUND

When deciding whether to do a clean installation or an upgrade to Windows 10, you need to consider the condition of your current system. If the Windows 8/7 system is giving you trouble, performing a clean installation is a good idea so that current problems don't follow you into the new installation. Also, you might do a clean installation if your computer does not already have an OS installed, such as on a new virtual machine or right after you have replaced a hard drive in a computer.

ESTIMATED COMPLETION TIME: 60 MINUTES

 Activity

Follow these steps to perform a clean installation using a Windows 10 setup DVD on a computer or the Windows 10 setup ISO file in a VM:

1. If you are installing Windows 10 on a computer, do the following:

   a. Start up your computer, and access BIOS/UEFI setup. Change the boot sequence so the optical drive is the first boot device.

   > **Notes** If the installation files are on a USB flash drive, change BIOS/UEFI to first boot to USB.

   b. Insert the Windows 10 DVD into the optical drive.

   c. Shut down your computer and start it up again.

   d. You might be asked to press any key on your keyboard to boot from the DVD. The computer should boot the DVD and begin the installation process.

2. If you are installing Windows 10 in a VM in Hyper-V, do the following (these steps are covered in Lab 12.2):

   a. Open Hyper-V, create the VM, open its **Settings** box, mount the ISO file to the virtual optical drive, and verify that the boot priority order lists the optical drive first.

   b. Start the VM. The Windows 10 installation process begins.

3. A Windows Setup dialog box appears and asks you to select your language, time and currency format, and keyboard input method. Make the appropriate selections. Click **Next**.

4. In the next Windows Setup dialog box, click **Install now**.

5. A Windows Setup dialog box asks for the product key that is used to activate Windows. Do one of the following:

   ◢ Enter the product key for Windows 10 and click **Next**.

   ◢ If you do not want to enter a product key at this time, click **I don't have a product key**. On the next screen, select the Windows 10 edition you want to install and click **Next**.

6. The License terms dialog box appears. Check **I accept the license terms** and click **Next**.

7. When prompted for the type of installation, select **Custom: Install Windows only (advanced)**.

8. In the next dialog box, select a drive and volume, and then click **Next**. (If you need clarification at this point in the installation, ask your instructor for assistance.) The installation process begins; it can take several minutes. What is the size of the partition that will hold Windows 10?

12

9. The computer or VM might restart by itself several times as part of the installation process. If prompted to press any key to boot the DVD, *ignore the message* because pressing any key will start the installation again from scratch.

10. Follow instructions through the Basics screens to choose a region and keyboard layout.

11. On the Account screen, select **Set up for personal use** and click **Next**.

12. You will set up a local account to sign in to Windows. On the *Sign in with Microsoft* screen, select **Offline account** and click **Next**.

13. On the *Sign in with Microsoft Instead?* screen, click **No**. (Microsoft strongly encourages you to use a Microsoft account with Windows.)

14. On the next few screens, enter a user account name, password, and answers to security questions. What are the user account name, password, and answers to the questions?

_____

15. On the next few screens, decline to use Cortana and the activity history and accept the default privacy settings.

16. After the system restarts, sign in to Windows 10. On the Services screen, select your privacy settings and click **Accept**. The upgrade to Windows 10 is complete.

17. Microsoft Edge is already open. Browse to a couple of websites to confirm you have a good Internet connection.

18. Open **File Explorer**. How much space on the hard drive did the Windows 10 installation use?

_____

REVIEW QUESTIONS

1. Was the Windows 10 installation a success? If so, what did you find most challenging about the installation process?

_____

2. When is a clean installation preferred over an upgrade to Windows 10?

_____

_____

_____

3. In this lab, you created a local account to sign in to Windows. Was it necessary to be connected to the Internet to create the account? If you had created a Microsoft account to sign in to Windows, would it have been necessary to be connected to the Internet to create the account?

_____

4. Why do you need to access BIOS/UEFI setup on a computer or BIOS settings on a VM before the installation process?

_____

5. Did Windows automatically activate during the installation? How can you find out if Windows is activated?

_____

_____

_____

LAB 12.4 PERFORM A CLEAN INSTALLATION OF WINDOWS 8.1

OBJECTIVES

The goal of this lab is to perform a clean installation of Windows 8.1. After completing this lab, you will be able to:

- Perform a clean installation of Windows 8.1

MATERIALS REQUIRED

This lab requires the following:

- To install Windows 8.1 on a computer, you need the Windows 8.1 setup DVD or installation files on another medium, such as a USB flash drive
- To install Windows 8.1 on a VM, you need the Windows 8.1 setup ISO file
- Product key from Windows 8.1 package or downloaded from the web (optional)

> **Notes** This lab provides steps for performing a clean installation of Windows 8.1. You can install Windows 8.1 on a computer or in a VM. Also, you have the option of not entering a product key during the installation.

12

LAB PREPARATION

Before the lab begins, the instructor or lab assistant needs to do the following:

- Verify that the computer powers up properly
- Provide each student with access to the Windows 8.1 installation files and product key
- Verify that any necessary Windows 8.1 drivers are available

ACTIVITY BACKGROUND

Most likely you will never be called on to upgrade from Windows 7 to Windows 8.1, because the current best practice is to upgrade from Windows 7 to Windows 10. However, if a current installation of Windows 8.1 fails or gives problems or the hard drive fails, you may need to perform a clean installation of Windows 8.1. Also, when learning to support computers, you might need to install Windows 8.1 in a VM so that you can practice using this OS. In this lab, you learn how to perform a clean installation of Windows 8.1 on a computer or on a VM.

> **Notes** To download the Windows 8.1 installation ISO file, go to *microsoft.com/en-us/software-download/windows8ISO*. You can use the ISO file to create a bootable Windows 8.1 setup DVD.

ESTIMATED COMPLETION TIME: 60 MINUTES

 Activity

PART 1: INSTALL WINDOWS 8.1

Follow these steps to perform a clean installation of Windows 8.1:

1. If you are installing Windows 8.1 on a computer, do the following:

   a. Start up your computer, and access BIOS/UEFI setup. Change the boot sequence so the optical drive is the first boot device.

   > **Notes** If the installation files are on a USB flash drive, change BIOS/UEFI to first boot to USB.

   b. Insert the Windows 8.1 DVD into the optical drive.

   c. Shut down your computer and start it up again.

   d. You might be asked to press any key on your keyboard to boot from the DVD. The computer should boot the DVD and begin the installation process.

2. If you are installing Windows 8.1 in a VM in Hyper-V, do the following (these steps are covered in more detail in Lab 12.2):

   a. Open Hyper-V, create the VM, open its **Settings** box, verify that the ISO file is mounted to the virtual optical drive, and verify that the boot priority order lists the optical drive first.

   b. Start the VM. The Windows 8.1 installation process begins.

3. A Windows Setup dialog box appears and asks you to select your language, time and currency format, and keyboard input method. Make the appropriate selections. Click **Next**.

4. In the next Windows Setup dialog box, click **Install now**.

5. A Windows Setup dialog box asks for the product key that is used to activate Windows. Enter the product key for Windows 8.1 and click **Next**.

   > **Notes** If you don't plan to activate Windows 8.1, you can use this product key to install Windows: GCRJD-8NW9H-F2CDX-CCM8D-9D6T9

6. The License terms dialog box appears. Check **I accept the license terms**, and click **Next**.

7. When prompted for the type of installation, select **Custom: Install Windows only (advanced)**.

8. In the next dialog box, select a drive and volume, and then click **Next**. (If you need clarification at this point in the installation, ask your instructor for assistance.) The installation process begins; it can take several minutes. What is the size of the partition that will hold Windows 8.1?

---

9. The computer might restart by itself several times as part of the installation process. If prompted to press any key to boot the DVD, *ignore the message* because pressing any key will start the installation again from scratch.

10. The Personalize screen asks you to choose a screen color and type the PC name. Enter the PC name as assigned by your instructor. Click **Next**.

11. In the Settings window, click **Use express settings**.

12. You will set up a local account to sign in to Windows. In the *Sign in to your Microsoft account* window, click **Create a new account** from the options at the bottom of the screen. Click **Sign in without a Microsoft account** to create a local account. Type the user name, the password (in both boxes), and the password hint. Click **Finish**. So you do not forget your password, write your user name and password here:

_____

13. The computer takes a few minutes while Windows 8.1 finalizes settings, and then the Start screen appears. You are finished performing a clean installation of Windows 8.1.

14. Open **File Explorer**. How much space on the hard drive did the Windows 8.1 installation use?

_____

15. Open **Internet Explorer** and verify that you have Internet access.

PART 2: CLONE A VM IN HYPER-V

If you have installed Windows 8.1 in a VM, you might want to duplicate or clone the VM so that you can have two VMs with Windows 8.1 installed. This is handy if you want to use the first VM to keep an installation of Windows 8.1 and use the second VM in Lab 12.5 where you upgrade Windows 8.1 to Windows 10. There are several methods to clone a VM in Hyper-V. In the following steps, you use one of these methods, which is to make a copy of the virtual hard drive and use it to create a new VM:

1. Shut down the VM you want to clone.

2. Open File Explorer or Windows Explorer and drill down into the folder where your VM is stored. Open the Virtual Hard Disks subfolder. The subfolder should contain two files. The .vhdx file is the virtual hard drive for the VM.

3. Copy the .vhdx file to a new folder. Rename the new .vhdx file so there is no confusion over which virtual hard drive belongs to which VM. What is the file name and path to the copy of your virtual hard drive file?

_____

4. To create a new VM, click **New** in the Actions pane of Hyper-V Manager. Select **Virtual Machine**. Click **Next**.

5. Assign a name to the new VM, select where you want to store the VM, and click **Next**. What is the name and path to the VM?

_____

6. Select **Generation 1** and click **Next**. Assign a value to Startup memory and click **Next**.

7. Assign your virtual switch to the VM and click **Next**.

8. In the Connect Virtual Hard Disk box, select **Use an existing virtual hard disk**. Click **Browse** and point to the copy of the .vhdx file you made earlier. Click **Open**.

9. Click **Next** and click **Finish**. Your VM clone is created.

10. Start the new VM and verify that it has Windows 8.1 installed.

12

> 📝 **Notes** If you have already activated Windows 8.1 in the first VM, you will have problems using both VMs, as only one activates. However, these VMs should work fine in these labs to practice installing and using Windows 8.1, where it is not necessary to activate Windows.

REVIEW QUESTIONS

1. Why is it unlikely you'll ever perform an upgrade from Windows 7 to Windows 8.1?

   _____

   _____

2. Why do you think Microsoft still provides a free ISO download for Windows 8.1 even though its latest OS is Windows 10?

   _____

3. Describe the purpose of the Export and Import commands, which are available in Hyper-V in the shortcut menu when you right-click a VM.

   _____

   _____

   _____

4. What is the file extension Hyper-V assigns to a virtual hard drive file?

   _____

LAB 12.5 UPGRADE TO WINDOWS 10

OBJECTIVES

The goal of this lab is to upgrade a current installation of Windows to Windows 10. After completing this lab, you will be able to:

▲ Upgrade to Windows 10

MATERIALS REQUIRED

This lab requires the following:

▲ Windows 10/8/7 computer or VM

▲ Internet access

▲ Windows 10 setup DVD or installation files on another medium, such as a USB flash drive or the Windows 10 setup ISO file

▲ Product key from Windows 10 package or available on the web (optional)

> 📝 **Notes** To activate Windows 10, the Windows 8/7 edition must qualify for the upgrade license for the Windows 10 edition. Home editions of Windows 8/7 can upgrade to Home editions of Windows 10. Professional and Business editions of Windows 8/7 can upgrade to Windows 10 Pro.

LAB PREPARATION

Before the lab begins, the instructor or lab assistant needs to do the following:

▲ Verify that Windows starts with no errors

▲ Verify Internet access

▲ Provide each student with access to the Windows 10 installation files and optional product key

▲ Verify that any necessary Windows 10 drivers are available

ACTIVITY BACKGROUND

Performing an upgrade to Windows 10 takes less time than performing a clean installation of Windows 10. It also has the advantages that user preferences and settings are not lost and applications are left in working condition. If there isn't a reason for a clean installation, an upgrade is recommended.

ESTIMATED COMPLETION TIME: 45 MINUTES

 Activity

The following steps are representative of a typical upgrade. Don't be alarmed if your experience differs slightly. Use your knowledge to solve any problems on your own, and ask your instructor for help if you get stuck. You might want to record any differences between these steps and your own experience. Also, record any decisions you make and any information you enter during the installation process.

Follow these steps to perform an in-place upgrade to Windows 10:

1. As with any upgrade installation, do the following before you start the upgrade:

   a. Scan the system for malware using an updated version of anti-malware software. When you're done, be sure to close the anti-malware application so it's not running in the background.

   b. Uninstall any applications or device drivers you don't intend to use in the new installation.

   c. Make sure your backups of important data are up to date, and then close any backup software running in the background.

2. To make the setup files available to Windows, do one of the following:

   ▲ On a computer, boot to the Windows 8/7 desktop, and insert the Windows 10 setup DVD.

   ▲ On a computer, if you are using the Windows ISO setup file, boot to the Windows 8/7 desktop, right-click the ISO file in Explorer, and click **Mount**.

   ▲ On a VM in Hyper-V, open the **Settings** box. Mount the Windows 10 ISO file to the virtual optical drive in the VM. Click **Apply** to apply your change.

3. The setup files should now be available to Windows, and Windows 10 setup should automatically start. If it does not start, open File Explorer or Windows Explorer and double-click the DVD or virtual DVD. The Windows 10 setup program launches.

4. Respond to any UAC dialog boxes.

5. Setup asks permission to go online for updates. Make your selection and click **Next**. The setup program loads files, examines the system, and reports any problems it finds.

6. If the setup program finds that the system meets minimum hardware requirements, it requests the product key. Enter the product key and click **Next**.

> **📓 Notes** If you don't plan to activate Windows 10, use this product key:
> W269N-WFGWX-YVC9B-4J6C9-T83GX

7. The product key is verified, and then the License terms window appears. Click **Accept**. To carry forward personal files and apps in the old OS to Windows 10, click **Install** without making any changes.

8. The computer or VM might restart by itself several times as part of the installation process. If prompted to press any key to boot the DVD, *ignore the message* because pressing any key will start the installation again from scratch.

9. When you see the Windows 10 sign-in screen, sign in to Windows 10.

10. Open **File Explorer**. What is the size of the Windows.old folder?

_____

11. Open **Microsoft Edge** to confirm you have a good Internet connection.

REVIEW QUESTIONS

1. What type of information is stored in the Windows.old folder?

_____

2. List two reasons you might need to use the Windows.old folder.

_____

_____

3. When performing a clean installation of Windows, setup gives you the opportunity to create a user account and password. Why do you think setup skipped this step in an upgrade installation?

_____

_____

4. Why is it a good idea to scan your system for malware before performing an upgrade?

_____

_____

5. When preparing for an upgrade, is it more important to make sure you have Windows 10 drivers for your network adapter or your sound card? Explain your answer:

_____

_____

_____

LAB 12.6 INSTALL WINDOWS 7 IN A HYPER-V VM

OBJECTIVES

The goal of this lab is to install Windows 7 in a VM. After completing this lab, you will be able to:

⊿ Install Windows 7 in a VM in Hyper-V

> **Notes** You can use Windows 7 installed in a VM to practice using Windows 7 in future chapters. The A+ Core 2 exam expects you to know how to support Windows 7, even though Microsoft has announced it will stop supporting Windows 7 in January 2020.

MATERIALS REQUIRED

This lab requires the following:

⊿ A computer with Hyper-V installed

⊿ Internet access

LAB PREPARATION

Before the lab begins, the instructor or lab assistant needs to do the following:

⊿ Verify that the computer starts with no errors and that Hyper-V is installed

⊿ Verify that Internet access is available

⊿ Make the Windows 7 setup ISO file available (optional)

12

ACTIVITY BACKGROUND

IT support technicians are expected to know how to support older operating systems. In this lab, you install Windows 7 in a VM. To practice the skills needed to support Windows 7, keep the VM for future labs.

If your instructor has provided access to the Windows 7 setup ISO image file that you will use to install Windows 7, ask your instructor for the following information:

⊿ What is the name and path to this ISO file?

_____

⊿ What is the edition of Windows 7 in the ISO image?

_____

⊿ What is the product key for the Windows installation?

_____

ESTIMATED COMPLETION TIME: 60–120 MINUTES

 Activity

If your instructor has not provided access to the Windows 7 setup ISO file, follow these steps to download it:

1. You must first get the download tool. Go to **heidoc.net**, click **Technology & Science**, click **Microsoft**, and click **Microsoft Windows and Office ISO Download Tool**. Near the top of the page, click **Windows-ISO-Downloader.exe**. The file downloads.

2. Double-click the downloaded file to launch it. In the HeiDoc.net Windows ISO Downloader window, select the latest release of Windows 7. (At the time of this writing, the latest release was in August 2018.)

3. In the drop-down list of Windows 7 editions, select **Windows 7 Professional 64-Bit**. In the list of product languages, select **English, US**.

4. Click **Download** and select the location to download the ISO file, such as your Downloads folder or the desktop.

5. Close any open windows.

Follow these steps to create a new VM in Hyper-V and install Windows 7 in it:

1. Open **Hyper-V Manager**. In the Hyper-V Manager window, click **New**, click **Virtual Machine**, and step through the New Virtual Machine Wizard to create a new VM, as you learned to do earlier in Lab 12.2. As you create the VM, set it up to install an OS from the Windows 7 setup ISO file that was made available by your instructor or that you downloaded from the web.

   ◢ What is the name of the VM? _____

   ◢ What is the path to the VM files? _____

   ◢ How much RAM does the VM have? _____

2. The VM should start automatically, booting from the Windows 7 setup ISO image and launching Windows 7 setup. Complete the installation of Windows 7, which is similar to installing Windows 10 or Windows 8.

3. When asked for a product key, use the key provided by your instructor. If you choose not to enter a product key, uncheck **Automatically activate Windows when I'm online**, and click **Skip**.

   ◢ What is the name of the user account you created during the Windows 7 installation?

   _____

   ◢ What is the computer name you created during the installation?

   _____

   ◢ What is the password to the user account?

   _____

4. After Windows is installed, the Windows 7 desktop appears. Open **Internet Explorer** and verify that you have Internet access.

5. Use the Windows 7 Start menu in the VM to shut down the VM.

You will use this virtual machine installation of Windows 7 in future labs in this lab manual.

REVIEW QUESTIONS

1. How much memory or RAM does Hyper-V assign to a VM by default?

   _____

2. By default, where does Hyper-V store the files for a virtual machine?

   _____

3. After you installed Windows 7 in the VM, what is the size of the folder holding the VM files?

   _____

4. How would you configure your virtual machine if you wanted to install Windows 7 from a DVD rather than an ISO image?

   _____

   _____

5. In this lab, we used a third-party download tool to download the Windows 7 ISO file from the Microsoft website. Why were we not able to use the Microsoft Media Creation Tool for this purpose?

   _____

12

LAB 12.7 INSTALL AND REMOVE A WINDOWS DUAL BOOT CONFIGURATION

OBJECTIVES

The goal of this lab is to install Windows 10 in a dual boot configuration with another OS and then remove the original OS. After completing this lab, you will be able to:

- ◢ Install Windows 10 in a dual boot configuration with another Windows OS
- ◢ Remove the original OS from the dual boot configuration

MATERIALS REQUIRED

This lab requires the following:

- ◢ Windows 10/8/7 computer or VM
- ◢ Windows 10 64-bit installation media
- ◢ Windows 10 product key (optional)

Notes This lab can be completed in a virtual machine.

LAB PREPARATION

Before the lab begins, the instructor or lab assistant needs to do the following:

▲ Verify that the Windows computer or VM starts with no errors

▲ Provide each student with access to the Windows 10 installation files and product key (optional)

▲ Verify that any necessary Windows 10 drivers are available

ACTIVITY BACKGROUND

When installing a new OS, it might be important to save the original OS in a dual boot configuration. Reasons to create a dual boot include the need to use both operating systems or to verify that applications or hardware drivers work in the new OS before you remove the old OS. Sometimes you might want access to both OSs for several weeks or months before you decide to remove the original OS.

In this lab, you install Windows 10 in a dual boot with another OS. After you have confirmed the dual boot works, you remove the original OS.

ESTIMATED COMPLETION TIME: 60 MINUTES

 Activity

Complete the following steps to install Windows 10 as a dual boot:

1. Boot the computer or VM, and sign in to Windows. Answer the following questions:

   ▲ Which edition of Windows is currently installed in the system?

   _____

   ▲ How much free space is on the hard drive? (At least 15 GB of free space is required to install Windows 10 in a dual boot.)

   _____

2. Open **Disk Management**. Examine the hard drives installed in the system. Do you have a hard drive with at least 15 GB of space marked as Unallocated? If there is not enough unallocated space, do the following to shrink the Windows volume and create some unallocated space:

   a. Right-click the C: volume where Windows is installed and click **Shrink Volume** in the shortcut menu (see Figure 12-2).

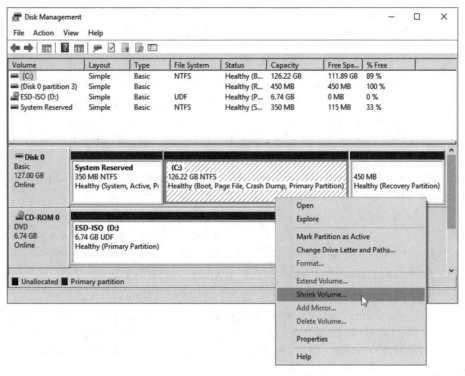

Figure 12-2 Shrink the Windows volume to make room for the new Windows 10 installation

    b. Enter the amount of space to shrink in MB and click **Shrink**. You should shrink about half of the available space to shrink. How much space did you shrink?

_____

    c. Verify that the space you shrank is listed as Unallocated. This is the space where you will install Windows 10.

    d. Close the Disk Management window.

  3. Shut down Windows.

You are now ready to install Windows 10 in the unallocated space on the hard drive. Follow these steps:

  1. Reboot the system, booting from the Windows 10 setup media (either a bootable Windows 10 setup DVD or flash drive or an ISO file mounted to an optical drive in the VM). Windows 10 setup is launched.

  2. Select language and regional preferences and click **Next**. On the next screen, click **Install now**.

  3. Enter a product key and click **Next** or click **I don't have a product key**. If you did not enter a product key, select the edition of Windows 10 you want to install and click **Next**.

  4. Accept the license terms and click **Next**.

  5. On the *Which type of installation do you want?* screen, click **Custom: Install Windows only (advanced)**.

  6. On the next screen, select the unallocated space and click **Next**. Windows setup creates a new partition from this unallocated space to hold Windows 10 and continues with the installation.

12

7. Continue to respond to questions asked by Windows setup, as you learned to do in earlier labs. Create an offline (local) account. What is the name and password of the local account?

8. After the installation completes, shut down the system. Boot the computer or VM. The *Choose an operating system* screen appears. Click the original OS and sign in to it. Shut down the system.

9. Boot the computer or VM again. In the *Choose an operating system* screen, select the new Windows 10 installation, and sign in to it.

After you have created a dual boot for Windows 10 and the original OS and verified that the dual boot works, you are ready to uninstall the original OS. Follow these steps:

1. Be sure you are signed in to the new Windows 10 installation and not the original OS. To remove the original OS from the *Choose an operating system* screen so that only one OS launches, open **Control Panel** in Classic view, and click **System**.

2. In the System window, click **Advanced system settings**.

3. In the System Properties box, click **Settings** in the Startup and Recovery group.

4. In the Startup and Recovery box, uncheck **Time to display list of operating systems** (see Figure 12-3). Click **OK** twice to close both boxes. Close the System window. The system will now always boot to the new installation of Windows 10.

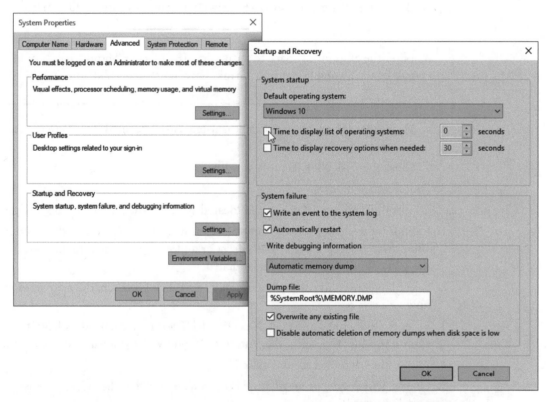

Figure 12-3   Remove the old Windows installation from the list of available operating systems

5. To free up the space on the hard drive taken up by the original Windows installation, open **File Explorer**. Look for a volume other than drive C: that holds the original Windows folder, such as drive D:. Delete all folders and files on drive D:, including its Windows folder. Drive D: is now ready to hold data.

REVIEW QUESTIONS

1. In the field, before you remove an original OS from a dual boot, why is it important to first back up all data on the original OS volume?

_____

_____

2. In this lab, what was the purpose of using Disk Management?

_____

_____

3. Why can you not have both installations of Windows on the same volume?

_____

4. Suppose you want to use Disk Management to increase the size of a volume. You right-click the volume and see that Extend Volume is grayed and not available. What are two possible reasons the option is not available?

_____

_____

LAB 12.8 PARTITION A HARD DRIVE USING GPT BEFORE A WINDOWS INSTALLATION

OBJECTIVES

The goal of this lab is to convert a hard disk drive partitioned using MBR to GPT before installing Windows 10. After completing this lab, you will be able to:

▲ Convert a hard disk drive from MBR to GPT from the command prompt

▲ Install Windows 10

▲ Verify that a hard drive is using GPT partitioning

MATERIALS REQUIRED

This lab requires the following:

▲ Windows 10 64-bit installation media

▲ Windows 10 product key

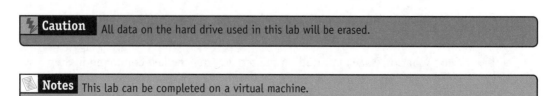

Caution All data on the hard drive used in this lab will be erased.

Notes This lab can be completed on a virtual machine.

12

LAB PREPARATION

Before the lab begins, the instructor or lab assistant needs to do the following:

⯈ Verify that the computer powers up properly

⯈ Provide each student with access to the Windows 10 installation files and product key

⯈ Verify that any necessary Windows 10 drivers are available

ACTIVITY BACKGROUND

Before installing Windows 10, setup first determines if the computer has been booted using UEFI mode or BIOS-compatibility mode in firmware on the motherboard. For a UEFI boot, Windows setup installs the GPT partitioning method on the hard drive. For a BIOS-compatibility boot, setup installs the MBR partitioning method.

However, many hard disk drives come from the manufacturer already partitioned with MBR. A problem can arise if you attempt to boot such a computer in UEFI mode. For instance, during Windows setup, you might see the message "Windows cannot be installed to this disk. The selected disk is not of the GPT partition style."

To solve this problem, you need to convert the hard drive to GPT. In this lab, you learn one method to perform the conversion using the diskpart command.

ESTIMATED COMPLETION TIME: 60 MINUTES

 Activity

Complete the following steps to convert a hard disk drive to GPT and then install Windows 10 on the drive:

1. Create a Windows 10 64-bit installation DVD or flash drive following the steps in Lab 12.1. Alternatively, your instructor might have installation media for you to use.

2. Boot from the installation media. Change the boot order in BIOS/UEFI setup, if necessary.

3. After booting to the installation media, select the language and regional preferences and click **Next**. Do *not* continue with the installation beyond this point.

4. On your keyboard, press **Shift+F10** to open a command prompt window.

5. Enter each of the following commands to partition the disk using GPT. The second command lists the number assigned to the disk (0, 1, or 2). If only one hard drive is installed, the disk number is 0, and you will use that number in the third command: select disk 0. If multiple hard drives are installed, use the size of the disk to determine the number of the disk you want to convert.

   diskpart

   list disk

   select disk #

   clean

   convert gpt

6. What message appeared on the screen after the last command in Step 5 was entered? Type **exit** and press **Enter**.

7. Close the command prompt window.

8. Click **Install now**.

9. Enter the product key and click **Next**. Alternately, you can continue the installation without entering a product key. If you don't enter a product key, setup then asks whether you want to install Windows 10 Home or Windows 10 Pro.

10. Accept the terms and click **Next**.

11. Click **Custom: Install Windows only (advanced)**.

12. On the next screen, verify that **Drive 0** is already selected. Click **Next**.

13. Windows Setup begins to install Windows. Complete the Windows installation following the process you learned earlier in this chapter.

14. After the Windows installation is complete and you see the Windows 10 desktop, right-click **Start** and click **Disk Management**. What volumes are listed for Disk 0? Which partitioning system is the hard drive using?

_____

_____

REVIEW QUESTIONS

1. What partition structure is required to support a hard drive greater than 2 TB?

_____

2. What happens to the data on the hard drive when it is repartitioned using the convert gpt command?

_____

3. In general, what is the purpose of the diskpart command?

_____

4. What is the keyboard shortcut for opening the command prompt window during a Windows installation?

_____

5. What is one partition on the hard drive that is evidence of GPT partitioning?

_____

6. What is the command, new to Windows 10, that can be used to convert a hard drive from MBR or GPT without erasing all the data on the drive?

_____

12

CHAPTER 13

Maintaining Windows

Labs included in this chapter:

- **Lab 13.1:** Perform Routine Hard Drive Maintenance
- **Lab 13.2:** Back Up and Restore Files in Windows 10
- **Lab 13.3:** Manage Hard Drive Partitions Using a Virtual Machine (VM)
- **Lab 13.4:** Set Up a Virtual Hard Drive in Windows
- **Lab 13.5:** Learn to Work from the Command Line
- **Lab 13.6:** Use the Xcopy and Robocopy Commands
- **Lab 13.7:** Use Remote Desktop

LAB 13.1 PERFORM ROUTINE HARD DRIVE MAINTENANCE

OBJECTIVES

The goal of this lab is to perform routine maintenance on a hard drive. After completing this lab, you will be able to:

- Adjust Automatic Maintenance settings in Windows 10
- Delete unneeded files on a hard drive
- Uninstall unneeded apps
- Remove unneeded apps from the Windows startup list
- Scan a hard drive for errors
- Verify defragment and optimized settings on a hard drive

MATERIALS REQUIRED

This lab requires the following:

- Windows 10/8 operating system

LAB PREPARATION

Before the lab begins, the instructor or lab assistant needs to do the following:

- Verify that Windows starts with no errors

ACTIVITY BACKGROUND

To ensure that Windows and your hard drive operate in peak condition, you should perform some routine maintenance tasks regularly. Many of the maintenance tasks required in earlier versions of Windows are now done automatically by Windows 10. Other tasks, however, require human decision making and can optimize efficiency and responsiveness in Windows 10 or Windows 8.

For starters, you can adjust the automatic maintenance tasks that Windows 10 performs by default. You can ensure that your hard drive has enough unused space by removing unnecessary files and uninstalling unneeded apps. You can also eliminate unnecessary apps from the Windows startup list. Other routine maintenance tasks include scanning the hard drive for errors and repairing those errors. In addition, files on a hard drive sometimes become fragmented over time; defragmenting the drive can improve performance because files can be read sequentially without jumping around on the drive. In this lab, you learn about these important disk maintenance tools and techniques. You should use these tools on a scheduled basis to keep your hard drive error free and performing well.

ESTIMATED COMPLETION TIME: 30–45 MINUTES

 Activity

PART 1: ADJUST WINDOWS 10 AUTOMATIC MAINTENANCE SETTINGS

For a Windows 10 system, complete the following steps to check and adjust the Automatic Maintenance settings:

1. Close all open applications.

2. Open **Control Panel**. In the Large icons view, click **Security and Maintenance**. Click the down arrow next to *Maintenance*. Under *Automatic Maintenance*, click **Change maintenance settings**.

3. Set a time for daily maintenance tasks that works best for your schedule. If you change the time, click **OK**. Otherwise, click **Cancel**.

PART 2: USE THE DISK CLEANUP TOOL

For Windows 10/8, follow these steps to delete unnecessary files on your hard drive:

1. Close all open applications.

2. Open **Control Panel**. Open **Administrative Tools**, and then open **Disk Cleanup**.

3. If the Disk Cleanup Drive Selection dialog box opens, select the drive you want to clean up in the drop-down list, and click **OK** to close the dialog box.

4. The Disk Cleanup dialog box opens, listing the various types of files you can clean up. To include more items in the list, click **Clean up system files**. If a UAC dialog box appears, respond to it. If the Disk Cleanup Drive Selection dialog box appears, select the drive you want to clean up, and click **OK** to close the dialog box.

5. Select the types of files you want Disk Cleanup to delete. Depending on your system, these options might include Downloaded Program Files, Recycle Bin, Temporary files, and Temporary Internet Files.

   ◢ How much disk space does each group of files take up?

   _____

   _____

   _____

   _____

   ◢ Click the name of a file group you might want to delete, and read a description of the files included in that group. Based on information in the Disk Cleanup dialog box, what is the purpose of each group of files listed in the dialog box? Record that information here:

Windows Update Cleanup	
Windows Defender	
Downloaded Program Files	
Temporary Internet Files	
Device driver packages	
Recycle Bin	
Temporary files	
Thumbnails	
Downloaded files (Windows 10 only)	

   ◢ What is the total amount of disk space you would gain by deleting all of these files?

   _____

13

◢ What types of files might you not want to delete during Disk Cleanup? Why?

_____

_____

6. Click **OK** to delete the selected groups of files.

7. When asked to confirm the deletion, click **Delete Files**. The Disk Cleanup dialog box closes, and a progress indicator appears while the cleanup is under way. The progress indicator closes when the cleanup is finished, returning you to the desktop.

PART 3: UNINSTALL UNUSED APPS

Complete the following steps to uninstall unused apps:

1. Close all open applications.

2. Right-click the **Start** button, and click **Apps and Features** (for Windows 8, click **Programs and Features**).

3. Scroll through the list of installed apps. If there's an app that you don't recognize, do a search online to determine if it's one you want to keep.

4. To uninstall an app, click to select it, and then click **Uninstall**. Click **Uninstall** again to confirm removal of the app. Which programs did you decide to remove?

_____

_____

_____

_____

PART 4: REDUCE APPS AT STARTUP

Complete the following steps to reduce the number of apps that begin at startup:

1. Close all open applications.

2. To open Task Manager, right-click **Start,** and click **Task Manager**. If necessary, click **More details**, and then click the **Startup** tab.

3. Scroll through the list of startup programs. If there's a program you don't recognize, do a search online to determine if it's a program you want to run automatically on your computer.

4. To prevent the program from starting at startup, click to select it, and then click **Disable**. Which programs did you decide to disable?

_____

_____

_____

_____

5. While you're in Task Manager, click the **Processes** tab. Scroll through the list of running Apps and Background processes to determine if any are using too much CPU or memory resources. If so, and if the process is not currently necessary, end the task and go back to the Startup tab to see if the related program should be disabled at startup.

PART 5: USE THE CHKDSK TOOL

The next step in routine maintenance is to use Windows Chkdsk to examine the hard drive and repair errors. Follow these steps:

1. Close any open applications so they can't write to the hard drive while it's being repaired.

2. In the Windows 10 search box, type **cmd**, right-click **Command Prompt**, and click **Run as administrator**. For Windows 8, right-click **Start** and click **Command Prompt** (**Admin**). Respond to the UAC dialog box. The elevated command prompt window opens.

3. Several switches (options) are associated with the Chkdsk utility. To show all available switches, enter **chkdsk /?** at the command prompt. Answer the following:

   ▲ What are two switches used to fix errors that Chkdsk finds?

   _____

   ▲ Why do the /I and /C switches in Chkdsk reduce the amount of time needed to run the scan?

   _____

4. To use the Chkdsk utility to scan the C: drive for errors and repair them, type **chkdsk C: /R** and press **Enter**. (*Note:* You may have to substitute a different drive letter depending on your computer's configuration.) A message reports that Chkdsk cannot run because the volume is in use by another process. Type **Y** and then press **Enter** to run Chkdsk the next time the system is restarted. Close the command prompt window, and restart your computer.

5. After Chkdsk runs, sign back in to Windows.

PART 6: VERIFY DEFRAGMENT AND OPTIMIZED DRIVE SETTINGS

Windows 10/8 automatically defragments magnetic hard drives and optimizes SSDs. Follow these steps to verify the settings:

1. Open **Control Panel**. Open **Administrative Tools**, and then open **Defragment and Optimize Drives**.

2. Confirm that your primary hard drive is included in the system's list of drives to be optimized and that scheduled optimization is turned on. To view and adjust the schedule, click **Change settings**.

3. Make any necessary changes to turn on scheduled optimization or to adjust the schedule, and click **OK**. If no changes are necessary, click **Cancel**.

REVIEW QUESTIONS

1. You discover a hard drive is not being optimized on an automatic schedule. Before you run the Optimize Drives tool, why should you first run Disk Cleanup?

   _____

   _____

2. How does defragmentation improve performance?

   _____

   _____

13

3. When you ran the Chkdsk command in this lab, it had to run during the startup process. Why was this necessary? What form of the Chkdsk command can you use in a command prompt window that does not require a restart to run?

_____

_____

4. Based on what you learned in this lab along with your other experiences with Disk Cleanup, which type of files removed by Disk Cleanup took up the most space?

_____

_____

5. Why might you want to uninstall unused apps?

_____

_____

6. What is one type of app that should absolutely begin at startup in order to protect your computer from attack?

_____

LAB 13.2 BACK UP AND RESTORE FILES IN WINDOWS 10

OBJECTIVES

The goal of this lab is to use Windows 10 Backup and Restore to back up and recover lost files. After completing this lab, you will be able to:

▲ Set up a Windows backup and back up files

▲ Restore deleted or modified files

MATERIALS REQUIRED

This lab requires the following:

▲ Windows 10 operating system

▲ An account with administrator privileges

LAB PREPARATION

Before the lab begins, the instructor or lab assistant needs to do the following:

▲ Verify that Windows starts with no errors

▲ Verify that each student has access to a user account with administrator privileges

▲ Decide which backup media will be used—for example, an external hard drive, a CD/DVD/BRD drive, or a USB flash drive

ACTIVITY BACKGROUND

Windows provides the Backup and Restore tool in Windows 10/7 and the File History tool in Windows 10/8 to help you safeguard data and Windows system files. Using these tools, you can back up one or more folders, or even an entire drive. You should back up your files from your hard drive to a different storage device, such as a CD, DVD, or Blu-ray disc, an external hard drive, or a USB flash drive. Windows professional and business editions also allow you to back up files to a network server. The File History tool is well suited for users to back up their personal data, and the Backup and Restore tool is suited for backing up data for multiple users and for system files.

In this lab, you use Windows 10 Backup and Restore to back up and restore your Documents Library and desktop.

ESTIMATED COMPLETION TIME: 45 MINUTES

 Activity

Follow these steps to create some files in the Documents library and on your desktop and then back up both:

1. Start Windows and sign in using an administrator account. Connect or plug in your backup media (a USB flash drive or other storage device) to the computer.

2. To make sure your storage device is large enough to hold all the files and folders in your Documents library and desktop, open **File Explorer** and use it to answer these questions:

   ◢ What backup storage device are you using? (For example, are you using a USB flash drive or an external hard drive?) What is the drive letter assigned to this device?

   _____

   ◢ What is the storage capacity of your backup storage device? How much free space is on the device?

   _____

   ◢ What is the size of your Documents library and the size of your Windows desktop?

   _____

   ◢ Does your storage device have enough free space to hold the backup of the Documents library and desktop?

   _____

3. Using Notepad, create a text file named **File1.txt** in your Documents library. Enter your name and address and the name of your favorite movie. Close the file.

4. Using Notepad, create a second text file named **File2.txt** in your Documents library. Enter your email address. Close the file.

5. Using Notepad, create a file named **File3.txt** on your desktop. Enter your favorite color. Close the file.

13

6. Open **Control Panel** in Classic view and click **Backup and Restore (Windows 7)**. The Backup and Restore window opens. What options are shown at the top of the left pane of the window?

_____

_____

_____

7. If a backup schedule has never been configured on this system, the *Set up backup* link appears in the upper-right area of the window. If a backup schedule has previously been configured, you will see the backup schedule information and the link *Change settings*.

   ◢ Does your computer already have a backup schedule in place?

   _____

8. If you are creating the first backup schedule for this system, click **Set up backup**. If a backup schedule is already in place, click **Change settings**. Follow the steps in the Backup Wizard to decide where to save the backup. What is the drive letter and name of the device that will receive your backup?

   _____

9. When asked what you want to back up, click **Let me choose**, and then click **Next**. Uncheck all items designated for backup. Be sure you uncheck **Include a system image of drives: System Reserved, (C:)**. In this lab, you are not backing up the system image.

10. Drill down to your **Documents Library**, and then check it. Drill down in the **Additional Locations** group, and check **Desktop**.

11. Follow the wizard to review your backup information, and verify that you are backing up the Documents library and desktop. What is the day and time the backup is scheduled to run? Save your changes and run the backup now.

    _____

12. The Backup and Restore window shows the progress of the backup. After the backup completes, close the window.

13. Now you will make some changes to the files you backed up. Open the **Documents** library, delete **File1.txt**, and then empty the Recycle Bin. Open **File2.txt** and add another email address. Save and close the document. Open **File3.txt** on your desktop and add another color. What steps did you use to empty the Recycle Bin?

    _____

Follow these steps to restore the deleted file from backup:

1. Open the Backup and Restore window and click **Restore my files**. The Restore Files dialog box appears.

2. Click **Browse for files**, and drill down to the **File1** text file. What is the path to the file?

   _____

3. Click on the file to select it, and then click **Add files**. File1 is listed in the Restore Files box. Click **Next**.

4. In the next box, decide where you want to restore the file. The default setting is the original location, but you can also change that to a new location. For this lab, restore the

file to the original location. Click **Restore**. Click **Finish**. (If the file already existed at the selected location, you would have had to choose whether to Copy and Replace, Don't Copy, or Copy, but keep both files.)

5. Open the Documents library and verify that File1 is restored. Open File1. Are the file contents as you created them?

Sometimes a file gets corrupted or you make changes to a file that you wish you could undo. If your file is backed up, you can restore it to a previous version. Follow these steps to find out how:

1. Open the Backup and Restore window to run a backup. In the window, click **Back up now**.

2. Open **File3** on your desktop and add a third color. Close the file.

3. Use the Backup and Restore window to run the backup. You should now have three backups of File3.

4. To see the different backups of File3 from which you can choose, open File Explorer and locate File3. Right-click **File3.txt** and click **Properties**. The Properties dialog box for the file appears. Click the **Previous Versions** tab. See Figure 13-1.

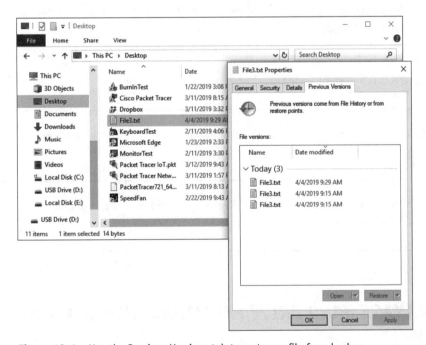

Figure 13-1   Use the Previous Versions tab to restore a file from backup

5. To restore a file, select it and then click **Restore**. A box appears and gives you the options to Copy and Replace, Don't Copy, or Copy but keep both files. Choose the last option, **Copy, but keep both files**, and then click **Finish**.

6. Keep restoring previous versions of File3 until you have one copy of File3 that has one color in it, another copy of File3 with two colors in it, and a third copy of File3 with three colors in it.

   ◢ What is the name of the file that contains one color? Two colors? Three colors?

⊿ The Previous Versions tab indicates that some backups of File3 may be stored at the backup location and others are stored in a restore point. Where does Windows store a restore point? Why would a backup of a file in a restore point not be available if the hard drive crashes?

REVIEW QUESTIONS

1. Is it more important to back up Windows system files or data files? Why?

2. By default, how often does Windows back up?

3. In the lab, you saw two ways to restore files: Use the Backup and Restore window or use the Previous Versions tab. Which method is better when you want to restore a corrupted file? Three deleted folders? When you want to recover a folder from a backup made over three weeks ago?

4. What is a system image, and how do you create one?

5. In the lab, File2 appears in the Documents library. What is the actual path and folder where File2 is stored?

6. Why do you think Backup and Restore is listed in Control Panel as Backup and Restore (Windows 7)?

LAB 13.3 MANAGE HARD DRIVE PARTITIONS USING A VIRTUAL MACHINE (VM)

OBJECTIVES

Your goal in this lab is to explore the features of the Disk Management utility using a virtual machine. After completing this lab, you will be able to:

⊿ Create a virtual hard disk drive in a virtual machine

⊿ Format a partition using the Disk Management utility

⊿ Assign a drive letter to a partition using the Disk Management utility

⊿ Split a partition using the Disk Management utility

MATERIALS REQUIRED

This lab requires the following:

⊿ Windows 10/8 Pro with Hyper-V installed

⊿ Installation of Windows in a VM

LAB PREPARATION

Before the lab begins, the instructor or lab assistant needs to do the following:

⊿ Verify that Windows starts with no errors

⊿ Verify that Windows is installed in a VM in Hyper-V

⊿ Verify that Windows starts in the VM with no errors

ACTIVITY BACKGROUND

Disk Management is a Windows utility that can be used to perform disk-related tasks, such as creating and formatting partitions and volumes and assigning drive letters. Additionally, Disk Management can be used to extend, shrink, or split partitions and to manage unallocated space. In most cases, you can perform Disk Management tasks without having to restart the system or interrupt users. Most configuration changes take effect immediately.

In the field, you might be required by your client to install a second hard drive—either physically or virtually—to increase the storage capacity of a system. In this lab, you'll gain some experience installing a second hard drive in a VM and preparing it for first use. A VM is a great tool to use when learning to use Disk Management, because you can install a new hard drive in a virtual machine without having to physically install a hard drive in a computer case. In this lab, you use a VM managed by Hyper-V, which you created in earlier labs in Chapter 12.

ESTIMATED COMPLETION TIME: 30 MINUTES

13

 Activity

PART 1: INSTALL A NEW HARD DRIVE IN THE VM

In addition to the powerful features of Disk Management, the utility in its most basic form displays installed disks' configurations, which can be useful if you need to document current information before making a decision on disk-related tasks. To learn more, first start Hyper-V and start a VM that has Windows installed in it. Follow these steps:

1. Start **Hyper-V Manager**. In the Hyper-V Manager window, start a VM that has Windows installed. Sign in to Windows in the VM.

2. In the VM, open **Disk Management**. Use the current disk configuration to answer the following questions:

   ⊿ How many hard drives does your VM currently have? What is the size of each drive?

   _____

   ⊿ How many volumes are currently configured on the system?

   _____

◢ What drive letter is assigned to each volume?

_____

◢ What is the size of the primary partition for drive C:?

_____

3. Close the Disk Management window, and shut down Windows in the VM.

Follow these steps to install a second hard drive in your VM:

1. In the Hyper-V Manager window, click the Windows VM to select it.

2. On the Actions pane, click **Settings**. The Settings dialog box displays.

3. In the left pane of the dialog box, click **IDE Controller 0**. In the IDE Controller pane, select **Hard Drive** and click **Add**.

4. With Virtual hard disk selected, click **New**. The New Virtual Hard Disk Wizard opens. Click **Next**.

5. Under Choose Disk Format, select **VHD** and click **Next**. In the next box, select **Dynamically expanding** and click **Next**.

6. In the next box, assign a name to the VHD file. What is the name of the VHD file?

_____

7. If you want to store the file in another location, click **Browse**, navigate to the location, and click **Select Folder**. What is the path to the VHD file? Click **Finish**. The virtual hard drive is created.

_____

8. Verify that the VM has two hard drives installed, and then close the VM's Settings box.

PART 2: PREPARE THE NEW HARD DRIVE FOR USE

You have created a new virtual hard disk and added it to the VM. Further configuration is required to allow the operating system to acknowledge the drive's existence so that you can begin taking advantage of the newly acquired storage space. To learn more, follow these steps:

1. Start your VM and sign in to Windows in the VM.

2. In the VM, open **File Explorer**. Answer the following questions:

◢ How many drives does File Explorer display?

_____

◢ Which drive letters have been assigned to the displayed drives, including optical drives?

_____

3. Close all windows.

When a new hard drive is installed, File Explorer is unable to see it. You need to use Disk Management to initialize, partition, and format the drive. Follow these steps:

1. Right-click **Start** and click **Disk Management**.

2. The Initialize Disk dialog box displays automatically because the system has detected the presence of a new storage device. In the Initialize Disk dialog box, select **GPT (GUID**

Partition Table), and click **OK**. The newly installed disk is displayed as a Basic disk with unallocated space.

3. Right-click in the unallocated space and click **New Simple Volume** in the shortcut menu. The New Simple Volume Wizard displays. Click **Next**.

4. In the Specify Volume Size dialog box, leave the size of the volume at the maximum size, and click **Next**.

5. In the Assign Drive Letter or Path dialog box, select **F** in the drop-down list next to *Assign the following drive letter*. (This letter is the default value.) Click **Next**.

6. In the Format Partition dialog box, enter your name as the Volume label, and click **Next**.

7. To close the wizard, click **Finish**. The newly created partition is displayed.

8. Right-click in the New Volume (F:) area. A shortcut menu displays, listing 11 items. List each item in the shortcut menu, and write a brief description of its purpose:

_____

_____

_____

_____

_____

_____

_____

_____

_____

_____

_____

_____

9. Close all windows.

10. Open **File Explorer**. How many drives do you see? List the drive letter and size of each drive:

_____

_____

PART 3: SHRINK AND EXTEND PARTITIONS

Let's use Disk Management to split the new volume you just created on the new virtual hard disk.

1. Use File Explorer, Windows Explorer, or a command prompt window to copy all the files in the \Program Files\internet explorer folder to a new folder named Copytest on the new hard drive. How large is the Copytest folder?

_____

2. Without erasing the Copytest folder, use Disk Management to split the volume on the new hard drive into two volumes that are about equal in size. List the steps you took to split the volume:

_____

_____

_____

_____

3. Format the new partition using the NTFS file system.

◢ What is the drive letter of the new volume?

_____

◢ Which volume is listed on the left side of the Disk Management window for the new disk?

_____

◢ Which volume is listed on the right side of the Disk Management window for the new disk?

_____

Suppose you need to combine two partitions into a single partition or volume. Because of the file system structure on a volume, Disk Management allows you to extend a volume to include unallocated space on the disk only if the unallocated space is to the right of the volume in the Disk Management window. To create the unallocated space, you can move all the data from the volume on the right to the volume on the left, delete the volume on the right, and then extend the volume on the left to include the unallocated space on the right. To practice this skill, do the following:

1. Using Explorer, verify that the Copytest folder is stored on the volume listed on the left side of the Disk Management window. If it is not, move the Copytest folder to the volume listed on the left.

2. In Disk Management, right-click the volume on the right, click **Delete Volume**, and click **Yes**. The volume is deleted and its space is again unallocated.

3. Right-click the volume on the left, and click **Extend Volume**. Using the Extend Volume Wizard, extend the volume to include all the unallocated space. The volume extends to include the entire disk.

4. Return to File Explorer and verify that the Copytest folder is present in the volume.

REVIEW QUESTIONS

1. When a partition on a hard drive has a file system installed on it, the partition is called a(n) _____.

2. Why is it better to practice installing a second hard disk by using a VM rather than a physical computer?

_____

3. When installing a new virtual hard disk, why is it better to use a dynamically expanding virtual hard disk rather than a fixed-size virtual hard disk?

_____

_____

4. What is the purpose of formatting a partition using Disk Management?

_____

_____

5. What must you do in Disk Management so that File Explorer can recognize and use a new hard disk?

_____

_____

6. Why might the Extend Volume option be gray and not available in the shortcut menu when you right-click a volume in Disk Management?

_____

7. What is the command to launch the Disk Management utility?

_____

LAB 13.4 SET UP A VIRTUAL HARD DRIVE IN WINDOWS

OBJECTIVES

The goal of this lab is to create a virtual hard drive in Windows. After completing this lab, you will be able to:

- Create a virtual hard drive (VHD)
- Use File Explorer or Windows Explorer to explore the VHD

MATERIALS REQUIRED

This lab requires the following:

- Windows 10/8/7 operating system

LAB PREPARATION

Before the lab begins, the instructor or lab assistant needs to do the following:

- Verify that Windows starts with no errors

ACTIVITY BACKGROUND

A virtual hard drive (VHD) is a file that acts like a hard drive. You can create a VHD and access it through File Explorer or Windows Explorer. You can also attach an existing VHD to your Windows installation. A Windows system image is stored in a VHD. A VHD is sometimes used to hold a deployment image when the image is deployed to computers over the network. Using Windows, you can boot a computer to Windows installed on a VHD. A VHD can be used as a hard drive in a virtual machine. In this lab, you create a VHD in your regular Windows installation and then use Explorer to explore the contents of the VHD.

13

ESTIMATED COMPLETION TIME: 30 MINUTES

 Activity

Follow these steps to create a new VHD:

1. Open **Disk Management**. How many disks are installed in your system? List the disk number and size of each disk:

   _____

   _____

2. To create the VHD, click the **Action** menu, and then click **Create VHD**. In the Create and Attach Virtual Hard Disk window, click **Browse**, and then browse to the location where you want to store the VHD. Enter the name of your VHD as **VHD001**. Click **Save**.

3. Enter **5000** for the virtual hard disk size in MB. Under Virtual hard disk format, select **Dynamically expanding**. Click **OK** to create the VHD.

   ◢ What is the number assigned to the disk by Disk Management? What is the status of your VHD in the Disk Management window?

   _____

   ◢ What is the reported size of the disk?

   _____

4. To initialize the disk, right-click in the Disk area, and select **Initialize Disk** in the shortcut menu. In the Initialize Disk box, if necessary, select **GPT (GUID Partition Table)**, and then click **OK**.

5. The next step to prepare the disk for use is to create and format a volume on the disk. To start the process, right-click in unallocated space on the disk, and select **New Simple Volume** in the shortcut menu. The New Simple Volume Wizard starts. Step through the wizard to assign all unallocated space to the volume and format the volume using the NTFS file system. What drive letter did Windows assign to the volume?

   _____

6. Open **File Explorer** or **Windows Explorer**. What capacity does it report for the new volume? How much free space is available?

   _____

7. Locate the VHD001 file.

   ◢ What is the file size? What is the file name, including the file extension?

   _____

   ◢ What happens when you double-click or otherwise attempt to open the VHD001 file?

   _____

8. Right-click the **VHD001** file, and click **Eject** in the shortcut menu. What happens to the virtual hard drive disk in the Disk Management window?

   _____

9. In Explorer, right-click the **VHD001** file, and click **Mount** in the shortcut menu. What happens to the virtual hard drive disk in the Disk Management window?

_____

REVIEW QUESTIONS

1. How does Windows use a VHD when creating a backup of the Windows volume?

_____

2. How is a VHD sometimes used when deploying Windows in an enterprise?

_____

3. Why can you not use an array of VHDs to create a striped volume in a Windows system?

_____

4. List two ways to install an existing VHD in Windows so that you can view the contents of the VHD.

_____

_____

5. List the steps to delete a VHD file that is currently installed as a virtual hard drive.

_____

_____

LAB 13.5 LEARN TO WORK FROM THE COMMAND LINE

OBJECTIVES

Your goal in this lab is to explore some commands used when working from the command line. After completing this lab, you will be able to:

◢ Examine directories

◢ Switch drives and directories

◢ Use various commands at the command prompt

MATERIALS REQUIRED

This lab requires the following:

◢ Windows 10/8/7 operating system

◢ USB flash drive

LAB PREPARATION

Before the lab begins, the instructor or lab assistant needs to do the following:

◢ Verify that Windows starts with no errors

ACTIVITY BACKGROUND

Experienced technicians use the command line for tasks that just can't be done in a graphical interface, especially when troubleshooting a system. For most tasks, however, you'll rely on a graphical interface, such as File Explorer. In this lab, you use the command line to perform several tasks you can also do in Explorer. It's assumed in this lab that Windows is installed on the C: drive. If your installation is on a different drive, substitute that drive letter in the following steps.

ESTIMATED COMPLETION TIME: 30 MINUTES

 Activity

To practice using the command-line environment, follow these steps:

1. Enter the **cmd** command in the Windows 10/7 search box or the Windows 8 Run box. In the command prompt window, notice that the cursor is flashing at the command prompt.

2. The title bar of the command prompt window varies with different versions of Windows and depends on the user name of the person currently signed in. Here's an example:

   C:\Users\James Clark>

   The command prompt indicates the working drive (drive C:) and the working directory (for example, the \Users\James Clark directory). Commands issued from this prompt apply to the folder shown unless you indicate otherwise.

3. Type **dir** and press **Enter**. Remember that dir is the command used to list a directory's contents. If the list of files and directories that dir displays is too large to fit on one screen, you see only the last few entries. Entries with the <DIR> label indicate that they are directories (folders), which can contain files or other directories. Also listed for each directory and file are the time and date it was created and the number of bytes a file contains. (This information is displayed differently depending on which version of Windows you're using.) The last two lines in the list summarize the number of files and directories in the current directory, the space they consume, and the free space available on the drive.

As you'll see in the next set of steps, there are two ways to view any files that aren't displayed because of the length of the list and the window size. To learn more about displaying lists of files in the command-line environment, perform the following steps:

1. First, go to a particularly large directory so you have more files to experiment with. Enter the command **cd c:\windows**. The new command prompt should look like this: c:\Windows>

2. Maximize the command prompt window.

3. Enter **dir /?** to display Help information for the directory command. You can view Help information for any command by entering the command followed by the /? parameter (also called a "switch").

4. Enter the **dir /w** command. What happened?

   _____

   _____

5. Enter the **dir /p** command. What happened?

   _____

   _____

6. Enter the **dir /os** command. What happened?

_____

_____

7. Enter the **dir /o-s** command. What happened? What do you think the hyphen between O and S accomplishes?

_____

_____

8. Insert a USB flash drive in a USB port.

9. Use File Explorer or Windows Explorer to find out what drive letter Windows assigned to the flash drive. (The drive will be listed in the left pane with the assigned drive letter in parentheses.) What is the drive letter? The following steps assume that the drive letter is H:, but yours might be different.

_____

10. Create a new folder named **Tools** on the flash drive. Use Notepad to create a file named **deleteme.txt** in the H:\Tools folder.

11. Close **File Explorer** or **Windows Explorer**. In the command prompt window, enter the **h:** command. The resulting prompt should look like this: H:\>. What does the H: indicate?

_____

12. What do you think you would see if you issued the dir command at this prompt?

_____

_____

13. Enter the **dir** command. Did you see what you were expecting?

_____

14. Enter the **dir h:\tools** command. This command tells the computer to list the contents of a specific directory without actually changing to that directory. In the resulting file list, you should see the file you created earlier, deleteme.txt.

File attributes are managed by using the Attrib command. Follow these steps to learn how to view and manage file attributes:

1. To make H:\Tools the default directory, enter the **cd h:\tools** command.

2. To view the attributes of the Deleteme.txt file, enter the **attrib deleteme.txt** command.

3. To change the file to a hidden file, enter the **attrib +h deleteme.txt** command.

4. View the attributes of the Deleteme.txt file again.

◢ What command did you use?

_____

◢ How have the attributes changed?

_____

5. To view the contents of the H:\Tools directory, enter the **dir** command. Why doesn't the Deleteme.txt file appear in the directory list?

6. To change the attributes so that the file is a system file, enter the **attrib +s deleteme.txt** command. What error message did you get?

7. Because you can't change the attributes of a hidden file, first remove the hidden attribute by entering the **attrib -h deleteme.txt** command.

8. Now try to make the file a system file. What command did you use?

9. Use the **dir** command to list the contents of the H:\Tools directory. Are system files listed?

10. To remove the file's system attribute, enter the **attrib -s deleteme.txt** command.

11. To move to the root directory, enter the **cd h:** command.

To learn how to delete a file from the command prompt, follow these steps:

1. Enter the **del deleteme.txt** command to instruct the computer to delete that file. You'll see a message stating that the file couldn't be found because the system assumes that commands refer to the working directory unless a specific path is given. What command could you use to delete the file without changing to that directory?

2. The current prompt should be H:\>. The \ in the command you typed indicates the root directory.

3. Enter the **cd tools** command. The prompt now ends with "Tools>" (indicating that Tools is the current working directory).

4. Now enter the **del deleteme.txt /p** command. You're prompted to type **Y** for Yes or **N** for No to confirm the deletion. If you don't enter the /p switch (which means "prompt for verification"), the file is deleted automatically without a confirmation message. It's a good practice to use this /p switch, especially when deleting multiple files with wildcard characters. Also, when you delete a file from the command line, the file doesn't go to the Recycle Bin, as it would if you deleted it in File Explorer or Windows Explorer. Because deletion from the command line bypasses the Recycle Bin, recovering accidentally deleted files is more difficult.

5. Type **Y** and press **Enter** to delete the Deleteme.txt file. You're returned to the Tools directory.

To display certain files in a directory, you can use an asterisk (*) or a question mark (?) as wildcard characters. Wildcard characters are placeholders that represent other unspecified characters. The asterisk can represent one or more characters, and the question mark represents any single character. The asterisk is the most useful wildcard, so it's the one you'll encounter most often. To learn more, follow these steps:

1. Return to the root directory of drive C:. What command did you use?

2. Enter the **dir *.*** command. How many files are displayed? How many directories are displayed?

_____

3. Enter the **dir u*.*** command. How many files are displayed? How many directories are displayed?

_____

4. Explain why the results differed in the previous two commands:

_____

_____

> **ESTIMATED COMPLETION TIME: 30 MINUTES**

CHALLENGE ACTIVITY

Follow these steps to practice using additional commands at the command prompt:

1. Copy the program file Notepad.exe from the \Windows directory on the hard drive to the \Tools directory on the flash drive. What command did you use?

_____

2. Rename the file in the \Tools directory as **Newfile.exe**. What command did you use?

_____

3. Change the attributes of Newfile.exe to make it a hidden file. What command did you use?

_____

4. Enter the **dir** command. Is the Newfile.exe file displayed?

_____

5. Unhide Newfile.exe. What command did you use?

_____

6. List all files in the \Windows directory that have an .exe file extension. What command did you use?

_____

_____

7. Create a new directory named **\New** in the root directory of drive C:, and then copy Newfile.exe to the \New directory. What commands did you use?

_____

_____

13

8. Using the /p switch to prompt for verification, delete the \New directory. What commands did you use?

_____

_____

9. Open Windows Help and Support. Use the Search text box or the Internet to answer the following questions:

▲ What is the purpose of the Recover command?

_____

_____

▲ What is the purpose of the Assoc command?

_____

_____

REVIEW QUESTIONS

1. What command/switch do you use to view Help information for the dir command?

_____

2. What do you add to the dir command to list the contents of a directory that's not the current working directory?

_____

3. What command do you use to change directories?

_____

4. What command do you use to delete a file?

_____

5. What command do you use to switch from drive H: to drive C:?

_____

LAB 13.6 USE THE XCOPY AND ROBOCOPY COMMANDS

OBJECTIVES

The goal of this lab is to demonstrate the differences in the xcopy and robocopy commands. After completing this lab, you will be able to:

▲ Copy files and folders with the xcopy or robocopy command

MATERIALS REQUIRED

This lab requires the following:

▲ Windows 10/8/7 operating system

▲ A USB flash drive or another form of removable media

LAB PREPARATION

Before the lab begins, the instructor or lab assistant needs to do the following:

◢ Verify that Windows starts with no errors

ACTIVITY BACKGROUND

The copy command allows you to copy files from one folder to another folder. Using a single xcopy command, you can copy files from multiple folders, duplicating an entire file structure in another location. The robocopy command is basically an improved version of xcopy with a few more features, including the ability to schedule copying to run automatically and the ability to delete the source files when the copying is finished. In this lab, you learn to copy files using either of these commands.

ESTIMATED COMPLETION TIME: 30 MINUTES

 Activity

Before you begin using the xcopy and robocopy commands, you need to create a test directory to use when copying files. Follow these steps:

1. Open a command prompt window, and make the root of drive C: the current directory. The quickest way to change to the root of a drive is to type **T:** (where T is the drive letter), and then press **Enter**.

2. Make a directory called **copytest** in the drive C: root.

Now you can begin experimenting with the xcopy command. Follow these steps:

1. Enter the **xcopy /?** command. Help information is displayed for the xcopy command. Notice all the switches you can use to modify the xcopy command. In particular, you can use the /e switch to instruct xcopy to copy all files and subdirectories in a directory, including any empty subdirectories, to a new location.

2. Enter the **robocopy /?** command. What are some new features unique to robocopy?

_____

_____

_____

_____

3. Enter the **xcopy "c:\program files\internet explorer" c:\copytest /e** command. (You must use quotation marks in the command line to surround a path, file name, or folder name containing spaces.) You'll see a list of files scroll by as they are copied from the C:\program files\internet explorer folder to the C:\copytest folder.

4. When the copy operation is finished, check the copytest folder to see that the files have been copied and the subdirectories created.

5. Enter a dir command with switches that will give you the total size of the copytest directory, including all the files in the directory and its subdirectories.

   ◢ What command did you use?

_____

13

◢ What is the total size of the copytest directory in bytes, including all files in the directory and its subdirectories?

_____

◢ What is the total size in MB? In GB?

_____

6. Insert a USB flash drive or attach an equivalent removable device. To find the capacity of your USB flash drive, enter the command dir H:. (You might have to substitute the drive letter assigned to your storage device for H:.) Add the bytes of used space and free space to determine the capacity of the drive.

   ◢ What is the capacity of your USB flash drive in MB? In GB?

_____

   ◢ How much free space is on your USB flash drive?

_____

   ◢ Will all the files in the C:\copytest directory fit on your flash drive?

_____

7. Enter the **md H:\copytest** command. This command creates a directory named copytest on the H: drive. (Remember to use the letter for the drive assigned to your media device.)

8. To copy all files in the copytest directory on the hard drive to the copytest directory on drive H:, enter the **Xcopy C:\copytest H:\copytest** command.

9. The system begins copying files. If the flash drive does not have enough free space to hold the entire C:\copytest directory, the system displays a message stating that the device is out of space and asks you to insert another device. Did you get this error message? If so, what is the exact error message?

_____

_____

10. If you don't have enough free space, stop the copying process by pressing **Ctrl+Pause/ Break**. You're returned to the command prompt.

REVIEW QUESTIONS

1. Can a single copy command copy files from more than one directory?

_____

2. What switch do you use with xcopy or robocopy to copy subdirectories?

_____

3. Why might you want to schedule a robocopy command to occur at a later time?

_____

_____

4. Which xcopy switch suppresses overwrite confirmation?

_____

LAB 13.7 USE REMOTE DESKTOP

OBJECTIVES

Your goal in this lab is to learn how to sign in to another computer remotely by using Windows Remote Desktop. After completing this lab, you will be able to:

◢ Configure Remote Desktop

◢ Use Remote Desktop to sign in to another computer remotely

MATERIALS REQUIRED

This lab requires the following:

◢ Windows 10/8/7 Professional, Ultimate, or Enterprise edition

◢ An account with administrator privileges

◢ A network workgroup consisting of two or more computers

◢ A team of two or more students

LAB PREPARATION

Before the lab begins, the instructor or lab assistant needs to do the following:

◢ Verify that Windows starts with no errors

◢ Verify that a network connection is available

◢ Verify that each student has access to a user account with administrator privileges

ACTIVITY BACKGROUND

Windows allows users to connect remotely from other Windows machines. With a remote connection, you can control a computer from another location, such as work or home. Remote Desktop is different from Remote Assistance because Remote Desktop does not need the end users' permission to connect their computers. Remote Desktop is also useful for connecting to servers, database servers, file servers, or other machines you access. For example, as a support technician, you might find Remote Desktop useful when you need to update or reset software on a server but you are working at your desk and the server is in the data center.

Remote Desktop is only available in Windows 10, Windows 8, or Windows 7 Professional, Ultimate, and Enterprise versions. Using Home editions of Windows 7, you cannot host Remote Desktop, but you can remote in to a computer that is hosting Remote Desktop.

Remote Desktop is not enabled by default in the operating system. When enabled, members of the administrators group can connect to the computer from another machine. When you use Remote Desktop, you are signed in to the remote computer as if you were actually sitting in front of the machine with full rights and access. Standard users must be placed on a remote access list to use Remote Desktop.

In this lab, you configure one computer to accept a remote connection, and then allow someone in your class workgroup to connect to it from her machine.

13

Activity

In this lab, you set up your computer to allow a remote connection. Then, you remote in to another computer in your workgroup that is also configured to use Remote Desktop. To configure your computer to accept a remote connection, follow these steps:

1. Sign in using an account with administrator privileges.

2. To determine the computer name and IP address, open a command prompt window, and enter the **ipconfig / all** command. Write down the computer name (host name) and IP address:

   _____

3. Open the **System** window, and click **Remote settings** in the left pane. The System Properties dialog box opens with the Remote tab selected.

4. Select the **Allow connections only from computers running Remote Desktop with Network Level Authentication** option. If a dialog box appears and warns about a Power Options setting, click **OK** to continue. Click **Apply**.

5. Click **Select Users**. In the Remote Desktop Users dialog box, you can add or remove users who are allowed to use a Remote Desktop connection. The users listed here and the user currently signed in have access to Remote Desktop. On the following line, list those users:

   _____

Remote Desktop will not work in Windows 10 unless it is enabled in both the System Properties dialog box and the Settings app. Follow these steps to configure Remote Desktop using the Settings app:

1. Open the **Settings** app, navigate to **System**, and then select **Remote Desktop**.

2. Turn on the switch for **Enable Remote Desktop** if it isn't on already. If a dialog box appears, click **Confirm**.

3. Click **Advanced settings** to make sure Network Level Authentication is required to connect. If a dialog box appears, click **Confirm**.

4. Click **Select users that can remotely access this PC** to review the user list you found using the System Properties dialog box earlier.

5. Close all windows.

Follow these steps to connect to a computer using Remote Desktop:

1. Find someone in your group who has set up Remote Desktop on his or her computer. Ask for the computer's name and IP address so that you can connect to it using Remote Desktop. What computer name and IP address will you connect to?

   _____

2. Open **Remote Desktop Connection**.

> **Notes** All local users are automatically signed off a computer when it is being remotely accessed. Also, only one computer can remotely access a single computer at a time.

3. In the Remote Desktop Connection dialog box, enter the IP address or computer name of the remote computer in the Computer text box, and click **Connect**.

4. A Windows security window appears and asks for the sign-in credentials of the computer you are connecting to. Enter the credentials for one of the user accounts that is allowed access. For the user name, you might need to include the computer name—for example, LenovoLaptop\Jean Andrews.

5. An identity warning window might appear because the system cannot authenticate the certificate. If you see this window, click **Yes** to accept. You can also check the **Don't ask me again for connections to this computer** box so that the warning doesn't appear again.

6. After a moment, the screen of the computer to which you now have remote access appears.

Follow these steps to use the remote machine:

1. Notice the toolbar at the top of the screen. What is the name of the computer that you are accessing?

_____

2. Open the **Documents** folder. Create a test document on the remote computer. What is the name of the document you created?

_____

3. Using Control Panel, adjust the time by a half-hour. What is the new time?

_____

4. Click **OK**, and close all windows.

5. Close the Remote Desktop Connection window, which ends the remote connection session.

6. Sign in to the remote machine you just used, change the time back to the correct time, and verify that the file has been created.

REVIEW QUESTIONS

1. Describe two situations in which you might want to use Remote Desktop:

_____

_____

_____

2. How can you tell if you are connected remotely to another computer?

_____

_____

3. How can you determine the name of the remote computer before connecting? How can you determine the IP address of the remote computer?

_____

_____

13

4. How might other programs, such as firewalls, interfere with a remote connection?

_____

_____

5. When a connection was made to the remote computer in the lab, what changed on that computer?

_____

6. What is the advantage of a host computer not displaying the Windows desktop locally when a Remote Desktop session is active?

_____

_____

Troubleshooting Windows After Startup

Labs included in this chapter:

- **Lab 14.1:** Use the Microsoft Management Console

- **Lab 14.2:** Use Task Manager

- **Lab 14.3:** Edit the Registry with Regedit

- **Lab 14.4:** Identify a Hard Drive Bottleneck by Using Performance Tools

- **Lab 14.5:** Use the System Configuration Utility

- **Lab 14.6:** Apply a Restore Point

- **Lab 14.7:** Use Windows Setup Media to Apply a Restore Point

- **Lab 14.8:** Use Windows Utilities to Speed Up a System

- **Lab 14.9:** Research Data Recovery Software

LAB 14.1 USE THE MICROSOFT MANAGEMENT CONSOLE

OBJECTIVES

The goal of this lab is to add snap-ins and save settings using the Microsoft Management Console (MMC) to create a customized console. After completing this lab, you will be able to:

- Use the MMC to add snap-ins
- Save a customized console
- Identify how to launch a console from the Start menu

MATERIALS REQUIRED

This lab requires the following:

- Windows 10/8/7 Professional or Business edition computer
- An account with administrator privileges

> **Notes** This lab works great in a Windows VM.

LAB PREPARATION

Before the lab begins, the instructor or lab assistant needs to do the following:

- Verify that Windows starts with no errors
- Verify that each student has access to a user account with administrator privileges

ACTIVITY BACKGROUND

The Microsoft Management Console (MMC) is a standard management tool you can use to create a customized console by adding administrative tools called snap-ins. You can use snap-ins provided by Microsoft as well as those from other vendors. Many of the administrative tools you have already used (such as Device Manager) can be added to a console as a snap-in. The console itself serves as a convenient interface that helps you organize and manage the administrative tools you use most often. In this lab, you use the MMC to create a customized console.

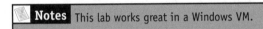

ESTIMATED COMPLETION TIME: 30 MINUTES

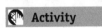

Follow these steps to build a customized console:

1. Sign in to Windows as an administrator.
2. In the Windows 10/7 search box or the Windows 8 Run box, enter the **mmc.exe** command. If necessary, respond to the UAC box. An MMC window for Console1 opens. The left pane displays the list of snap-ins in the console. Currently, nothing appears in this list because no snap-ins have been added to Console1 yet.
3. On the Console1 menu bar, click **File**, and then click **Add/Remove Snap-in**. The Add or Remove Snap-ins dialog box opens. Available snap-ins are listed on the left side of this dialog box (see Figure 14-1). Note that this list includes some administrative tools you have already used, such as Device Manager and Event Viewer. To add Device Manager as a snap-in, click **Device Manager**, and then click **Add**.

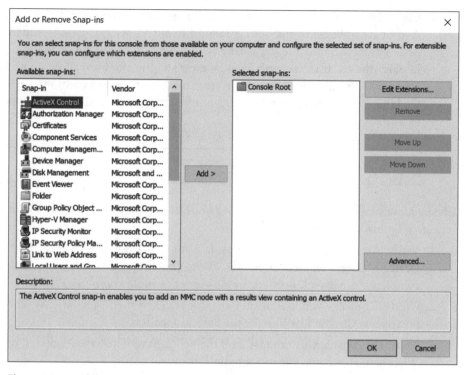

Figure 14-1 Adding snap-ins to the Microsoft Management Console

4. For Windows 8/7, the Device Manager dialog box opens, and you can specify here which computer you want this Device Manager snap-in to manage. You want it to manage the computer you're currently working on, so verify that the **Local computer** button is selected, and then click **Finish**. (Windows 10 assumes the local computer for Device Manager.)

5. Next, you add Event Viewer as a snap-in. Click **Event Viewer** in the Available snap-ins list, and then click **Add**. The Select Computer dialog box opens.

6. Verify that the **Local computer** button is selected, and then click **OK**.

7. Click **OK** to close the Add or Remove Snap-ins dialog box. The two new snap-ins are listed in the left and middle panes of the Console1 window.

You have finished adding snap-ins for the local computer to your console. Next, you add another Event Viewer snap-in to be used on a network computer. If your computer isn't connected to a network, you can read the following set of steps, but you won't be able to perform them because Windows won't be able to find any networked computers. If your computer is connected to a network, follow these steps:

1. Add another Event Viewer snap-in, and then click the **Another computer** button in the Select Computer dialog box. Now you need to specify the name of the computer to which you want this Event Viewer snap-in to apply. You could type the name of the computer, but it's easier to select the computer by using the Browse button.

2. Click the **Browse** button. A different Select Computer dialog box opens. Click **Advanced** to open a third Select Computer dialog box. Click **Find Now** to begin searching the network for eligible computers. Eventually, a list of eligible computers is displayed.

3. Click the name of the computer to which you want to apply this Event Viewer snap-in, and then click **OK**. The third Select Computer dialog box closes, and you return to the second Select Computer dialog box.

14

4. Click **OK** twice to close the two remaining Select Computer dialog boxes. Close the Add or Remove Snap-ins box. A second Event Viewer snap-in is added below the first. The new Event Viewer listing is followed by the name of the remote computer in parentheses. If the second Event Viewer snap-in does not show up and you get an error message instead, write the error message here and continue with the rest of the lab. The remote computer might not be configured to allow event logging on the network.

_____

_____

You're finished adding snap-ins and are ready to save your new, customized console so you can use it whenever you need it. Follow these steps:

1. Verify that the left pane of the Console Root folder now contains the following items: Device Manager on local computer, Event Viewer (Local), and, if you were able to complete the network portion, Event Viewer (*remote computer name*).

2. On the Console1 window menu bar, click **File**, and then click **Save As**. The Save As dialog box opens. Choose **Desktop** for the Save in location.

3. Name the console **Custom.msc**, and then click **Save**. The Save As dialog box closes. What is the file name and exact path to the console?

_____

4. Close the Console window.

Follow these steps to open and use your customized console:

1. Open the Custom console from the Desktop. If the UAC dialog box opens, click **Yes**. Your customized console opens in a window named Custom - [Console Root].

2. Maximize the console window, if necessary.

3. In the left pane, click **Device Manager on local computer**, and observe the options in the middle pane.

4. In the left pane, click the arrow next to Event Viewer (Local). Subcategories are displayed below Event Viewer (Local). List the subcategories you see:

_____

_____

_____

_____

5. Click **Event Viewer** (*remote computer name*) and observe that the events displayed are events occurring on the remote computer.

6. On the Custom - [Console Root] menu bar, click **File**, and then click **Exit**. A message box opens, asking if you want to save the current settings.

7. Click **Yes**. The console closes.

8. Launch the customized console again, and record the items listed in the middle pane when the console opens:

_____

REVIEW QUESTIONS

1. What term is used to refer to the specialized tools you can add to a console with the MMC? What are they used for?

_____

2. Suppose you haven't created a customized MMC yet. How would you start the MMC?

_____

3. How can a customized console be used to monitor many computers from a single machine?

_____

4. Why might you want the ability to monitor or manage a remote computer through a network?

_____

5. In what folder do you put a console so that it appears in the Start menu for all users?

_____

LAB 14.2 USE TASK MANAGER

OBJECTIVES

The goal of this lab is to use Task Manager to examine your system. After completing this lab, you will be able to:

- ◢ Identify applications that are currently running
- ◢ Launch an application
- ◢ Display general system performance and process information in Task Manager

MATERIALS REQUIRED

This lab requires the following:

- ◢ Windows 10/8/7 Professional or Business edition computer
- ◢ Installed optical drive, installed/onboard sound card, and an audio CD
- ◢ An account with administrator privileges

LAB PREPARATION

Before the lab begins, the instructor or lab assistant needs to do the following:

- ◢ Verify that Windows starts with no errors
- ◢ Verify that an optical drive and sound card have been installed on all student computers
- ◢ Verify that each student has access to a user account with administrator privileges

ACTIVITY BACKGROUND

Task Manager is a useful tool that allows you to switch between tasks, end tasks, and observe system use and performance. In this lab, you use Task Manager to manage applications and observe system performance.

14

Activity

Follow these steps to use Task Manager:

1. Sign in to Windows as an administrator.

2. Press **Ctrl+Alt+Del** and then click **Task Manager** in Windows 10/8 or **Start Task Manager** in Windows 7. Alternatively, you can right-click any blank area on the taskbar and then click **Task Manager** in Windows 10/8 or **Start Task Manager** in Windows 7 in the shortcut menu. The Task Manager window opens, with tabs you can use to find information about applications, processes, and programs running on the computer and information on system performance.

3. If necessary, click the **Processes** tab in Windows 10/8 or the **Applications** tab in Windows 7. If you see *More details* at the bottom of the Task Manager window, click it to see the details. For Windows 10/8, click **View** in the menu bar, and select **Group by type** in the submenu list. For Windows 10/8, what are the three groups of processes or applications in the list that appears?

_____

_____

_____

4. Open the **Paint** app. What change occurred in the list of Windows 10/8 processes or Windows 7 applications?

_____

5. In Windows 10/8, click **File** on the Task Manager menu bar, and then click **Run new task**. In Windows 7, click the **New Task** button in the lower-right corner of the window. The Create new task dialog box opens, showing the last command entered.

6. Use the Create new task box to open a command prompt window.

   ◢ What command did you use?

_____

   ◢ What new process is listed in the Task Manager window? Include the path to the program file in your answer.

_____

7. Press and drag the command prompt window so it overlaps the Task Manager window. The command prompt window is the active window and appears on top of Task Manager.

You can customize Task Manager to suit your preferences. Among other things, you can change the setting that determines whether Task Manager is displayed on top of all other open windows, and you can change the way information is displayed. To learn more about changing Task Manager settings, make sure the command prompt window is still open and is on top of the Task Manager window. Follow these steps:

1. In Task Manager, click **Options** on the menu bar. A menu with a list of options opens. Note that the check marks indicate which options are currently applied.

Check **Always on top**, which keeps the Task Manager window on top of all other open windows. List other options in the Options menu here:

_____

_____

_____

2. Click on the command prompt window. What happens?

_____

3. On the Task Manager menu bar, click **View**. You can use the options on the Update Speed submenu to change how quickly the information is updated. List the available and current settings:

_____

_____

_____

Follow these steps in Task Manager to end a task and observe system use information:

1. Notice the information listed in columns in Windows 10/8, and in the bar at the bottom of Task Manager in Windows 7. What information do you see, and what are the values?

_____

_____

_____

2. While observing these values, move your pointer around the screen for several seconds and then stop. Did any of the values change?

_____

3. Next, move your pointer to drag an open window around the screen for several seconds, and then stop. How did this affect the values?

_____

4. End the Paint app using Task Manager. Because Paint is not critical to core Windows functions, it's safe to end this process. In the list of applications, click **Paint** and then click the **End Task** button.

> ⚡ **Caution** Be careful about ending processes; ending a potentially essential process (one that other processes depend on) could have serious consequences.

5. Compare the memory usage with the information recorded in Step 1. How much memory was Paint using?

_____

14

Follow these steps in Task Manager to observe performance information:

1. Click the **Performance** tab, which displays CPU usage and memory usage in bar graphs. What other categories of information are displayed on the Performance tab?

   _____

   _____

2. Insert and play an audio CD. Observe the CPU and memory usage values, and record them here:

   _____

   _____

3. Stop the CD from playing, and again observe the CPU usage and memory usage. Compare these values with the values from Step 2. Which value changed the most?

   _____

4. When you're finished, close all open windows.

REVIEW QUESTIONS

1. Record the steps for one way to launch Task Manager:

   _____

2. Which Task Manager tab do you use to switch between applications and end a task?

   _____

3. Why could it be dangerous to end a process with Task Manager?

   _____

4. How could you tell whether the processor had recently completed a period of intensive use but is now idle?

   _____

5. Did the playback of an audio CD use more system resources than moving the pointer? Explain:

   _____

LAB 14.3 EDIT THE REGISTRY WITH REGEDIT

OBJECTIVES

Your goal in this lab is to learn how to save, modify, and restore the Windows registry. After completing this lab, you will be able to:

◢ Back up and modify the registry

◢ Observe the effects of a modified registry

◢ Restore the registry

MATERIALS REQUIRED

This lab requires the following:

◢ Windows 10/8/7 operating system

> **Notes** This lab works great in a Windows 10/8/7 virtual machine.

LAB PREPARATION

Before the lab begins, the instructor or lab assistant needs to do the following:

◢ Verify that Windows starts with no errors

ACTIVITY BACKGROUND

The registry is a database of configuration information stored in files called hives. Each time Windows boots, it rebuilds the registry from the configuration files and stores it in RAM. When you need to modify the behavior of Windows, you should consider editing the registry only as a last resort. Errors in the registry can make your system inoperable, and there's no way for Windows to inform you that you have made a mistake. For this reason, many people are hesitant to edit the registry. If you follow the rule of backing up the system before you make any change, however, you can feel confident that even if you make a mistake, you can restore the system to its original condition. In this lab, you back up, change, and restore the registry.

ESTIMATED COMPLETION TIME: 45 MINUTES

 Activity

Windows allows you to create a restore point so that you can restore Windows to a time before any changes were made. Follow these directions to back up the system (including the registry):

1. Open Control Panel in Classic view, and open the **System** window. In the System window, click **System protection**. The System Properties dialog box opens with the System Protection tab selected.

2. Select drive **C**.

3. Click **Create** and then type a name for your restore point. The current time and date will be added automatically. Click **Create** again to create the restore point.

4. When the restore point is completed, close all open windows and dialog boxes.

5. Open the System Properties dialog box again, and then click **System Restore** on the System Protection tab. In the System Restore Wizard, click **Next**, and check the **Show more restore points** check box. Make sure the name and description of the backup you just created are listed by checking the date and time the file was created. Record the name, date, and time of this file:

_____

6. Click **Cancel** to close the System Restore Wizard, and then click **Cancel** again to exit from System Properties.

7. Close any open windows.

As you know, you can use Windows tools such as Control Panel to modify many Windows settings, ranging from the color of the background to power-saving features. Control Panel provides a safe,

14

user-friendly graphical interface that modifies the registry in the background. Sometimes, however, the only way to edit the registry is to do it yourself. These modifications are sometimes referred to as registry tweaks or hacks. In the following steps, you will make a relatively small change to the registry by editing the name of the Recycle Bin. To open the registry using the registry editor, do the following:

1. In the Windows 10/7 search box or the Windows 8 Run box, enter the **regedit** command.

2. If Windows presents a UAC dialog box, click **Yes**. The Registry Editor opens, displaying the system's registry hierarchy in the left pane along with any entries for the selected registry item in the right pane.

The registry is large, and searching through it requires a little bit of practice. The section of the registry that governs the naming of the Recycle Bin is HKEY_CURRENT_USER\Software\Microsoft\Windows\CurrentVersion\Explorer\CLSID\{645FF040-5081-101B-9F08-00AA002F954E}. See Figure 14-2.

Figure 14-2 The status bar at the top of the Registry Editor window shows the currently selected key

To navigate to this section and rename the Recycle Bin, follow these steps:

1. Click the arrow on the left side of the **HKEY_CURRENT_USER** key.

2. Click the arrows next to **Software**, and then **Microsoft**. Scroll down the list, and then click the arrows next to **Windows, CurrentVersion, Explorer**, and, finally, **CLSID**.

3. Click **{645FF040-5081-101B-9F08-00AA002F954E}** to select it.

4. In the right pane, double-click **Default** to open the Edit String dialog box.

5. To rename the Recycle Bin as Trash Bin, type **Trash Bin** in the Value data box, and then click **OK**.

6. Notice that Trash Bin now displays under the Data column.

7. Right-click the desktop and click **Refresh** in the shortcut menu. Note that the Recycle Bin icon is now named Trash Bin.

8. To close the Registry Editor, click **File** on the menu bar, and then click **Exit**. You weren't prompted to save your changes to the registry because they were saved the instant you made them. This is why editing the registry is so unforgiving: There are no safeguards. You can't undo your work by choosing to exit without saving changes, as you can in Microsoft Word, for instance.

Finally, you need to undo your changes to the Recycle Bin. Follow these steps to use System Restore to restore the registry's previous version:

1. Open the System Properties dialog box again, and then click **System Restore** on the System Protection tab. In the System Restore Wizard, click **Next**. Check the **Show more restore points** check box.

2. Choose the restore point you created earlier, and then click **Next**.

3. When you're asked to confirm your restore point, click **Finish**. Click **Yes** when the system warns you that a system restore cannot be undone.

4. After the system restore, the computer will have to reboot.

5. After the boot is completed, notice that the name of the Recycle Bin has been restored.

Use the web or Windows Help and Support to answer the following questions about the registry:

◢ How often does Windows back up the registry automatically?

_____

◢ Where are registry backups usually stored?

_____

◢ What files constitute the Windows registry? What type of file are they saved as during backup?

_____

_____

REVIEW QUESTIONS

1. Why does Windows automatically back up the registry?

_____

2. Where is the registry stored while Windows is running?

_____

3. What type of safeguards does the Registry Editor have to keep you from making mistakes?

_____

4. What do you call the files that make up the registry on your system?

_____

5. In this lab, how did you check to make sure your registry was restored?

_____

_____

14

LAB 14.4 IDENTIFY A HARD DRIVE BOTTLENECK BY USING PERFORMANCE TOOLS

OBJECTIVES

Your goal in this lab is to learn to use Performance Monitor in Windows to identify bottlenecks in the system caused by the hard drive or the applications using it. After completing this lab, you will be able to:

▲ Use the Windows Performance Monitor

▲ Identify a hard drive performance bottleneck

MATERIALS REQUIRED

This lab requires the following:

▲ Windows 10/8/7 operating system

▲ Internet access

▲ An account with administrator privileges

LAB PREPARATION

Before the lab begins, the instructor or lab assistant needs to do the following:

▲ Verify that Windows starts with no errors

▲ Verify that Internet access is available

▲ Verify that each student has access to a user account with administrator privileges

ACTIVITY BACKGROUND

A problem with slow Windows performance can be caused by hardware or software. Key hardware components that can cause a bottleneck include the processor, memory, and hard drive. Several factors can affect hard drive performance: the speed of the drive, the amount of free space on the drive, file fragmentation on the drive, hard drive thrashing, and applications that make excessive demands on the drive. In this lab, you determine if the hard drive is a bottleneck to your system by examining all these factors.

Performance Monitor offers hundreds of counters used to examine various aspects of the system related to performance. Two hard drive counters you will use in this lab are the % Disk Time counter and the Avg. Disk Queue Length counter. The % Disk Time counter represents the percentage of time the hard drive is in use. The Avg. Disk Queue Length counter represents the average number of processes waiting to use the hard drive. If the Avg. Disk Queue Length is above two and the % Disk Time is more than 80 percent, you can conclude that the hard drive is working excessively hard and processes are slowed down waiting on the drive. Anytime a process must wait to access the hard drive, you are likely to see degradation in overall system performance.

ESTIMATED COMPLETION TIME: 45 MINUTES

 Activity

Performance Monitor is in the Administrative Tools group of Control Panel and works by displaying counters related to hardware and software components. Follow these steps to use Performance Monitor to display two counters related to the hard drive:

1. In the Windows 10/7 search box or the Windows 8 Run box, enter the **perfmon.msc** command. The Performance Monitor window opens.

2. If necessary, expand **Monitoring Tools** in the left pane. Under Monitoring Tools, click **Performance Monitor**.

3. By default, current activity of the processor information object displays in a line graph, and the line is red (see Figure 14-3). The list of counters currently selected for display appears at the bottom of the window. In the figure, the one counter selected is % Processor Time. You should delete any counters you do not need so that you will not unnecessarily use system resources to monitor these counters. To delete the % Processor Time counter, click somewhere in the row to select it. Next, click the **red X** above the graph to delete the counter from the graph. The graph is now empty.

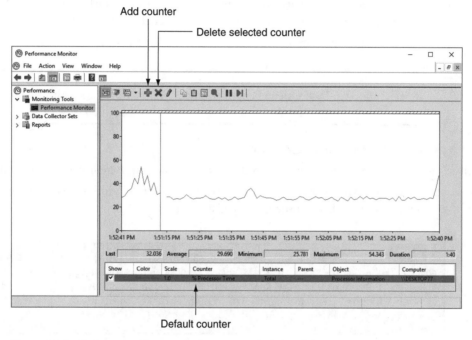

Figure 14-3 Performance Monitor displays current activity of the processor information object

4. To add a new object and counter to the graph, click the **green plus sign** above the graph. The Add Counters box opens.

5. To add a counter for hard drive activity, scroll through the *Available counters* and expand the items in the **PhysicalDisk** object. The counters under the PhysicalDisk object appear, and all these counters are selected. In the list of counters, click **% Disk Time**. This action selects the counter and causes all the other counters to be deselected. Click **Add**. The % Disk Time counter appears in the Added counters area.

6. In the list of counters, click **Avg. Disk Queue Length**, and then click **Add**. The Avg. Disk Queue Length counter appears in the Added counters area. To close the box, click **OK**.

7. The two hard drive counters appear in the Performance Monitor line graph. Answer these questions:

   ◢ What is the color of the line for the % Disk Time counter?

   _____

   ◢ What is the color of the line for the Avg. Disk Queue Length counter?

   _____

8. Keep the Performance Monitor window open as you perform other activities on your computer. In a real-life situation, you would open the applications a user normally uses and work as the user would normally do to attempt to produce a typical working environment needed to monitor performance. In this lab, try playing a game or surfing the web, keeping both the game and the browser open at the same time. As you work, watch the Performance Monitor window as it shows peaks in both counters.

9. Reading the counters by watching peaks is not as accurate as reading the actual data. To read actual values of the counters, hover over a line with your pointer and read the counter value that appears in a bubble window.

10. Performance Monitor also records the average, minimum, and maximum counter values under the graph. In the list of counters at the bottom of the Performance Monitor window, select the **% Disk Time** counter and answer these questions:

    ◢ What is the maximum value for the % Disk Time counter?

    _____

    ◢ Select the **Avg. Disk Queue Length** counter. What is the maximum value for this counter?

    _____

11. Close the Performance Monitor window.

Follow these steps to use Task Manager to identify a process that might be hogging hard drive resources:

1. Open **Task Manager** and select the **Processes** tab. For Windows 10/8, click the **Disk** column to sort the list of processes by disk usage.

> **Notes** Windows 7 Task Manager does not normally monitor disk usage, but you can configure it to do so. Click **View** on the menu bar, and then click **Select Columns**. In the Select Process Page Columns dialog box, select three items: **I/O Read Bytes**, **I/O Write Bytes**, and **Description**. A process that shows either the I/O Read Bytes column or the I/O Write Bytes column constantly changing indicates that the process is hogging hard drive resources.

2. Search the Task Manager processes for constantly changing values, and answer these questions:

    ◢ List the processes that show constantly changing values, and include in your list the description of each process:

    _____

    _____

    _____

    _____

    ◢ Of the processes you listed, which processes belong to Windows?

    _____

    _____

    ◢ Of the processes you listed, which processes do not belong to Windows?

    _____

    _____

3. Close the Task Manager window.

If processes that belong to Windows are constantly changing, most likely the problem is caused by hard drive thrashing. Hard drive thrashing happens when the system is short on memory and must therefore constantly swap data from memory to the page file and back to memory. This situation can best be corrected by installing more memory.

If a particular process that belongs to an application is hogging resources, consider upgrading or replacing the application with a more efficient version or product.

If you suspect the hard drive is a performance bottleneck, you should investigate whether the drive has enough free space and whether files on the drive are fragmented. Follow these steps to check these two possibilities:

1. A hard drive needs a minimum of 15 percent free space on the drive. For Windows 10/8, open **File Explorer** and click **This PC**. For Windows 7, open **Windows Explorer** and click **Computer**. Answer these questions:

   ◢ What is the total size of the hard drive?

   _____

   ◢ What is the free space on the hard drive?

   _____

   ◢ What is the percentage of free space on the hard drive?

   _____

2. Examine the hard drive and answer these questions:

   ◢ How much space can be cleared up on the drive by performing a complete disk cleanup?

   _____

   ◢ Describe how you found your answer:

   _____

   _____

3. Fragmented files can also slow down hard drive performance. If the default setting has not been changed, Windows automatically defragments a magnetic hard drive and optimizes an SSD weekly. Answer these questions:

   ◢ Is Windows configured to defragment or optimize the drive weekly?

   _____

   ◢ What day of the week and time of day is defragmentation or optimization scheduled?

   _____

   ◢ Describe how you found your answers:

   _____

If you've eliminated processes that might be hogging hard drive resources and determined that you have adequate free space on the hard drive, but you still suspect the hard drive is a performance bottleneck, you might consider upgrading the hard drive to a faster or larger drive. Follow these steps to determine the speed of your drive:

1. Open **Device Manager**. In the Device Manager window, expand the **Disk drives** category. Answer this question:

   ◢ What is the brand and model of your hard drive?

   _____

14

2. Open your browser and go to **google.com**. In the Google search box, enter the brand and model number of your drive exactly as it appears in the Device Manager window. Click links to find the website of the hard drive manufacturer or other sites where you can find specifications for your drive. Answer these questions:

◢ Is the drive a solid-state drive or a magnetic drive?

_____

◢ If the drive is a magnetic drive, what is the RPM rating for the drive?

_____

◢ Standard RPM ratings for a PC hard drive are 5400, 7200, and 10,000 RPM. Do you consider your drive a slow, moderate, or fast drive?

_____

3. Close all open windows.

Windows 10/8 offers a command-line Windows Experience Index that gives results similar to the Windows 7 graphical Windows Experience Index you can find in the System window. For Windows 10/8, follow these steps to use the command-line utility:

1. Open a command prompt with administrator privileges. Enter the **winsat prepop** command. This command runs a benchmark utility and stores the results in an XML file.

2. Open Windows PowerShell and enter the **Get-WmiObject -Class Win32_WinSAT** command. This command analyzes the results of the benchmark utility and then displays the results as scores, similar to the Windows Experience Index in Windows 7.

◢ What is the system's base score (WinSPRLevel)?

_____

◢ What are the scores for each category?
   ◢ Processor (CPU) score: _____
   ◢ 3D graphics capabilities score: _____
   ◢ Hard disk score: _____
   ◢ Graphics score: _____
   ◢ Memory score: _____

REVIEW QUESTIONS

1. If you determine that the hard drive is experiencing excessive use but the Windows Experience Index reports that memory is the system bottleneck, which component do you upgrade first: memory or the hard drive? Why?

_____

_____

2. What values for the % Disk Time and Avg. Disk Queue Length counters of Performance Monitor collectively indicate the hard drive is a performance bottleneck?

_____

3. Based on the maximum values for both hard drive counters you measured using Performance Monitor in this lab and the criteria for the two counters given in the

Activity Background section of this lab, is the hard drive a performance bottleneck in your system? Why or why not?

4. What can you conclude if a Windows process is constantly reading and writing to the hard drive?

5. How much free space does a hard drive need to prevent a performance slowdown?

LAB 14.5 USE THE SYSTEM CONFIGURATION UTILITY

OBJECTIVES

Your goal in this lab is to learn to diagnose problems using the System Configuration utility. After completing this lab, you will be able to:

◢ Use options in System Configuration that can later help you troubleshoot Windows startup problems

◢ Explore the startup functions of Windows

MATERIALS REQUIRED

This lab requires the following:

◢ Windows 10/8/7 operating system

◢ For Windows 7, two or more applications installed that appear in the All Programs menu off the Start menu (for example, Adobe Reader, Microsoft Security Essentials, or other freeware)

◢ An account with administrator privileges

LAB PREPARATION

Before the lab begins, the instructor or lab assistant needs to do the following:

◢ Verify that Windows starts with no errors

◢ For Windows 7, verify that two or more applications are installed that appear in the All Programs menu off the Start menu

◢ Verify that each student has access to a user account with administrator privileges

ACTIVITY BACKGROUND

Windows offers many wizards and utilities that technicians use to troubleshoot a malfunctioning computer. One of these utilities, the System Configuration utility (also called Msconfig), is used to troubleshoot Windows startup problems. This utility allows you to make changes to boot files and startup parameters, which can help you determine which boot file, startup parameter, or startup program is causing a problem.

In this lab, you work with the features included in System Configuration to learn how to detect problems that might occur when a Windows service, application service, or application fails to load at Windows startup.

14

Activity

Follow these steps to learn about two methods to start the System Configuration utility:

1. Sign in to Windows using an administrator account. An administrator account is required to use all the features of System Configuration.

2. To launch System Configuration, enter the **msconfig.exe** command in the Windows 10/7 search box or the Windows 8 Run box. The System Configuration dialog box opens (see Figure 14-4).

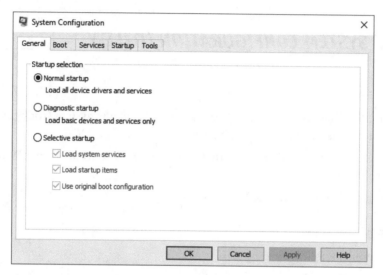

Figure 14-4   The System Configuration utility with the General tab open

3. A technician needs to know more than one method to reach utilities and tools in an operating system. To see an alternate way to open the System Configuration utility, close the System Configuration dialog box, and then open **Control Panel**.

4. In Control Panel, click **Administrative Tools**, and then double-click **System Configuration**. The System Configuration dialog box opens. Answer the following questions:

   ◢ Of the three startup selections listed on the General tab, which one loads all device drivers and services set to load when Windows starts?

   _____

   ◢ Which startup selection loads only basic devices and services?

   _____

   ◢ Which startup selection allows you to load only system services and no startup applications?

   _____

   ◢ Which startup selection is currently selected?

   _____

Diagnostic startup allows you to start the computer with only the most basic devices and services that are needed for the computer to run. This clean environment can help with Windows troubleshooting. Do the following to find out more:

1. To perform a diagnostic startup, click **Diagnostic startup** on the General tab, and then click **Apply**. The wait icon appears while Windows processes this change. If it encounters a problem, it rejects Diagnostic startup and reverts to Selective startup. Which startup selections are chosen when the wait icon disappears?

   _____

2. If Diagnostic startup is not still selected, select **Diagnostic startup**. Click **OK** to close the System Configuration dialog box. A new System Configuration dialog box appears and states that your computer must be restarted to apply this change. Click **Restart**.

3. As Windows restarts, sign back in to Windows as an administrator, and watch carefully for error messages.

   ◢ Record any problems or error messages you see during the restart:

   _____

   ◢ What changes do you notice to your Windows desktop, video, and taskbar?

   _____

   ◢ If the system gives an error message using this bare-bones startup method, how might that be helpful when troubleshooting the system?

   _____

4. Open the System Configuration utility. Record any differences you noted when starting the utility compared with how it started earlier in the lab:

   _____

Now let's explore the Selective startup option, which can be used to limit Windows startup only to services, but not to other programs. Doing so can help you eliminate startup programs that are not services from the types of programs that might be causing a Windows startup problem. Follow these steps to find out more:

1. Click **Selective startup**. Check the **Load system services** check box. Uncheck **Load startup items**. Click **OK**. In the new dialog box that appears, click **Restart**.

2. Windows restarts. Sign back in to the system as an administrator. Record any problems or error messages you see during the restart, and record any differences in the video, desktop, and taskbar compared with a normal startup:

   _____

3. Open the System Configuration utility again. Record any differences you noted when starting the utility compared with how it started at the beginning of this lab:

   _____

Now let's explore the Services tab of System Configuration. The Services tab can help you troubleshoot problems related to system and application services that load at startup. Follow these steps:

1. If necessary, open the System Configuration utility again.

2. To reset startup settings, click **Normal startup** on the General tab.

14

3. Click the **Services** tab. On this tab, check the **Hide all Microsoft services** check box. List the non-Microsoft services installed on this machine and the status of each:

_____

_____

_____

_____

_____

_____

_____

4. To disable all the non-Microsoft services, click **Disable all**. To restart the system using this setting, click **OK**. In the next dialog box, click **Restart**.

5. Windows restarts. Sign in again as an administrator. What do you notice about the system that is different from a normal startup?

_____

In a real troubleshooting situation, you would not need to disable all Microsoft services except in the most extreme circumstances. In many cases, you might choose to disable all non-Microsoft services and only disable a particular system service that you suspect is causing a problem. Follow these steps to practice disabling all non-Microsoft and system services:

1. Open the System Configuration utility again. Go to the **Services** tab and uncheck the **Hide all Microsoft services** check box. Click **Disable all**, and then click **OK**. In the dialog box that appears, click **Restart**.

2. Windows restarts. Sign in as an administrator. Carefully watch what happens as the Windows desktop loads. Record any error messages and differences in the video, desktop, or taskbar compared with a normal startup:

_____

3. Because many system services are not running, Windows functions differently than it does during a normal startup. To see some of these differences, open **Control Panel** and the **Network and Sharing Center**. Describe any differences you notice in these tools compared with a normal startup:

_____

_____

_____

4. Open the System Configuration utility and return startup to a Normal startup with all services enabled. Click **OK** and restart the system. Windows restarts normally. Sign in to the system as an administrator.

5. Open the System Configuration utility, and select the **Boot** tab. List each operating system installed and the drive and folder where it is installed:

_____

_____

Here is an explanation of each option on the Boot tab:

Safe boot: Minimal. Boots to Safe Mode with networking disabled.

Safe boot: Alternate shell. Boots to a Windows command prompt in Safe Mode; networking is disabled.

Safe boot: Active Directory repair. Boots to Safe Mode; used to repair Active Directory on a domain.

Safe boot: Network. Boots to Safe Mode with Networking.

No GUI boot. No Windows splash screen is displayed when booting.

Boot log. Boot logging is stored in *%SystemRoot%\Ntbtlog.txt.*

Base video. Boots to minimal VGA mode.

OS boot information. Displays driver names as the drivers are loaded during the boot.

Make all boot settings permanent. Changes you have made in System Configuration are permanent; you cannot roll back your changes by selecting Normal startup on the General tab.

The Windows 10/8 Startup tab in Task Manager or the Windows 7 Startup tab in System Configuration lists applications launched at startup, including how they are launched from a startup folder or registry key. This information can be really useful when you are investigating how a program is launched at startup. For example, malware that launches at startup might not be found by anti-malware software. You can use this tab to find the folder or registry key where a program is launched so that you can delete the entry. Follow these steps to find out more:

1. Select the **Startup** tab. In Windows 10/8, click **Open Task Manager** to see the Startup tab in Task Manager. In Windows 7, it might be necessary to select the first item in the list to view the Command column. Record the following for the first item in the list:

   ◢ Startup item: _____

   ◢ Publisher/manufacturer: _____

   ◢ Windows 10/8 Status: _____

   ◢ Windows 10/8 Startup impact: _____

   ◢ Windows 7 Command: _____

The System Configuration Tools tab provides a convenient list of diagnostic tools and other advanced tools that you can run from System Configuration. Follow these steps to find out more:

1. Click the **Tools** tab, and then click **Change UAC Settings**. What is the path and program name of the utility to change UAC settings?

   _____

2. Click the **Launch** button. What was the result of your action?

   _____

3. Close all windows and the System Configuration utility.

14

REVIEW QUESTIONS

1. Which tab in System Configuration can you use to find out if the computer is using a dual-boot configuration? What information on this tab tells you that two operating systems are installed?

_____

2. How can enabling and disabling items listed on the Task Manager or System Configuration Startup tab be useful when you are troubleshooting a problem boot?

_____

_____

3. Which tab in System Configuration can be used to restart the system in Safe Mode?

_____

4. Which tab in System Configuration can you use to find out if a service is currently running?

_____

5. How can the Tools tab in System Configuration be useful to a technician?

_____

6. You are attempting to install software, but errors occur during the installation. How can System Configuration help with this problem?

_____

LAB 14.6 APPLY A RESTORE POINT

OBJECTIVES

The goal of this lab is to restore the system state on a Windows 10/8/7 computer. After completing this lab, you will be able to:

- Create a restore point by using System Restore
- Change system settings
- Restore the system state with the restore point you created

MATERIALS REQUIRED

This lab requires the following:

- Windows 10/8/7 computer

LAB PREPARATION

Before the lab begins, the instructor or lab assistant needs to do the following:

- Verify that Windows starts with no errors

ACTIVITY BACKGROUND

Using the System Restore tool in Windows, you can restore the system to the state it was in when a snapshot, called a "restore point," was taken of the system state. The settings recorded in a restore point include system settings and configurations and files needed for a successful boot. When the system state is restored to a restore point, user data on the hard drive isn't affected, but software and hardware might be. Restore points are useful if, for example, something goes wrong with a software or hardware installation and you need to undo these changes. In this lab, you create a restore point, make changes to system settings, and then use the restore point to restore the system state.

ESTIMATED COMPLETION TIME: 30 MINUTES

 Activity

To use the System Restore tool to create a restore point, follow these steps:

1. Open **Control Panel** in Classic view, and click **System**. The System window opens. Select the **System Protection** tab, and then click **System Restore**. The System Restore dialog box opens.

2. In the System Restore box, click **Next**. Check **Show more restore points**. (If this check box is not available, your system has no more restore points to show.)

   ◢ What are the dates of the three most recent restore points?

   _____

   ◢ What types of recent events prompted Windows to automatically create restore points?

   _____

   _____

3. Close the System Restore box.

4. On the System protection tab of the System Properties box, verify that protection is turned on for the drive on which Windows is installed.

5. To create a new restore point, click **Create**. Name your restore point, and then click **Create**. A restore point is created.

6. Close any open windows.

Next, you make changes to the system.

1. Do one of the following to change the desktop background:

   ◢ For Windows 10, right-click the desktop and click **Personalize** in the shortcut menu. Click **Background** and select a new background picture.

   ◢ For Windows 8/7, right-click the desktop and click **Personalize** in the shortcut menu. Click **Desktop Background**. Select a new background picture, and click **Save changes**.

2. Notice that the desktop background or desktop theme has changed to the one you selected. Close any open windows.

14

3. To install utility software, open your browser and go to **cpuid.com**. As you work, be careful not to click an advertisement that has a download link. Under CPU-Z, click **for WINDOWS**. On the next page, click **Setup-English** to download the setup program in English. On the next page, click **DOWNLOAD NOW** and download the file to your Windows desktop. At the time of this writing, the file name was cpu-z_1.88-en.exe.

4. Double-click the downloaded file to install CPU-Z, following directions on the screen and accepting all default settings.

5. Run the CPU-Z program. CPU-Z results display, including information about your processor.

Follow these steps to use the restore point you created to restore the system state:

1. Open the **System Restore** dialog box. Click **Next**.

2. Select the restore point you created earlier in the lab, and then click **Next**.

3. When a confirmation window is displayed, click **Finish** to continue. If necessary, click **Yes** to proceed.

◢ Describe what happens when you proceed with a restore:

_____

_____

4. After the system restarts, sign in to Windows. A message is displayed stating that the restoration is complete. Click **Close**.

◢ Did the desktop background change back to the original setting?

_____

◢ Is the CPU-Z software still installed?

_____

◢ Is the CPU-Z setup file you downloaded from the web still on your desktop?

_____

5. You can undo a system restore. To find out how, open the **System Restore** dialog box. Describe what you must do to undo the system restore you just performed.

_____

REVIEW QUESTIONS

1. List three situations in which you might want to create a restore point.

_____

_____

2. What types of restore points are created by the system, and what types are created by users?

_____

_____

_____

3. Windows 7 automatically creates a restore point daily. In the past, Windows 10 automatically created restore points weekly, but that has changed. Does Windows 10 automatically create restore points on a regular basis? If so, how often?

   _____

4. Can more than one restore point be made on a specific date?

   _____

5. What is the command to execute the System Restore utility?

   _____

6. If you do a system restore while in Safe Mode, can you undo the system restore?

   _____

LAB 14.7 USE WINDOWS SETUP MEDIA TO APPLY A RESTORE POINT

OBJECTIVES

Your goal in this lab is to learn to repair a computer that won't start or that generates an error during reset. After completing this lab, you will be able to:

▲ Create a restore point

▲ Use Windows setup media to apply a restore point

MATERIALS REQUIRED

This lab requires the following:

▲ Windows 10/8 operating system

▲ Windows setup on DVD, flash drive, or ISO file

▲ Internet access

> **Notes** This lab works great on Windows 10/8 installed in a VM. If you use a VM, the Windows setup media can be an ISO file mounted to the VM's virtual optical drive.

LAB PREPARATION

Before the lab begins, the instructor or lab assistant needs to do the following:

▲ Verify that Windows starts with no errors

▲ Verify that Internet access is available

▲ Perform a backup of important files if necessary

ACTIVITY BACKGROUND

When you have a computer that won't start or is generating an error during a reset, you can use a recovery drive to restore or recover your system. System Restore will not affect your documents, pictures, or other personal data; however, it might uninstall programs or drivers that have been installed since the last restore point was created. When Windows will not

14

start from the hard drive, you can boot from the Windows setup media and use the Windows Recovery Environment to apply a restore point.

In this lab, you'll first create a restore point on the computer. Then you use Windows setup on bootable media to boot the system and apply the restore point.

ESTIMATED COMPLETION TIME: 30 MINUTES

 Activity

Follow these steps to create a system restore point on your computer and later make changes to your system:

1. Open **Control Panel** in Classic or Icon view, and click **System**. The System window opens.

2. Select the **System Protection** tab, and verify that protection is turned on for the drive on which Windows is installed.

3. To create a new restore point, click **Create**. Name your restore point, and then click **Create**. A restore point is created.

4. Close any open windows.

5. Now let's make two changes to the system. First, install a free program, such as CPU-Z from *cpuid.com*. Then create a document in your Documents folder. Write down the name of the program you installed and the name of the document you created:

_____

_____

6. Shut down the system.

Now that you have created a restore point and made changes to your system, follow these steps to use Windows setup on bootable media to restore your computer back to the restore point you created:

1. If you are using a physical computer (not a VM), insert the Windows setup DVD or flash drive. If necessary, change the boot order in BIOS/UEFI to boot first to your Windows setup DVD or flash drive.

2. If you are using a VM, do the following:

   a. Select the VM and open the VM's Settings dialog box.

   b. Mount the Windows setup ISO image to the VM's optical drive.

   c. If necessary, change the VM settings to boot first from the optical drive. For VirtualBox, change the *Boot Order* on the System Motherboard tab of the Settings box. For Hyper-V, select BIOS in the Settings box, and then change *Startup order*.

3. Turn on your physical machine or start your VM. To boot to the optical drive, you will need to press a key during the boot. The computer boots from the optical drive to Windows setup.

4. Select your language and other preferences, and click **Next**.

5. In the next Windows Setup screen, click **Repair your computer**.

6. In the Choose an option screen, select **Troubleshoot**. For Windows 8, click **Advanced options**.

7. In the Advanced options screen, choose **System Restore** to use the restore point you created. If requested, select a Windows account and enter the account password. Be sure to select an administrator account.

8. In the System Restore screen, select Windows as the target operating system.

9. The System Restore box opens. Click **Next**.

10. Choose the restore point you created, and then click **Next**.

11. Confirm that you chose the correct restore point on the local disk, and then click **Finish**. To confirm you want to continue, click **Yes**.

12. When the restore is complete, System Restore needs to restart the system. Click **Restart**. Boot into Windows.

13. Windows informs you that you have used a restore point. Click **Close**.

◢ Is the program you installed still installed?

_____

◢ Is the document you created still there?

_____

REVIEW QUESTIONS

1. When using System Restore, how will a system be affected? What will not be affected?

_____

_____

_____

2. When Windows refuses to start, why would you use Windows setup on bootable media to apply a system restore point rather than use a USB recovery drive to recover from the drive?

_____

_____

3. What should you do before you make changes to a system, such as installing a new program?

_____

_____

4. Why might the option to manually create a new restore point be faded and unavailable? What can you do to fix the problem?

_____

_____

_____

_____

14

LAB 14.8 USE WINDOWS UTILITIES TO SPEED UP A SYSTEM

OBJECTIVES

Your goal for this lab is to learn how to clean up processes that might slow Windows performance. After completing this lab, you will be able to:

◢ Use Windows tools to clean up the startup process

◢ Investigate processes that are slowing down Windows

◢ Configure the system to keep it clean and free of malware

MATERIALS REQUIRED

This lab requires the following:

◢ Windows 10/8/7 operating system

◢ An account with administrator privileges

◢ Internet access

LAB PREPARATION

Before the lab begins, the instructor or lab assistant needs to do the following:

◢ Verify that Windows starts with no errors; for the best student experience, try to use systems that are not optimized and need the benefits of this lab. For example, you can do this lab using your own computer or a friend's, or one your instructor assigns to you that gets heavy student use.

◢ Verify that each student has access to a user account with administrator privileges

◢ Verify that Internet access is available

ACTIVITY BACKGROUND

A troubleshooting problem you'll often face as an IT support technician is a sluggish Windows system. Customers might tell you that when their Windows computer was new, it ran smoothly and fast, with no errors, but that it now hangs occasionally, is slow to start up or shut down, and is slow when working. One particular problem doesn't stand out above the rest. The customer just wants you to make the system work faster. When solving these types of general problems, it helps to have a game plan. This activity gives you just that. You'll learn how to speed up Windows, ridding it of unneeded and unwanted processes that are slowing it down.

ESTIMATED COMPLETION TIME: 60 MINUTES

 Activity

Use an administrator account to sign in to the system each time you need to sign in during this lab. Before you make any changes to the system, first get a benchmark of how long it takes for Windows to start up. Do the following:

1. Power down the computer, and then turn it back on. Using a watch with a second hand, note how many minutes it takes the system to start. Startup is completed after you have signed in to Windows, the hard drive activity light has stopped, and the pointer looks like an arrow. How long does startup take?

---

2. Describe any problems you observed during startup:

_____

_____

This lab assumes that Windows might be slow starting but that it does start up without errors. If you see error messages on the screen or the system refuses to boot, you need to solve these problems before you continue with a general cleanup in the following steps.

When you're ready to begin a general cleanup, do the following:

1. If valuable data on the hard drive is not backed up, back up that data now.

2. Run anti-malware software. Here are your options:

   ◢ If anti-malware software is not installed and you have the anti-malware software setup CD, install it. If it fails to install (some malware can block software installations), boot into Safe Mode, and install and run the software from there.

   ◢ If you don't have access to the anti-malware software setup CD, you can download software from the Internet. If your computer cannot connect to the Internet (possibly because Internet access is being blocked by malware), try to connect to the Internet using the Safe Mode with Networking option on the Advanced Boot Options menu. (This option might disable malware that is preventing Internet access.) If that doesn't work, then download the software on another computer, and burn a CD with the downloaded file.

   ◢ If you don't have anti-malware software installed and don't have access to an anti-malware software setup CD, but you can connect the computer to the Internet, you can run an online anti-malware scan from an anti-malware website. For example, Trend Micro (*trendmicro.com*) offers a free online anti-malware scan. (This free online scan has been known to find malware that other scans do not.)

   List the steps you took to run the anti-malware software:

   _____

   _____

   _____

   List any malware the anti-malware software found:

   _____

   _____

   _____

3. Reboot the system. Is there a performance improvement? How long does startup take?

   _____

   _____

4. Use the Programs and Features window to uninstall applications that are no longer needed. If the system is still running so slowly you find it difficult to work, you can temporarily turn off startup processes that are hogging system resources. In Windows 10/8, use Task Manager to manage startup processes, and in Windows 7, use the System Configuration utility.

14

5. You can keep services from starting by unchecking them on the Startup tab. List all of the non-Microsoft services that are run at startup, and use the Internet to determine the purpose of each of them:

_____

_____

_____

_____

_____

6. Uncheck all the services except the ones associated with your anti-malware program. Reboot the system to cause these changes to take effect.

7. Is there a performance improvement? How long does startup take?

_____

8. Clean up the hard drive. Delete temporary files and check the drive for errors. If the system is slow while doing these tasks, do them from Safe Mode. Note that you need about 15 percent free hard drive space to defragment the drive. Windows requires this much free space to run well. If you don't have that much free space, find some folders and files you can move to different media.

9. Reboot the system. Is there a performance improvement? How long does startup take?

_____

10. Check Device Manager for hardware devices that are installed but not working and for devices that are no longer needed and should be uninstalled. Did you find any devices that need fixing or uninstalling? How did you handle the situation?

_____

_____

Task Manager in Windows 10/8 and System Configuration in Windows 7 do not necessarily show all the processes that run at startup. To get a more thorough list, you need to use a more powerful startup manager, such as Autoruns from Sysinternals.

1. Go to **docs.microsoft.com/en-us/sysinternals/downloads/autoruns** and download and install the latest version of Autoruns.

2. Run Autoruns, and then select the **Logon** tab, as shown in Figure 14-5. Note in the figure that Autoruns marks in yellow the startup commands or processes that give errors.

3. How does the list of startup processes differ from the list generated by Windows 10/8 Task Manager or Windows 7 System Configuration? List any additional processes identified:

_____

_____

_____

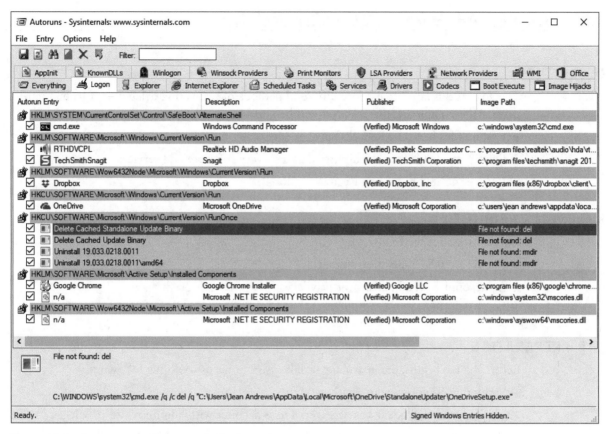

Figure 14-5 Autoruns startup manager by Sysinternals

REVIEW QUESTIONS

1. If anti-malware software is not installed and you don't have access to the Internet, how can you install the software?

2. Which window or dialog box is used to check a hard drive for errors?

3. What two folders can contain programs to be launched when a specific user signs in to the system?

4. When cleaning up the startup process, you notice a program file in a startup folder that you don't recognize. What should you do first before you decide what to do with the file?

5. What Windows utility lists all currently running processes?

LAB 14.9 RESEARCH DATA RECOVERY SOFTWARE

OBJECTIVES

The goal of this lab is to explore different methods of recovering deleted data from a hard drive. After completing this lab, you will be able to:

- ◢ Restore files from the Recycle Bin
- ◢ Identify the benefits of third-party data recovery software and services
- ◢ Recover deleted files using Recuva (optional)

MATERIALS REQUIRED

This lab requires the following:

- ◢ Windows 10/8/7 operating system
- ◢ An account with administrator privileges
- ◢ Internet access

LAB PREPARATION

Before the lab begins, the instructor or lab assistant needs to do the following:

- ◢ Verify that Windows starts with no errors
- ◢ Verify that each student has access to a user account with administrator privileges
- ◢ Verify that Internet access is available

ACTIVITY BACKGROUND

A client has contacted you because she accidentally deleted a group of files that hold very sensitive and important financial information. She is unable to find the files in the Recycle Bin and is panicked because her job may depend on retrieving them. To retrieve the data, you will need to install third-party data recovery software to scan the drive and attempt retrieval.

ESTIMATED COMPLETION TIME: 30 MINUTES

 Activity

Let's first see how to recover files from the Recycle Bin. To begin, you need to create a folder and files. Follow these steps to create the folder and files, delete them, and then recover them from the Recycle Bin:

1. Create a folder named **Important Files** on your desktop.
2. Open the **Important Files** folder. In the folder, create a text document file named **Monthly budget**. Open the text file, type your name in the document, and close the file, saving your changes.
3. Create a second text document, and name it **Financial statement**. Enter some text in the document, and then save and close it.
4. Select both files and right-click your selection. In the shortcut menu, click **Delete**. If necessary, confirm your deletion. The files are deleted and placed in the Recycle Bin.
5. Double-click the Recycle Bin on your desktop, and search for the deleted files. Click a column heading to sort by that field. Right-click one of the files you just deleted. In the

shortcut menu, click **Restore**. The file is restored to the Important Files folder. Restore the second file in the same way.

6. Check the Important Files folder, and confirm that the two files are restored. You may need to click the Refresh icon in File Explorer or Windows Explorer.

Sometimes deleted files cannot be found in the Recycle Bin. In this situation, third-party data recovery software, such as Recuva by Piriform, might help. To learn about the Recuva data recovery software, follow these steps:

1. Open your browser and go to **ccleaner.com/recuva/download**.

2. Review the features and information provided about Recuva, and answer the following questions:

   ▲ What is a deep scan?

   _____

   _____

   ▲ How can you use a portable version of Recuva if you can't or don't want to install the software on the computer on which you're trying to recover files?

   _____

   _____

   ▲ What are the editions of Recuva and their respective prices?

   _____

   _____

Another company that offers data recovery software is Stellar Information Technology. To learn about this third-party software, follow these steps:

1. Go to **stellarinfo.com**.

2. Review the features and information provided for Stellar Data Recovery software, and answer the following questions:

   ▲ Can the software recover data from a corrupted virtual machine?

   _____

   ▲ How much does a one-year subscription to Stellar Data Recovery Professional cost for personal use on a single system?

   _____

   _____

   ▲ List three applications for which the recovery software is especially designed to handle data recovery.

   _____

Sometimes, storage devices experience mechanical failure or are damaged by fire or a natural disaster. Occasionally, someone even intentionally tries to destroy data to cover a crime. Third-party software might not be able to retrieve data that has been damaged to this point. In these situations, special, almost surgical, procedures are needed to physically open a hard drive housing and retrieve the data in a secured clean room. To learn about these processes, follow these steps:

1. Go to **drivesaversdatarecovery.com**.

2. Search the website and answer the following questions:

   ◢ You can mail a hard drive to a DriveSavers center or drop it off. Where is your nearest drop-off location?

   _____

   ◢ What level of clean room does DriveSavers maintain?

   _____

   ◢ What security compliance qualifies DriveSavers to handle confidential medical records?

   _____

   ◢ What are two kinds of devices that DriveSavers can recover data from?

   _____

   _____

   ◢ If DriveSavers opens your hard drive, what happens to your manufacturer's warranty?

   _____

   _____

ESTIMATED COMPLETION TIME: 45 MINUTES

CHALLENGE ACTIVITY

Recuva is a powerful freeware utility that can be used to restore files that have been deleted and cannot be restored from the Recycle Bin. To practice using Recuva, follow these steps:

1. Create a new Microsoft Word document titled **My Resume** in the Important Files folder. (If you don't have Microsoft Word installed, create a text file instead.) Open the file, type **This is a test of My Resume**, and then save and close the file. What is the specific path and file name for your file?

   _____

2. Delete the **My Resume** file from the Important Files folder.

3. To empty the Recycle Bin, right-click the **Recycle Bin** on your desktop. In the shortcut menu, click **Empty Recycle Bin**. When prompted to confirm deletion, click **Yes**.

4. Open your browser and go to **ccleaner.com/recuva**. Download the latest version of Recuva and install it. As you install it, be careful not to install other freeware offered during the installation. Close all open windows.

5. Launch Recuva. If a UAC dialog box appears, click **Yes**. The Recuva Wizard opens. Click **Next**. If you created a Microsoft Word document in Step 1, select **Documents** for the File type. If you created a text file, select **All Files** for the File type. Click **Next**.

6. On the next screen in the wizard, select **In the Recycle Bin** for the file location (see Figure 14-6). Click **Next**.

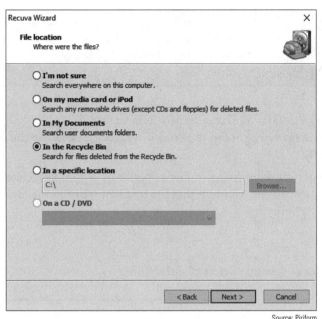

Source: Piriform

Figure 14-6 Recuva asks where to search for files to recover

7. Click **Start**. Recuva will run a scan on your computer, which might take several minutes depending on the size of your drive(s). If Recuva does not find any files, close and then relaunch Recuva. Rescan your computer using the deep scan option on the final screen, where you click Start.

8. When the program presents its scan results, look for a .docx or .txt file created at the same time you created the My Resume file. Figure 14-7 shows one search results window, but yours might look different. The file name might be an unintelligible mix of letters, numbers, and symbols, but you can identify the correct file by checking the date and time it was last modified. (To sort the list by date last modified, click the Last Modified column heading.) Check the box next to the file, as shown in the figure, and then click **Recover**.

14

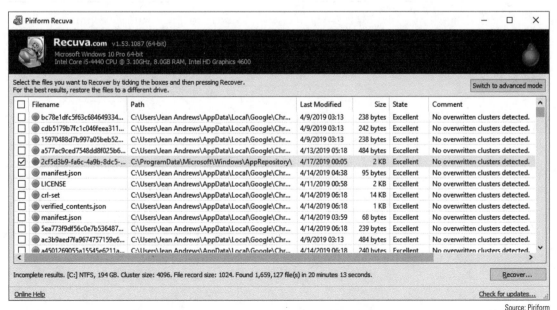

Source: Piriform

Figure 14-7 In this example, the file name is not the same as the original, but sometimes it is the same

> **Notes** Sometimes the data in a deleted file is corrupted and cannot be recovered easily by Recuva. A red dot next to the file indicates it is corrupted, and a green dot indicates a good file. If your file has a red dot, you can still go through the steps of recovering the file, but you will get an error message when you try to open the file.

9. In the Browse For Folder dialog box, select the **Important Files** folder, and then click **OK**. When asked if you want to restore to the same drive, click **Yes**. When the operation is completed, click **OK**.

10. Go back to the Important Files folder in File Explorer or Windows Explorer, and double-click the recovered file. Confirm that the text you typed in the file earlier has been successfully recovered.

REVIEW QUESTIONS

1. What happens to files when you delete them?

   _____

2. How do you recover a deleted file using the Recycle Bin?

   _____

3. What is a clean room, and how is it used by data recovery services?

   _____

   _____

   _____

4. What are three methods of restoring data that you learned about in this lab?

   _____

   _____

   _____

Troubleshooting
Windows Startup

Labs included in this chapter:

- **Lab 15.1:** Create a Windows 10/7 Repair Disc

- **Lab 15.2:** Create and Use a Custom Refresh Image in Windows 8

- **Lab 15.3:** Launch and Explore Windows Recovery Environment (RE)

- **Lab 15.4:** Investigate Startup Processes

- **Lab 15.5:** Explore Tools to Solve Windows 10 Startup Problems

- **Lab 15.6:** Reimage the Windows Volume

- **Lab 15.7:** Recover Data from a Computer That Will Not Boot

- **Lab 15.8:** Roll Back to a Previous Version of Windows

- **Lab 15.9:** Use Fresh Start

- **Lab 15.10:** Sabotage and Repair Windows

LAB 15.1 CREATE A WINDOWS 10/7 REPAIR DISC

OBJECTIVES

Your goal in this lab is to learn to create a Windows 10/7 repair disc, which can be used in the event the hard drive will not boot and the Windows 10/7 setup DVD is not available. After completing this lab, you will be able to:

⬧ Create a Windows 10/7 repair disc

⬧ Verify that the disc boots without errors

MATERIALS REQUIRED

This lab requires the following:

⬧ Windows 10/7 operating system

⬧ A computer with a DVD drive or other optical drive that will burn a DVD

⬧ Blank DVD disc

⬧ Permanent marker to label the disc

LAB PREPARATION

Before the lab begins, the instructor or lab assistant needs to do the following:

⬧ Verify that Windows starts with no errors

⬧ Verify that the boot priority order in BIOS/UEFI is set so that the system can boot to a DVD before turning to the hard drive; if you expect the students to change the boot priority order during the lab, verify the key to press at startup to access setup BIOS/UEFI.

ACTIVITY BACKGROUND

Windows 10/7 allows you to create a bootable repair disc that holds the Windows Recovery Environment (RE). The repair disc can be used in place of the Windows 10/7 setup DVD to fix a corrupted Windows installation. When Windows creates the repair disc, a 32-bit version of Windows creates a 32-bit version of Windows RE, and a 64-bit version of Windows creates a 64-bit version of Windows RE. These discs are not interchangeable; you must use a 32-bit repair disc to repair a 32-bit installation of Windows, and a 64-bit repair disc must be used to repair a 64-bit installation. You can, however, use a repair disc created by one edition of Windows 10/7 to repair another edition. For example, a repair disc created by Windows 10 Home can be used to repair a Windows 10 Pro installation.

In this lab, you create the repair disc. Then, in a later lab, you will use the repair disc to explore Windows RE.

ESTIMATED COMPLETION TIME: 15 MINUTES

 Activity

Follow these steps to create a Windows 10 repair disc:

    1. To find out if your version of Windows 10 is a 32-bit or 64-bit OS, open the System window, and answer these questions:

        ⬧ Is your system type a 32-bit operating system or a 64-bit operating system?

◢ What edition of Windows 10 is installed?

2. Insert a blank DVD in your optical drive that has the ability to burn a DVD.

3. There are several ways to launch the utility to build the repair disc. In this lab, you use the Backup and Restore (Windows 7) window. In Control Panel, open the **Backup and Restore (Windows 7)** applet.

4. In the left pane, click **Create a system repair disc**, and follow the on-screen directions to create the disc.

5. When the process is finished, remove the DVD from the drive, and label it "Windows 10 32-bit Repair Disc" for a 32-bit version of Windows or "Windows 10 64-bit Repair Disc" for a 64-bit version of Windows. Also include on the label the edition of Windows 10 used to create the disc.

Follow these steps to test the repair disc, verifying that you can use it to boot the system and launch Windows RE:

1. Insert the repair disc in the optical drive, and restart the system. A message might appear: "Press any key to boot from DVD or CD." If so, press any key.

2. If the system does not boot from the disc, chances are BIOS/UEFI setup is configured to look first to the hard drive before turning to the optical drive for a boot device. Check BIOS/UEFI setup and change the boot sequence so that it looks to the optical drive before it turns to the hard drive for an OS. The method for accessing BIOS/UEFI setup varies, depending on your computer. Look for a message that prompts you to "Press Del to access setup" or "Press F2 for setup" or a similar message when the system is first started. After you have made your changes, save your BIOS/UEFI settings and reboot. This time you should be able to boot from the disc.

3. After you have booted from the DVD, the first screen shows the Windows RE window where you can select your keyboard input method. When you see this window, you know you have successfully created a bootable repair disc.

4. Remove the disc and restart the system to the Windows 10 desktop.

5. Save the repair disc to use in a later lab.

REVIEW QUESTIONS

1. What Windows utility is used to create a Windows 10 repair disc?

2. Is your system a 32-bit or 64-bit operating system?

3. Why do you think it is important to label the Windows repair disc as a 32-bit or 64-bit version?

15

4. Sometimes a computer boots directly to the hard drive even when a bootable DVD is inserted in the optical drive. Explain why this happens and how you can fix the problem so that the computer boots from the DVD:

_____

_____

_____

_____

5. What key do you press on your computer to access BIOS/UEFI setup and change the boot sequence?

_____

LAB 15.2 CREATE AND USE A CUSTOM REFRESH IMAGE IN WINDOWS 8

OBJECTIVES

The goal of this lab is to create and use a custom refresh image. After completing this lab, you will be able to:

▲ Create a custom refresh image

▲ Refresh your system using your custom refresh image

MATERIALS REQUIRED

This lab requires the following:

▲ Windows 8 operating system

▲ Internet access

▲ An account with administrator privileges

LAB PREPARATION

Before the lab begins, the instructor or lab assistant needs to do the following:

▲ Verify that Windows starts with no errors

▲ Verify that Internet access is available

▲ Verify that each student has access to a user account with administrator privileges

ACTIVITY BACKGROUND

If your system isn't running well, you might want to refresh or reset it. A refresh is preferred to a reset because a refresh retains user settings, data, and Windows 8 apps. A refresh works even better if you have created a custom refresh image to use during the refresh. Using the image, the system is restored to its state when the image was created, and then any user settings, data, or Windows 8 apps that were installed or changed since the image was created are also restored. After you refresh your system using a custom refresh image, you will need to reinstall any desktop applications that were not installed at the time you created the custom refresh image.

The best practice is to create a custom refresh image after you have the system configured just the way you want it. A custom refresh image takes a snapshot or image of the current system and stores the Windows installation, all installed applications, and user settings and data.

In this lab, you make some changes to user settings, data files, and installed apps. Then, you create a custom refresh image and make additional changes to user settings, data files, and installed apps. Next, you refresh the system and then examine the system to find out which changes are retained by the refresh. By working your way through this lab, you can be confident you understand exactly how a refresh works and what to expect from one.

ESTIMATED COMPLETION TIME: 60–120 MINUTES

 Activity

Follow these steps to customize your computer:

1. Sign in using an administrator account.
2. From the Start screen, click the **Settings** charm on the charms bar. Click **Personalize**. Select a picture for the Start screen background, and then select a background color. Describe the picture and color you selected:

   _____

3. Visit **google.com/chrome**, and download and install Google Chrome, the free web browser.
4. Create a new document and save it in your Documents folder. What is the file name and the path to your document?

   _____

Follow these steps to create a custom refresh image:

1. Move your pointer to the bottom of the Start screen, and click the **down arrow**. On the Apps screen, scroll to the right, and in the Windows System section, find the Command Prompt tile. Right-click **Command Prompt**. In the status bar, click **Run as administrator**. Respond to the UAC dialog box. The command prompt window opens.
2. Enter this command, substituting your own drive and folder name:

   recimg /createimage C:\MyImage

3. The image is created and registered. In the command prompt, enter this command:

   recimg /showcurrent

4. The location of the image is displayed. Write down the location of the image:

   _____

5. Close the command prompt window. Open File Explorer and browse to the image file. What is the location given in your address bar? What is the size of the image file?

   _____

   _____

Follow these steps to make additional changes to your system:

1. From the Start screen, open the **Settings** charm, and click **Personalize**. Select a picture for the Start screen background and a background color different from those you selected at the beginning of this lab. Describe the new picture and color you selected:

   _____

15

2. Go to **mozilla.org/firefox** and download and install the Mozilla Firefox browser.

3. Open the **Store** app, and install a Windows 8 app. Which application did you install?

_____

4. Delete the file you stored in your Documents folder earlier in the lab.

Follow these steps to refresh the system using the custom refresh image you created earlier:

1. Open the **Settings** charm, and then click **Change PC settings**.

2. On the PC settings page, click **Update and recovery** in the left pane.

3. On the Update and recovery page, click **Recovery** in the left pane.

4. Under _Refresh your PC without affecting your files_, click **Get started**.

5. On the Refresh your PC screen, review what will happen when you perform a refresh. Click **Next**.

6. Click **Refresh**. During the refresh process, your system restarts.

Do the following to find out the results of the refresh:

1. Sign in to your system, and answer the following questions:

   ◢ Does the Start screen use the latest picture and background color you selected? Why or why not?

   _____

   ◢ Is the app you installed from the Windows Store still installed? Why or why not?

   _____

   ◢ Is the file you stored in your Documents folder there? Why or why not?

   _____

   ◢ Is Google Chrome installed as a desktop app? Why or why not?

   _____

   ◢ Is Mozilla Firefox installed as a desktop app? Why or why not?

   _____

2. Browse to the root of drive C:. What is the size of the Windows.old folder?

   _____

3. Open the file stored on the Windows desktop that lists the desktop applications removed from your computer during the refresh. Which application(s) were removed during the refresh?

   _____

Now it's time to clean up the system. Do the following:

1. To keep your hard drive clean, it's best to delete the Windows.old folder after you have confirmed that the refresh was successful. Delete the Windows.old folder.

2. Uninstall any Windows 8 apps or desktop applications that you installed in this lab and are still installed.

3. If your instructor requests it, delete the custom refresh image you created in this lab.

REVIEW QUESTIONS

1. What command line can you enter into the command prompt window to view the location of the active recovery image?

   _____

2. What is the file name of the refresh image?

   _____

3. When you perform a system refresh, how will your computer settings be changed?

   _____

4. When you perform a system refresh without the help of a custom refresh image, some apps are kept and some are removed. Which apps are kept? Which are removed? How do you know which apps were removed?

   _____

   _____

   _____

LAB 15.3 LAUNCH AND EXPLORE WINDOWS RECOVERY ENVIRONMENT (RE)

OBJECTIVES

Your goal in this lab is to learn how to use the repair disc and the Windows RE to solve problems with Windows startup. After completing this lab, you will be able to:

▲ Boot to the Windows RE user interface using multiple methods

▲ Use the tools in Windows RE to solve startup problems

MATERIALS REQUIRED

This lab requires the following:

▲ Windows 10 operating system

▲ An account with administrator privileges

▲ Repair disc created in a previous lab

LAB PREPARATION

Before the lab begins, the instructor or lab assistant needs to do the following:

▲ Verify that Windows boots with no errors

▲ Verify that each student has access to a user account with administrator privileges

▲ Verify that each student has access to Windows recovery media, such as the repair disc created in a previous lab

15

ACTIVITY BACKGROUND

Windows RE is an operating system designed to be used to recover from a corrupted Windows installation. Windows RE can be loaded from the Windows setup DVD, the repair disc, or the operating system. It contains graphical and command-line tools used to troubleshoot a failed Windows startup.

ESTIMATED COMPLETION TIME: 45 MINUTES

 Activity

If Windows will start, you can load Windows RE from a few entry points. Use each of these methods to load the Windows RE operating system from the operating system:

1. Launch Windows RE by holding the **Shift key** while selecting **Restart** from the power options on the Windows sign-in screen.

2. Launch Windows RE by holding the **Shift key** while selecting **Restart** from the power options on the Start menu.

3. Open the **Settings** app and navigate to **Update & Security**, then **Recovery**. Under Advanced startup, select **Restart now**.

Starting Windows RE from the operating system will not work if the hard drive is corrupted. In this situation, try these other methods to launch Windows RE:

1. Boot from a repair disc or recovery drive. Follow prompts as needed.

2. Boot from the Windows setup DVD. Follow prompts as needed. On the Install screen, select **Repair your computer**.

3. Turn off the computer two to four times in a row during the Windows boot process to automatically launch Windows RE.

Follow these steps to explore Windows RE:

1. The first tool to try in almost every troubleshooting situation is Startup Repair, which examines key system files used to start the system and replaces or rebuilds them if a problem is detected. It's easy to use, and you can't do any harm using it. Select **Troubleshoot, Advanced options**, and then click **Startup Repair**.

2. Select the account and enter the password. The system is checked for errors, and an error report is generated. When Startup Repair is finished, return to the Advanced options menu in Windows RE.

3. Sometimes a problem can be resolved by applying a restore point. To explore this option, click **System Restore**, and then click **Next**. A list of restore points appears.

▲ What types of problems can you solve by successfully applying a restore point?

_____

_____

▲ What problems might you create when you successfully apply a restore point?

_____

_____

4. To continue without applying a restore point, click **Cancel**. Return to the Advanced options menu in Windows RE.

5. In a troubleshooting situation, you might decide to completely restore the volume on which Windows is installed to the time the last system image was created. To explore this option, click **System Image Recovery**. If a system image is found, information about the system image appears, and you can continue with the restore. Describe what changes you would make to the system if you continued with System Image Recovery:

   _____

   _____

6. Return to the Advanced options menu in Windows RE.

7. Some problems can be resolved by using commands in a command prompt window. To explore the command prompt window, click **Command Prompt**. A command prompt window opens where you can enter commands.

   ◢ What is the default drive and path showing in the command prompt?

   _____

8. At the command prompt, enter the command to list the contents of the current folder. What command did you use?

   _____

9. Enter the command to move up one level in the directory tree to the parent folder of the current folder. What command did you use?

   _____

10. Enter the command to close the command prompt window. What command did you use?

    _____

11. Return to the first menu in Windows RE, and select **Continue** to load Windows 10.

REVIEW QUESTIONS

1. Which Windows RE option should you use to solve a problem with a corrupted device driver that was just installed and causes the system not to boot?

   _____

2. Which Windows RE option should you use if a recent update to Windows started causing problems?

   _____

3. Suppose that after you insert the repair disc in the drive and restart the system, the Windows desktop loads. Why did the system not boot from the disc?

   _____

4. Which Windows RE option should you use if you have decided to restore the Windows volume to the last image created?

   _____

5. Which Windows RE option will make less intrusive changes to the system: System Restore or Startup Repair?

   _____

15

LAB 15.4 INVESTIGATE STARTUP PROCESSES

OBJECTIVES

The goal of this lab is to identify malicious software running on your computer by examining all running processes. After completing this lab, you will be able to:

◢ Identify all processes running on your computer at startup

◢ Use the Internet to determine the function of each process

MATERIALS REQUIRED

This lab requires the following:

◢ Windows 10/8/7 operating system

◢ An account with administrator privileges

◢ Internet access

LAB PREPARATION

Before the lab begins, the instructor or lab assistant needs to do the following:

◢ Verify that Windows starts with no errors

◢ Verify that each student has access to a user account with administrator privileges

◢ Verify that Internet access is available

ACTIVITY BACKGROUND

As more add-ons, utilities, and applications are installed on a system over time, they can cause Windows to slow down and give errors. When a program automatically launches at startup, it takes up valuable computer resources behind the scenes and can cause startup errors. In this lab, you learn to investigate all the startup processes on your computer and to identify those you should remove.

ESTIMATED COMPLETION TIME: 45 MINUTES

 Activity

Follow these steps to investigate the startup processes on your computer:

1. Restart your computer and sign in as an administrator.

2. Use Task Manager to display all the running processes on your machine. In Windows 10/8, use the Details tab in Task Manager, and in Windows 7, use the Processes tab. Be sure to view processes for all users.

3. How many processes are running? Note that many processes are listed twice, but you should count each process only once. To help you identify processes listed more than once, click the **Name** column in Windows 10/8 or the **Image Name** column in Windows 7 to sort the processes by process name. Figure 15-1 shows the running processes for one system, but yours will be different. On a separate piece of paper, make a list of each process running on the computer, or create and print screenshots that show these processes.

> **Notes** To change which columns are displayed, right-click a column heading, and then click **Select columns.**

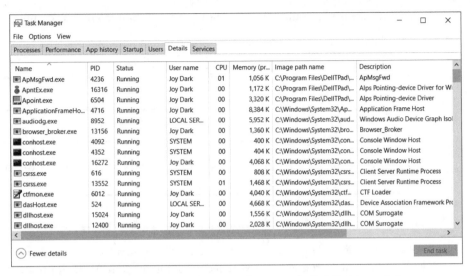

Figure 15-1 The Name and Image path name columns on the Details tab can help you identify a process and how it is loaded

4. Now reboot the computer in Safe Mode, and use Task Manager to list the running processes for all users again. How many processes are running now? (Remember: Count each process only once.)

_____

5. Which processes didn't load when the system was booted in Safe Mode?

_____

_____

_____

_____

6. Use the web to research each process identified in Step 5, and write a one-sentence explanation of each process on a separate piece of paper.

⊿ Did you find any malicious processes running? If so, list them:

_____

_____

_____

⊿ Did you find any programs that should be uninstalled from the system? If so, list them:

_____

_____

_____

15

◢ Suppose one of the processes running on your computer is named whAgent.exe. What program is associated with this process?

_____

◢ List the steps you could take to remove this program from your computer:

_____

_____

_____

_____

◢ How could you use the System Configuration utility to temporarily disable a process?

_____

_____

7. To improve the computer's performance, use the System Configuration utility to temporarily disable any program that you decide is not necessary. Which program, if any, did you disable?

_____

8. If the system works fine with the program disabled, go ahead and uninstall the program.

REVIEW QUESTIONS

1. Why is it a good idea to temporarily disable a program before removing it altogether?

_____

_____

2. Why might anti-malware software not detect malicious software?

_____

_____

3. Why would you expect fewer processes to be running in Safe Mode?

_____

_____

4. Why is disabling the Lsass.exe process not a good idea?

_____

5. What method did you use to launch Safe Mode?

_____

LAB 15.5 EXPLORE TOOLS TO SOLVE WINDOWS 10 STARTUP PROBLEMS

OBJECTIVES

The goal of this lab is to explore tools to solve Windows 10 startup problems. After completing this lab, you will be able to:

▲ Find troubleshooting tools for Windows startup problems

▲ Use the Startup Repair process

▲ Boot to Safe Mode with Networking

MATERIALS REQUIRED

This lab requires the following:

▲ Windows 10 operating system

▲ Windows 10 recovery drive

▲ An account with administrator privileges

▲ Internet access

LAB PREPARATION

Before the lab begins, the instructor or lab assistant needs to do the following:

▲ Verify that Windows starts with no errors and the Windows 10 recovery drive is available

▲ Verify that each student has access to a user account with administrator privileges

▲ Verify that Internet access is available

ACTIVITY BACKGROUND

Startup problems can be annoying, and Windows 10 has taken great effort to minimize this pain. Windows 10 is one of the most stable operating systems with the fewest errors at startup. On the fourth sequential reboot, Windows 10 automatically starts a self-healing process. If you still encounter a hang-up, error message, stop error, or hardware error after Windows 10 has attempted to heal itself, you can use the startup repair tools discussed in this lab to help you resolve startup problems.

15

ESTIMATED COMPLETION TIME: 30 MINUTES

 Activity

As you work through this lab, reference Figure 15-2 to keep track of where you find each of the startup troubleshooting tools. Follow these steps to locate startup repair tools:

1. Sign in to your system with an administrator account.

2. Open the **Settings** app. Navigate to **Update & Security** and then **Recovery**.

3. List the computer recovery options that can be accessed through the Settings app, and briefly describe the purpose of each one:

_____

_____

_____

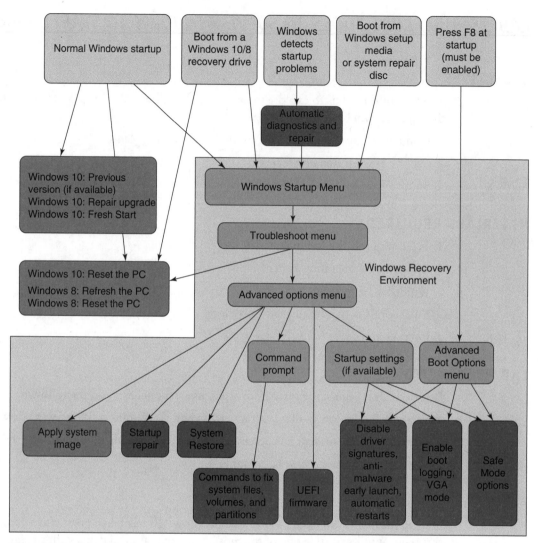

Figure 15-2   Methods to boot the system, including menus and tools for troubleshooting startup problems

4. Under More recovery options, click **Learn how to start fresh with a clean installation of Windows.** If necessary, respond to a dialog box. Describe the purpose of a fresh start.

_____

_____

5. Return to the Recovery page in the Settings app. Click **Restart now** under the Advanced startup option to launch Windows RE. Your computer restarts. When given an option, click **Troubleshoot,** and then click **Advanced options.** List the tools available under Advanced options for troubleshooting startup problems, and briefly describe the purpose of each:

_____

_____

_____

_____

_____

_____

_____

6. Select **Startup Repair**. Your computer restarts into Startup Repair.

7. Choose your account name, and enter your password. Click **Continue**.

8. Startup Repair diagnoses your system and reports its findings. Click **Advanced options** to return to the Windows Startup menu.

9. Click **Troubleshoot**, and then click **Advanced options**.

10. Click **Startup Settings**, and then click **Restart**.

> **Notes** You might need to select **See more recovery options** to find Startup Settings.

11. Listed are options for changing startup behavior. Press **5** or **F5** on your keyboard to select **Enable Safe Mode with Networking**. The system reboots. After you sign in, Safe Mode with Networking loads.

12. Open **Internet Explorer**, and make sure the Internet is available.

13. Restart the computer.

There are a few ways to launch Windows RE, such as holding down the Shift key while using the Restart button from the Start menu. However, if the hard drive is so corrupted you cannot boot to it, you must boot from other bootable media. Follow these steps to explore the troubleshooting tools available when booting from other bootable media:

1. Boot from the Windows recovery drive, and select your language and keyboard layout. (Before you can boot to media other than the hard drive, you might need to first change the boot priority order in BIOS/UEFI setup.)

2. When the Windows Setup screen appears, click **Repair your computer**. Next, select the correct troubleshooting options on each screen until you reach the Advanced options screen.

   ◢ List the tools available under Advanced options:

   _____

   _____

   _____

   _____

   ◢ Which tool is not available on the Advanced options screen that was available in Step 5 earlier, when you used the Settings app to launch Windows RE?

   _____

3. Launch Windows normally and remove the bootable media from your computer.

15

REVIEW QUESTIONS

1. Why is Windows 10 considered to be a more stable system than previous Windows editions in terms of startup problems?

_____

_____

2. List the steps you take to find the Reset this PC option using the Settings app:

_____

_____

_____

3. What is the difference between a fresh start and a reset?

_____

_____

_____

4. What are two methods for launching Windows RE?

_____

_____

5. If the hard drive is so corrupted that Windows won't load, how should you boot the system so you can attempt to repair the Windows installation?

_____

LAB 15.6 REIMAGE THE WINDOWS VOLUME

OBJECTIVES

Your goal in this lab is to learn how to create a system image and use it to restore the Windows volume. After completing this lab, you will be able to:

▲ Create a system image using a second hard drive installed in a system

▲ Use the system image to reimage the Windows volume

MATERIALS REQUIRED

This lab requires the following:

▲ Windows 10/8/7 operating system

▲ A second internal or external hard drive

▲ Alternately, you can use Windows installed in a virtual machine. (If you are using a VM, this lab creates a second virtual hard drive in the VM.)

LAB PREPARATION

Before the lab begins, the instructor or lab assistant needs to do the following:

⊿ Verify that Windows starts with no errors

⊿ Verify that a second hard drive is available

⊿ Alternately, if you plan to use a VM for this lab, verify that Windows is installed in the VM

ACTIVITY BACKGROUND

A system image backs up the entire Windows volume and can be stored on an external or internal hard drive or on DVDs. (For professional and higher Windows editions, you can install the system image in a network location.) When the Windows volume is corrupted or data on the drive is totally lost, you can use a system image to restore the entire Windows volume to the time the system image was last updated.

You can do this lab using a Windows computer with a second hard drive. Alternately, you can use Windows installed in a virtual machine and create a second hard drive in the VM. Directions for both methods are included.

ESTIMATED COMPLETION TIME: 45 MINUTES

 Activity

If you are using a Windows computer and a second hard drive, follow the steps in Part 1 of this lab. If you are using Windows in a VM, follow the steps in Part 2 of this lab.

PART 1: USE A WINDOWS COMPUTER TO CREATE AND USE A SYSTEM IMAGE

1. Plug in an external hard drive, or install a second internal hard drive in your computer.

2. If the hard drive is new and needs to be partitioned and formatted, open Disk Management, and partition and format the hard drive using the NTFS file system.

3. Using File Explorer or Windows Explorer, find out how much space is used on drive C:. Find out how much space is free on the second hard drive. The free space needed to hold the system image on the second hard drive will be about 80 percent of the space used on drive C:.

   ⊿ How much space is used on drive C:?

   _____

   ⊿ How much space is free on the second hard drive? Do you have enough room on the second drive for the system image?

   _____

4. To create the system image in Windows 10/7, open the Backup and Restore utility in Control Panel, and then click **Create a system image**. In Windows 8, open File History in Control Panel, and then click **System Image Backup**. Follow the on-screen directions to create the image.

   ⊿ Other than the second hard drive, what locations or devices can you use for the image?

   _____

15

◢ What is the name of the subfolder in the WindowsImageBackup folder that holds the system image? What is the size of this subfolder?

5. Now let's make some changes to the Windows volume. Use File Explorer or Windows Explorer to go to your user profile in C:\Users*username*. On the following lines, record the exact path to your Documents, Music, Pictures, and Videos folders, and then delete these four folders.

6. Shut down Windows.

7. Boot up the computer and launch Windows RE. (For details on how to do that, see Lab 15.3.) What steps did you use to launch Windows RE?

8. To start the process of reimaging the drive, do one of the following:

◢ For Windows 10/8, on the *Choose an option* screen, click **Troubleshoot**, click **Advanced options**, and then click **System Image Recovery**.

◢ For Windows 7, in the *System Recovery Options* window, click **System Image Recovery**.

9. Follow the on-screen directions to reimage the drive. What decisions and responses did you need to make during this process?

10. When the imaging is complete, Windows restarts and the Windows desktop loads. Look in your user profile. Are the deleted folders restored?

PART 2: USE WINDOWS IN A VM TO CREATE AND USE A SYSTEM IMAGE

1. Using a VM that has Windows installed, install a second virtual hard drive (VHD) in the VM, if necessary. Make the VHD a dynamically expanding drive with a maximum capacity of at least 50 GB. For the details of installing a second VHD in a VM in Hyper-V, see Lab 13.3.

2. Start the VM. If you have just installed a new VHD, use Disk Management to partition and format this drive using the NTFS file system.

3. Open File Explorer, Windows Explorer, or Disk Management to help you answer these questions:

◢ How much space is used on drive C:?

◢ How much space is free on the second hard drive? Do you have enough room on the second drive for the system image?

_____

4. Open Windows 10/7 Backup and Restore or Windows 8 File History, and use it to create a system image on the second hard drive.

◢ What other locations or devices can you use for the image other than the second hard drive?

_____

◢ What is the name of the subfolder in the WindowsImageBackup folder that holds the system image? What is the size of this subfolder?

_____

5. Now let's make some drastic changes to the Windows volume. List the exact paths to several folders on drive C:, and then delete these folders. Include Windows subfolders and Users subfolders in your list of folders to delete.

_____

_____

_____

6. Shut down the Windows VM.

7. Mount the Windows ISO setup file to the virtual optical drive in the VM so that you can use the ISO file to launch Windows RE.

8. Start the VM again and load the Advanced Boot Options menu. Launch Windows RE. What responses did you make to launch Windows RE?

_____

9. To start the process of reimaging the drive, do one of the following:

◢ For Windows 10/8, on the _Choose an option_ screen, click **Troubleshoot**, click **Advanced options**, and then click **System Image Recovery**.

◢ For Windows 7, in the _System Recovery Options_ window, click **System Image Recovery**.

10. Follow the on-screen directions to reimage the drive. What decisions and responses did you need to make during this process?

_____

_____

_____

11. When the imaging is complete, the VM restarts and the Windows desktop loads. Did Windows launch successfully? Are the deleted folders restored?

_____

15

ESTIMATED COMPLETION TIME: 20 MINUTES

CHALLENGE ACTIVITY

Interestingly enough, Windows stores the system image in a VHD. If you drill down into the WindowsImageBackup subfolders, you will find a very large VHD file that contains the image. Mount (attach) this VHD file as a virtual hard drive installed on your computer or virtual machine. Then, use File Explorer or Windows Explorer to explore the VHD. Copy a file in the system image to the Windows desktop.

Answer the following questions:

◢ What utility did you use to attach the VHD file to your system as an installed virtual hard drive? What drive letter did Windows assign the VHD?

_____

◢ What is the size of the VHD file in the WindowsImageBackup folder that holds the system image you created in this lab?

_____

◢ Why is it unreasonable to ask you the name of the VHD file?

_____

REVIEW QUESTIONS

1. If you were using single-sided recordable DVDs to hold the system image you created in this lab, how many DVDs would be required? How did you arrive at your answer?

_____

_____

2. What Windows 10 utility is used to create a system image? To restore the system using a system image? To mount a VHD to the Windows system?

_____

_____

_____

3. Why is it useful to know that you can mount the VHD that holds the system image into the Windows system?

_____

_____

4. Describe one situation in the field when you might want to recover the Windows volume using the system image. Describe a situation when you might want to mount the VHD that holds the system image into the Windows system:

_____

_____

LAB 15.7 RECOVER DATA FROM A COMPUTER THAT WILL NOT BOOT

OBJECTIVES

Your goal in this lab is to learn how to recover data from a computer that will not boot. After completing this lab, you will be able to:

◢ Copy data from a nonbooting computer

MATERIALS REQUIRED

This lab requires the following:

◢ Two Windows 10/8/7 computers designated for this lab

◢ An account with administrator privileges

◢ Internet access

LAB PREPARATION

Before the lab begins, the instructor or lab assistant needs to do the following:

◢ Verify that Windows works with no errors

◢ Verify that each student has access to a user account with administrator privileges

◢ Verify that Internet access is available

ACTIVITY BACKGROUND

If Windows is corrupted and the system will not boot, recovering your data might be your first priority. One way to get to the data is to remove your hard drive from your computer and install it as a second nonbooting hard drive in another working system. After you boot up the system, you should be able to use File Explorer or Windows Explorer to copy the data to another medium, such as a USB flash drive. If the data is corrupted, you can try to use data recovery software. In this lab, you will remove the hard drive from a computer and attempt to recover information from it.

> **ESTIMATED COMPLETION TIME: 45 MINUTES**

 Activity

First, create some data that will need to be rescued on the first computer:

1. Boot the first computer, and sign in as administrator.

2. Using Control Panel, create a new user called **User1**.

3. Sign in as User1.

4. You will now create some files to represent important information that might be saved in various locations on this computer. Use Notepad to create three text files named **file1.txt**, **file2.txt**, and **file3.txt**, and save one in each of the following locations:

   ◢ Save **file1.txt** in User1's My Documents folder.

   ◢ Save **file2.txt** in the Public Documents subfolder within the \Users\Public folder.

   ◢ Save **file3.txt** in the root (probably C:\).

5. Open Internet Explorer, and bookmark at least three locations on the web.

6. Sign out and shut down this computer.

Now pretend this computer is no longer able to boot. Because a backup or restore point has not been created recently, you will remove the hard drive and attempt to recover your important files before attempting to determine why the computer won't boot.

1. Remove the main hard drive, and install it as a second hard drive in another Windows machine. If you are not trained to work inside a computer, ask your instructor for assistance.

> **Notes** You can save time by purchasing an external IDE/SATA-to-USB converter kit (for about $15), which can be used to temporarily connect a hard drive to a USB port on a working computer.

2. Boot this computer, and sign in as an administrator.

3. Use File Explorer or Windows Explorer to locate the three text files on the hard drive you just installed.

4. List the path where each of these files can be found:

   ◢ file1.txt

   _____

   ◢ file2.txt

   _____

   ◢ file3.txt

   _____

5. Determine the name and location of the file containing your Internet Explorer bookmarks:

   _____

6. Can you think of any other locations that could contain information a user might want to recover?

   _____

   _____

In some cases, the files you are trying to recover might be corrupt, or you might not be able to access the drive at all. In these cases, you can attempt to use file-recovery software.

1. Open a command prompt window. Use the chkdsk command to check for errors on the hard drive where you have important data stored, and then attempt to fix the errors. What chkdsk command line did you use?

   _____

2. Shut down the system you're using, and return the hard drive to its original computer.

3. Boot both computers back up, and ensure that everything is working before shutting them both down.

CHALLENGE ACTIVITY

You can simulate this lab using two virtual machines. Go through the steps in the lab again using Windows 10/8/7 installed in a virtual machine in either Hyper-V Manager, Virtual PC, or VirtualBox. Then "move" the virtual hard drive (VHD) to a second VM that has Windows 10/8/7 installed. Install the VHD as the second hard drive in this VM. Then use Windows 10/8/7 on this second VM to recover the data on your virtual hard drive. Finally, return the VHD to the original VM, and start up both VMs to make sure everything is working as it should. Answer the following questions:

1. List the steps you took to "move" the VHD in the first VM to the second VM:

_____

_____

_____

2. List the steps you took to locate and use the second virtual hard drive when you started the second VM:

_____

_____

_____

3. List the steps you took to return the VHD to the first VM:

_____

_____

_____

4. What problems did you encounter while performing this Challenge Activity, and how did you solve them?

_____

_____

REVIEW QUESTIONS

1. Why might you want to recover lost data before attempting to resolve a boot problem?

_____

_____

2. How could scheduled backups save you a lot of time if your system will not boot?

_____

_____

15

3. What types of errors might cause a computer not to boot? List three possible causes:

_____

_____

_____

4. If you suspect the first computer is not booting because it is infected with a virus, what should you ensure before installing its hard drive in a second computer?

_____

_____

LAB 15.8 ROLL BACK TO A PREVIOUS VERSION OF WINDOWS

OBJECTIVES

Your goal in this lab is to learn to return to a previous version of Windows. After completing this lab, you will be able to:

▲ Roll back to a previous version of Windows

MATERIALS REQUIRED

This lab requires the following:

▲ Windows 8/7 operating system

▲ Windows 10 setup flash drive or installation files

> 📝 **Notes** This lab works great on Windows 8/7 installed in a VM.

LAB PREPARATION

Before the lab begins, the instructor or lab assistant should do the following:

▲ Verify that Windows 8/7 starts with no errors

▲ Perform a backup of important files if necessary

ACTIVITY BACKGROUND

When you upgrade from Windows 8/7 to Windows 10, you might encounter unexpected issues. For instance, a program or hardware driver might turn out to be incompatible with the new version. Usually within 10 days of an upgrade to Windows 10, you can use the Roll Back feature in the Settings app to easily uninstall Windows 10 and return to the previous version of Windows. If more than 10 days have passed since an upgrade to Windows 10, you must reinstall the previous version of Windows using the installation files for that version.

ESTIMATED COMPLETION TIME: 30 MINUTES

Activity

1. Follow the steps in Chapter 12 of this book to perform an upgrade from Windows 8/7 to Windows 10.

2. Boot to Windows 10 and sign in. Open the **Settings** app, click the **Update & Security** group, and then select **Recovery**.

3. Under *Go back to Windows 8.1* (or *Go back to Windows 7*), click **Get started**.

4. Select a reason for why you are going back. If you were going through this rollback in response to a problem, you could choose to contact Microsoft to troubleshoot the issue by clicking the "contact support" link. Click **Next**.

5. If you are connected to the Internet, you now have a chance to check for updates to see if that resolves your issue. Click **No, thanks**.

6. Review what you need to know before performing the rollback, and then click **Next**.

7. Verify that you have the password for the Windows 8/7 user account. Click **Next**.

8. Click **Go back to earlier build** (or Go back to Windows 8.1 or Go back to Windows 7). The computer restarts and restores the previous version of Windows.

9. Finally, make sure you can still sign in to your previous version of Windows.

REVIEW QUESTIONS

1. What are two reasons you might want to roll back to a previous version of Windows?

_____

_____

2. How long after an upgrade to Windows 10 is the rollback to a previous version available in the Settings app?

_____

3. How can you return to a previous version of Windows if 10 days have passed since the upgrade to Windows 10?

_____

_____

4. What options during the rollback process does Microsoft offer to try to resolve any issues and help make Windows 10 work better for you?

_____

_____

15

LAB 15.9 USE FRESH START

OBJECTIVES

The goal of this lab is to restore a sluggish computer back to like-new condition by removing unneeded apps preinstalled by the manufacturer (known as bloatware), as well as other unwanted apps, all the while leaving personal files and data untouched. After completing this lab, you will be able to:

◢ Use Fresh Start in the Windows Defender Security Center

MATERIALS REQUIRED

This lab requires the following:

◢ Windows 10 operating system

◢ Internet access

> **Notes** This lab works great on Windows 10 installed in a VM.

LAB PREPARATION

Before the lab begins, the instructor or lab assistant should do the following:

◢ Verify that Windows starts with no errors

◢ Verify that Internet access is available

◢ Perform a backup of important files if necessary

ACTIVITY BACKGROUND

Too many programs can bog down system resources, causing a computer to act sluggish. Fresh Start downloads and installs the latest version of Windows 10 while removing manufacturer bloatware. User data and files are kept; however, if there is data stored in a program being removed, that data will be lost. Fresh Start requires Internet access and at least 3 GB of space to download the Windows image.

ESTIMATED COMPLETION TIME: 45 MINUTES

 Activity

Follow these steps to create a new user account and install a program so you can test the results of Fresh Start:

1. Create another user on the system. Sign in as that user, and create a text document. Where is the text document stored? Write down the name of the document file.

_____

_____

2. Sign out of the new user account, and sign back in to your administrator account. Create a text document. Write down the name and location of the file.

_____

3. Install a free program, such as CPU-Z from *cpuid.com*. Write down the name of the program.

Follow these steps to test the results of Fresh Start:

1. Open the **Settings** app, click the **Update & Security** group, and then select **Recovery**. Under *More recovery options*, click **Learn how to start fresh with a clean installation of Windows**. Click **Yes** to switch to the Windows Defender Security Center.

2. The Windows Defender Security Center opens to the Fresh Start window (see Figure 15-3). Click **Get started**. Respond to the UAC box.

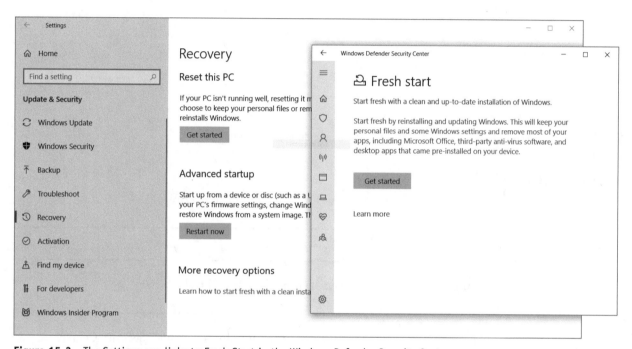

Figure 15-3 The Settings app links to Fresh Start in the Windows Defender Security Center

3. On the Fresh Start screen, review what happens when you use Fresh Start. Click **Next**.

4. Review the list of apps that will be removed. Notice if the program you installed earlier is listed. Write down the list of apps to be removed. Use another sheet of paper if you need more space. Click **Next**.

5. On the next screen, click **Start**. While installing Windows 10, Fresh Start might restart your computer a few times.

6. When your computer returns to the Windows 10 sign-in screen, sign in to your account.

7. On the desktop, open the Removed Apps file, compare this list to the list you wrote down earlier, and verify that the program you installed is listed as removed (see Figure 15-4).

8. Verify that the files you created on both user accounts are still there.

15

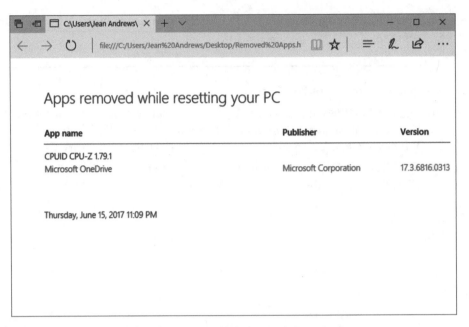

Figure 15-4 Review the list of apps removed during Fresh Start

REVIEW QUESTIONS

1. How is using Fresh Start different from System Image Recovery?

_____

_____

2. When might personal files or data be lost when using Fresh Start?

_____

3. Why do you think Fresh Start is a part of the Windows Defender Security Center?

_____

4. Where do you find a list of programs that have been removed after using Fresh Start?

_____

5. List information you need to collect about a system before running Fresh Start.

_____

_____

_____

LAB 15.10 SABOTAGE AND REPAIR WINDOWS

OBJECTIVES

Your goal in this lab is to learn to troubleshoot Windows by repairing a sabotaged system. After completing this lab, you will be able to:

▲ Troubleshoot and repair a system that isn't working correctly

MATERIALS REQUIRED

This lab requires the following:

- Windows 10/8/7 installed on a computer designated for sabotage
- Windows 10/8/7 setup flash drive/DVD or installation files
- A workgroup of two to four students

> **Notes** This lab works great on Windows 10/8/7 installed in a VM.

LAB PREPARATION

Before the lab begins, the instructor or lab assistant needs to do the following:

- Verify that Windows starts with no errors
- Provide each workgroup with access to the Windows 8 or Windows 7 installation files, if needed

ACTIVITY BACKGROUND

You have learned about several tools and methods you can use to recover Windows when it fails. This lab gives you the opportunity to use these skills in a troubleshooting situation. Your group will sabotage another group's system while that group sabotages your system. Then your group will repair its own system.

ESTIMATED COMPLETION TIME: 45 MINUTES

 Activity

Follow these steps to sabotage a Windows 10/8/7 system for another group and then repair your Windows 10/8/7 system that the other group has sabotaged:

1. If your system's hard drive contains important data, back it up to another medium. Is there anything else you would like to back up before another group sabotages the system? Record the name of that item here, and then back it up:

   _____

2. Trade systems with another group, and sabotage the other group's system while they sabotage your system. Think of one thing that will cause the system to fail to boot, display errors after the boot, or prevent a device or application from working. The following list offers some sabotage suggestions. Do something in the following list, or think of another option. (Do not alter the hardware.)

   - Find a system file in the root directory that's required to boot the computer, and rename it or move it to a different directory. (Don't delete the file.)
   - Using the Registry Editor (Regedit.exe), delete several important keys or values in the registry.
   - Locate important system files in the \Windows folder or its subfolders, and rename them or move them to another directory.

> **Notes** To move, delete, or rename a Windows system file, you might need to first take ownership of the file using the takeown and icacls commands. The Microsoft Knowledge Base Article 929833 at *support.microsoft.com/en-us/help/929833/* explains how to use these two commands.

15

◢ Put a corrupted program file in the Windows folder that will cause the program to launch automatically at startup. Record the name of that program file and folder here:

_____

◢ Use display settings that make text unreadable—such as black text on a black background.

◢ Disable a critical device driver or Windows service.

3. Reboot the system and verify that a problem exists.

4. How did you sabotage the other team's system?

_____

_____

5. Return to your system and troubleshoot it.

6. Describe the problem as a user would describe it to you if you were working at a help desk:

_____

_____

_____

7. What is your first guess as to the source of the problem?

_____

8. An expert problem solver always tries the simple things first. What is an easy fix that you can try? Try the fix and record the results.

_____

_____

9. As you troubleshoot the system, list the high-level steps you are taking in the troubleshooting process:

_____

_____

_____

_____

10. How did you finally solve the problem and return the system to good working order?

_____

_____

REVIEW QUESTIONS

1. What would you do differently the next time you encountered the same symptoms that you encountered in this lab?

   _____

   _____

2. What Windows utilities did you use—or could you have used—to solve the problem in the lab?

   _____

3. What might cause the problem in the lab to occur in real life? List three possible causes:

   _____

   _____

   _____

4. If you were the IT support technician responsible for this computer in an office environment, what could you do to prevent this problem from happening in the future or at least limit its impact on users if it did happen?

   _____

   _____

15

Securing and Sharing Windows Resources

Labs included in this chapter:

LAB 16.1 MAP A NETWORK DRIVE AND USE WAKE-ON-LAN

OBJECTIVES

Your goal in this lab is to learn to map a network drive and remotely power on your computer. After completing this lab, you will be able to:

▲ Map a network drive in Windows

▲ Set up Wake-on-LAN

MATERIALS REQUIRED

This lab requires the following:

▲ Two or more Windows 10/8/7 computers on the same wired network (not wireless)

▲ Internet access (optional and used for research only)

LAB PREPARATION

Before the lab begins, the instructor or lab assistant needs to do the following:

▲ Verify that Windows starts with no errors

▲ Verify that Internet access is available

▲ Set up a peer-to-peer network with two or more computers

ACTIVITY BACKGROUND

When using more than one computer (for example, a laptop and a desktop), it is sometimes necessary to pass files between them. Having a mapped network drive on a computer makes it easy to access the files on another computer. On a small network, you might be accessing a resource on a desktop instead of a server, and the hosting computer might go to sleep. Setting up Wake-on-LAN allows you to wake up the hosting computer and access your files. This can be useful if you're accessing your files remotely over a VPN from the other side of the country or if you're just tired of getting up and walking across the room to turn on the computer or wake it from sleep mode.

ESTIMATED COMPLETION TIME: 45 MINUTES

 Activity

> 📝 **Notes** Sometimes HomeGroup does not play well with others when sharing. Before beginning this lab in Windows 8/7, open the **Network and Sharing Center**, and click **Change advanced sharing settings**. Make sure HomeGroup is turned off. Repeat these steps on the second computer.

In this lab, Computer 1 is acting as the server that is serving up a network resource (for example, a folder named Downloads or Resources), and Computer 2 is acting as the client that is using this shared resource.

1. Begin with two networked Windows computers. Designate one computer to be Computer 1 and the other computer to be Computer 2.

2. On Computer 1, which will be your server, open File Explorer or Windows Explorer, navigate to your C: drive, and display the root of drive C:.

3. Create a new folder in the root of drive C:, and name the folder **Resources**.

4. To grant access to all users on the network, right-click your new **Resources** folder, select **Properties**, and select the **Sharing** tab. Click **Share**.

5. Select **Everyone** from the drop-down list, and then click **Add**. Under Permission Level for Everyone, grant **Read/Write** access (see Figure 16-1), and then click the **Share** button. Windows confirms that the folder is shared.

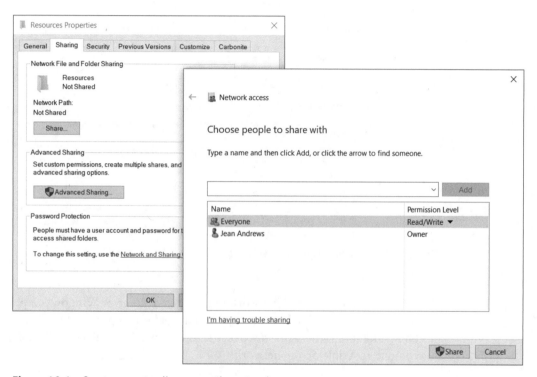

Figure 16-1 Grant access to all users on the network

6. To make sure network discovery and file and printer sharing are turned on, open the **Network and Sharing Center**, click **Change advanced sharing settings**, and verify that **Turn on network discovery** and **Turn on file and printer sharing** are selected (see Figure 16-2).

7. To see a list of all network shares on this computer, open a command prompt window, and enter the **net share** command at the command prompt. Record on the following lines all the shared resources on the computer. Close the command prompt window.

_____

_____

_____

8. Go to Computer 2, open the **Network and Sharing Center**, and verify that network discovery and file sharing are turned on for Computer 2.

16

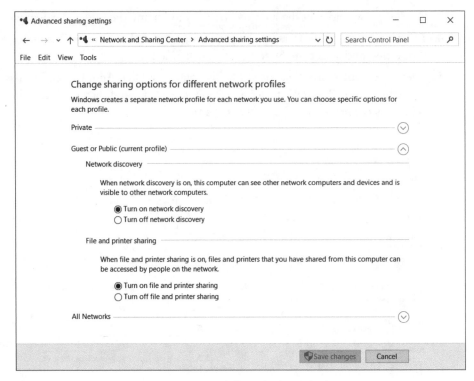

Figure 16-2   Turn on network discovery and file and printer sharing

9. On Computer 2, expand **Network** in the File Explorer or Windows Explorer navigation pane. Computer 1 should be in the list of available computers. If it isn't, check Computer 1 and make sure its network discovery settings are correct. Record the names of all the computers visible on the network:

_____

10. To view the shared resources on Computer 1, open Computer 1. You might have to enter your user name and password if you haven't previously opened the network resource and saved your credentials.

11. You see a list of the shared resources on Computer 1. Does the list match the list of shared resources you wrote down in Step 7?

_____

12. Right-click the **Resources** folder, and select **Map network drive**. Windows assigns a drive letter by default, starting at Z and working backward through the alphabet. However, you can change this drive letter. What drive letter did you assign to the network drive? Check **Reconnect at sign-in** or **Reconnect at logon** if it is not already checked, and then click **Finish**.

_____

13. To test the functionality of your new network drive, create a test document on the mapped drive.

14. Go back to Computer 1 and verify that the test document you created is in the Resources folder on the C: drive.

Now you will activate the Wake-on-LAN functionality. Follow these steps:

1. On Computer 1, open the **Network and Sharing Center**.

2. In the left pane, click **Change adapter settings**.

3. Right-click the network adapter for the wired connection and select **Properties**.

4. Click **Configure** and then select the **Power Management** tab. Which boxes are checked on the Power Management tab?

   _____

   _____

5. Make sure that the **Allow the computer to turn off this device to save power** option is selected. This enables power management in Windows.

6. Check **Allow this device to wake the computer**. Why shouldn't you select *Only allow a magic packet to wake this computer*?

   _____

   _____

   _____

7. Click **OK**.

8. Shut down Computer 1.

9. Boot Computer 1 and access BIOS/UEFI setup. Find the power management configuration screen in BIOS/UEFI, and confirm that Wake-on-LAN is enabled. Did you need to enable Wake-on-LAN?

   _____

10. Exit BIOS/UEFI setup and start Windows.

11. Put Computer 1 in sleep mode.

12. On Computer 2, go to File Explorer or Windows Explorer, and try to open your mapped network drive. What happens?

    _____

13. Shut down Computer 1.

14. On Computer 2, go to File Explorer or Windows Explorer, and try to open your mapped network drive. What happens?

    _____

16

REVIEW QUESTIONS

1. What is the purpose of the net share command? When network discovery and file and printer sharing are turned off, does the net share command still report a shared folder as shared?

   _____

2. What drive letter does Windows first attempt to assign a mapped network drive? What is the second letter used?

   _____

3. Why should you map a network drive rather than just access your network resource from the Network group in File Explorer or Windows Explorer?

_____

_____

4. In what two locations must you enable Wake-on-LAN to use it?

_____

5. Why is Wake-on-LAN typically disabled on laptops?

_____

_____

6. Why would you choose to disable the Wake-on-LAN functionality?

_____

_____

_____

LAB 16.2 MANAGE USER ACCOUNTS IN WINDOWS 10/8

OBJECTIVES

Your goal in this lab is to gain experience adding and modifying user accounts by using the Settings app in Windows 10 or the PC settings page in Windows 8. After completing this lab, you will be able to:

▲ Add users

▲ Reset passwords

▲ Control user account access

MATERIALS REQUIRED

This lab requires the following:

▲ Windows 10/8 operating system

▲ An account with administrator privileges

LAB PREPARATION

Before the lab begins, the instructor or lab assistant needs to do the following:

▲ Verify that Windows starts with no errors

▲ Verify that each student has access to a user account with administrator privileges

ACTIVITY BACKGROUND

Maintaining Windows involves more than just managing physical resources like hard drives; you also need to manage users and their access to these resources. Managing users can be very time consuming, however. Much of this time is typically spent helping users who have forgotten their passwords or entered their passwords incorrectly multiple times, causing Windows to lock their accounts. In this lab, you practice managing user accounts and passwords using the Windows 10 Settings app or the Windows 8 PC settings page and the Windows 10/8 Manage Accounts window in Control Panel. For more advanced user account management, you can use the Computer Management console, which is not covered in this lab.

ESTIMATED COMPLETION TIME: 30 MINUTES

 Activity

To examine the user account information available via the Windows 10 Settings app or the Windows 8 PC settings page, follow these steps:

1. Sign in using an account with administrator privileges.

2. Open **Control Panel** in Classic view. Click **User Accounts,** and then click **Manage another account.** The Manage Accounts window opens. Your screen will resemble Figure 16-3. For Windows 8, notice a Guest account is present. By default, Windows 10 disables the Guest account.

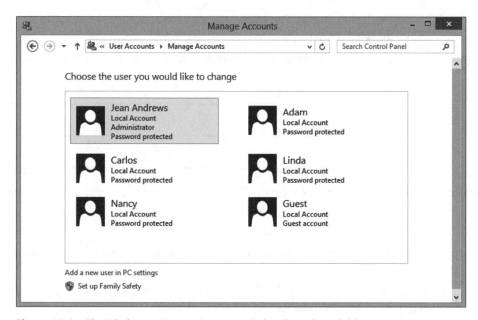

Figure 16-3 The Windows 8 Manage Accounts window lists all available user accounts

Microsoft strongly encourages you to set up Microsoft accounts rather than local accounts on a computer, as you will see in the following steps. To add a new local user, follow these steps:

1. In the Manage Accounts window, click **Add a new user in PC settings**.

2. For Windows 8, do the following:

   a. On the PC settings page, verify that **Other accounts** is selected. Click **Add an account.**

   b. At the bottom of the *How will this person sign in?* screen, click **Sign in without a Microsoft account.** Review the two options for signing in, and then select **Local account.**

3. For Windows 10, do the following:

    a. Verify that the **Family & other people** page opens in the Settings app. Click **Add someone else to this PC**.

    b. Click **I don't have this person's sign-in information**. On the next page, click **Add a user without a Microsoft account**.

4. You are now able to set up a local account. In the User name text box, type **James Clark**.

5. In the Password text box, type **changeme** and confirm the password in the next text box. Enter a password hint in case the password is forgotten.

6. For Windows 8, click **Next** and click **Finish**. Windows 10 makes it more difficult to set up a local account and requires you to enter security questions and answers. Enter this information and click **Next**. The local account is created.

7. Close all open windows.

New users in Windows 10/8 are set up as Standard user accounts by default. A Standard user account can't create, delete, or change other accounts, make system-wide changes, change security settings, or install some types of software. To give the account administrator privileges, do the following:

1. Open **Control Panel** in Classic view, and click **User Accounts**. Click **Manage another account**. In the Manage Accounts window, select the **James Clark** account, and then click **Change the account type**.

2. In the Change Account Type window, change the account type to **Administrator**, and click **Change Account Type**.

3. Sign out of your computer, and sign in as James Clark. List the steps you took to accomplish this task:

_____

_____

_____

Occasionally, administrators have to reset user passwords. To reset a user's password, do the following:

1. Sign out of the James Clark account, and sign in again using the original administrator account.

2. Open the Manage Accounts window in Control Panel, and select the James Clark account.

3. Click **Change the password**. What information does a user lose when the password is changed by an administrator?

_____

_____

_____

4. Enter the password as **newpass**, confirm the password, enter a new password hint, and then click **Change password**.

5. Close all open windows and try to sign in with the James Clark account using the old password. What error do you get? Click **OK**.

_____

6. If a user does not know his or her password, the user might be able to reset it using the sign-in screen. Under the password box on the sign-in screen, click **Reset password**. What does a user need to have to reset a password? Click **OK**.

_____

7. Sign in using the new password.

8. Finally, sign out of the James Clark account, sign in as the administrator, and delete the James Clark account. List the steps that you took to delete the account:

_____

_____

_____

REVIEW QUESTIONS

1. Which Windows operating system was the first one to accept Microsoft accounts to sign in?

_____

2. Which editions of Windows allow you to use the Computer Management console to manage user accounts?

_____

3. When setting up a new user account, when does Windows create the user profile for the account?

_____

4. Why is it a good idea to primarily use a Standard account instead of an Administrator account for normal computer activity?

_____

_____

LAB 16.3 MANAGE USER ACCOUNTS IN WINDOWS 7

16

OBJECTIVES

Your goal in this lab is to gain experience adding and modifying user accounts by using Control Panel in Windows 7. After completing this lab, you will be able to:

◢ Add users

◢ Control user account access

MATERIALS REQUIRED

This lab requires the following:

◢ Windows 7 operating system

◢ An account with administrator privileges

LAB PREPARATION

Before the lab begins, the instructor or lab assistant needs to do the following:

◢ Verify that Windows starts with no errors

◢ Verify that each student has access to a user account with administrator privileges

ACTIVITY BACKGROUND

IT technicians are often called on to support older software and hardware. Managing user accounts in Windows 7 is different than in Windows 10/8. In Windows 7, you can access most of the necessary functions in just the Manage Accounts window in Control Panel. Because changing the password is almost exactly the same in Windows 7 as it is in Windows 10/8, you can refer to Lab 16.2 for those instructions. In this lab, you practice adding and editing user accounts using the Manage Accounts window in Control Panel. For more advanced user account management, you can use the Computer Management console, which is not covered in this lab.

ESTIMATED COMPLETION TIME: 30 MINUTES

 Activity

To examine the user account information available via the Windows 7 Control Panel, follow these steps:

1. Sign in using an account with administrator privileges.

2. Click **Start**, click **Control Panel**, and then click **Add or remove user accounts**. The Manage Accounts window appears.

3. Examine the Manage Accounts window, and answer the following questions:

◢ What three types of user accounts are included on a Windows 7 system by default?

_____

_____

_____

◢ Does your system contain any individual user accounts? If so, list them here:

_____

Using the Manage Accounts window, add and configure users on your local computer by following these steps:

1. In the Manage Accounts window, click **Create a new account**.

2. In the New account name text box, type **James Clark**.

3. Click **Standard user**, if it is not selected, and then click **Create Account**.

4. To create a password for the new account, click the **James Clark** account in the Manage Accounts window. Click **Create a password**.

5. In the New password text box, type **newuser**, and confirm the password in the next text box.

6. Click **Create password**, and then close all open windows.

A Standard user account can't create, delete, or change other accounts, make system-wide changes, change security settings, or install some types of software. To give the account administrator privileges, do the following:

1. Open the Manage Accounts window in Control Panel, and select the **James Clark** account.

2. Click **Change the account type**, and select **Administrator**.

3. Click **Change Account Type**.

4. Sign out of your computer, and sign in as James Clark. List the steps you took to accomplish this task:

_____

_____

_____

REVIEW QUESTIONS

1. Besides adding, editing, and deleting users, what additional tasks can you perform in the Manage Accounts window of Control Panel in Windows 7?

_____

2. What are the differences between Standard and Administrator accounts?

_____

_____

_____

3. Why do you think new user accounts are not automatically assigned administrator privileges?

_____

_____

4. Why might it be a good idea to have users reset their passwords instead of having an administrator do it for them?

_____

_____

16

LAB 16.4 USE NTFS PERMISSIONS TO SHARE FILES AND FOLDERS

OBJECTIVES

Your goal in this lab is to learn to use the advanced sharing and security tools in Windows to give folder permissions to specific local users and to control a network connection sharing specific folders with specific users and/or groups. After completing this lab, you will be able to:

▲ Configure a network connection for secured access

▲ Share folders with others on the network using NTFS permissions

MATERIALS REQUIRED

This lab requires the following:

⊿ Two computers networked together; one computer must use a Professional or higher edition of Windows 10/8/7, and the other computer can use any edition of Windows 10/8/7

⊿ An account with administrator privileges

⊿ A workgroup of two students

LAB PREPARATION

Before the lab begins, the instructor or lab assistant needs to do the following:

⊿ Verify that both Windows computers start with no errors

⊿ Verify that the local network is working

⊿ Verify that each student has access to a user account with administrator privileges

ACTIVITY BACKGROUND

On a Windows 10/8/7 Professional or higher computer, you can control which specific users or groups have access to specific folders. Microsoft best practices recommend that you set up a user group for each classification of data and assign permissions to a folder or other shared resources according to user groups. Assigning permissions to user groups is easier to maintain than assigning permissions to specific users because you can add or remove users from the group easier than you can change the permissions on each folder.

In this lab, you set up the security for a peer-to-peer network in a doctor's office. Two computers are connected to the small company network; one of these computers (Computer 1) acts as the file server for the other computer (Computer 2). You create two classifications of data, Financial and Medical. Two workers (Nancy and Adam) require access to the Medical data, and two workers (Linda and Carlos) require access to the Financial folder. In addition, the doctor, Lucas, requires access to both categories of data.

This lab is divided into four parts, which accomplish the following:

⊿ Part 1: On Computer 1, you create folders named Financial and Medical, and you create five user accounts—for Lucas, Nancy, Adam, Linda, and Carlos. All the accounts belong to the standard user group. You also create two new user groups, Financial and Medical.

⊿ Part 2: You set the NTFS permissions on the Financial and Medical folders so that only the members of the appropriate group can access each folder.

⊿ Part 3: You test your security settings for local users.

⊿ Part 4: For each user on Computer 2, you test the access to both folders across the network.

ESTIMATED COMPLETION TIME: 60 MINUTES

 Activity

Working with your partner, perform all four parts of this lab. Begin by designating one computer as Computer 1 (the file server) and the other computer as Computer 2 (the client computer).

PART 1: CREATE FOLDERS, USER ACCOUNTS, AND USER GROUPS

> **Notes** Sometimes HomeGroup does not play well with others when sharing. Before beginning this lab in Windows 8/7, open the **Network and Sharing Center** and click **Change advanced sharing settings**. Make sure HomeGroup is turned off. Repeat these steps on the second computer.

Follow these steps to create the folders, user accounts, and user groups on Computer 1 (the file server), which is using Windows 10/8/7 Professional or a higher edition:

1. Sign in to Computer 1 as an administrator.

2. Create two folders: **C:\Financial** and **C:\Medical**. In each folder, create a test document. What is the name of the test document in the Financial folder? In the Medical folder?

   _____

3. To open the Computer Management console in Windows 10/8, right-click **Start** and then click **Computer Management**. In Windows 7, enter **Computer Management** in the search box.

4. Using the console, create user accounts for Lucas, Nancy, Adam, Linda, and Carlos. To create the first new user, right-click **Users** under Local Users and Groups, and then select **New User** in the shortcut menu. Make the password for each user the same as the name of the user. Uncheck the **User must change password at next logon** check box. What are the other three check box options when creating user accounts?

   _____

   _____

   _____

5. Click **Create**. The user will automatically be added to the Users group. Create all the user accounts, and click **Close** after the last user account is created.

6. To create the Financial user group, right-click **Groups** under Local Users and Groups, and then select **New Group** in the shortcut menu. The New Group dialog box appears. Enter **Financial** as the name of the group. Enter the description **Users have access to the Financial folder**.

7. To add members to the Financial group, click **Add**. The Select Users dialog box opens. In the _Enter the object names to select_ box, enter the name of a user, and then click **OK**. Add all the user account names that need access to this folder, separated by semicolons, as in **Carlos; Linda; Lucas**. (Alternatively, you can click **Advanced** to open a new dialog box and then click **Find Now** to view a list of user names. Then, hold down the **Ctrl** key and select multiple names, and then click **OK**.) To create the group, click **Create** in the New Group box.

8. Next, create the **Medical** group, and add Lucas, Nancy, and Adam to the group.

9. Close the Computer Management console.

16

PART 2: SET NTFS PERMISSIONS ON FOLDERS

Follow these steps to set the permissions for the two folders:

1. Open File Explorer or Windows Explorer, right-click the **Financial** folder, and then select **Properties** in the shortcut menu. The Properties dialog box for the folder appears. Click the **Security** tab (see the right side of Figure 16-4). What groups and users already have access to the C:\Financial folder?

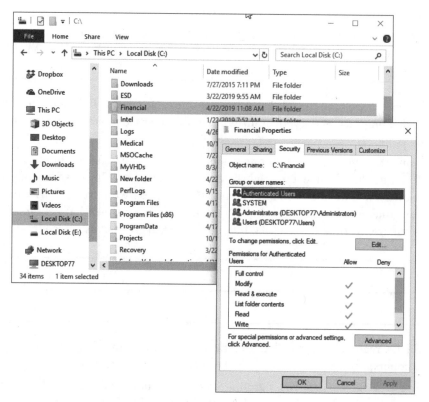

Figure 16-4   Permissions assigned to the Financial folder

2. When you select a user group in the Group or user names section, the type of permissions assigned to that group appears in the Permissions section. Note that the Administrators group has full control of the folder. Also notice the checks under Allow are dimmed. These permissions are dimmed because they have been inherited from the Windows parent object.

3. To remove the inherited status from these permissions so that you can change them, click **Advanced**. The Advanced Security Settings window appears. Do one of the following:

   ◢ For Windows 10/8, click **Disable inheritance** (see Figure 16-5).

   ◢ For Windows 7, click **Change Permissions**. You can now uncheck **Include inheritable permissions from this object's parent**.

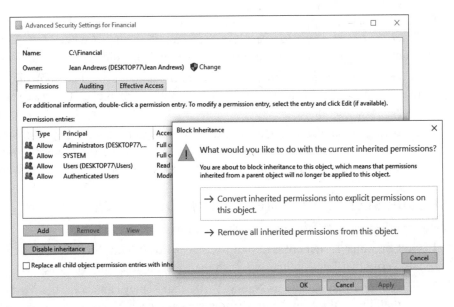

Figure 16-5 Remove the inherited status from the current permissions

4. To keep the current permissions but remove the inherited status placed on them, click **Convert inherited permissions into explicit permissions on this object.**

5. Click **Apply,** and click **OK** to close the Advanced Security Settings window.

6. In the Financial Properties dialog box, notice the permissions are now checked in black, indicating they are no longer inherited permissions and can be changed. What permissions are allowed to the standard Users group by default?

_____

7. Click **Edit** to change these permissions.

8. The Permissions for Financial dialog box opens (see Figure 16-6). Select the **Users** group, and then click **Remove.** Also remove the **Authenticated Users** group. Don't remove the SYSTEM group or the Administrators group. That way, an administrator can always access the data.

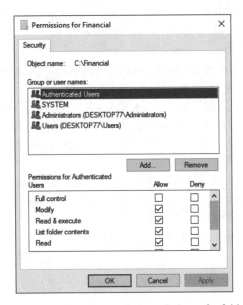

Figure 16-6 Change the permissions of a folder

9. To add a new group, click **Add**. The Select Users or Groups dialog box opens. In the *Enter the object names to select* box, type **Financial**, and then click **OK**. The Financial group is added to the list of groups and users for this folder.

10. In the Permissions for Financial section, check **Allow** for the **Full control** option to give that permission to this user group. Click **Apply**, and then click **OK** twice to close the Properties dialog box.

11. Following the same process, change the permissions of the C:\Medical folder so that Authenticated Users and Users are not allowed access and the Medical group is allowed full control. Don't forget to first disable inheritable permissions in the advanced settings.

PART 3: TEST YOUR SECURITY SETTINGS WITH LOCAL USERS

Do the following to test the share permissions on each shared folder:

1. On Computer 1, sign out and sign back in as **Lucas** with the password set earlier in this lab. Verify that Lucas can access both the Medical and Financial folders.

2. Sign out and sign back in as **Nancy**. Verify that Nancy can access the Medical folder but not the Financial folder. What warning appears when Nancy tries to access the Financial folder?

———————————————————————————————————

———————————————————————————————————

3. Sign out and sign back in as **Adam**. Verify that Adam can access the Medical folder but not the Financial folder.

4. Sign out and sign back in as **Linda**. Verify that Linda can access the Financial folder but not the Medical folder.

5. Sign out and sign back in as **Carlos**. Verify that Carlos can access the Financial folder but not the Medical folder.

PART 4: TEST YOUR SECURITY SETTINGS ON THE NETWORK FOR EACH USER ON COMPUTER 2

NTFS permissions and share permissions both control access over the network, and the more restrictive permission setting applies. The best practice is to give full access using share permissions and restrictive access using NTFS permissions. Do the following to set share permissions so that all network users are given full control of both folders:

1. Sign in to Computer 1 as an administrator. Open the Properties dialog box for the Medical folder, and click the **Sharing** tab. Do one of the following:

   ◢ For Windows 10/8, click **Advanced Sharing**. Check **Share this folder,** and then click **Permissions**. If necessary, add the Everyone group. Select **Everyone**, and check **Allow** next to **Full Control**. Click **Apply**, and then click **OK**. Click **Apply** again, and then click **OK**.

   ◢ For Windows 7, click **Share**. In the drop-down list, select **Everyone**, and click **Add**. In the Name column, click **Everyone**, and in the Permission Level column, select **Read/Write**. Click **Share**. Close the Properties dialog box.

2. In the same way, set share permissions for the Financial folder.

Even though share permissions allow full access, the NTFS permissions set earlier in this lab will limit access. Do the following to test your security settings for network users:

1. On Computer 2, sign in as an administrator.

2. Create user accounts for Lucas, Nancy, Adam, Linda, and Carlos. Make the password for each account the name of the user.

> **Notes** If Computer 2 uses a Windows Home edition, you must use the Windows 10 Settings app, the Windows 8 PC settings page, or Windows 7 Control Panel to create user accounts.

3. Sign out and sign back in to Computer 2 as Lucas. Verify that Lucas can access both the Medical and Financial folders on Computer 1. If you have a problem accessing the folders, go back and check your work, making sure all settings are correct. If you still have a problem, try signing out and signing back in. If that doesn't work, try restarting both computers.

4. Sign out and sign back in to Computer 2 as Nancy. Verify that Nancy can access the Medical share but not the Financial share on Computer 1. What text appears in the Network Error box when Nancy tries to access the Financial share?

_____

_____

5. Sign out and sign back in to Computer 2 as Adam. Verify that Adam can access the Medical share but not the Financial share on Computer 1.

6. Sign out and sign back in to Computer 2 as Linda. Verify that Linda can access the Financial share but not the Medical share on Computer 1.

7. Sign out and sign back in to Computer 2 as Carlos. Verify that Carlos can access the Financial share but not the Medical share on Computer 1.

REVIEW QUESTIONS

1. Why is it necessary that Computer 1 run Windows Professional or a higher edition to implement the security used in this lab?

_____

_____

2. When viewing the permissions assigned to a folder, why might these permissions be grayed out so that you cannot change them?

_____

3. When assigning permissions to a folder, why might you allow full permissions to the Administrators group?

_____

4. What is the purpose of turning on the *Use user accounts and passwords to connect to other computers* option in the Advanced sharing settings window?

_____

_____

16

LAB 16.5 WORK WITH OFFLINE FILES AND THE SYNC CENTER

OBJECTIVES

The goal of this lab is to work with offline files and the Sync Center. After completing this lab, you will be able to:

▲ Enable offline files in Windows

▲ Make network files available offline

▲ Sync offline files with the network

MATERIALS REQUIRED

This lab requires the following:

▲ Two or more Windows 10/8/7 computers networked together; at least one computer must use Windows 10/8/7 Professional or higher

▲ Internet access

> 📝 **Notes** It is recommended that you complete Lab 16.1 in this chapter before tackling this lab.

LAB PREPARATION

Before the lab begins, the instructor or lab assistant needs to do the following:

▲ Verify that Windows starts with no errors

▲ Verify that Internet access is available

▲ Set up a simple network with two or more computers

ACTIVITY BACKGROUND

Sometimes, you need access to network files when the network is not available. Maybe you're traveling and you can't find a wireless connection or maybe the server is being updated and it's temporarily unavailable. Windows allows you to work with offline files and then sync up the changes with the network files later. In this lab, you set up some network files so they can be changed offline. Then, when you're connected to the network, the files on your computer sync up with the files on the network server.

ESTIMATED COMPLETION TIME: 45 MINUTES

 Activity

In this lab, Computer 1 is serving up a folder that is used by Computer 2. Computer 2 will use offline files to use the folder even when it is not connected to Computer 1. Offline files are a feature of Windows 10/8/7 Professional or higher editions. Therefore, Computer 2 must be using one of these editions.

1. Begin with two networked Windows computers and test your network connection. What method or utility did you use? Designate one computer as Computer 1 (the file server) and the other computer as Computer 2, the client computer. Computer 2 must be using Windows 10/8/7 Professional or higher.

2. Computer 1 will be your server. Using Computer 1, create a folder named **Offline Files** in the root of drive C:. Share this folder with the Everyone group. (If you need help sharing the folder, see Lab 16.1 in this chapter.) In the folder, create a small text document. What is the exact name and path of your shared folder and file?

_____

3. Sign in to Computer 2, and create a mapped network drive to the shared folder. If you need help with this step, see Lab 16.1 in this chapter. What is the drive letter used for the network map?

_____

4. Still using Computer 2, open the text file to test your connection.

5. In File Explorer or Windows Explorer, right-click the drive you just mapped, and select **Always available offline** in the shortcut menu. The offline files service launches.

6. To open the Sync Center, open **Control Panel** in Classic view, and click **Sync Center**. In the left pane of the Sync Center, click **View sync partnerships**, if it is not already selected. The window reports progress syncing the files (see Figure 16-7). Note any messages or conflicts here:

_____

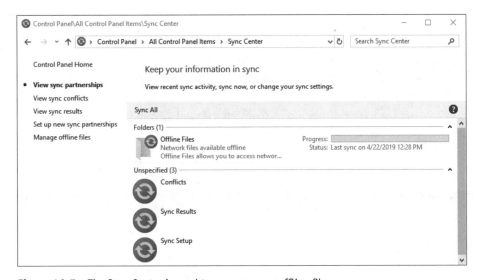

Figure 16-7   The Sync Center is used to manage your offline files

16

7. Close all open windows.

You can work with offline files by following these steps:

1. Temporarily remove Computer 2 from the network by unplugging the network cable or disabling the network adapter. Windows will automatically enable offline files whenever the network is not available.

2. Open File Explorer or Windows Explorer, and open the offline version of the shared text file.

3. Make a small change to this file. What change did you make?

   _____

4. Open the Sync Center, and click **Manage offline files**. The Offline Files dialog box opens. Answer the following questions:

   ◢ What objects are listed when you click **View your offline files**?

   _____

   _____

   ◢ How can you change the amount of space available for storing offline files on your computer?

   _____

   _____

   ◢ How can offline files help you when you are experiencing a slow network connection?

   _____

   _____

   _____

5. Now reconnect Computer 2 with the network.

6. Windows updates offline files automatically but not continuously. To make sure the offline file is updated, go to the Sync Center, right-click **Offline Files**, and then click **Sync Offline Files.**

7. After the sync finishes, go to Computer 1 and sign in if necessary. Open the shared file. Did the file update with offline changes made from Computer 2?

   _____

ESTIMATED COMPLETION TIME: 20 MINUTES

CHALLENGE ACTIVITY

Suppose you are working with offline files while disconnected from the network, and you make a change to the file on your local computer while another change is made to the same file stored on the host computer. What happens when you reconnect to the network and sync your offline files? Which change is kept and which change is lost? Set up this scenario, and describe what happens:

_____

_____

_____

REVIEW QUESTIONS

1. What are some reasons you might choose to set up offline files?

_____

_____

_____

2. How is working with offline files different from simply making a second copy of the files you need to access?

_____

3. Why might encrypting your offline files be necessary? Describe at least one situation in which encrypting your offline files might be appropriate:

_____

_____

_____

4. Why might you choose to work with offline files even if the network is available?

_____

_____

_____

5. What is the path on your local computer where offline files are stored?

_____

LAB 16.6 USE ACTIVE DIRECTORY IN THE CLOUD

OBJECTIVES

The goal of this lab is to set up Windows Server and Active Directory in the cloud and set up users in the domain. After completing this lab, you will be able to:

◢ Set up Windows Server using Amazon Web Services (AWS)

◢ Set up Active Directory to manage a domain

◢ Use Active Directory to manage users

MATERIALS REQUIRED

This lab requires the following:

◢ A credit card that can be used to set up an AWS account (the card will not be charged)

◢ Internet access on a Windows computer

16

LAB PREPARATION

Before the lab begins, the instructor or lab assistant needs to do the following:

◢ Verify that Windows starts with no errors

◢ Verify that Internet access is available

ACTIVITY BACKGROUND

Active Directory is a service provided by Windows Server to manage a domain on a network. Amazon Web Services (AWS) makes available cloud services that can be used to create a virtual machine with Windows Server installed. You can use Windows Server to set up Active Directory as a domain controller.

Amazon Elastic Compute Cloud (Amazon EC2) provides scalable computing capacity in the AWS cloud. Use it to create and launch virtual servers and set up security, networking, and storage for these servers.

In this lab, you set up an account in AWS, a Windows Server virtual machine, and Active Directory. You then use Active Directory to manage users on the domain you have created.

ESTIMATED COMPLETION TIME: 60 MINUTES

 Activity

PART 1: SET UP AN AWS ACCOUNT

An AWS account includes 12 months of free access, although you do need a credit card to sign up for this service. If you don't already have an account, follow these steps to sign up for an AWS account:

1. Go to **aws.amazon.com** and click either **Sign Up** or **Create an AWS Account**.

2. Enter your email address, password, password confirmation, and AWS account name. Click **Continue**. Write down your email address, password, and account name:

_____

_____

3. On the next screen, select **Personal** for the Account type. Enter your full name, phone number, country, and mailing address.

4. Read and then accept the AWS Customer Agreement. Then click **Create Account and Continue**.

5. Enter your credit card information, and click **Secure Submit**.

6. Complete the next screen by deciding how you want to receive a verification code (text or voice) and entering the security check.

7. When you receive the verification code, enter it on the next screen, and click **Continue**. Click **Continue** again.

8. In the list of support plans available, click **Free** to select the Basic Plan.

9. Follow directions on the screen to sign up. You will need to enter your email address and create a password. The AWS Management Console window appears. Your account is working and ready to go.

10. To sign out of AWS, click **Sign Out** under your account name in the menu bar.

PART 2: CREATE A WINDOWS SERVER VM

Follow these steps to create a VM instance in AWS:

1. Go to **aws.amazon.com** and click **Sign In to the Console**. If necessary, enter your email address and password.

2. In the AWS Management Console window, click **Launch a virtual machine**. The VM will be created using Amazon EC2 services.

3. Notice the seven steps listed across the top of the window to create your instance. In the first step, *Choose AMI*, you select an existing Amazon machine image. Click **Community AMIs** in the left pane.

4. Select the type of VM. Be sure to select one that has Windows Server installed. For example, select **Windows_Server-2019-English-Full-Base-2019.04.26**, which is the one we used in this lab. Click **Select** on the right side of the instance you want to use.

5. The second step is *Choose Instance Type*. The *Free tier eligible* option is selected, which gives low to moderate performance. Click **Next: Configure Instance Details**.

6. In the third step, *Configure Instance*, glance over the details already selected, and click **Next: Add Storage**.

7. In the fourth step, *Add Storage*, verify that the storage capacity is 30 GB, and click **Next: Add Tags**.

8. In the fifth step, *Add Tags*, verify that the instance has no tags. (Optional AWS tags allow you to label your AWS resources so that you can better manage many resources of the same type.) Click **Next: Configure Security Group**.

9. In the sixth step, *Configure Security Group*, note that the first time you set up an instance, *Create a new security group* is selected. See Figure 16-8. A security group is a list of firewall rules that control access to the VM. The group has a default name and one firewall rule that allows incoming RDP traffic to the instance from any IP address. Leave these default settings, and click **Review and Launch**. What is the security group name?

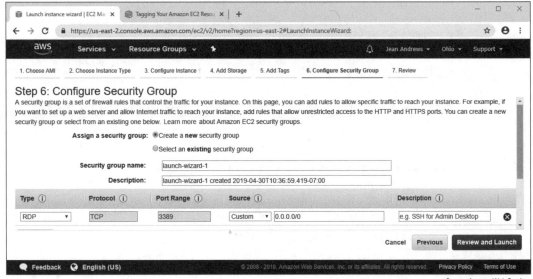

Source: Amazon Web Services

Figure 16-8   Configure the security group that controls access to the VM

10. In the seventh and final step, *Review*, review your selections and click **Launch**. What is the type and port range allowed for incoming traffic?

_____

11. The *Select an existing key pair or create a new key pair* box appears. A key pair is a public key and private key used for encryption when communicating with the VM. The first time you create an AWS VM, you must create a new key pair. In the first drop-down list, select **Create a new key pair**. Enter a Key pair name and click **Download Key Pair**. Save the key pair file to your desktop or a USB flash drive; the key pair file will have a PEM file extension. What is the path and file name of your PEM key pair file?

_____

> **📓 Notes** The next time you create an AWS VM, you can select *Choose an existing key pair*, point to your existing key pair file, and acknowledge you have access to the key pair.

12. Click **Launch Instances**. The instance is launched, initialized, and set to a running state, which can take a few minutes. To see your list of instances, click **View Instances**. It will take some time for your new instance to be created and then appear in the list. See Figure 16-9.

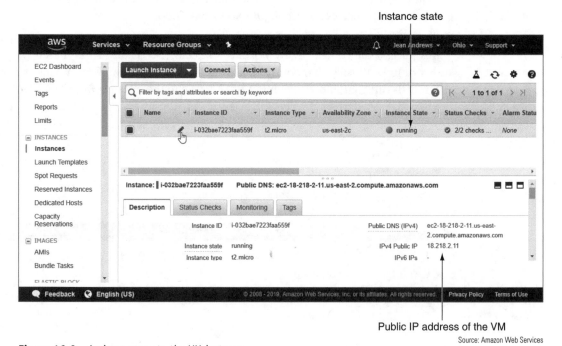

Figure 16-9   Assign a name to the VM instance

13. To change the name of your VM instance, click in the Name field, and enter a name.

◢ What is the name of your VM?

_____

◢ What is the IPv4 Public IP address of your VM?

_____

14. To connect to your VM, select it and click **Connect**. The *Connect To Your Instance* box appears (see Figure 16-10). What is the user name to your VM?

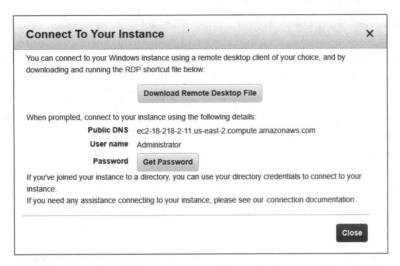

Connect To Your Instance   ✕

You can connect to your Windows instance using a remote desktop client of your choice, and by downloading and running the RDP shortcut file below:

    Download Remote Desktop File

When prompted, connect to your instance using the following details:

       Public DNS ec2-18-218-2-11.us-east-2.compute.amazonaws.com
       User name Administrator
       Password   Get Password

If you've joined your instance to a directory, you can use your directory credentials to connect to your instance.
If you need any assistance connecting to your instance, please see our connection documentation.

                                                                    Close

Figure 16-10 The Administrator password is required to connect to your VM

15. Click **Get Password**.

> **Notes** If AWS reports that the password is not yet available, click Close, wait a few moments, and try again. The VM is not yet fully initialized.

16. To communicate with the VM, you must provide the key pair. Click **Choose File** and point to the PEM file you saved earlier. Click **Open**. Click **Decrypt Password**.

17. The password appears in the *Connect To Your Instance* box. Select and copy the password. Open Notepad and paste the password into the Notepad file. Save the file to the same location as your key pair file. What is the name and path to the Notepad file that holds your VM password?

18. Your AWS VM instance is now created and ready to use. To practice stopping and starting your VM, click **Actions**, point to **Instance State** in the drop-down menu, and click **Stop**. Then click **Yes, Stop**. The VM takes a few moments to stop. Notice the Instance State is stopped.

19. To start your VM, click **Actions**, point to **Instance State**, and click **Start**. Click **Yes, Start**.

When you are finished working with AWS, it's a good habit to turn off all your VMs before you sign out.

PART 3: SET UP ACTIVE DIRECTORY DOMAIN SERVICES

To configure Active Directory Domain Services in Windows Server, follow these steps:

1. If necessary, go to **aws.amazon.com**, sign in to your AWS account, and click **EC2**. In the left pane, click **Instances**. Your list of VM instances appears. If necessary, start your VM. What is the IPv4 public IP address of your VM?

16

2. You can remote in to a Windows Server VM using Remote Desktop Connection or by downloading and running the RDP shortcut file provided by AWS. To use Remote Desktop Connection, enter the **mstsc** command in the Windows 10/7 search box or the Windows 8 Run box. In the Remote Desktop Connection box, enter the public IP address of your VM. Click **Connect**.

3. The Windows Security box appears. Enter **Administrator** as the user name. Open the Notepad file you saved earlier, and copy and paste the password stored in the file to the Windows Security box. Click **OK**. Click **Yes**. The Windows Server desktop appears in the Remote Desktop Connection window.

You are now ready to set up your Windows Active Directory domain. Follow these steps:

1. Click **Start** and click **Server Manager**. In the Server Manager window, under *Configure this local server*, click **Add roles and features**. The Add Roles and Features Wizard opens. Click **Next**.

2. In the *Select installation type* box, select **Role-based or feature-based installation**, and click **Next**.

3. In the *Select destination server* box, accept the default values and click **Next**.

4. Under *Select server roles*, check **Active Directory Domain Services**, and click **Add Features**.

5. Click **Next** three times to step through boxes in the wizard, accepting default values. The *Confirm installation selections* box appears. Check **Restart the destination server automatically if required**, and click **Yes**. Then click **Install**. Wait while the installation happens. You can click the flag in the upper-right corner of the Server Manager window to view the progress. When the installation completes, click **Close** to close the Add Roles and Features Wizard.

6. Click the notification flag in the Server Manager window, and then click **Promote this server to a domain controller**. The Deployment Configuration window appears. Select **Add a new forest**. Enter your root domain name. You can use **homerun.com**, as in the example in the main text, or another domain name. Click **Next**. What is your domain name?

_____

7. Wait while the Domain Controller Options window loads and completes initializing—it can take some time. Then enter the DSRM password twice, and click **Next**. (The Directory Services Restore Mode password is used when a technician needs to take Active Directory offline. Use a password that contains uppercase and lowercase letters, numbers, and at least eight characters.) Ignore any warning messages and click **Next** several times to step through the wizard. Finally, click **Install**. After the system reboots, you have a working domain controller.

PART 4: CONFIGURE AN OU, USER GROUP, AND USER

Follow these steps to set up one organizational unit (OU), one user group, and one user in your domain:

1. Return to your list of VM instances in AWS. If necessary, start your VM. What is the IPv4 public IP address for your VM?

_____

2. Remote in to your VM using Remote Desktop Connection. Open **Server Manager**.

3. To manage OUs, user groups, and users, click **Tools** and then click **Active Directory Users and Computers**. In the Active Directory Users and Computers window, expand the list under your domain name.

4. By default, your domain has one OU: Domain Controllers. To create an OU named Finances directly under the domain, right-click the domain name, point to **New**, and click **Organizational Unit**. Name the OU **Finances**. Click **OK**. The Finances OU is created.

5. To create the Accountants user group in the Finances OU, right-click **Finances**, point to **New**, and click **Group**. Enter **Accountants** for the group name and click **OK**.

6. To add a user to the Finances OU, right-click **Finances**, point to **New**, and click **User**. Enter the information for **Samuel Adams**, whose sign-in name is **Samuel**. Enter **Passw0rd** for the password.

7. To add Samuel to the Accountants group, right-click **Samuel Adams** and click **Add to a group**. In the object names area, type **Accountants** and click **OK**. Click **OK** again.

8. To verify that Samuel is in the Accountants group, double-click the **Accountants** group and click the **Members** tab. Click **Cancel**.

9. When you're finished working with your VM, avoid accumulating any charges against your free quota by shutting down the server VM in the Remote Desktop Connection box or in the AWS window of your browser.

> **Notes** If you are finished with your AWS account, you can close the account. (If you close the account, you will not be allowed to open another AWS account using the same email address.) To close the account, click your account name in the AWS window, and click **My Account**. Scroll down to the bottom of the page, and check all boxes under Close Account. Then click **Close Account**.

REVIEW QUESTIONS

1. In this lab, you allowed access to your VM from any source IP address. How could you limit access to only one subnet of IP addresses?

2. In your security group, which port did you open to allow incoming traffic to your VM?

3. Describe the purpose of a key pair file in AWS.

4. In this lab, did your VM use a dynamic public IP address or a static public IP address?

5. After you installed Active Directory in Windows Server, what did you have to do next before you could set up a domain in Active Directory?

6. If you want to access your AWS VM from various computers, what file must you have available?

16

Security Strategies

Labs included in this chapter:

- **Lab 17.1:** Monitor Security Events
- **Lab 17.2:** Audit Access to Private Folders
- **Lab 17.3:** Use Encryption
- **Lab 17.4:** Secure a Workstation
- **Lab 17.5:** Design for Physical Security
- **Lab 17.6:** Protect against Malware
- **Lab 17.7:** Download and Use Microsoft Security Essentials in Windows 7

LAB 17.1 MONITOR SECURITY EVENTS

OBJECTIVES

The goal of this lab is to use Event Viewer to monitor security events such as failed attempts to sign in to the system or changes to files and folders. Multiple failed attempts at signing in to a system can indicate a potential hacker, and sometimes audit reports can help identify unauthorized use of a file or folder. After completing this lab, you will be able to:

▲ Use the Local Security Policy tool in Control Panel to set policies to monitor failed sign-in attempts and changes to files and folders

▲ Use Event Viewer to monitor the events of failed sign-ins and changes to files and folders

MATERIALS REQUIRED

This lab requires the following:

▲ Windows 10/8/7 operating system, Professional or higher edition

▲ An account with administrator privileges

LAB PREPARATION

Before the lab begins, the instructor or lab assistant needs to do the following:

▲ Verify that Windows starts with no errors

▲ Verify that each student has access to a user account with administrator privileges

ACTIVITY BACKGROUND

As part of its efforts to manage the security of a computer or network, your organization might ask you to report incidents of suspicious events, such as failed attempts to sign in (indicating a potential hacker) or unauthorized changes to certain files. For example, suppose an employee is suspected of stealing from the company; you might be called on to monitor any changes to the bookkeeping files to which this employee has read-and-write access but would not normally edit.

You can track auditing events by setting policies using the Local Security Policy tool and then by using Event Viewer to monitor the logged events.

The Local Security Policy tool is one of the Administrative tools available in Control Panel. The tool creates security policies that apply only to the local computer. If you had to set other policies, you would need to use Group Policy, which covers a wider range of policies than does the Local Security Policy tool.

ESTIMATED COMPLETION TIME: 30 MINUTES

 Activity

Repeated failures to sign in to a system might indicate someone is trying to guess a password and gain unauthorized access to a user account. Follow these steps to use Local Security Policy to monitor failures when someone is attempting to sign in to the system:

1. Sign in as an administrator, and create a new standard user account called **Newuser**. Create a password for this new user account. What is the password?

2. Using Control Panel, open **Administrative Tools**. Double-click **Local Security Policy**. The Local Security Policy window opens.

3. Expand the **Local Policies** group, and select **Audit Policy**. How many policies appear in the right pane for the Audit Policy group?

4. Double-click **Audit account logon events** to open the Audit account logon events Properties dialog box. Check the **Failure** check box, as shown in Figure 17-1, and then click **OK**. Also enable failure auditing for the **Audit logon events policy**.

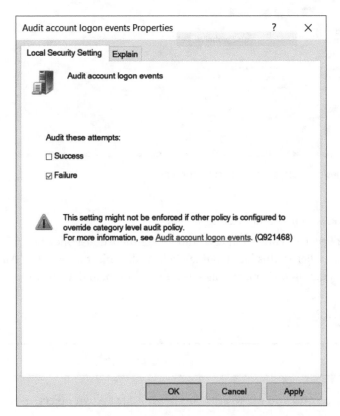

Figure 17-1 Local Security Policy set to audit failed sign-in events

5. Examine the other Audit Policy policies. Which one would you use to monitor when a password is changed? Close the Local Security Policy window.

6. To see the logged audit events, open **Event Viewer** from the Administrative Tools window. In the left pane, click **Windows Logs**, and then click **Security**. How many events are logged in this group of events? Open the Security logs. Does Event Viewer currently list any sign-in failures?

7. Sign out, and attempt to sign in to the Newuser account using an incorrect password.

8. Sign back in using an administrator account.

9. Open **Event Viewer** and again click **Security**, as shown in Figure 17-2. What is the date and time that Windows recorded for the failed sign-in attempt?

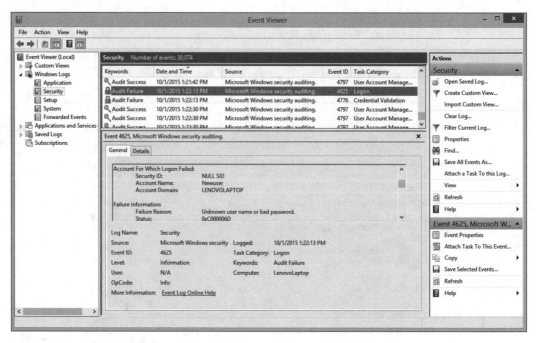

Figure 17-2   Event Viewer displays the failed sign-in event

Follow these steps to monitor changes to files and folders:

1. Open the **Local Security Policy** window, and locate the Audit Policy policies, as you did in Steps 2 and 3 earlier in this lab. Double-click **Audit object access**. The Audit object access Properties dialog box opens. Click the **Explain** tab, and answer the following questions:

   ◢ What is a SACL?

   _____

   _____

   ◢ Which dialog box do you use to set a SACL for a file system object?

   _____

2. On the Local Security Setting tab, check the **Success** and **Failure** check boxes, and then click **OK**.

3. Close the Local Security Policy window.

4. Now let's set Windows to audit activity in the Public folder. To do so, open **File Explorer** or **Windows Explorer**, open the **Properties** dialog box of the C:\Users\Public folder, and click the **Security** tab.

5. Click **Advanced**, select the **Auditing** tab, and then click **Continue**.

6. The Advanced Security Settings for Public dialog box opens. You can now add users or groups that you want to monitor. Click **Add**. In Windows 10/8, click **Select a principal**. Add the Newuser profile.

7. Close the Select User or Group window.

8. In Windows 10/8, change the Type to **All**, and check **Full Control**. Close the Auditing Entry for Public dialog box. In Windows 7, check the **Full control** check boxes in the

Successful and Failed columns, and close the Auditing Entry for Public dialog box. Close the Advanced Security Settings for Public dialog box. If errors appear, click **Continue** to close each box.

9. Close all windows and sign out of the system.

10. Sign in as **Newuser** and open the **C:\Users\Public** folder. While you're there, use Notepad to create a short text file, and save it to this location. What did you name your text file?

_____

11. Sign out as Newuser, and sign back in using your administrator account.

12. Open **Event Viewer**. In the left pane, select **Event Viewer (Local)**. In the Summary of Administrative Events section, double-click **Audit Success** to open that group of events. Double-click the first event in the group named **Microsoft Windows security auditing**. Maximize the window so you can easily view information about each event.

13. Explore the recent events in this section until you find the ones that are associated with Newuser's activity in the C:\Users\Public folder. You might need to search other Microsoft Windows security auditing events to find the relevant events. About how many events were created?

_____

14. List one event that is related to the creation of the new text file:

_____

15. Close all open windows.

REVIEW QUESTIONS

1. How can you use Local Security Policy to determine if someone has tried to hack into a user account?

_____

_____

2. When securing a system, why is it important to audit failed attempts to access files?

_____

_____

3. Which policy would you use to monitor when a user changes her password?

_____

4. In this lab, you monitored the activity of a single user. What would be a more efficient way to monitor the activities of a collection of users?

_____

5. Why does accessing one file create multiple events?

_____

_____

17

LAB 17.2 AUDIT ACCESS TO PRIVATE FOLDERS

OBJECTIVES

Your goal in this lab is to learn how to set up folder auditing so that you can determine if unauthorized users attempt to access a private folder. After completing this lab, you will be able to:

▲ Use a local security policy to require a password for all user accounts

▲ Configure Windows to log attempts to access a private folder

▲ View the event log for folder access attempts

MATERIALS REQUIRED

This lab requires the following:

▲ Windows 10/8/7 operating system, Professional or higher edition

▲ An account with administrator privileges

LAB PREPARATION

Before the lab begins, the instructor or lab assistant needs to do the following:

▲ Verify that Windows starts with no errors

▲ Verify that each student has access to a user account with administrator privileges

ACTIVITY BACKGROUND

Although auditing of file and folder access is usually not necessary for home computers with only a few trusted users, it can be useful in a networked environment with many users where all users are not trusted with complete access to all resources. You can set up Windows to audit activity on a file or folder so that whenever the file or folder is accessed, this activity is recorded in a log. Each user has a user profile in the C:\Users folder, and a standard user should not be able to access the folders that belong to another user. In this lab, you set up a user profile, configure Windows to audit the folder, attempt to access the folder, and verify that the access attempt was logged.

ESTIMATED COMPLETION TIME: 30 MINUTES

 Activity

PART 1: SET A LOCAL SECURITY POLICY TO REQUIRE PASSWORDS FOR USER ACCOUNTS

In the first part of the lab, you set a local security policy to require a password on all accounts. To see the effect of the policy, you create one standard user before you set the security policy in order to verify that a password is not required for the account. Then, you create another user after you set the policy and verify that a password is now required. Recall that the Local Group Policy Editor is only available in Windows 10/8 Professional and Enterprise editions or Windows 7 Professional, Ultimate, and Enterprise editions, and can be run only by an administrator. Do the following to create a standard user account:

1. Sign in to the computer as an administrator.

2. Using the Computer Management window, create a standard user named **User1**, without a password.

3. Sign out and sign back in as **User1**. Note that you are not prompted for a password. When a user first signs in, his user profile namespace is created in the C:\Users folder. These folders are private and can be accessed only by the owner of the folder and administrators.

Do the following to set the local security policy:

1. Sign out and sign back in as an administrator. Use **gpedit.msc** to open the Local Group Policy Editor console.

2. In the left pane, navigate to **Computer Configuration, Windows Settings, Security Settings**, and **Account Policies**, and then select **Password Policy**.

3. Double-click **Minimum password length** in the right pane. When the Minimum password length Properties dialog box opens, click the **Explain** tab, and read the information about password length.

4. Click the **Local Security Setting** tab, enter a non-zero value in the text box, and then click **OK**. Close the Local Group Policy Editor console.

Any new user accounts created will now need a password. Existing user accounts will not be affected until their passwords are created or changed. To verify this, you'll create another user account, and then sign in with that account. Follow these steps:

1. Create a standard user named **User2**, without a password. An error message reports that the minimum password requirement was not met. Add the password and create the user. Write down the password for User2 here:

_____

2. Sign out of the computer. Sign in as **User2**.

PART 2: ATTEMPT TO ACCESS A PRIVATE FOLDER

To verify that User1's folders are not accessible to other users, attempt to access the folders while you are signed in as User2. Follow these steps:

1. In the address bar of File Explorer or Windows Explorer, type **C:\Users\User2** to navigate to the folders that belong to this user. A user has full access to his own private folders.

2. In the address bar of File Explorer or Windows Explorer, type **C:\Users\User1**. A message informs you that you don't have access to the folder. Click **Continue**, and note that you must supply an administrator password to open the folder. Click **No**, and sign out of the computer.

PART 3: AUDIT FOLDER ACCESS

In this part of the lab, you configure Windows to audit access attempts on the private folders that belong to another user. First, you enable auditing in Group Policy, and then you configure auditing options on a specific folder in the folder's Properties window. Follow these steps:

1. Sign in to the computer as an administrator. Use **gpedit.msc** to open the Local Group Policy Editor console again.

2. In the left pane, navigate to **Computer Configuration, Windows Settings, Security Settings**, and **Local Policies**, and then click **Audit Policy**.

3. Open the **Audit object access Properties** dialog box. Note that you can audit successful attempts, failures, or both. For the purposes of this lab, you'll audit failures only. Check the **Failure** check box, and if necessary, uncheck the **Success** check box. See Figure 17-3. Click **OK**. Close the Local Group Policy Editor console.

17

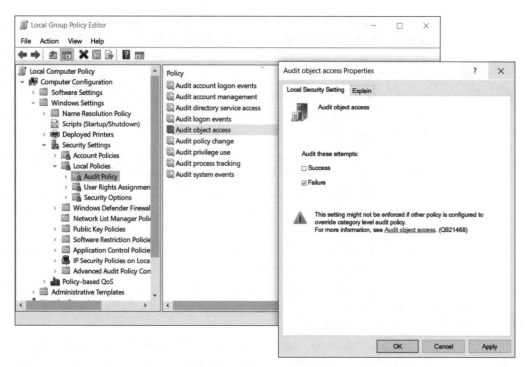

Figure 17-3   Only audit failed attempts to access an object

Next, you edit the properties of the C:\Users\User1 folder to enable auditing for that folder. Follow these steps:

1. In File Explorer or Windows Explorer, navigate to C:\Users, and right-click the **User1** folder. If a warning dialog box opens, click **Continue** to access the User1 folder.

2. Select **Properties** in the shortcut menu, and then click the **Security** tab. Click **Advanced**, click the **Auditing** tab, and then click **Continue** to view the folder's auditing properties. The Advanced Security Settings for User1 dialog box opens.

> **Notes**   Only administrator accounts are able to use the Advanced Security Settings dialog box.

3. The auditing entries box will be blank because no entries have been added yet. Click the **Add** button, and in Windows 10/8, click **Select a principal**, type **Everyone** in the Select User or Group dialog box, and then click **OK**.

> **Notes**   To delete an auditing entry you find already listed, select it and then click **Remove**.

4. In Windows 10/8, change the type to **Fail**. If necessary, click **Show advanced permissions**. Check the **Traverse folder/execute file** check box and the **List folder/read data** check box, as shown in Figure 17-4. In Windows 7, open the **Auditing Entry for User1** dialog box, and place check marks in the **Failed** column for Traverse folder/execute file and List folder/read data. At the bottom of the dialog box, select the option to apply these auditing settings only to objects and/or containers within this container. Close the open dialog boxes. When you click OK to apply the changes, you might receive an Error Applying Security message. Some folders will not allow this audit policy to be applied. Click **Continue** to continue applying the audit policy to other folders. You might have to address this error message several times.

5. Sign out of the administrator account.

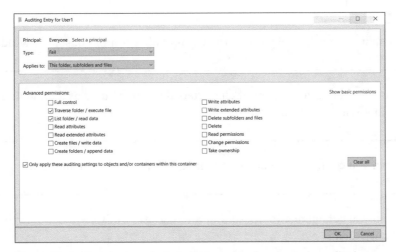

Figure 17-4 Use check marks to indicate types of access to be audited

Next, you attempt to access the User1 folder with an unauthorized account. Then, you view the event that is logged in the Event Viewer. Follow these steps:

1. Sign in to the computer as User2. As you did before, attempt to navigate to the **C:\Users\User1** folder. You should get the same message informing you that you don't have access to the folder.

2. Sign out as User2, and sign back in as an administrator. Use **eventvwr.msc** to open Event Viewer.

3. In the left pane, expand **Windows Logs**, and then select **Security**.

4. In the middle pane, scroll through the list of events (if necessary), and look for an event for which "Audit Failure" appears in the Keywords column and "File System" appears in the Task Category column. There might be more than one event listed.

5. Double-click the event and read the description in the top section of the General tab of the Event Properties dialog box. (You might need to scroll or resize the window to see all the details.) Note that the account name (User2) and the object name (C:\Users\User1) are both listed, as shown in Figure 17-5.

6. Close any open windows.

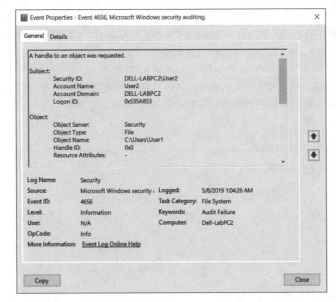

Figure 17-5 Use Event Properties to display details of an event

REVIEW QUESTIONS

1. Why might you not be able to find the Group Policy Editor console in Windows?

_____

2. What is the maximum number of characters that can be used as a minimum password length in a Windows 10 password?

_____

3. How can you configure Windows so that passwords are not required for user accounts?

_____

4. How can you configure a folder so that another user can view the files in the folder but not change them?

_____

_____

5. What group policy needs to be set to allow auditing of folder access attempts?

_____

6. Why is it important to require passwords for all user accounts on a computer when you want to audit access to a folder?

_____

7. What prevents a standard user from disabling auditing on a Windows computer?

_____

LAB 17.3 USE ENCRYPTION

OBJECTIVES

The goal of this lab is to work with Windows file and folder encryption. File or folder encryption is one method you can use when you want to secure important and private data. In this lab, you learn how to encrypt a folder and how to back up your encryption key. You also learn what happens when someone tries to use an encrypted file without permission, and how to move encrypted files from one storage device to another and from one computer to another. After completing this lab, you will be able to:

◢ Encrypt a folder

◢ Save files to the encrypted folder

◢ Back up the encryption certificate key

◢ Attempt to access the encrypted files as a different user

◢ Observe what happens when you move or copy an encrypted file or folder to another computer

MATERIALS REQUIRED

This lab requires the following:

▲ Windows 10/8/7 operating system, Professional or higher edition

▲ An account with administrator privileges

LAB PREPARATION

Before the lab begins, the instructor or lab assistant needs to do the following:

▲ Verify that Windows starts with no errors

▲ Verify that each student has access to a user account with administrator privileges

ACTIVITY BACKGROUND

Despite your best efforts to set secured permissions to files and folders, unauthorized users might still gain access to sensitive files. To further decrease the possibility of this type of security breach, you can use file encryption, which prevents unauthorized users from being able to view files, even if they do manage to gain access to them. The EFS (Encrypting File System) is a Windows feature that allows a user to store information on her hard drive in an encrypted format.

You can encrypt individual files or entire folders. Encryption is the strongest protection that the operating system offers to keep your information secure. The EFS is available on hard drives that are set up as NTFS drives. In this lab, you create and encrypt a folder and its contents. Then, you test the encryption and back up the encryption certificate key. Finally, you learn how to decrypt a file and move an encrypted file to another computer.

ESTIMATED COMPLETION TIME: 30 MINUTES

 Activity

Follow these steps to prepare your system for this lab:

1. Sign in as an administrator.

2. Create a new standard user account. Assign a password to the account. List the name and password of the new account:

_____

3. In File Explorer or Windows Explorer, open the **Documents** folder.

4. Create two folders named **Normal Test** and **Encrypted Test** in the Documents folder.

5. Create a text document in each folder. Name each document **TestFile**.

Now that you have the system prepared, let's work with the Encrypting File System. Follow these steps:

1. In the Documents folder, right-click the **Encrypted Test** folder, and select **Properties** in the shortcut menu.

2. On the General tab of the Encrypted Test Properties dialog box, click **Advanced**.

3. The Advanced Attributes dialog box appears. Check the **Encrypt contents to secure data** check box, and click **OK**.

4. Click **OK** to close the Encrypted Test Properties dialog box.

5. A Confirm Attribute Changes dialog box opens. This dialog box indicates that the attribute *encrypt* has been chosen and asks how you want to apply this attribute. Select **Apply changes to this folder, subfolders and files**. Click **OK** to close the dialog box. A notification might appear and remind you to back up your file encryption certificate and key.

17

When you start encrypting information, it is important to back up your encryption certificate. This is your key that unlocks the data. If you lose this key or the key becomes damaged and you didn't make a backup, the encrypted information can forever remain locked.

Follow these steps to create a backup of the encryption certificate:

1. Use **certmgr.msc** to open the certmgr window (see the left side of Figure 17-6).

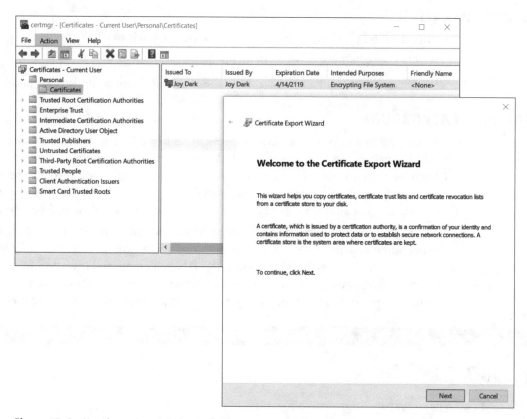

Figure 17-6   Use the certmgr window to back up encryption keys

2. In the left pane, select **Personal**, and then **Certificates**. In the right pane, select the certificate that shows **Encrypting File System** in the Intended Purposes column, as shown in Figure 17-6. If more than one certificate is listed, select them all.

3. On the menu bar, click **Action**, click **All Tasks**, and then click **Export**. The Certificate Export Wizard opens, as shown on the right side of Figure 17-6. Click **Next**.

4. Select **Yes, export the private key**, and click **Next**.

5. Select **Personal Information Exchange** for the file format and click **Next**. The backup of the key will be saved in a PFX (.pfx) file.

6. Create a password for your key. Click **Next**. Write the password:

_____

7. Click **Browse**. Navigate to where you want to save the file, name the file **Encryption Key Backup,** and click **Save**. What is the exact path and name of the file, including the file extension?

_____

8. To complete the process, click **Next,** click **Finish,** and then click **OK**.

Now that you have encrypted a folder and backed up the encryption key, let's investigate how an encrypted folder works. Follow these steps:

1. Open **File Explorer** or **Windows Explorer**. In the Documents folder, what is the new color of the Encrypted Test folder name? What is the color of the file name in this folder?

> **Notes** If the folder is not shown in a different color, you can adjust that setting. In Windows 10/8, open the **View ribbon**, and then click **Options** to open the Folder Options dialog box. In Windows 7, click **Organize** in the window toolbar, and then click **Folder and search options**. In the Folder Options dialog box, click the **View** tab, and check the **Show encrypted or compressed NTFS files in color** check box (see Figure 17-7). Click **OK**.

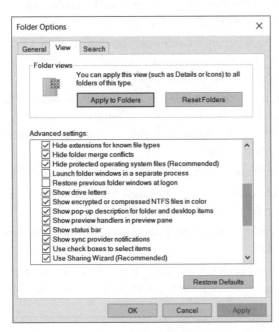

Figure 17-7 Change the way folders and files appear in File Explorer or Windows Explorer

2. Verify that the file in the Encrypted Test folder is encrypted. How did you verify that encryption is applied?

---

3. Copy both the **Normal Test** folder and **Encrypted Test** folder to the root of drive C:. Are the contents of the *copied* Encrypted Test folder encrypted? How do you know?

---

4. Copy the **Normal Test** folder and the **Encrypted Test** folder to a USB flash drive. Are the contents of the *copied* Encrypted Test folder encrypted? How do you know?

---

5. Sign out, and then sign in using the standard user account you created earlier in this lab.

17

6. Open **File Explorer** or **Windows Explorer**, and locate the Normal Test folder in the root of drive C:. Describe what happens when you double-click the file in the Normal Test folder:

_____

7. Locate the Encrypted Test folder in the root of drive C:. Describe what happens when you double-click the file in the Encrypted Test folder:

_____

8. Sign out, and then sign in using your administrator account.

9. Upon reaching the desktop, return to the encrypted folder in the Documents folder.

Let's assume you have used a USB flash drive to move your files to another computer that supports the Encrypting File System. When you do so, the files are still encrypted. However, you will not be able to use them unless you use your private key to access the files. You must import the private key to the new computer. Follow these steps to see how the process works:

1. To import or install your private key on a computer, you must use the Certificate Import Wizard. To launch it, double-click the **Encryption Key Backup** file you created earlier. The Certificate Import Wizard opens. Click **Next** two times.

2. Enter the password you created for the private key file, and then click **Next**. In the Certificate Store box, click **Next**. Click **Finish**. The wizard reports the import was successful. Click **OK**. Now that your private key is installed, you can use the encrypted files and folders you have moved to this computer.

At times you may need to decrypt a folder or file to return it to unrestricted use. Follow these steps:

1. In the Documents folder, right-click the **Encrypted Test** folder that you made earlier. Click **Properties**. On the **General** tab, click **Advanced**.

2. In the Advanced Attributes dialog box, uncheck the **Encrypt contents to secure data** check box. Click **OK**. Click **OK** again.

3. To confirm the attribute change, click **OK**. Verify that the file in the Encrypted Test folder is no longer encrypted. Explain how you know the file is no longer encrypted:

_____

_____

REVIEW QUESTIONS

1. Which file system must be used to enable encryption?

_____

2. What is necessary so that a USB flash drive can be used to hold encrypted files and folders?

_____

3. When you move an encrypted file from one computer to a second computer, what must you do first before you can open the encrypted file on the second computer?

_____

_____

4. What happens to encryption when you move an encrypted file to a Windows 8 or Windows 7 Home Premium computer? Explain your answer:

_____

_____

5. What is the file extension for an exported certificate backup file?

_____

6. Why is it necessary to back up or export your encryption certificate key?

_____

_____

7. (Challenge Question) Why is encryption available in the NTFS file system but not in the FAT32 file system?

_____

_____

LAB 17.4 SECURE A WORKSTATION

OBJECTIVES

Your goal in this lab is to learn how to secure a Windows workstation. After completing this lab, you will be able to:

◢ Require that all users press Ctrl+Alt+Del to sign in

◢ Require a password after the computer goes to sleep or screen saver mode

◢ Set a local security policy

MATERIALS REQUIRED

This lab requires the following:

◢ Windows 10/8/7 operating system, Professional or higher edition

◢ An account with administrator privileges

LAB PREPARATION

Before the lab begins, the instructor or lab assistant needs to do the following:

◢ Verify that Windows starts with no errors

◢ Verify that each student has access to a user account with administrator privileges

ACTIVITY BACKGROUND

Securing a workstation is one of the most important tasks you can perform when setting up security for an organization or individual. Windows provides some default security settings; however, these default settings are often exploited by malicious programs, thieves, and hackers. A few simple tweaks to your computer's security policy greatly improve the security of your system.

17

Activity

Follow these steps to require that a user press Ctrl+Alt+Del to sign in:

1. Use **netplwiz** to open the User Accounts dialog box. Write down the user names displayed in the User Accounts dialog box:

---

2. Select the **Advanced** tab, and under *Secure sign-in* or *Secure logon,* check the **Require users to press Ctrl+Alt+Delete** check box.

> **Notes** If the option in Step 2 is grayed out, you can change the option in the Local Group Policy Editor. To do this, open the **Local Group Policy Editor**, and navigate to **Computer Configuration, Windows Settings, Security Settings, Local Policies,** and then **Security Options.** Open the **Interactive logon: Do not require CTRL+ALT+DEL** policy, and disable it.

3. Apply the changes. Restart the computer to confirm that the change has taken effect.

Follow these steps to secure the computer using a screen saver and sleep mode:

1. In Windows 10, open the **Settings** app, navigate to **Accounts,** and then navigate to **Sign-in options.** Under Require sign-in, select **When PC wakes up from sleep.** In Windows 8/7, open **Control Panel.** Select **Power Options,** and select **Require a password on wakeup** or **Require a password when the computer wakes.**

2. Under "Password protection on wakeup," make sure **Require a password (recommended)** is selected. If you need to change this setting, you might need to first click **Change settings that are currently unavailable.**

3. Save your changes and close all windows.

4. In Windows 10, open the **Settings** app, navigate to **Personalization** and then **Lock screen,** and select **Screen saver settings.** In Windows 8, from the Start screen, type **Screen Saver,** and select **Change screen saver** from the search results. In Windows 7, click **Start,** type **Screen Saver** in the search box, and press **Enter.** The Screen Saver Settings dialog box opens.

5. Select a screen saver from the drop-down menu to activate the screen saver function.

6. Check the **On Resume, display logon screen** check box. Apply your changes, and close all windows.

Follow these steps to require that all users have a password:

1. Open the **Local Group Policy Editor** console.

2. Navigate to **Computer Configuration, Windows Settings, Security Settings, Account Policies,** and then the **Password Policy** group.

3. Change the Minimum password length policy to a value higher than zero. How many characters did you require?

Follow these steps to secure the computer using BIOS/UEFI settings:

1. Restart the computer, and access BIOS/UEFI setup. To access this setup, you need to press a key or combination of keys at the beginning of the boot. Look for a message to tell you which key(s) to press (for example, F2, Del, or F12).

2. After you are in the BIOS/UEFI setup utility, find the screen to change the security settings.

3. Enter a value for the password that must be entered in order to boot up the computer. This password might be called the power-on password, system password, boot password, or another name. Write down the name for this password given on your BIOS/UEFI setup screen and the password you assigned:

   _____

4. Enter a value for the password that must be entered in order to make changes to the BIOS/UEFI settings. This password might be called the admin password, the supervisor password, or another name. Answer the following questions:

   ◢ What is the name for the admin password as described on your BIOS/UEFI setup screen, and what is the password you assigned to it?

   _____

   ◢ Does your BIOS/UEFI setup support encrypting the hard drive? If so, describe the feature in BIOS/UEFI setup:

   _____

   _____

   ◢ What other passwords does your BIOS/UEFI setup offer that can be used to secure the computer? Name and describe each password:

   _____

   _____

   _____

5. Save your changes and restart the computer.

Do the following to test the security settings you created in this lab and record the results of your test:

1. When the computer starts up, what message appears and asks you for the power-on password?

   _____

2. Were you required to press Ctrl+Alt+Del before you could see the Windows sign-in screen?

   _____

3. After you reach the Windows desktop, put the computer in sleep mode. Were you required to enter your Windows password before you could wake up the computer?

   _____

4. Use the Computer Management window to create a new user account with no password. Then, sign out and sign back in using the new user account. At what point

17

in this process did you receive a message that required you to create a password for the user account?

_____

5. Did any of the security measures you implemented in this lab fail during this testing process? If so, what was the cause of the problem?

_____

REVIEW QUESTIONS

1. Why is it preferable to require the Ctrl+Alt+Del key combination for sign-in?

_____

_____

2. Why would you want to require a password to sign in after the screen saver activates or the computer comes back on from sleep mode?

_____

_____

3. How many characters should the minimum password length be for best security practice?

_____

4. What does setting the admin password (sometimes called the supervisor password) in BIOS/UEFI accomplish?

_____

5. Why would you want a power-on password?

_____

_____

_____

6. Should you rely only on the Windows password to protect your sensitive data stored on the hard drive? Explain your answer:

_____

_____

_____

_____

_____

LAB 17.5 DESIGN FOR PHYSICAL SECURITY

OBJECTIVES

The goal of this lab is to walk through methods of providing security for the computing infrastructure inside your organization. After completing this lab, you will be able to:

▲ Identify ways that your software-level security can be defeated

▲ Implement real-world access controls

▲ Consider the role that a building layout plays in your security design

MATERIALS REQUIRED

This lab requires the following:

▲ Pen and paper

▲ A computer or tablet with Internet access

LAB PREPARATION

Before the lab begins, the instructor or lab assistant needs to do the following:

▲ Verify that computers or tablets have Internet access

ACTIVITY BACKGROUND

You have learned how to use software to secure data, but there is no such thing as data that cannot be compromised. As we have seen several times, high-profile government agencies have lost sensitive data over the past 10 years. In this lab, you learn that good security must be built in from the ground up. First, you learn about some high-profile breaches and how they happened, and then you examine some security issues you need to consider before you even install equipment.

ESTIMATED COMPLETION TIME: 30–45 MINUTES

 Activity

PART 1: HOW DATA BREACHES HAPPEN

Let's do some quick research to see how some notable data breaches have happened. You can keep this information in mind as you plan for security.

1. Go online and search on **Bradley Manning** to read about how thousands of U.S. State Department documents were released to Wikileaks. Write a brief description of what happened.

_____

_____

17

2. What steps could the U.S. Army have taken to prevent this data breach?

_____

3. Now research **Reality Winner**. How did this breach happen?

_____

_____

4. What could the U.S. Air Force have done differently to prevent this data breach?

_____

_____

5. Research **Edward Snowden**. How did this breach happen?

_____

_____

6. What could the NSA have done to prevent the Snowden breach?

_____

_____

> **Notes** The Snowden breach reminds us that sometimes you can do everything well to secure a network but a breach can still happen. (In this case, however, the NSA did have some outdated software that partially enabled the breach.)

7. Research the **2017 Equifax Data Breach**. How did this happen?

_____

_____

8. What could Equifax have done differently to prevent this breach?

_____

_____

PART 2: NETWORK LAYOUT FOR SECURITY

Before you buy and install any computer equipment, you need to have a good plan in place because good security begins with good planning. An important part of your design is to provide a safe place for computer equipment. This is important not just for proper functioning but also for security. For example, if you have ever worked at a corporate job, you know that keys to the IT closets are tracked closely. As you begin your security plan, start with the architectural plans for the building. A snip of one plan is shown in Figure 17-8, which includes the location of a telecom closet. As you examine this plan, keep in mind how the breaches from the previous section occurred and what could have prevented them.

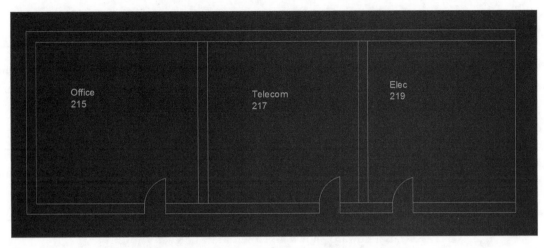

Figure 17-8 Section of a blueprint showing the location of an IT telecom closet

Follow these steps to go through the process of setting up computer equipment from the viewpoint of ensuring security:

1. Examine the location of the telecom closet in the blueprint in Figure 17-8. Why is it common for IT departments to have closets that they do not share with other groups inside the same company?

   _____

2. What is the minimum level of security that you would expect a telecom closet to have?

   _____

   _____

3. In many businesses, it is common to have a keycard-style access control to get in and out of the building or into other sections of the building. What major benefit does a centralized access control system offer that simple locks and keys cannot?

   _____

   _____

4. Figure 17-9 shows a typical server room. How many ways can you get into the server room?

   _____

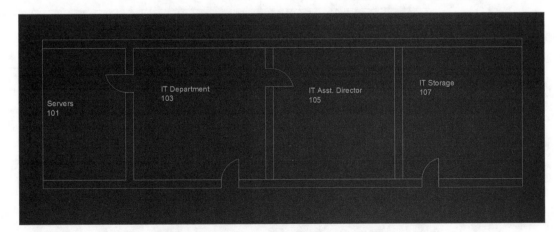

Figure 17-9 Section of a blueprint showing the location of a server room and IT staff

17

5. What is the benefit of having the server room located behind the IT staff?

_____

6. In Figure 17-9, you see a room dedicated to the IT staff. Why do you think this room has doors that can be closed and locked, as opposed to an open-air (cube farm) model?

_____

_____

7. Occasionally, somebody from outside your organization may need to access the server room. What policies should be in place for granting access, and why?

_____

_____

8. Why is it so important to keep track of who had access to the equipment, and servers in particular?

_____

_____

REVIEW QUESTIONS

1. Why is it important to enforce access controls and to keep logs regarding who has access to data closets?

_____

_____

2. What can you do to prevent credentialed users from causing data breaches?

_____

_____

3. What are effective ways to design a building for good security?

_____

_____

4. Who is responsible for security of computing infrastructure?

_____

LAB 17.6 PROTECT AGAINST MALWARE

OBJECTIVES

The goal of this lab is to verify that your computer is clean of malicious programs by using Windows Defender or free malware removal software. After completing this lab, you will be able to:

▲ Make sure Windows Defender is turned on

▲ Check for and install the latest Windows Defender updates

▲ Scan for spyware or other malicious software infecting your computer

MATERIALS REQUIRED

This lab requires the following:

▲ Windows 10/8 operating system

▲ Internet access

LAB PREPARATION

Before the lab begins, the instructor or lab assistant needs to do the following:

▲ Verify that Windows starts with no errors

▲ Verify that Internet access is available

▲ Perform a backup of important files if necessary

ACTIVITY BACKGROUND

Malware removal software is one of the largest-growing technology sectors today, as new malicious programs continually flood the Internet. Malware removal software is useful because malware hides from the user and is difficult to detect. As a user surfs the web, malware can be downloaded and installed without the user's knowledge or consent.

Microsoft Windows offers Windows Defender to protect a system against spyware, rootkits, viruses, and other malware. Once you turn on Windows Defender, it will run automatically to scan for malware or other unwanted programs. Definitions need to be updated daily to keep up with new malware.

> **Notes** Microsoft recommends Windows Defender as the only software you need in Windows 10 to protect against malware. If Windows finds another anti-malware program running on your computer, it automatically turns off Defender. When you turn off or uninstall the other anti-malware program, Windows Defender is automatically turned on.

17

ESTIMATED COMPLETION TIME: 15 MINUTES

 Activity

This lab is divided into two parts. Part 1 covers how to use the Windows 10 Windows Defender Security Center, and Part 2 covers how to use Windows Defender in Windows 8.

PART 1: WINDOWS 10 WINDOWS DEFENDER SECURITY CENTER

Windows Defender Security Center brings Windows 10 security features to one location. Follow these steps to turn off other anti-malware software and then explore the Windows 10 Windows Defender Security Center:

1. To find out if anti-malware software other than Windows Defender is running, open **Control Panel** in Large icons view. Click **Security and Maintenance**. Click the **Security** title to expand the Security section. Under Virus protection, click **View installed antivirus apps**. (If this link is missing, no anti-malware program other than Windows Defender is installed.) Figure 17-10 shows all installed anti-malware apps, including Windows Defender Antivirus. What anti-malware programs are listed?

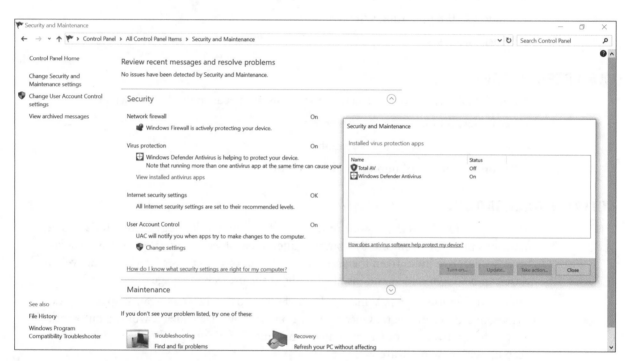

Figure 17-10   Use Control Panel to review installed anti-malware apps

2. If you find that anti-malware software other than Windows Defender is running, turn off this anti-malware program. Click **Close** and then close Control Panel.

3. To open the Windows Defender Security Center, open the **Settings** app, and click the **Update & Security** group. Click **Windows Security,** and then click **Open Windows Defender Security Center.** The Windows Defender Security Center window shown in Figure 17-11 indicates that the computer is potentially unprotected.

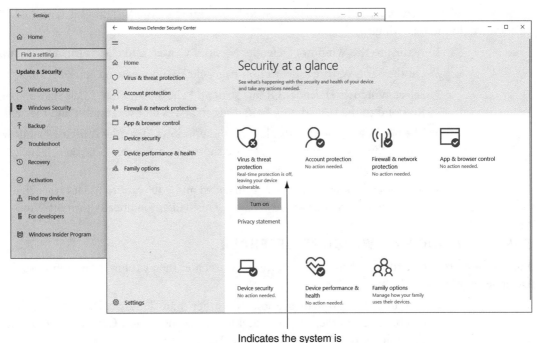

Indicates the system is
not protected

Figure 17-11 Windows Defender Security Center shows the computer's health and security risks to the
computer

4. If your real-time protection for viruses is currently turned off, as it is in Figure 17-11,
click the **Turn on** button. Respond to the UAC box if necessary.

5. Open the **Virus & threat protection** group, and then click **Virus & threat protection
updates**.

6. Click **Check for updates** to update your definitions.

After the virus and spyware definitions have finished updating, you can scan your computer with the
most recent defenses against malware that Windows Defender offers.

> **Notes** If you want to infect your computer with a test virus, go to *2016.eicar.org/86-0-Intended-
> use.html* and download the Anti-Malware Testfile.

To scan your computer, follow these steps:

1. Return to the Virus & threat protection page. Click **Scan now**.

2. After the scan is completed, examine the scan results. If any malicious software is found,
complete the action requested by Windows Defender to remove the threat.

3. Repeat the scan and remove any newly detected threats.

4. Keep repeating the scan until no threats are detected.

To change scan settings and delete quarantined items, follow these steps:

1. To change the scan settings, click **Virus & threat protection settings**. Explore the different
settings listed. Return to the Virus & threat protection page.

2. To remove quarantined items from your computer, click **Threat history**.

3. Under Quarantined threats, remove any threats that are found or individually review and
remove each threat.

Some malware, such as a rootkit, is best detected by scanning before Windows is launched. To see how this works, do the following:

1. Return to the **Windows Defender Security Center**, and click **Virus & threat protection**.

2. On the Virus & threat protection page, click **Run a new advanced scan**.

3. Select **Windows Defender Offline scan** and click **Scan now**. Click **Scan** to confirm. Respond to the UAC dialog box, if necessary. Windows restarts and the scan begins.

4. The progress of the scan displays on the Windows Defender Antivirus window; the scan can take as long as 15 minutes. If you are short on time in this lab, you can click **Cancel scan** to stop the scan.

5. If other anti-malware software is installed and you want to use it rather than Windows Defender, turn that software back on. This will automatically turn off Windows Defender.

PART 2: WINDOWS 8 WINDOWS DEFENDER

Follow these steps to turn off other anti-malware software, and then explore how Windows 8 Windows Defender works:

1. To find out if anti-malware software other than Windows Defender is running on your computer, go to the Windows desktop, click the **Action Center** flag in the taskbar, and then click **Open Action Center**. The Action Center opens.

2. Click the **Security** title to expand the Security section. If you find in the Security section that anti-malware software other than Windows Defender is running, turn off this anti-malware program. Close the Action Center.

3. To open the Windows Defender window, go to the **Start** screen, and type **defender**. Click the **Windows Defender** tile in the search results. The Windows Defender window opens (see Figure 17-12). In the figure, Windows Defender shows the computer is potentially unprotected.

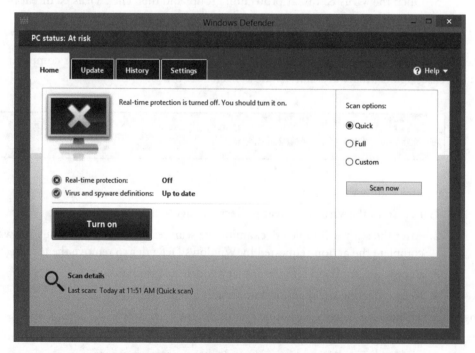

Figure 17-12 Windows Defender warns that this computer is at risk

4. If your real-time protection is off, click the **Turn on** button.

5. Click the **Update** tab, and then click **Update** to update your definitions.

After the virus and spyware definitions have finished updating, you can scan your computer with the most recent defenses against malware that Windows Defender offers.

> **Notes** If you want to infect your computer with a test virus, go to *2016.eicar.org/86-0-Intended-use.html* and download the Anti-Malware Testfile.

To scan your computer, follow these steps:

1. Return to the **Home** tab. With **Quick** selected as the scan option in the right pane, click the **Scan now** button.

2. After the scan is completed, you can see results from the scan. If any malicious software is found, complete the action requested by Windows Defender to remove the threat.

3. Repeat the scan and remove any newly detected threats.

4. Keep repeating the scan until no threats are detected.

To change scan settings and delete quarantined items, follow these steps:

1. To change the scan settings, click the **Settings** tab. Explore the different setting groups in the left pane, and then click the **Advanced** group.

2. Select the boxes next to the options you want Windows Defender to use in future scans. If you made any changes, click the **Save changes** button.

3. To remove quarantined items from your computer, click the **History** tab. If necessary, with **Quarantined items** selected, click the **View details** button.

4. If any quarantined items are found, remove all threats or individually review and remove each threat.

REVIEW QUESTIONS

1. Why is it important to use a malware removal program, such as Windows Defender, rather than just being careful while surfing the web?

_____

_____

_____

2. Why is it important to update virus and spyware definitions on malware removal programs, and how often should they be updated?

_____

_____

3. Why would you want to quarantine malware, and how do you delete quarantined malware from your system? Why could this be important?

_____

_____

_____

_____

_____

17

4. What options are available in the Windows Defender settings? Why is the Real-time protection option important?

_____

_____

_____

_____

LAB 17.7 DOWNLOAD AND USE MICROSOFT SECURITY ESSENTIALS IN WINDOWS 7

OBJECTIVES

Your goal in this lab is to learn how to use Microsoft Security Essentials to protect a Windows 7 computer from malware such as viruses, spyware, rootkits, and worms. After completing this lab, you will be able to:

▲ Download and install Microsoft Security Essentials

▲ Configure and use Microsoft Security Essentials

▲ Use the EICAR anti-malware test file to confirm that anti-malware protection is active

MATERIALS REQUIRED

This lab requires the following:

▲ Windows 7 computer or VM

▲ An account with administrator privileges

▲ Internet access

LAB PREPARATION

Before the lab begins, the instructor or lab assistant needs to do the following:

▲ Verify that Windows starts with no errors

▲ Verify that Internet access is available

▲ Verify that each student has access to a user account with administrator privileges

ACTIVITY BACKGROUND

As an IT support technician, you need to know how to support both old and new operating systems. For every computer or VM you support, you need to make sure it has anti-malware software installed and that it is configured to receive automatic updates and run in the background. Many free and paid-by-subscription anti-malware products are available and can be downloaded from the Internet. Among the free products, Microsoft Security Essentials is well rated and does a good job of protecting a Windows 7 system against malware. (Windows 10/8 uses Windows Defender for malware protection, which is built into the OS.) In this lab, you learn to download Microsoft Security Essentials, install it, configure it, and make sure it is running in the background to protect a Windows 7 system against malware.

ESTIMATED COMPLETION TIME: 20 MINUTES

 Activity

> **Notes** Websites change from time to time, so you might need to adjust the following steps to accommodate changes to the Microsoft site.

Follow these steps to download and install Microsoft Security Essentials:

1. Sign in to Windows 7 using an account with administrator privileges.

2. Open **Control Panel** and then open the **System** window. Is 32-bit or 64-bit Windows 7 installed?

   _____

3. Using your browser, go to **microsoft.com/en-us/download/windows.aspx**.

4. Click **Microsoft Security Essentials**. Click **Download**.

5. Select either the 64-bit version or 32-bit version of the software to match the version of Windows 7 installed on your system. Click **Next**. If necessary, click **Allow once** to allow the pop-up from Microsoft.

6. Internet Explorer asks if you want to run or save MSEInstall.exe. Select **Save**; Internet Explorer will automatically save the file to the Downloads folder in the current user's home directory. When the download is complete, click **View downloads**.

7. In the View Downloads window, click **Downloads** beside the file name you just downloaded.

   ◢ What is the path and file name (including file extension) of the downloaded file? What is the size of the file?

   _____

8. Close your browser.

9. To execute the downloaded file, double-click it in your Downloads folder. If necessary, respond to the UAC dialog box.

10. The Microsoft Security Essentials window appears. Click **Next**.

11. On the next screen, click **I accept** to agree to the license agreement.

12. On the next screen, choose whether you would like to participate in the Microsoft Customer Experience Improvement Program, and then click **Next**.

13. When the "If no firewall is turned on, turn on Windows Firewall (Recommended)" option appears, leave this box checked, and click **Next**.

14. On the next screen, click **Install**.

15. On the next screen, uncheck the **Scan my computer for potential threats after getting the latest updates** check box. Click **Finish**.

16. The Microsoft Security Essentials window opens with the Update tab active and the update process already running. This process installs the latest virus and spyware definitions and then scans your computer for malware. Wait for the entire process to complete, which might take several minutes.

17. If necessary, click the **Home** tab. On the Home tab, look for the large green check mark, which indicates that the software is configured to automatically scan for malware and that the software is up to date (see Figure 17-13).

17

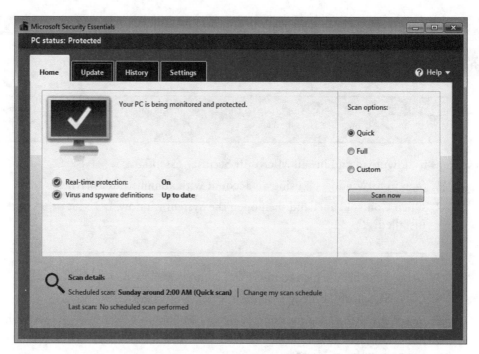

Figure 17-13 Microsoft Security Essentials for Windows 7 is up to date with the latest virus and spyware definitions

18. Click the **History** tab. List any suspicious items the scan recorded:

_____

_____

_____

19. Click the **Settings** tab. Answer the following questions:
    ◢ On what day of the week and time of day is a scan scheduled?

    _____

    ◢ Is the software configured to check for the latest updates before running a scan?

    _____

20. Click **Real-time protection**. What is the purpose of having real-time protection enabled?

    _____

    _____

21. List the steps to configure the software to scan removable drives:

    _____

    _____

    _____

22. Close the Microsoft Security Essentials window.

23. To clean up your computer, delete the downloaded file in your Downloads folder. Which file did you delete?

_____

The EICAR anti-malware test file can be used to confirm that your anti-malware software is working. Follow these steps to find out more:

1. Open **Internet Explorer** and navigate to **eicar.org/?page_id=3950**.

2. Read the instructions for using the test file. To test whether Microsoft Security Essentials detects malware that is downloaded, click **eicar.com** in the list of files to download. When Internet Explorer asks if you want to run or save the file, save it to your Downloads folder.

   ◢ What is the error message you receive?

   _____

   ◢ Why do you think Internet Explorer did not allow you to download the file?

   _____

3. Try to download other versions of the file listed for download. Were you able to download any of these files?

   _____

4. To get the file to your computer, you can copy the text that creates the digital signature of a virus. To do so, scroll down the page, and copy the 68-character ASCII string to your Windows Clipboard.

5. Open **Notepad**. Paste the string into Notepad, save the file to your Windows desktop, and name the file **eicar.txt**. What happens when you save the file?

   _____

6. Open the **Microsoft Security Essentials** window, and click the **History** tab. Note any changes from when you viewed the list in Step 18 earlier in this lab:

   _____

   _____

REVIEW QUESTIONS

1. Why does EICAR release the anti-malware test string?

   _____

   _____

2. What is the name of the executable program file for Microsoft Security Essentials (not the downloaded file)?

   _____

17

3. Why does Microsoft Security Essentials prompt you to activate Windows Firewall if a firewall is not active?

_____

4. Which tab on the Microsoft Security Essentials window do you use to find out the Virus definitions version and the Spyware definitions version?

_____

5. In this lab, you verified that Microsoft Security Essentials stops malware from downloading. In which three types of programs, as identified by their file extensions, did you verify that Microsoft Security Essentials could find potential malware?

_____

macOS, Linux, and Scripting

Labs included in this chapter:

- **Lab 18.1:** Investigate Apple Operating Systems

- **Lab 18.2:** Investigate Linux and Create a Bootable Ubuntu Flash Drive

- **Lab 18.3:** Use TeamViewer to Remotely Access Another Computer

- **Lab 18.4:** Compare Operating Systems

- **Lab 18.5:** Create and Run a PowerShell Script

- **Lab 18.6:** Use Wireshark to Compare Security in Telnet and SSH

LAB 18.1 INVESTIGATE APPLE OPERATING SYSTEMS

OBJECTIVES

The goal of this lab is to become familiar with the various Apple operating systems and the hardware they support. After completing this lab, you will be able to:

▲ Describe the various Apple operating systems, hardware, and applications

▲ Research Apple technology on the Apple website (*apple.com*)

MATERIALS REQUIRED

This lab requires the following:

▲ Internet access

LAB PREPARATION

Before the lab begins, the instructor or lab assistant needs to do the following:

▲ Verify that Internet access is available

ACTIVITY BACKGROUND

Mac operating systems are designed to be used only on Apple Mac servers, desktops, and laptops. Apple and many other developers have created applications for Apple products, including applications for the Mac computer, the iPad, the iPhone, and Apple's other mobile devices. The Apple website (*apple.com*) is the best source of information about its products. In this lab, you investigate different Apple operating systems, hardware, and applications for both computers and mobile devices.

ESTIMATED COMPLETION TIME: 30 MINUTES

 Activity

1. Open your browser and go to **apple.com**. Explore the site, and when you are done, return to the main page. Use the links on the site (see Figure 18-1) to answer the questions in this lab.

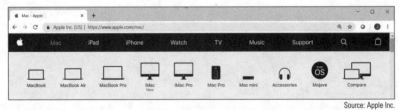

Source: Apple Inc.

Figure 18-1   Apple Mac products

2. What is the latest version of the Mac operating system available for a new iMac?

3. What is the cost of upgrading a Mac operating system to the latest version?

Compare the iPhone, iMac, Mac mini, MacBook Pro, and MacBook Air systems available for sale on the Apple website, and answer these questions:

1. What are the highest speeds or frequencies of the processors in each product?

2. How much does the fastest 27-inch iMac cost?

3. What software comes bundled with an iMac?

4. What is a MacBook?

5. How much does the most expensive MacBook Pro cost?

6. What features are included with the least expensive MacBook?

7. Describe the features of an Apple Magic Mouse:

8. List three functions of a 2big Dock Thunderbolt device.

9. What operating systems are available for Apple mobile devices?

10. What is the latest operating system available for the iPhone?

11. Describe the iCloud service:

12. Describe the purposes of the FaceTime app for iPhone and iPad:

_____

_____

13. What is the purpose of QuickTime software?

_____

_____

REVIEW QUESTIONS

1. What is one advantage of using an Apple computer instead of a Windows computer?

_____

_____

_____

2. What is one disadvantage of using an Apple computer instead of a Windows computer?

_____

_____

_____

3. Can macOS run on a Windows computer? Explain:

_____

_____

_____

4. Describe the advantages of an iPad over a traditional laptop:

_____

_____

LAB 18.2 INVESTIGATE LINUX AND CREATE A BOOTABLE UBUNTU FLASH DRIVE

OBJECTIVES

Your goal in this lab is to find information about Linux operating systems and use a distribution of Linux to create a bootable USB flash drive. After completing this lab, you will be able to:

▲ Create a bootable Ubuntu flash drive

▲ Explore the different distributions of Linux

▲ Compare Linux to other operating systems

MATERIALS REQUIRED

This lab requires the following:

- ◢ Internet access
- ◢ A USB flash drive (thumb drive)
- ◢ A computer capable of booting from a USB flash drive

LAB PREPARATION

Before the lab begins, the instructor or lab assistant needs to do the following:

- ◢ Verify that Internet access is available
- ◢ Inform students they will need a flash drive with at least 4 GB of capacity

ACTIVITY BACKGROUND

Linux—a scaled-down version of the UNIX operating system that is provided free of charge in its basic form—allows open access to its programming code. Linux can be used as both a server platform and a desktop platform; additionally, Linux is a portable operating system, meaning that it can be installed on any hardware platform. Ubuntu is one of the various Linux distributions.

Imagine the power of having a bootable Linux flash drive (called a live USB) that gives you the ability to boot into any computer to perform troubleshooting steps. By the end of this lab, you will have that ability in your hands, using the Ubuntu distribution.

ESTIMATED COMPLETION TIME: 60 MINUTES

 Activity

1. Open a browser and go to **ubuntu.com**. Spend a few minutes exploring the site on your own.
2. Click the **Download** tab. Click **Ubuntu Desktop**.
3. Download the latest LTS (long-term support) version of Ubuntu. At the time of this writing, Ubuntu 18.04 LTS was available. Answer the following questions:

   - ◢ What is the size of the downloaded file?

   _____

   - ◢ What is the path and file name of the downloaded file?

   _____

   - ◢ Depending on the speed of your Internet connection, the download may take a while. How long did the file take to download?

   _____

   - ◢ What is the file extension of the downloaded file?

   _____

18

The next step is to download a program called the LinuxLive USB Creator app. This program is used to make the USB flash drive bootable and provide persistent storage. Persistent storage means that you can write data to the drive and it will still be there the next time you boot from the live USB.

To download, install, and launch the LinuxLive (LiLi) USB Creator app, follow these steps:

1. Insert your flash drive in a USB port. (Keep in mind that *all* the data on the flash drive will be deleted.)

2. Go to **linuxliveusb.com/en/home** and download the LinuxLive (LiLi) USB Creator app. Be sure not to download or install other freeware also available on the site. At the time of this writing, the file name was LinuxLive USB Creator 2.9.2.exe. What is the path and file name of your downloaded file?

_____

3. Double-click the downloaded file to install and run the LiLi Creator app. If necessary, respond to the UAC box. Follow the on-screen directions to install the software. After the software installs, it automatically launches and the setup dialog box appears. Complete the following (as shown in Figure 18-2):

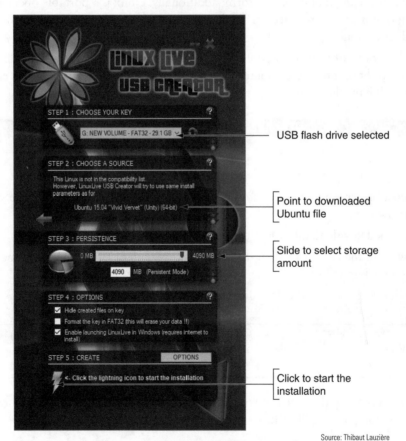

Source: Thibaut Lauzière

Figure 18-2 Settings to create a Linux live USB with persistent storage

a. In the Step 1 section, select your USB drive letter. (Make sure this selection is correct.)

b. In the Step 2 section, browse to the location of the Ubuntu downloaded file. The file has an .iso file extension.

c. In the Step 3 section, move the slider all the way to the right to select the maximum amount for persistent storage.

d. In the Step 4 section, no changes are needed.

4. In the Step 5 section, click the lightning icon to create the Linux live USB. The LiLi Creator app will format and configure your bootable flash drive. The process may take a few minutes to complete.

5. Close all open windows.

To test your Linux bootable flash drive, follow these steps:

1. Boot into the BIOS/UEFI setup on your computer. (To boot into BIOS/UEFI setup, press a key or key combination at startup. Near the beginning of the boot, look for a message such as "Press Del for setup" or "Press F10 to configure setup.")

2. Using the BIOS/UEFI setup utility, ensure that the boot sequence is adjusted to boot from USB first.

3. Exit BIOS/UEFI setup, saving any changes you made, and shut the computer completely off.

4. Plug the USB Linux bootable flash drive into a USB port.

5. Start the computer. Your computer should boot into the Linux operating system. Your desktop should look similar to Figure 18-3.

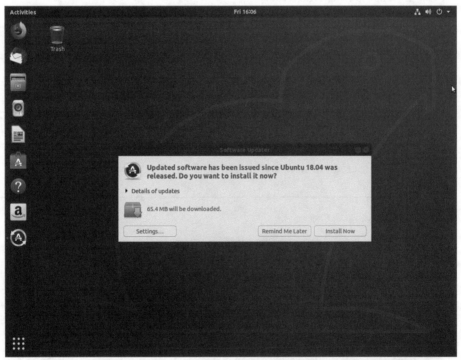

Source: Ubuntu.com

Figure 18-3 A typical Linux Ubuntu desktop

6. After Ubuntu boots up, open a browser and make sure you have connectivity to the Internet.

7. To test the persistent storage, create a text file on your Ubuntu desktop. What is the name of the file?

_____

8. Restart your computer, booting again to the Linux live USB. Is the text file still on your desktop?

_____

18

You have just created one of the most powerful tools you can have in your arsenal of software tools. Use it wisely. Label the flash drive and keep it in a safe place.

Ubuntu is not the only distribution of Linux. To learn about other distributions, open a browser and go to *linuxmint.com*. Answer the following questions:

◢ How does Linux Mint compare with Ubuntu?

_____

_____

◢ Linux Mint offers free tutorials. Examine a few, and describe how detailed they are:

_____

_____

_____

◢ What is DuckDuckGo?

_____

_____

◢ What other Linux distributions are popular?

_____

_____

◢ Who is credited with creating Linux?

_____

REVIEW QUESTIONS

1. Which file system was used to create your Linux live USB drive?

_____

2. What are some of the "costs" associated with installing a "free" operating system such as Linux?

_____

_____

_____

3. Why might a company not want to use Linux on its desktop computers?

_____

_____

4. What is one advantage of using Linux rather than a Windows operating system on a desktop?

_____

5. Based on what you learned from the Linux Mint website, how do you think companies that provide Linux make most of their profit?

LAB 18.3 USE TEAMVIEWER TO REMOTELY ACCESS ANOTHER COMPUTER

OBJECTIVES

The goal of this lab is to explore one method by which computers can be remotely accessed and controlled across an Internet connection. As an IT support technician, you can use TeamViewer when you are called on to support a client's computer remotely. The client can easily give you access to his or her computer if you both have Internet access. TeamViewer is also useful when you are working on a team project and you and your team members need to share information and collaborate about the project from remote locations. After completing this lab, you will be able to:

▲ Download and install TeamViewer

▲ Use TeamViewer to share desktops with other users over the Internet

▲ Use TeamViewer to remotely control other computers over the Internet

▲ Move files between computers over the Internet

MATERIALS REQUIRED

This lab requires the following:

▲ Two computers using Windows 10/8/7 (for best results, the two computers should be sitting side by side)

▲ An account with administrator privileges

▲ Internet access on both computers

▲ Workgroup of two students

LAB PREPARATION

Before the lab begins, the instructor or lab assistant needs to do the following:

▲ Verify that Windows starts with no errors

▲ Verify that each student has access to a user account with administrator privileges

▲ Verify that Internet access is available

ACTIVITY BACKGROUND

TeamViewer is remote control software that is free to noncommercial users. It can be used for such things as tech support, remote maintenance, web conferencing, online presentations and training, team meetings, or simple application and file transfers. TeamViewer uses two-factor authentication and 256-bit AES session encryption, thereby providing reasonable security for most situations.

After you have connected to a target computer using TeamViewer, you can take complete control over the computer. For example, an IT support technician tells the story of a client calling to say she lost almost 400 valuable data files on her computer and desperately asking

18

for help to recover them. The technician connected to her computer over the Internet using TeamViewer. He then used this connection to download and install the Recuva software, which you learned to use earlier. The technician was able to use the Recuva software to recover 98 percent of her missing files. He became her hero that evening! (True story.)

In this lab, you and your partner each download and install the free full version of TeamViewer on your computers. Then, together you remotely access one computer from the other over the Internet and explore the settings and capabilities of the software. For best results, the two computers should be side by side so that you can easily see what happens on each computer after each action is performed. Note that this lab can also be completed by one person using two computers. Each partner should answer all of the questions in his or her own lab manual.

ESTIMATED COMPLETION TIME: 45 MINUTES

 Activity

In this lab, you work with a partner and two computers. The host computer will use TeamViewer to access and remotely control the target computer. Designate one partner as the host partner using the host computer and the other partner as the target partner using the target computer.

◢ Who is the host partner?

_____

◢ Who is the target partner?

_____

Note that later in the lab, the host and target roles are reversed and Parts 2–4 are repeated so that each partner has the opportunity to do all the steps in this lab.

PART 1: DOWNLOAD AND INSTALL TEAMVIEWER

Both partners follow these steps to download and install TeamViewer on their computers:

1. Sign in to your computer with a user account that has administrator privileges.

2. Using your browser, go to **teamviewer.com**.

   ◢ Besides the free version of TeamViewer, what other versions are available?

   _____

   _____

   _____

   ◢ What is the current version number of the free version available for download?

   _____

3. To download the free version of TeamViewer, click **DOWNLOAD FOR FREE**. What is the path and file name of the downloaded file?

   _____

4. Double-click the executable file that downloaded to begin the installation. Make sure **Basic installation** is selected, select **Personal/Non-commercial use,** and then click **Accept – finish.** If necessary, click **Yes** to respond to the UAC dialog box.

5. You will see the progress bar as TeamViewer is installed, and then TeamViewer opens (see Figure 18-4). Minimize or close any browser windows that are blocking the TeamViewer window. What is the ID number and password displayed in TeamViewer?

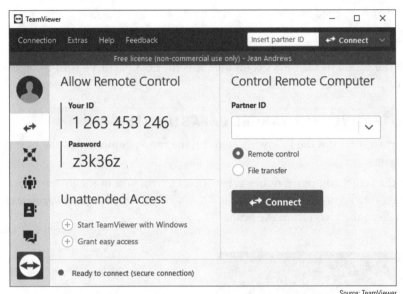

Figure 18-4 TeamViewer displays the ID and password needed for someone to connect to your computer

PART 2: REMOTELY ACCESS THE TARGET COMPUTER

The host partner uses the host computer to establish access to the target computer. If you are the host partner, follow these steps as the target partner observes:

1. On the host computer, in the Partner ID box in the TeamViewer window, type the ID generated by TeamViewer on the target computer. Click **Connect**. The TeamViewer Authentication dialog box appears. Let's take a few minutes to explore the advanced settings before signing in to the target system. Click **Advanced** in the lower-left corner.

2. Full Access is selected by default. Click **Access control** to open the Access Control Details dialog box. These are the specific settings that are allowed with Full Access. Review each of these settings, and then click **Close** to close the Access Control Details dialog box.

3. Click the **Full Access** button. What other three choices appear in the drop-down menu?

4. Select **Confirm all**, and then click **Access control** again. How have the settings changed?

5. Click **Close** to close the Access Control Details dialog box. Click **Confirm all**, and then select **Custom settings**. Click **Access control** again. Notice that each setting now has a customizable drop-down menu for configuring each setting individually. What are the three choices for configuring each setting in the drop-down menu (all settings have the same three choices)?

18

6. Click **Cancel** to close the Access Control Details dialog box. Using the drop-down menu, change Custom settings back to **Full Access**. Type the TeamViewer password of the target computer, and then click **Log On**.

◢ What happened on the target computer to indicate the session is live?

_____

◢ What happened on the host computer?

_____

Now we will switch the action to the target computer. It is the host partner's turn to observe as the target partner proceeds to Part 3.

PART 3: EXPLORE TEAMVIEWER TARGET CAPABILITIES

If you are the target partner, perform the following steps on the target computer as the host partner observes:

1. On the target computer, notice the session control box in the lower-right corner of the screen (see Figure 18-5). Do *not* click the X; if you do, TeamViewer will close all sessions and disconnect you from the host.

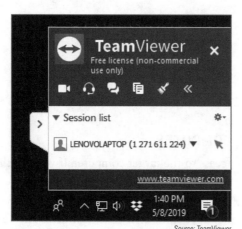

Source: TeamViewer

Figure 18-5   Use the session control box to access tools for TeamViewer

2. Hover the mouse over each icon on the toolbar of the session control box, and list what each of these five tools does:

_____

_____

_____

_____

_____

3. Click each of the five tool icons one at a time to see what happens. Type a sentence into the chat section and click **Send**. What happened on the host?

_____

4. Create a text document on your desktop, and use the File box feature to move the file to the host computer. After the document is moved, the host user can right-click the document and download it to any folder on his or her computer (don't do that now).

5. Create a Rich Text document on your desktop, and leave it there. The host user will retrieve it later in this lab. Write down the name of the file:

_____

6. In the Session list section, hover the mouse over the blue arrow icon on the right side of the host computer's name. What is the purpose of this icon?

_____

7. Sometimes you might want to stop a host user from remotely controlling your computer. To do so, click the **blue arrow**. Then tell the host user to try to do something (like open the Start menu) on your computer from the TeamViewer host window. Nothing will happen because you have denied the host computer remote control.

8. Use the blue arrow again to allow the host to remotely control your target computer.

Now we will switch the action back to the host computer. It is the target partner's turn to observe again as the host partner proceeds to Part 4.

PART 4: EXPLORE TEAMVIEWER HOST CAPABILITIES

To find out how the host can control the target computer, the host partner performs the following steps as the target partner observes:

1. To verify that you can control the target computer, open its **System** window. Then close the window.

2. Remember that Rich Text document your partner created on the desktop of the target computer? Rather than asking your partner to move it to the File box so that you can download it, drag and drop it into the File box. You can then download the file.

3. Take a few minutes to review each of the options under each of the five menu items on the toolbar that is displayed at the top of the target computer window on your desktop.

   ◢ List the steps to reboot the target computer.

   _____

   ◢ List the steps to reboot the target computer in safe mode.

   _____

   ◢ List the steps to switch the target computer's desktop to full screen mode on your desktop.

   _____

   ◢ List the steps to switch the host and target computers (switch sides with your partner). Are you able to do this using the free version of TeamViewer?

   _____

4. To close the session, close the TeamViewer pop-up box on the target computer.

5. Now switch roles with your partner, and repeat this lab beginning with Part 2.

18

REVIEW QUESTIONS

1. Does TeamViewer have to be running on both the host and the target computer in order to establish a session?

2. What does the host user require from the target user in order to establish a connection?

3. In what general ways can a target user limit the access of the host user?

4. After a TeamViewer session is opened, list four types of actions that can be performed between the two computers using either the free or paid version:

5. Do the ID and password assigned by TeamViewer remain the same after closing and relaunching TeamViewer?

6. Under what circumstances might you, as the target user, want to limit the access of the host user connecting to your machine?

7. Under what circumstances might you, as the target user, want to give full access to the host user?

8. What are some useful TeamViewer host tools that a technician might need to use on the target system, and why might they be used?

LAB 18.4 COMPARE OPERATING SYSTEMS

OBJECTIVES

Your goal in this lab is to investigate the history of computer operating systems and learn why many of today's operating systems share similar features. After completing this lab, you will be able to:

◢ Better understand the relationships among operating systems

MATERIALS REQUIRED

This lab requires the following:

◢ Internet access

LAB PREPARATION

Before the lab begins, the instructor or lab assistant needs to do the following:

◢ Verify that Internet access is available

ACTIVITY BACKGROUND

Modern operating systems—such as Windows, Ubuntu Linux, and macOS—have many similar features because they share a common history. Some of them have a direct or indirect connection with earlier operating systems. Figure 18-6 shows some highlights of this history. The arrows indicate a direct or indirect influence from an earlier operating system.

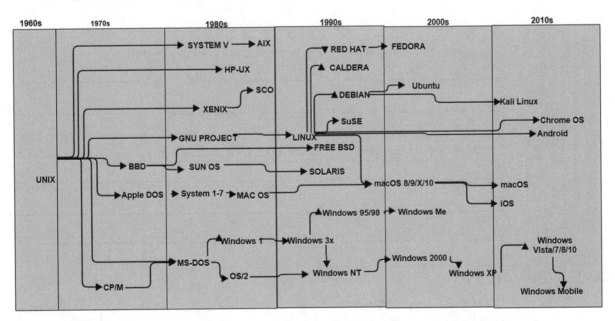

Figure 18-6 An operating system timeline

18

Activity

Using your favorite search engine, answer the following questions:

1. Search for the "history of operating systems." List the URLs of three sites that you think do a good job of explaining this history:

   _____

   _____

   _____

2. What are two similarities and two differences between the original Mac OS and Windows?

   _____

   _____

   _____

3. How is OS/2 loosely connected to Windows 10?

   _____

   _____

4. What is the relationship of QDOS to CP/M and MS-DOS?

   _____

   _____

5. List three mobile device operating systems that are currently popular:

   _____

   _____

6. Several operating systems have appeared since the year 2000 that have evolved from Linux. List three of them that are not listed in Figure 18-6, and list a primary purpose of each OS.

   _____

   _____

   _____

REVIEW QUESTIONS

Using a search engine, research operating system timelines; then, based on the OS timelines that you find, answer the following questions:

1. Why do you think Linux and UNIX share more commands than Windows 10 and UNIX?

   _____

2. Which type of operating system—macOS or Windows—is more similar to UNIX?

   _____

3. Why do you think most versions of Linux and Windows use the cd command to change directories?

4. What is the primary purpose of Kali Linux?

LAB 18.5 CREATE AND RUN A POWERSHELL SCRIPT

OBJECTIVES

The goal of this lab is to explore the potential of PowerShell by running a PowerShell script. After completing this lab, you will be able to:

◢ Set up PowerShell to run scripts

◢ Create and run a simple PowerShell script

MATERIALS REQUIRED

This lab requires the following:

◢ Windows 10 computer

LAB PREPARATION

Before the lab begins, the instructor or lab assistant needs to do the following:

◢ Verify that Windows starts with no errors

ACTIVITY BACKGROUND

PowerShell is a Windows shell and scripting tool. The shell is a basic command-line interface that supports hundreds of cmdlets and aliases. In addition, PowerShell is a scripting tool that can store a list of cmdlets in a text file and execute the cmdlets as a group. PowerShell scripting text files have a .ps1 file extension. To use scripts in PowerShell, you must first set the PowerShell execution policy, create the scripting text file with its cmdlets, and then execute the script. This lab steps you through this simple yet powerful process. Although you can use the Windows PowerShell Integrated Scripting Environment (ISE) to write, test, and run PowerShell scripts, in this lab we use a simple tool, Notepad.

ESTIMATED COMPLETION TIME: 15 MINUTES

 Activity

18

By default, PowerShell won't run scripts. To set the execution policy so that you can run scripts in PowerShell, do the following:

1. Open an elevated PowerShell window.

2. By default, the execution policy is Restricted, meaning scripts will not run. To see the current execution policy, use this command:

```
Get-ExecutionPolicy
```

3. To set the execution policy so that scripts will run except those downloaded from the Internet without a valid digital signature, use the following cmdlet, and then type **Y** to confirm the policy change.

```
Set-ExecutionPolicy RemoteSigned
```

4. To view the new policy, enter this cmdlet:

```
Get-ExecutionPolicy
```

When writing scripts, know that when the script is executed, PowerShell does not use the current directory to interpret cmdlets in a script. Therefore, it's important to use the full path with file names in a script. Now let's create and run a script:

1. Open File Explorer and create a folder (for example, C:\Scripts) to hold your scripts. What is your folder name and path?

_____

2. Open Notepad and then enter the following cmdlets, which you learned about in Chapter 13 of the main text:

```
Get-ChildItem C:\
```

```
Get-ChildItem C:\Users
```

```
Get-ChildItem C:\Users -recurse -depth 1
```

3. Save the file to your scripts folder, naming the script **MyScript1.ps1**. When you save the file in Notepad, be sure to change the *Save as type* option to **All Files** so that you can specify the file extension (see Figure 18-7).

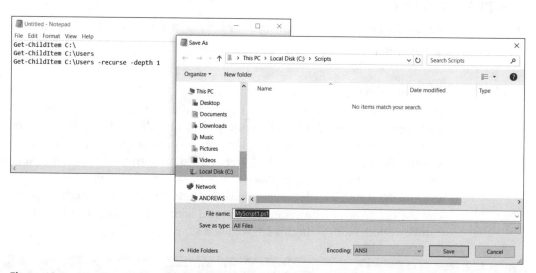

Figure 18-7 Use Notepad to create the MyScript1.ps1 script file

4. Return to your PowerShell window. Enter this cmdlet to go to your Scripts folder:

```
Set-Location C:\Scripts
```

5. To execute a script in the current folder, you must precede the script file name with ./ or .\. Enter the following cmdlets. All three cmdlets should execute the script:

```
./MyScript1.ps1
```

```
.\MyScript1.ps1
```

```
./MyScript1
```

6. When the script executes, check the results for errors. If you see an error, go back to the Notepad window, and correct the error in the script file. Don't forget to save the file again. Then return to the PowerShell window, and execute the script again.

7. Close all open windows.

REVIEW QUESTIONS

1. What is the file extension of a PowerShell script file?

2. Is it necessary to enter the file extension when you execute a script in PowerShell?

3. What is the default policy for executing scripts in PowerShell?

4. What type of file is a .ps1 PowerShell script file?

LAB 18.6 USE WIRESHARK TO COMPARE SECURITY IN TELNET AND SSH

OBJECTIVES

The goal of this lab is to use an Ubuntu Linux VM to examine security when using Telnet and SSH to remote in to Ubuntu. You will use Wireshark to watch data move from a remote client to the Telnet or SSH server and verify the data's security. After completing this lab, you will be able to:

▲ Use SSH for secure terminal functions
▲ Use Wireshark to look for an insecure app

MATERIALS REQUIRED

This lab requires the following:

▲ A computer with Windows 10/8 and Hyper-V
▲ Internet access

LAB PREPARATION

Before the lab begins, the instructor or lab assistant needs to do the following:

▲ Verify that the Windows computer works with no errors and is able to connect to the Internet and run Hyper-V

ACTIVITY BACKGROUND

Telnet was one of the earliest protocols used in networking computers. First ratified in 1969, Telnet was widely used on almost all servers. However, because Telnet sends all data in the clear, Secure Shell (SSH) was developed to replace it. Originally ratified in 1995, SSH has

18

completely replaced Telnet in applications that involve the Internet or where security matters. However, many devices still have Telnet enabled on them. Sometimes, it's because they are simple devices, such as a webcam or IoT thermostat, that cannot support encryption. In this lab, we contrast SSH connections with Telnet connections so that you can evaluate the security risk of Telnet on your network. In your career as an IT support technician, you are likely to encounter the need to validate the security of an application, and this lab shows you how to do that.

ESTIMATED COMPLETION TIME: 30–45 MINUTES

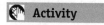 **Activity**

PART 1: CREATE AN UBUNTU LINUX VM

Follow these steps to use Client Hyper-V to create an Ubuntu Desktop VM:

1. The Ubuntu Desktop installation file was downloaded in Lab 18.2. If you have not already downloaded the file, go to **ubuntu.com** and download the Ubuntu Desktop OS to your hard drive. This is a free download, so you can decline to make any donations. The file that downloads is an ISO file. Ubuntu is a well-known version of Linux and offers both desktop and server editions. What is the path and file name of the Ubuntu installation ISO file on your computer?

   _____

2. Open the Hyper-V Manager, and create a new VM. Mount the ISO file that contains the Ubuntu Desktop download to a virtual DVD in your VM. What is the name of your VM?

   _____

> **Notes** If you need help creating or managing the VM in Hyper-V, see Lab 12.2. If you use the Quick Create option to create the new virtual machine, be sure to uncheck the **This virtual machine will run Windows** box before you create the VM.

3. Start the VM and install Ubuntu Desktop, accepting all default settings. When given the option, don't install any extra software bundled with the OS. You'll need to restart the VM when the installation is finished.

PART 2: INSTALL AND RUN WIRESHARK IN THE UBUNTU VM

Wireshark is free, open-source software that can read and analyze packets on a network to help with troubleshooting, protocol development, and education. Wireshark can be installed in Windows, macOS, and Linux. Follow these steps to install Wireshark in your Ubuntu Linux VM:

1. Open Hyper-V and start the Ubuntu Desktop VM. Sign in to Ubuntu.

2. To open the Terminal window, click **Activities**, and type **terminal** in the search box. Then click **Terminal** in the list that appears. See Figure 18-8.

Figure 18-8 Open a terminal window in Ubuntu Desktop

Source: ubuntu.com

3. To install and configure Wireshark in Ubuntu, enter the commands listed in Table 18-1.

Command	Description
`sudo apt-add-repository universe`	Add the universe repository to the list of places Ubuntu can find apps. This is an official repository of apps, but it is not supported by Ubuntu. (Note that when you attempt to add the repository and it is already available, a message reports that the component is already enabled.)
`sudo apt-get update`	Download and update all apps available to Ubuntu, including the ones in the universe repository.
`sudo apt-get install wireshark`	Install Wireshark. When asked if non-superusers should be able to capture packets, use the arrow keys to point to Yes and press Enter.
`sudo dpkg-reconfigure wireshark-common`	Allows all users to use Wireshark. When asked if non-superusers should be able to capture packets, respond with Yes.
`sudo addgroup wireshark`	Create a user group for Wireshark users. (Ubuntu might tell you the group already exists.)
`sudo usermod -a -G wireshark $USER`	Add the current user to the Wireshark group.
`grep "wireshark" /etc/group`	Verify that the Wireshark group and current user is in the group file. (The /etc/group file lists user groups.)
`sudo setcap 'CAP_NET_RAW+eip CAP_NET_ADMIN+eip' /usr/bin/dumpcap`	Assign appropriate permissions to the dumpcap daemon, which is the part of Wireshark that captures packets.

Table 18-1 Commands to set up and run Wireshark in Ubuntu

18

4. Sign off and sign back in to your Ubuntu VM. Recall that to sign out of Ubuntu, you click the down arrow in the upper-left corner of the screen, click your user name, and click **Log Out**.

5. To start Wireshark, open the Launcher (the icon is a square of dots) in the lower-left corner of the screen, and type the app name in the search box. Alternately, you can search for and double-click the Wireshark icon.

6. On the Wireshark home page (see Figure 18-9), select the Ethernet interface. Most likely, its name is **eth0**. Start the Wireshark capture (click the blue fin icon) to verify that Wireshark is working as it should. Stop the capture by clicking the red square icon.

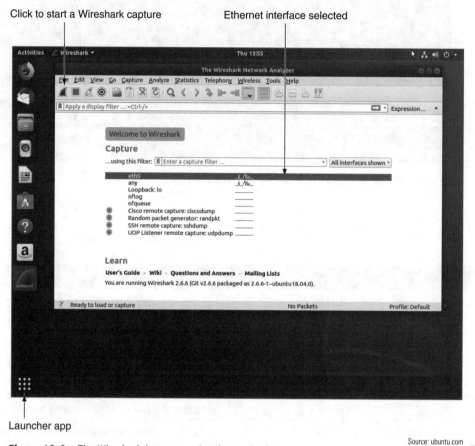

Figure 18-9   The Wireshark home page in Ubuntu Desktop

PART 3: INSTALL AND USE THE SSH AND TELNET DAEMONS

Telnet and SSH are daemons, which run as servers in the background to allow remote client computers to sign in to Ubuntu and use the OS. These servers are useful when you need to remotely control an Ubuntu Linux computer. Follow these steps to install and use Telnet and SSH and capture their packets:

1. To install the SSH daemon, open the Terminal and enter this command:

```
sudo apt-get install openssh-server
```

> **Notes** If you get an error when trying to install SSH, perhaps Ubuntu needs updating. Enter these two commands to download and apply all Ubuntu updates:
>
> ```
> sudo apt-get update
> sudo apt-get upgrade
> ```

2. Enter this command to install the network commands, including ifconfig:

```
sudo apt install net-tools
```

3. Enter this command to find your Ubuntu VM's IP address:

`ifconfig`

◢ What is the IP address of the VM?

_____

4. Next, enter this command to install and start Telnet:

`sudo apt install telnetd`

5. In Wireshark, start packet tracing to monitor your network interface. When you start the trace, you are asked if you want to save the previous trace. It's not necessary to save it.

Your Windows computer is the host computer supporting the VM; however, you can also use it as a remote client to Ubuntu. PuTTY is an SSH and Telnet client that you can use in Windows as your remote client software to access Ubuntu. (Note that you could also use any computer on your network as the remote client.) Follow these steps to install and use PuTTY to remote in to the VM:

1. In Windows, find out the IP address of your computer.

◢ How did you discover the IP address?

_____

◢ What is the IP address of your computer?

_____

2. In Windows, go to **putty.org** and follow the directions to download the MSI Windows installer file for either the 32-bit or 64-bit version. Double-click the installer file to launch it and follow instructions on the screen to install PuTTY, accepting all default settings. Is your Windows installation a 32-bit or 64-bit installation?

_____

3. In Windows, launch PuTTY. Notice that, by default, PuTTY is set to use SSH and port 22. See Figure 18-10.

18

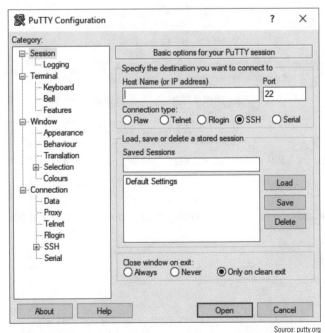

Source: putty.org

Figure 18-10 PuTTY client software is set to connect to a host using SSH

4. In PuTTY, make the selection to use Telnet. When you selected Telnet, what port was assigned for the Telnet session?

5. In PuTTY, enter the IP address of the Ubuntu machine in the Host Name text box. Open the Telnet connection. Telnet allows you to sign in to the Ubuntu VM with your user name and password.

6. Back in your VM, examine the Wireshark traffic. To find packets transmitting your user name and password, look for a packet where the destination IP address is to your Windows computer and the protocol is TCP. Right-click on this packet, select **Follow**, and then select **TCP Stream**. The entire stream of packets appears in a separate window, as shown in Figure 18-11. Are your user name and password encrypted or in plain text?

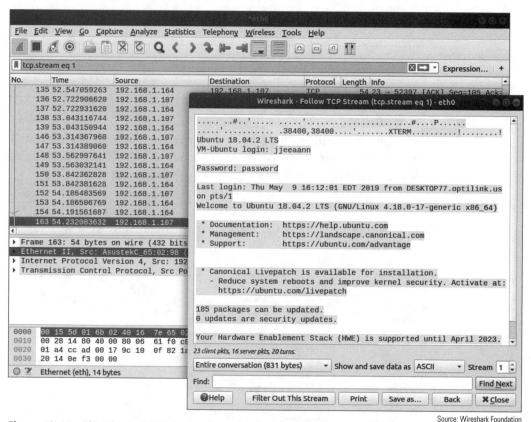

Source: Wireshark Foundation

Figure 18-11   The Wireshark TCP stream shows the user name and password in plain text

7. Enter these commands through Telnet so that you can see more Telnet traffic in Wireshark:

◢ `ls`

◢ `pwd`

◢ `ifconfig`

8. Enter the **exit** command to end the Telnet session and close PuTTY.

9. Reopen PuTTY and leave SSH and port 22 as the default protocol and port.

10. Open the SSH session, and use it to sign in to your Ubuntu VM.

11. In Wireshark in the VM, try to follow the TCP stream showing your user name and password. Can you find them in the stream? Why or why not?

_____

12. Enter the same commands you used in Step 7. Knowing what the data looks like from Step 7, can you identify which packets are which?

_____

REVIEW QUESTIONS

1. It is usually inadvisable to use Telnet because:

   a. Telnet does not support encryption.

   b. Telnet is outdated.

   c. Telnet clients aren't available on modern operating systems.

   d. Telnet is not supported on modern servers.

2. The development of SSH is:

   a. Open source

   b. Closed source

   c. No longer active

   d. A and B

3. The first time you connect to a server using SSH, you must accept a cryptographic key. This key is used to:

   a. Verify the identity of the computer you are connecting to.

   b. Create a secure passphrase.

   c. Determine the directories to which you have access.

   d. Create a random encryption scheme that is understandable by both the client and server.

4. Which operating system does _not_ include an SSH daemon or service by default?

   a. Windows

   b. UNIX

   c. Linux

   d. macOS

18